Measuring and Valuing Health Benefits for Economic Evaluation

Measuring and Valuing Health Benefits for Economic Evaluation

Professor John Brazier

Professor of Health Economics

School of Health and Related Research,
University of Sheffield, UK

Dr Julie Ratcliffe

Senior Research Fellow

School of Health and Related Research,
University of Sheffield, UK

Dr Joshua A. Salomon

Assistant Professor of International Health

Department of Population and International Health,
Harvard School of Public Health, Harvard University, USA

Dr Aki Tsuchiya

Senior Lecturer in Economics and Health Economics

School of Health and Related Research, and
the Department of Economics, University of Sheffield, UK

OXFORD
UNIVERSITY PRESS

OXFORD

UNIVERSITY PRESS

Great Clarendon Street, Oxford OX2 6DP

Oxford University Press is a department of the University of Oxford.
It furthers the University's objective of excellence in research, scholarship,
and education by publishing worldwide in

Oxford New York

Auckland   Cape   Town   Dar es Salaam   Hong Kong   Karachi
Kuala Lumpur   Madrid   Melbourne   Mexico City   Nairobi
New Delhi   Shanghai   Taipei   Toronto

With offices in

Argentina   Austria   Brazil   Chile   Czech   Republic   France   Greece
Guatemala   Hungary   Italy   Japan   South Korea   Poland   Portugal
Singapore   Switzerland   Thailand   Turkey   Ukraine   Vietnam

Oxford is a registered trade mark of Oxford University Press
in the UK and in certain other countries

Published in the United States
by Oxford University Press Inc., New York

© Oxford University Press, 2007

The moral rights of the author have been asserted

Database right Oxford University Press (maker)

First published 2007

A catalogue record for this title is available from the British Library

Library of Congress Cataloging in Publication Data
Measuring and valuing health benefits for economic evaluation/John
Brazier ... [et al.].
    p. ; cm.
Includes bibliographical references and index.
ISBN-13: 978-0-19-856982-4 (alk. paper)
ISBN-10: 0-19-856982-3 (alk. paper)
1. Outcome assessment (Medical care) 2. Medical economics.
I. Brazier, John.
[DNLM: 1. Economics, Medical. 2. Costs and Cost Analysis
--economics. 3. Models, Econometric. 4. Public Health--economics.
W 74.1 M481 2007]
R853.O87M428 2007
338.4'73621--dc22

2006032634

Typeset by Cepha Imaging Pvt Ltd, Bangalore, India
Printed in Minion
on acid-free paper by
Ashford Colour Press Ltd., Gosport, Hampshire.

ISBN 978-0-19-856982-4 (Pbk.)

10   9   8   7   6   5   4   3   2   1

Preface

There has been an increasing use of economic evaluation to assist policy makers concerned with the health impact of their programmes. Major users include agencies such as the National Institute for Health and Clinical Excellence (NICE) in England and Wales and similar bodies around the world (Scotland, Australia, Canada, The Netherlands and Sweden). In North America there is also an increasing interest in the potential role of cost-effectiveness analysis in the evaluation of non-health care as well as health care interventions that impact on health. This has resulted in a corresponding increase in the need for data on costs and benefits of these interventions for use in economic evaluation. This book is concerned with the measurement and valuation of health benefits.

This book is aimed to complement those that currently exist on economic evaluation and health outcome measures. The valuation of health benefits is a central concern in economic evaluation that raises different types of problems from those conventionally addressed in the psychometric literature on health and quality of life assessment. Our philosophy in writing this book has been to draw on these two fields and to forge a book that is comprehensive and above all useful to the practitioner in this field, whether they are academics, students, consultants or policy makers.

The writing of this book has been a collective enterprise, drawing on our different expertise in measuring and valuing health. Like many textbooks, it began life as teaching material delivered on courses, including Masters Degrees for health economists, health services researchers and public health physicians, and a commercial course delivered to pharmaceutical companies. It soon evolved into something much larger to take into account such a large and diffuse area of research. We hope this proves to be a useful source book to the wide range of readership to which it is aimed.

J.E.B
J.R
J.A.S
A.T

Acknowledgements

We owe a considerable debt to colleagues, particularly those at the Universities of Sheffield and Harvard, with whom we have worked with in this field over the years including Chris McCabe, Chris Murray, Jennifer Roberts, Paul Dolan, Jim Hammitt, Tony O'Hagan and Milt Weinstein. We are particularly grateful to those who kindly agreed to comment on sections of this book as it emerged in various draft forms. We would specifically like to thank: Simon Dixon, Richard Edlin, Enrico de Nigris, Jennifer Roberts, Katherine Stevens, Isabel Towers, and Yaling Yang. We would also like to extend our thanks to Sarah McEvoy for proof reading the manuscript and to Kathryn Aleixos for her clerical support. Any remaining errors or omissions are the responsibility of the authors alone.

John Brazier is funded by the UK Medical Research Council Health Services Research Collaboration. Joshua Salomon in funded by the National Institute on Aging, US National Institute of Health.

Finally we would like to acknowledge our collective intellectual debt to Alan Williams who was one of the pioneers in measuring and valuing health and has been such an inspiration to many of us working in this field.

Contents

Chapter 1

The purpose and scope of this book

The measurement and valuation of health benefits forms a major component of economic evaluation in health care. It continues to be a major source of contention, and yet at the same time the last three decades have seen major advancements in the methods of measuring and valuing health benefits. The range of tools has expanded considerably from the early notion of a 'health index' in the USA (Fanshel and Bush 1970) and the development of the Rosser Scale in the UK (Rosser and Watts 1972) in the 1970s, to the emergence of the EQ-5D in Europe (Brooks 1996) and the Health Utilities Index in Canada (Feeny *et al.* 2002). At the same time there have been important debates in the literature on a range of key issues such as the definition of health, the techniques of valuation, who should provide the values, techniques for modelling health state values, the appropriateness of valuation tools in children and vulnerable groups, cross-cultural issues and the problems of selecting instruments from the ever growing number available. These issues raise normative and positive problems that are core to the practice of economic evaluation. By addressing these issues in depth, this book aims to supplement a range of excellent texts on economic evaluation in health care (Gold *et al.* 1996; Drummond *et al.* 2005; Neumann 2005). Any reader of this book is encouraged to read one of these to provide them with the context for this book.

The issues addressed in this book are also important to health services research and to the field of quality of life research (sometimes known as patient-reported outcomes) in general, to which economics is but one contributing discipline. This field has seen contributions from an array of disciplines, including psychology and psychometrics, sociology, statistics, philosophy and the many health professions. The field of measuring health status and health-related quality of life already has a number of classic texts (Streiner and Norman 1989; Bowling 1991; Wilkin *et al.* 1992; McDowell and Newell 1996). These texts are primarily concerned with what economists would regard as measurement rather than valuation and are not concerned with the very specific requirements of economic evaluation. This book aims to help bridge the gap between conventional psychometric approaches to measuring health and the needs of economic evaluation.

We hope our book provides the reader with an in-depth knowledge of one of the key elements of economic evaluation in health care, the measurement and valuation of health. It is written as a textbook, aiming to be comprehensive in coverage of topics, but at the same time up to date at the time of going to press. We believe it fills an important gap that has been generated by the establishment of the National Institute for Health and Clinical Excellence (NICE) and similar bodies around the world that require cost-effectiveness evidence in the form of incremental cost per quality-adjusted life year (QALY). It is aimed at academics and students of health economics and other areas of economics concerned with the valuation of intangible benefits such as health; practitioners from economics and other disciplines engaged in generating economic evaluations for research bodies; governmental agencies in health care (such as NICE) and non-health care agencies whose programmes affect health (e.g. human services, environment and transport); pharmaceutical companies and management consultancies. The book should appeal to professional economists and comparative novices alike. The measurement and valuation of health is a multidisciplinary endeavour, and this book seeks to be inclusive by being accessible to a wide audience.

Chapter 2 is an introduction to the topic, and experienced health economists may prefer to skip it. It provides a justification for why health economists have entered an already crowded field. It presents the basic economic problem of scarcity and choice, and an overview of the techniques developed to assess the relative efficiency of different programmes. The chapter then considers the role and limitations of existing clinical and health-related quality of life measures in economic evaluation. These limitations provide the rationale for developing an alternative measure of the value of health, namely the QALY. The QALY is then briefly described. One of the best known examples of a measure to value health states to calculate QALYs is the generic preference-based measure, the EQ-5D (Brooks 1996). However, underpinning this and similar instruments are a number of core questions: what should be the measure of value, how should it be described, how should health states be valued, who should provide the values, and how should these values be aggregated? The remainder of this book addresses these questions from a number of different perspectives and examines the many methods used.

Chapter 3 examines the theoretical foundation of valuing health benefits and the appropriate measure of value. It starts with a review of welfare economics and market failure. It considers in some detail the theoretical foundation for assessing programmes using the Pareto criterion and the

Kaldor–Hicks compensation criteria. It then considers why the method of willingness to pay, which is often the preferred approach in economics to valuing intangibles, has not been as widely used in health care. The chapter then offers alternative justifications for the QALY including its foundations in welfare economics and non-welfare economic approaches. The chapter goes on to examine the foundation of the QALY in consumer theory, and specifically expected utility theory. For QALYs to represent preference-based utilities requires a number of restrictive assumptions to hold. The extent to which these assumptions are violated is reviewed, along with alternative preference-based measures such as the healthy year equivalent.

Chapter 4 deals with the second question, namely how should health be described. It considers the debates around the scope of a QALY from a narrow clinical definition of health through to a broad and all-encompassing definition of quality of life. This chapter reviews the pros and cons of generic and condition-specific measures in the context of economic evaluation. Can condition-specific measures, for example, be used to make cross-programme comparisons? If not, then what can be done when generic measures appear to be insensitive to a health change? The chapter also examines the more difficult conceptual issue of defining health, and considers the implications for health benefit measurement in economic evaluation. The chapter then moves on to consider more practical questions in the construction of health states: use of health state descriptive systems versus bespoke vignettes, generation and selection of dimensions and items, and the testing of the reliability and validity of the final measure (bearing in mind the context throughout is economic evaluation).

Chapter 5 turns to more familiar territory of how to value health states. It describes the range of techniques that are currently used and considers the arguments for and against each of them. It looks in some detail at the theory behind the methods and the issues in imputing health state values from these tasks. A more neglected topic has been the impact of different variants on the values obtained, which has been shown to be more important in some cases than the differences between techniques, which is also considered here.

Chapter 5 then examines the question of whose values. There is evidence that people's valuations for a state depend on who they are and the perspective they take. Values have been shown to differ systematically by a number of personal characteristics such as age and illness experience. It has also been shown that patients valuing their own state give different values from those given by members of the general population trying to imagine the state. The reasons for these differences are examined (with interesting parallels to the notion of response shift from the psychometric literature). In this chapter, we review the normative arguments for and against using patient experiences compared with the hypothetical preferences of members of the general population.

Most descriptive systems give rise to a larger number of possible health states than can be feasibly valued in a valuation survey, and so values are usually elicited for a subset. The problem is then how to model from this subset in order to value all possible states defined by the instrument's descriptive system. Chapter 6 addresses this problem. Two main approaches have been used to estimate utility values for all states: methods based on multiattribute utility theory and those based on statistical inference. This chapter considers the technical issues in applying these approaches and reviews some of the latest developments in the field, including the use of a non-parametric Bayesian approach.

This is followed in Chapter 7 by an examination of the rapidly developing area of modelling ordinal data, such as data generated from ranking and discrete choice experiments (DCEs) to estimate health state values. Given the complexity of conventional cardinal valuation techniques, there has been interest in using apparently simpler tasks such as ranking and discrete choice experiments to estimate mean health state values. While ordinal methods, especially DCEs, have been used for a number of years in health economics, it is only recently that they have been used to value health for use in economic evaluation. Ordinal methods offer a promising approach to obtaining valuation data from more vulnerable groups such as children and the very elderly. This chapter presents the theoretical basis for using ordinal data and its analysis, and reviews recent empirical work.

Chapter 8 provides a highly practical review of approaches to obtaining health state values. It describes the different approaches including: using generic preference-based measures (including a detailed review of the EQ-5D, HUI2, HUI3, SF-6D, QWB and AQoL), mapping from health status and health-related quality of life measures onto a preference-based measure, valuing vignettes (compared with using a descriptive system such as the EQ-5D), direct preference elicitation from patients, and finally the use of health state values published in the literature. This practical guide offers a useful question and answer approach to deciding on the best way to obtain health state values under different circumstances.

Chapter 9 examines the analytical issues raised in two contexts: economic evaluations alongside clinical trials and decision analytic modelling. Their use in economic evaluations alongside clinical trials raises important issues of design, such as the design of the data collection, mode of administration, who to ask and how frequently to administer the measure. It also raises important analytical problems of dealing with missing data and uncertainty. The second, and increasingly the more important application, is in the context of decision analytic modelling. Here the problem is built around the health states being used in the economic model, and the analyst must consider the best place to collect relevant data. This also raises the important problem of how to characterize the uncertainty around health state values for use in Monte Carlo models. The other consideration is whether QALYs should be discounted and, if so, at what rate.

Having calculated QALYs using one or other of the methods described in this book, the final question addressed in Chapter 10 is how such data should be aggregated. One important issue is whether a QALY to a group with one set of characteristics is the same as the QALY to another group that differs in terms of their socio-demographic variables, health status or even the extent to which they have brought the condition upon themselves.

Interest in using cost per QALY to inform resource allocation has mainly come from developed countries. Low- and middle-income countries have shown less interest, but for them it is arguably even more important. Chapter 11 reviews attempts to apply the ideas described in this book through the particular lens of the developing country perspective. We provide a brief introduction to the disability-adjusted life year (DALY), which is an alternative to the QALY that has been favoured in much of the cost-effectiveness work in developing countries, and extend the discussions of key issues in the definition, description and valuation of health to address some of the added considerations demanded by cross-cultural applications of the methods and tools that are the focus of this book.

The final chapter concludes with a discussion of the way forward in the light of the substantial methodological differences, the role of normative judgements and where further research is most likely to be productive in taking the field forward (at least in our opinion!).

References

Bowling A (1991). *Measuring health: a review of quality of life and measurement scales.* Open University Press, Milton Keynes, UK.

Brooks RG (1996). Euroqol: the current state of play. *Health Policy* 37:53–72

Drummond MF, Sculpher M, O'Brien B, Stoddart GL, Torrance GW (2005). *Methods for the economic evaluation of health care programmes.* Oxford Medical Publications, Oxford.

Fanshel S, Bush J (1970). A health status index and its application to health service outcomes. *Operations Research* 18:1021–66.

Feeny D, Furlong W, Torrance GW, Goldsmith CH, Zhu Z, DePauw S, Denton M, Boyle M (2002). Multiattribute and single-attribute utility functions for the health utilities index mark 3 system. *Medical Care* 40:113–28.

Gold MR, Siegel JE, Russell LB, Weinstein MC (1996). *Cost-effectiveness in health and medicine.* Oxford University Press, Oxford.

McDowell I, Newell, C. (1996). *Measuring health: a guide to rating scales and questionnaire.* Oxford University Press, Oxford.

Neumann PJ (2005). *Using cost-effectiveness analysis in health care.* Oxford University Press, New York.

Rosser RM, Watts, VC (1972). The measurement of hospital output. *International Journal of Epidemiolology* 1:361–8.

Streiner DL, Norman, GR (1989). *Health measurementscales: a practical guide to their development and use.* Oxford University Press, Oxford.

Wilkin D, Hallam L, Doggett MA (1992). *Measures of need and outcome for primary health care.* Oxford Medical Press, Oxford.

Chapter 2

Introduction to the measurement and valuation of health

The purpose of this chapter is to set the scene for the remainder of the book. It has been written in a non-technical style designed to be accessible to non-economists and economists alike. It begins by showing the trade-offs implied by the resource allocation decisions made by policy makers, particularly regarding different aspects of health. It then provides a non-technical introduction to the techniques of economic evaluation used by economists to help generate the information required to inform such decisions. This is followed by an introduction to health status measures (that will be very familiar to quality of life researchers) and the problems with using them in economic evaluation. We then provide a basic introduction to the quality-adjusted life year (QALY), followed by a discussion of the key issues in the construction of QALYs that are addressed in the rest of the book.

2.1 The rationale

It has long been recognized that health care, like other aspects of life, faces the problem that the resources available to spend are insufficient to meet all demands. The resources used to provide health care, including staff, facilities, equipment and knowledge, are scarce. Decisions about what services to provide, to whom, where and when, usually have resource implications. Pursuing one course of action, such as offering screening for a particular disease to a defined population in a given location at a given frequency, means that other possible decisions were not made regarding screening for that condition, and the resource costs will mean that fewer resources are available to provide for other services. In other words, there will be lost opportunities (known as opportunity costs).

In a publicly funded health care system with a limited budget, or even in an insurance-based system where premiums have to be competitive, such decisions have implications for health. The overall aim of economic evaluation is to aid decision makers to make efficient and equitable decisions by comparing the costs and benefits of health care interventions (Drummond *et al.* 2005). There has been an increasing use of economic evaluation to inform policy making over the last decade through the establishment of organizations such as the National Institute for Health and Clinical Excellence (NICE 2004) in England and Wales, and the Health Technology Board in Scotland (2002), and similar agencies in Australia (Commonwealth Department of Health and Ageing 2002), Canada (Ministry of Health 1994) and The Netherlands (Health Insurance Council 1999). In North America, there is also an increasing interest in the potential role of cost-effectiveness analysis in health care (Gold *et al.* 1996) and in the evaluation of non-health care interventions through the impact on health (Miller *et al.* 2006). This has resulted in a corresponding increase in the need for data on the benefits of these interventions for use in economic evaluation.

While it may seem quite obvious how to cost the direct resource consequences and even the less direct ones, such as any impact for the economy in the form of lost production from illness and its treatment, the health consequences are less tangible and it is rather less obvious how to assess them. Nonetheless, the health consequences are just as important, and indeed the main reason why most health services are provided.

One of the things that make health consequences difficult to assess is that they are multidimensional, uncertain and disparate. A person's life expectancy might be improved and/or the quality of their health may improve in various dimensions such as mobility, dexterity, sensory perception, social activities, pain relief and mental health. The assessment of the person's overall health presents major conceptual problems in the definition and description of health that are explored in Chapter 4. It is well recognized that traditional clinical and biomedically defined outcomes (such as blood pressure or respiratory function) are not adequate for describing the health consequences of health care for patients. Therefore, measures have been developed that focus on the concerns of the recipient of the service such as their ability to function, their social activities and their psychological well-being (Bowling 1997). Added to this is the fact that health care is uncertain on many levels. Most interventions cannot guarantee any given outcome, so there is usually a probability associated with a range of outcomes. Furthermore, medical knowledge is limited by the available evidence, and this in turn leads to more uncertainty. All this risk has potentially important implications for valuation. Furthermore, the outcomes may fall on different people at different points in time, and this has implications for equity.

The way that these different types of benefits are measured and valued is fundamental to economic evaluation in health care and ultimately for informing the decision maker. The next section looks at the different techniques of economic evaluation.

2.2 Techniques of economic evaluation

Economic evaluation is the comparative assessment of the costs and benefits of alternative health care interventions (Drummond *et al.* 2005). The techniques of economic evaluation are cost-effectiveness analysis, cost-utility analysis, cost-benefit analysis and cost-consequence analysis (though there is some dispute over whether the latter is truly a technique of economic evaluation). The unit for measuring the benefits of health care is the key feature that distinguishes the different techniques of economic evaluation (see summaries in Box 2.1). This section provides a brief overview of each technique to provide the context for the rest of this book. (Readers wanting to learn more about the techniques are encouraged to read Drummond *et al.* 2005.)

2.2.1 Cost-effectiveness analysis (CEA)

This technique compares the costs of alternative ways of achieving a given objective. Where two or more interventions are found to achieve the same level

---

Box 2.1 Techniques of economic evaluation

Cost-minimization analysis seeks to establish which is the least cost alternative, but is only a technique of economic evaluation if it can be shown that the alternatives achieve identical outcomes. However, in practice this is very rarely achieved since there is always uncertainty around the measure of outcome.

Cost-effectiveness analysis considers what is the best method of achieving a given objective, usually measured in 'natural' units, and presents results in terms of cost per unit of effect (e.g. cost per positive cancer detected or cost per symptom-free day).

Cost-utility analysis compares the costs of alternative health care programmes with their utility, usually measured in terms of quality-adjusted life years (QALYs). QALYs combine survival and quality of life into a single measure of value.

Cost-benefit analysis compares the benefits with costs of a health care programme, where all the benefits are valued in money terms including health improvement.

of benefits, the intervention with the least cost is the most cost-effective alternative. Under these circumstances, CEA is equivalent to cost-minimization analysis; however, this situation seldom arises, in part because of the uncertainty that usually exists around the estimates of benefits (Briggs and O'Brien 2001) that require a full probabilistic analysis of cost-effectiveness (see Chapter 9).

Where the benefits of competing interventions can be measured along a single dimension, then CEA can be used to rank interventions in terms of their ratio of cost per unit of effect. These effects are usually measured in 'natural' units. Typical examples of 'natural' measures used in CEA include life years saved or number of gallstone episodes avoided. CEAs can consider a wide range of end-points such as detecting cancers, reductions in blood pressure and improvements in bone mineral density. However, for any given analysis, only one outcome can be used. The important features of the measures that are used are that more of a good outcome is better than less, and that the measure lies on an interval scale over the range being examined, in other words a scale that allows meaningful comparisons of differences. An important question addressed later in this chapter is whether it is possible to conduct a CEA using the scores generated by measures of health-related quality of life.

The key characteristic of CEA is that the objective implied by the measure (e.g. detecting cancers) is not being questioned nor is its worth valued. In this sense, it is the most straightforward technique of economic evaluation. However, it is also very limited in terms of the questions it can address. It cannot be used to compare interventions that differ in more than one outcome e.g. (1) where a treatment improves survival at the expense of a poorer quality of life; or (2) where one intervention improves two outcomes because we do not know how much cost to attribute to each, so we cannot get the cost per unit health improvement. It is also unable to inform decisions on the efficient allocation of resources between disease groups or health care programmes with different outcomes. Nonetheless, it is a widely used technique, which can be extremely helpful in addressing those questions where the objective is not being questioned and no trade-off between outcomes is required.

2.2.2 Cost-utility analysis (CUA)

CUA is like CEA in that it compares interventions in terms of their cost per unit of effect and can be seen as a form of CEA (Drummond *et al.* 2005). Although much of the literature on economic evaluation, particularly in the USA, makes no distinction between CUA and CEA, the typology used by Drummond and colleagues regards CUA as a special case of CEA, in which the unit of effect is 'a year in full health' which combines length of life with health-related quality of life on a single scale. The most widely used measure of years in full health is the QALY. The number of QALYs is calculated by multiplying a person's life expectancy by the value of the health-related quality of life in each period measured on a scale between zero and one, where zero is dead and one is full health. Being on hospital renal dialysis, for example, may be assigned a quality adjustment value or weight of 0.8. A 20 year period on renal dialysis is 16 QALYs, and this is assumed to be equivalent to someone living for 16 years in full health. If being on dialysis affects more than one dimension of health (e.g. restricted activities and physical discomfort), then the 0.8 reflects two pieces of information: the value of the two dimensions of health relative to each other, and the relative value between the dialysis state and full health. For more complex health profiles, involving transitions between states of health, the QALY score is calculated by summing the product of the time spent in each state and the value attached to that state. A health state can take a value from negative infinity (though many instruments limit the lower end to negative one) to one. There are two components to the procedure for estimating the quality adjustment values for QALYs. The first is a description of the state or profile of a person's health and the second is the valuation of these descriptions. Because of this valuation component, health state descriptive systems accompanied by a set of health state values are often called 'preference-based' measures of health.

CEAs that use QALY measures have several advantages compared with general CEA. First, interventions with more than one kind of health outcome, including any side effects, can be analysed, since the preference-based measure will collapse the multidimensional change in health into a single number. Secondly, interventions of the same condition with different health outcomes can be compared against each other. Thirdly, interventions for different kinds of health problems with different health outcomes can be compared. The results are reported in terms of monetary costs per unit change in the preference-based health outcome measure. Although some authors have used the term CUA to represent this kind of analysis, in this book the term CEA with QALYs or cost per QALY analysis will be used instead. The reason for avoiding the term cost 'utility' analysis will become clear towards the end of Chapter 3.

Health care interventions can be compared in terms of their incremental cost per QALY (i.e. the extra cost of an intervention over the next best alternative divided by the extra QALY gain) within and between programmes (Williams 1985). It even permits comparisons between programmes primarily concerned with increasing survival and those which mainly improve health-related quality of life. The earliest application of the QALY measure was undertaken in North America by Weinstein and Stason (1977) and Torrance *et al.* (1972), and in the UK by Williams (1985).

A collection of CEAs with QALYs can be brought together to form an ordering of various alternatives, ranked in terms of effectiveness, accounting for dominance and weka dominance (Drummond *et al.* 2005). The important thing to note about CEAs on their own is that they indicate which is the best way to achieve something, provided that resources have already been committed towards the outcomes in question (e.g. that we will spend £100 billion on health care). On their own, CEAs do not help in this earlier, more fundamental, decision to be made elsewhere (i.e. how much to spend on health care). One practical solution to this shortcoming is the introduction of a 'threshold' cost per unit outcome. A single CEA, combined with an exogenously given threshold, can inform whether or not a given alternative should be taken or not.

The rationale behind the use of a common threshold is that if some treatments that cost more than the threshold cost per unit of output are funded and others that cost less than the threshold are not, then there is an inefficiency; more health will be produced from the same limited resources if the former treatment is dropped and the latter taken up. So, the use of a common threshold enables maximizing health gains from a fixed amount of resources. The policy implication is that, by inferring from the prevalence of different conditions and thus the volume of each selected intervention, the National Health Service (NHS) should be funded up to the point that enables the delivery of all health care interventions that clear the threshold, but not beyond.

The next issue is how the threshold is set at any particular level. In the context of the UK, this threshold has been perceived to be in the range £20 000–£30 000 per additional QALY (NICE 2004). The usual interpretation given to this threshold is that this represents the maximum amount of resources that is regarded as appropriate to divert towards the production of an additional QALY, taking into account the 'opportunity costs' of doing so. The concept of opportunity costs means the benefits that would have been achieved should the resources in question have been put to the next best alternative use. If the best thing that a resource of £20 000 can achieve outside health care is of less value than one QALY, then the benefit achieved by allocating this £20 000 to health care is larger than the opportunity cost of doing so, and therefore it is worth spending £20 000 to produce one QALY. However, if the best thing that can be achieved outside health care has more value than one QALY, then it does not make sense to divert that resource towards health care only to produce something of less value.

However, this explanation does not answer the more fundamental question of how a value of a QALY is determined. There are two schools of thought here. One argues that this value is derived from an aggregation of what individuals *as private consumers* are willing to pay from their own pockets for small changes in health for themselves. Put very simplistically, if on average people are willing to pay £100 to join a lottery that had a 5 per cent chance of improving their health by 0.1 QALYs, then that will aggregate up to a willingness to pay £20 000 for one QALY for certain. The other school of thought holds that since this is about the use of public resources, it should reflect what individuals *as public citizens* are willing to expend from the public purse for a QALY gain for some unspecified fellow citizen. In other words, the second school argues that the threshold value of one QALY in the context of CEA to influence public health care resource allocation should not be determined with reference to other private consumer goods, but should be determined with reference to all the other goods and services in areas such as education, criminal justice, environment and defence, that are publicly provided. This is not an issue where one line of thought is correct and the other wrong, but firstly a matter of ideology and judgement, and secondly an issue for consistency and comparability of different CEA results. The issues of these two schools will be described in more detail in Chapter 3 in the context of the interpretation of the concept of the QALY and what it represents.

2.2.3 Cost-benefit analysis (CBA)

The key feature of CBA is that all the benefits of an intervention are valued in monetary terms. This does not mean that only financial consequences are included, but that intangible outcomes, such as the effects on survival and health, have to be valued using money as the numeraire. An intervention is worthwhile if the monetary valuation of all the benefits exceeds the costs. This technique can be used to address the question of whether a treatment/-programme is worthwhile for society, rather than restricting it to the NHS budget or to a single objective. A further advantage of CBA is that the measure of benefit encompasses a wider range of benefits, and in particular non-health benefits. The theoretical justification for CBA comes from the notion of compensation, which is that those who gain (i.e. enjoy the benefits) could compensate the losers (i.e. incur the costs) (see Chapter 3 for a review of this claim).

There are a number of techniques for obtaining monetary valuations of benefits. One is to impute values from people's 'revealed preferences' in market settings in order to value benefits. One example of this is in valuing life where the extra earnings of construction workers in risky occupations over safe occupations are used to infer a value for a life. This is regarded as the most appropriate method where it is feasible since actual decisions are assumed to be a more valid reflection of people's preferences than what someone says he or she would do hypothetically. However, revealed preference methods are difficult in the health care field due to the well-documented features of health care, including consumer ignorance and zero or subsidised price at the point of use (Donaldson and Gerard 1993). This can be overcome in some cases by obtaining revealed preference data from outside the health care sector (such as value for life from the labour market), but these tend to be rather limited in terms of the nature of benefits they cover and the extent to which they reflect just differences in health effects.

These difficulties have led to the adoption of a range of techniques in applied micro-economics under the broad heading of 'stated preference' methods or contingent valuation. These methods ask respondents to express how much they would be 'willing to pay' for an intervention, though they are not required to pay.

The use of stated willingness to pay (WTP) has been popular in other areas such as transport and environments, but less so in health economics (Donaldson and Gerard 1993). This has arisen in part from a concern about the distributional implications of using WTP, since it assumes the current distribution of income is appropriate. However, there are ways of adjusting for this effect. Another problem arises from the fact that many health systems, such as the NHS, have a fixed budget, and hence the decision rule must be modified to examining the relative costs and benefits from different programmes. This technique is still widely used in health care as a means of valuing health and other benefits, and is reviewed further in the next chapter.

2.2.4 Cost-consequence analysis (CCA)

CCA is founded on scepticism concerning to what extent all the relevant considerations in an economic evaluation could be presented in one number, such as the monetary cost per unit outcome or net benefit of treatment. To give a few examples, these efficiency measures on their own do not tell us anything about the size of the health gain; about what severity of health the health improvement starts from; what happens to patients if they do not get the treatment; about the age and life stage or socio-economic situation of typical patients; or about the level of uncertainty associated with the treatment. All these might be relevant considerations in determining the relative ranking of different interventions. Therefore, the results of CCA are reported in the form of a table, where all the relevant factors are presented, but do not have a single number to enable a unique and complete ranking of different treatment options. This last stage is left to the 'decision maker', for whom the analyses were carried out.

The advantage of this approach is that it retains the way of thinking and discipline of economic evaluation (Coast 2004). To the extent that the data are helpful, it can be seen within the decision-aiding tradition of economic evaluation (Sugden and Williams 1978). The disadvantages are that the basis for a decision can often be unclear and will not be based on explicit values.

2.3 Measures for describing health

2.3.1 What is health?

Health has been variously defined, but one of the most enduring and influential definitions is the statement in the Constitution of the World Health Organization (1948) that health is: 'A state of complete physical, mental and social well-being, and not merely the absence of disease and infirmity'. While this definition has been highly influential in the development of measures in this field, it is very broad and not easy to operationalize. It could be argued, for example, that social well-being is not health *per se*, but an aspect of quality of life that is affected by health. Some developers have chosen to take a much narrower definition of health in the construction of their measure. As a consequence, measures of health or health-related quality of life often differ considerably in their content. To add to the potential for confusion, some measures claim to measure quality of life, and yet their content is narrowly focused around symptoms.

In the health literature terms such as health, health status, health related quality of life and quality of life are used to mean different things by different instrument developers. In a sense terminology in itself does not matter, but underlying this issue of semantics is an important implication for policy in terms of what should be counted as a benefit and what might be ignored for the purpose of informing health policy. Whether or not social activites are counted as health, health related quality of life or quality of life does not matter, the important question is whether impact on social activities should form the part of the description of the benefits of health care. benefit Chapter 4 addresses this question in some detail.

An important feature of health is that it includes elements (such as pain, affect or various symptoms) that are experienced by an individual but difficult to measure with any external instrument or test that is valid, reliable and comparable. There is evidence of significant differences between what professionals report on a patient and what the patients say themselves (Jachuck *et al.* 1982). It is increasingly recognized in clinical and health services research that descriptions of the experience of a health state should be elicited from the patients themselves or, where this is not possible, from others on their behalf, in order best to reflect the actual experience of the disease and its treatment (Fitzpatrick *et al.* 1998).

2.3.2 What are self-reported measures of health?

A common approach to describing an individual's health is to elicit self-reports of levels on various health dimensions using standardized numerical scoring systems. This approach aims to provide quantitative descriptions of health states in terms of the components of health regarded as most relevant to patients with health problems, caused either by disease, the treatment of disease or other processes such as natural ageing, trauma and pregnancy. The domains included in most self-reported health measures do not include bio-medical measures (such as blood pressure, forced expiratory volume, choles-terol levels,etc.) or relate to specific diagnostic instruments used in clinical practice. While both of these are important in the clinical management of a patient and potentially important in predicting a person's future health, they are less pertinent to understanding the health experience of a patient.

Self-reported measures of health have been available since the 1940s (Karnofsky and Burchenal 1949), but did not become widely used until the 1960s and 1970s. However, by 1987, there were over 200 measures of health identified by Spilker and colleagues (1990). They can assess symptoms, func-tion or well-being depending on the specific definition of health being used, and can be 'generic' and hence designed for use across all conditions, or specif-ically designed for a particular disease. See Chapter 4 for a further discussion on this topic.

Patient-perceived measures of health are increasingly used to assess the effi-cacy and effectiveness of health care interventions. Some researchers have attempted to use them in conducting economic evaluations alongside clinical trials (e.g. Buxton *et al.* 1985; Nichol *et al.* 1992; Brazier *et al.* 1999) but they were not designed to be used in this way. The use of these measures in eco-nomic evaluation has been criticized by health economists, largely because they do not have the necessary interval properties to undertake CEA. However, such measures will continue to be widely used in clinical trials and other stud-ies due to their popularity with clinicians and health services researchers who are seeking to gather evidence for other purposes. It is therefore important to examine the potential use of health status measures in economic evaluation, if only from an opportunistic viewpoint. More importantly, this provides an important background to the reasons why measures have been specially devel-oped for use in economic evaluation.

2.3.3 The content of instruments

Measures of health vary widely in terms of content, format and scaling. The principal features of a sample of five measures are presented in Table 2.1.

Table 2.1 Characteristics of five health status measures (from Brazier et al. 1999)

Questionnaire	No. of dimensions	Description of dimensions/items	No. of items	Source of responses	Method of administration	Source of values	Results
Condition specific							
St George's Respiratory Questionnaire	4	Symptoms (e.g. shortness of breath and wheezing), activity (e.g. walking and playing games), impacts (e.g.embarrassment)	50	Patient	Interview or self-completion	Patients (using VAS)	Profile and index
Chronic Respiratory Questionnaire	4	Dyspnoea, fatigue, emotional function, mastery	20	Patient	Interview	Assumed	Profile
Barthel	1	Mobility, grooming, dressing, continence	10	Professional	Professional assessment	Assumed	Index
Generic							
SF-36 health survey	8	Physical functioning, role limitations (physical and emotional problems), social functioning, pain, mental health, general health perception	36	Patient or proxy	Self-completion, interviewer administration	Assumed	Profile
Nottingham Health Profile	6	Mobility, social isolation, pain, emotional reactions, energy	38	Patient	Self-completion	Thurstone's method	Profile

Reprinted by permission of Sage Publications Ltd from Andrew Stevens, Keith Abrams, John Brazier, Ray Fitzpatrick and Richard Lilford, The Advanced Handbook of Methods in Evidence Based Healthcare, (©Andrew Stevens, 2001)

The instruments have been selected to demonstrate the diversity of measures in terms of their size, coverage of health domains, method of administration and sources of values, not for being typical or even representative.

The content varies considerably between the measures. They cover generic concepts of functioning (such as physical functioning), through to specific symptoms (e.g. dyspnoea for respiratory disease, dexterity for arthritis, and so forth). The methods of completing the questionnaires include clinical interview, professional assessment, researcher interview and self-completion, either in the clinic or at home. While most of these measures are self-reported, we note that the Barthel Index is an exeption, being completed by the health professional. The Chronic Respiratory Questionnaire incorporates a further development, where patients are asked to identify the important activities which make them breathless, as well as providing the assessment. The developers have argued that this approach has the advantage of generating a score more responsive to health change (Guyatt *et al.* 1987), though it is of doubtful use in interpersonal comparisons. Responses to items are combined into either a single index or a profile of several subindices of scores using a scoring algorithm.

Most measures of health have a simple 'summative' scoring system. The SF-36 health survey, for example, is a standardized questionnaire used to assess patient health across eight dimensions (Ware *et al.* 1993). It consists of items or questions which present respondents with choices about their perception of their health (see Table 2.2). The physical functioning dimension, for example, has 10 items to which the patient can make one of three responses: 'limited a lot', 'limited a little' or 'not limited at all'. These responses are coded 1, 2 and 3, respectively, and the 10 coded responses summed to produce a score from 10 to 30. The same procedure is used for all eight dimensions. These raw dimension scores are transformed linearly onto a 0–100 scale. The eight dimension scores of the SF-36 are not comparable across dimensions. This procedure has been mistakenly described in the psychometric literature as being 'unweighted' (Jenkinson 1991), yet implies an *equal* weighting.

Scoring can be more sophisticated, such as the use of statistical techniques like factor analysis for the SF-36 (Ware *et al.* 1993). More recently, Rasch models have been suggested to take into account degree of difficulty, or severity, of an item in relation to the underlying, unobserved (latent) scale that the item is presumed to measure. Some instruments, such as the St George's Respiratory questionnaire and the Sickness Impact Profile, weight items using explicit valuation procedures. This involves asking people to rate the importance of each item using a visual analogue scale (VAS). Other instruments ask the patients to record how bothersome they find the attribute described by the item, and this is then used to weight the item.

Table 2.2 An example of a measure of health status–the SF-36 health survey (from Brazier et al. 1999)

Dimension	No. of items	Summary of content	No. of response choices	Range of response choice
Physical functioning	10	Extent to which health limits physical activities such as self-care, walking, climbing stairs, bending, lifting, and moderate and vigorous exercises	3	'Yes limited a lot' to 'no, not limited at all'
Role limitations– physical	4	Extent to which physical health interferes with work or other daily activities, including accomplishing less than wanted, limitations in the kind of activities, or difficulty in performing activities	2	Yes/No
Bodily pain	2	Intensity of pain and effect of pain on normal work, both inside and outside the home	5 and 6	'None' to 'very severe' and 'not at all' to 'extremely'
General health	5	Personal evaluation of health, including current health, health outlook and resistance to illness	5	'All of the time' to 'none of the time'
Vitality	4	Feeling energetic and full of life versus feeling tired and worn out	6	'All of the time' to 'none of the time'
Social functioning	2	Extent to which physical health or emotional problems interfere with normal social activities	5	'Not at all' to 'extremely' and 'All of the time' to 'none of the time'
Role limitations– emotional	3	Extent to which emotional problems interfere with work or other daily activities, including decreased time spent on activities, accomplishing less and not working as carefully as usual	2	Yes/No
Mental health	5	General mental health, including depression, anxiety, behavioural–emotional control, general positive affect	6	'All of the time' to 'none of the time'

Health Technology Assessment 1999; 3(9) 'A Review of the use of Health Status Measures in Economic Evaluation' by Brazier, Deverill, Green, Harper, and Booth. © Crown copyright material is reproduced with the permission of the controller of HMSO and Queen's Printer for Scotland.

2.4 The use of non-preference-based measures of health in economic evaluation

2.4.1 Criticisms of non-preference-based health status measures

Scoring by dimension

The simple summative scoring algorithms described above have been used by most measures of perceived health. This assumes equal intervals between the response choices and that the items are of equal importance. However, there is no reason to suppose, for example, that patients perceive the intervals of the responses to items of the physical functioning dimension of the SF-36 of 'not limited at all' and 'limited a little' to be equivalent to the interval between 'limited a little' and 'limited a lot'. To take another example from the SF-36, the intervals for an item on how much bodily pain a person has had in the last 4 weeks are 'none' to 'very mild', 'very mild' to 'mild', 'mild' to 'moderate', 'moderate' to 'severe', and 'severe' to 'very severe'. This would imply that in a trial, a reduction in pain from 'mild' to 'very mild' would be equivalent to a reduction from 'severe' to 'moderate'. Yet evidence using visual analogue and standard gamble valuation techniques suggests that people are often unable to perceive a significant difference between 'very mild' and 'mild', but that there is a very large and significant difference between 'moderate' and 'severe' (Brazier *et al.* 1998, 2002).

The summing of scores across items makes equally untenable assumptions about the value people would place on different items. In the physical functioning scale of the SF-36, the item 'limitations in climbing one flight of stairs' is assumed to be of equal importance to 'limitations in walking more than one mile'. For someone living in a bungalow, limitations in walking would probably be regarded as a far worse problem. Given the lack of any empirical basis for these assumptions, there must be doubts about even the ordinal properties of these scales as indicators of people's preferences, particularly over small changes in the dimension scores.

The equal interval assumptions underlying most measures of health have been defended by some researchers. It has been claimed that the relative importance of the different health concepts (as perceived by the instrument developers) is in part taken account of by the number of items used to represent them. It has also been claimed that it makes little difference in practice whether or not equal interval weighting is used (Jenkinson 1991). However, the numerous valuation studies with the EQ-5D, SF-6D and HUI3 have all shown that intervals between response choices are not equal and that items do not have the same weight (see Chapter 8 for a review of these measures). Furthermore, studies have found only a low to moderate correlation between health status measures and various preference- or value-weighted measures (Brazier *et al.* 1999).

Some instruments have adopted more sophisticated scoring methods using factor analysis or Rasch modelling. Factor analysis weights items according to the extent to which they contribute to some underlying latent variable. The stronger the correlation, the larger the weight of an item or dimension (depending on the unit of analysis). This has been used to re-score the SF-36 dimensions into two summary scores, one for physical health and the other for mental health (Ware *et al.* 1993). The scores have also been transformed so that a score of 50 represents the mean level in the general population and each movement of 10 points from this score represents a standard deviation of the score in the general population. Whilst this scoring system offers a statistical basis for understanding score differences between populations, there is no reason why weights based on correlation between items should reflect their relative importance to people in their daily lives.

More recently there has been interest in using Rasch models to re-score instruments based on item response theory. This was originally developed in education to provide a way of estimating how difficult different questions are against a unidimensional construct, for example numeracy. In health, the analysis will estimate the degree of severity represented by different items, where the underlying construct can be physical functioning, or pain. It is claimed that Rasch models result in a linear interval scale against which any item, regardless of the instrument from which it came, can be calibrated. One example of its application was a re-scoring of the 10 item physical functioning of the SF-36 (Raczek *et al.* 1997).

Whilst Rasch models provide a useful technique for understanding the position of items within a construct, they do not provide an appropriate method for valuing health for economic evaluation (such as in a cost per QALY analysis). The fact that one item is found to be more difficult to do, say against the construct mobility, does not mean it is more or less important in people's lives. While it may represent an improvement on summative scoring and has an important role in constructing measures (this is discussed in the context of constructing preference-based measured in Chapter 4), it does not provide preference-based (or experienced-based) weights needed for cost per QALY analyses.

Over the years, there have been a number of interesting debates between psychometricians and economists. The main source of confusion seems to arise from the distinction between measuring the construct or constructs of health and the value of health. This difference is summarized in Box 2.2. Whilst the dichotomy may seem rather artificial, since measures of health do contain valuations (some items contain a degree of valuation—more on this in

Box 2.2 The difference between measuring and valuing health

A common source of confusion between economists and other health researchers is the distinction between measuring and valuing health. Whilst many psychometricians are seeking to measure or numerically describe health along its different dimensions, economists want to know the *relative value that patients or others* place on the dimensions and their components in order to undertake more than the most rudimentary form of economic evaluation. The value of a health improvement will be related to a measure of the size of the change, but these two concepts will not be perfectly correlated. For example, someone may regard a large health improvement (such as the ability to walk upstairs) as being of little or no benefit if they live in a bungalow. Conversely an apparently small improvement in pain may be highly valued by the patient.

Chapter 4—and all instruments are weighted in some way), it does provide a useful way to understand the difference between the two approaches.

Score profile

Most health status measures present a profile of scores. The generation of a single index score for health has been opposed by many developers of measures of health. The developers of the Nottingham Health Profile, for example, have argued: 'The simple addition of affirmative responses gives misleading results because of the features of pain, social life, emotion, and so on are qualitatively distinct and made up of different facets which cannot have common denominators' (Hunt *et al.* 1986). This view is understandable when the purpose is to derive a *measure* of different aspects of health, but this is not sufficient for use in economic evaluation. To undertake economic evaluation, it will often be necessary to be able to combine the dimensions into an overall indicator of health. In a comparison of surgical and medical management of a condition, for example, one might perform better against one dimension, but worse against another. At the end of a clinical trial it would not be possible to determine which treatment was most effective, let alone whether it was cost-effective. A trade-off needs to be made between dimensions in order to determine effectiveness, and for assessing cost-effectiveness some means of valuing the difference between interventions needs to be found.

Some measures of health combine dimensions to form a single index (e.g. St George's Respiratory questionnaire, the Sickness Impact Profile and the

Barthel Index). As for the aggregation of items, many assume an equal weighting between dimensions (e.g. Barthel), while others combine the items using item weights estimated using valuation techniques such as the VAS (a critique of VAS as a measure of preference is provided in Chapter 5). In addition to the criticisms of these methods of valuing, the scoring systems make an assumption of simple additivity between dimensions, where the value of one dimension is assumed to be unaltered by the level of another dimension. This rules out the prospect of any interaction between dimensions.

Health status and survival

An important limitation of conventional measures of health is that they do not include mortality. One criticism of separating mortality from health status is the same as that made of profiles in general (i.e. how to combine them in order to assess the overall cost-effectiveness of an intervention). Another is that it creates a statistical artefact known as the 'survivor' effect. In a clinical study, a lower survival rate in one arm of the trial can increase its mean health status score(s) compared with the other arms of the trial. This arises because the patients who have died probably have a lower than average health status. Assuming increased survival is regarded as a good thing, then the analyst is without any means for deciding which is the better treatment. There are some statistical solutions to this problem, but they fail to address the central problem that these outcomes need to be combined in some way (Billingham *et al.* 1999). This is a serious limitation of conventional measures of health status, since many health care interventions have consequences for survival and health status.

Time profile of outcomes

The outcome of a treatment is often estimated as the mean difference between health scores before and after the treatment of patients in the trial. A more sophisticated approach to analysing repeated measures is to estimate the health change as the difference between the mean pre-treatment scores and a weighted average of mean scores across the post-treatment assessments, with the weights proportional to the time between each assessment. In other words, it is the 'area under the curve' where levels of health are plotted against time along the horizontal axis (Matthews *et al.* 1990). However, this method of analysis ignores the impact of time on people's preferences over different outcomes.

Uncertainty in outcomes

Outcomes in health care are rarely certain. Even common interventions such as cholecystectomy are associated with a wide dispersion of outcomes, such as in the relief of pain (Nicholl *et al.* 1992) and mortality. Most interventions come with risks, including mortality in many cases, and numerous complications and side effects. When treatment begins, neither the doctor nor the patient knows the outcome for certain. Conventional analyses of measures of health assume people are risk-neutral (i.e. their decision is unaffected by the degree of uncertainty around the mean value). Yet, in health care, there is evidence that many people are averse to risk (Loomes and McKenzie 1989). Patients may choose a treatment that achieves a lower expected or mean improvement in the health than another, but is associated with less variance (below we consider how this concern also pertains to QALYs)

2.4.2 Limitations to using health status measures in economic evaluation

The usefulness of non-preference-based health status measures in assessing the relative efficiency of interventions depends on the results of the study. In Table 2.3 we present seven scenarios of costs and outcomes in a comparison of a new intervention with the existing one, and consider whether it is possible to assess cost-effectiveness using health status measures.

Table 2.3 Assessing the relative efficiency of two interventions given different cost and health outcome scenarios

Scenario	Cost	Health status measure	Can relative efficiency be evaluated?
1	Lower	Better in at least one dimension and no worse on any other	Yes, by dominance[1]
2	Same	Better in at least one dimension and no worse on any other	Yes[1]
3	Lower	Same across all dimensions	Yes, by cost minimization[1,2]
4	Lower	Better on some dimensions and worse on others	No
5	Same	Better on some dimensions and worse on others	No
6	Higher	Better in at least one dimension and no worse on any other	No
7	Higher	Better on some dimensions and worse on others	No

[1] Assuming the scale at least indicates ordinal preferences over the range being considered (see discussion in text).

[2] It has been argued that cost minimiztion is rarely achievable, given the uncertainty that exists around most estimates (see discussion in text).

From: © The EurQol Group. www.euroqol.org.

The first scenario is a case of dominance where new treatment is cheaper *and* better on at least one of the dimensions of the health status measures, while being no worse on any other. In the second scenario, it is also straightforward to assess relative efficiency, since it is simply a question of choosing the treatment with the better health status measure scores since the two have been found to cost the same. In the third scenario, the dimension scores are the same across all dimensions of the health status measure, and so the decision as to whether to adapt the new intervention could be seen as a *cost-minimization analysis*. Even for these three scenarios, however, it is necessary to demonstrate the ordinality of the scale of the health status measure scores in relation to preferences and that there are no differences on other outcomes, such as survival. Furthermore, it has been argued that in practice there will always be uncertainty around outcomes and so it is not possible to be sure that outcomes are equal (Briggs and O'Brien 2001) or that one intervention is always better than another. The handling of uncertainty is considered in Chapter 9, but essentially the best way to handle it would be through probabilistic sensitivity analysis (Claxton *et al.* 2006) and this requires a single measure of outcome. Health status measures would not be appropriate for this type of analysis.

The result is even less straightforward for scenarios 4–7. In scenarios 4 and 5 the new treatment performs better on some dimensions but worse on others, and hence it could have a lower cost per unit of health gain on some dimensions but higher on others. Even where one treatment is apparently more cost-effective across all the health dimensions, care must be taken in the interpretation. A review of the evidence found that health status measures do not possess the interval properties required to undertake such comparisons (Brazier *et al.* 1999). Furthermore, it is the incremental cost-effectiveness ratio that is important for resource allocation purposes. Therefore, where the least cost-effective intervention costs more and yields a higher benefit, then the greater benefit could be worth the extra cost.

For multiple outcomes, one approach is to present the costs and benefits of the alternatives in a CCA. This type of presentation uses an economic framework, but is unlikely to be helpful since scores on health status measures have no obvious intuitive meaning. Score differences cannot be compared between dimensions, nor can health status measures scores be compared with other outcomes, such as survival, or cost. Non-preference-based health status measures cannot be used to assess the efficiency of interventions in such circumstances.

Overall, health status measures have a very limited role in economic evaluation in their current form, if any at all. For this reason, a different class of health status measures has been developed, known variously as preference-based measures of health or multiattribute utility scales, for calculating QALYs. However, this is not to say that the descriptive data collected by these non-preference-based health measures could not be used in other ways. In Chapter 8 we review a range of methods for using these data in an economic evaluation, including mapping onto preference-based measures and constructing new preference-based measures from them (as has been done with the SF-36). The next section provides an introduction to QALYs and to preference-based measures of health.

2.5 **An introduction to quality-adjusted life years**

One of the great innovations in the subdiscipline of health economics has been the development of a new method for valuing benefits for use in economic evaluation, namely the QALY. The QALY attempts to value the benefits of health care in terms of a measure that combines the impact on longevity with quality of life into the common numeraire of a year in full health. Health economics has really broken with mainstream economics by using the QALY rather than the traditional WTP approach (see Chapter 3 for a review of theoretical foundation of the QALY and why it has gained prominence over the more conventional monetary approaches used by mainstream economists). This section introduces the reader to the QALY and preference-based health status measures that provide a key ingredient, the quality adjustment.

2.5.1 **Basic description**

Since health is a function of both length of life and quality of life, the QALY has been developed in an attempt to combine the value of these attributes into a single index number. It has been defined as 'a measure of health outcome which assigns to each period of time a weight, ranging from 0 to 1, corresponding to the health related quality of life during that period, where a weight of 1 corresponds to optimal health, and a weight of 0 corresponds to health state judged to be equivalent to death' (Gold *et al.* 1996). The basic idea is that, for any individual, the prospect of living Y years in less than full health, or 'optimal health', may be equated to a prospect of living X years in full health where X<Y. If different 'Ys' can be converted into equivalent 'Xs' (i.e. QALYs), and if more QALYs are preferred to fewer, then QALYs can be used to inform resource allocation decisions.

The QALY can be represented graphically. Figure 2.1 shows the expected quality and length of life profiles of patients with severe angina and left main vessel disease (Williams 1985). The graph shows the length of life along the horizontal axis and the quality of life, measured on the zero to one scale, along

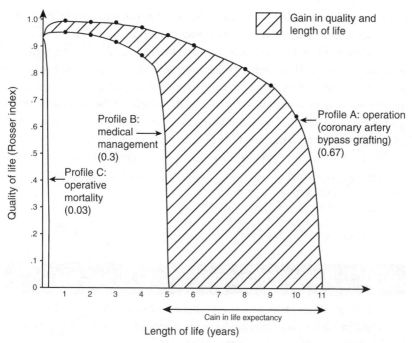

Fig. 2.1 Expected value of quality and length of life gained for patients with severe angina and left main vessel disease. From Williams A (1985). Economics of coronary artery bypass grafting. *British Medical Journal* 291:326–9. Reproduced with permission from the BMJ Publishing Group.

the vertical scale. Profile A is the expected profile following surgery where the patient lives for 11 years at different levels of quality. Profile B represents medical management and profile C the operative mortality from surgery. The number of QALYs associated with each profile is represented by the area under each curve. The net benefit of surgery is profile A minus profile C and minus profile B. This is one of the oldest representations of the QALY measure and it is worth saying that the expected survival and quality of life data come from a very low level of evidence (the opinion of three clinicians!), but there are instruments for obtaining such data from clinical studies.

More generally, the QALY is constructed as follows. The number of QALYs relating to *a health outcome* is expressed as the *value* given to a particular health state, multiplied by the *length of time* spent in that state. Since the outcomes of any given intervention are uncertain, the expected value of each possible outcome can be represented by the value weighted by its *probability*. Then, the expected outcome of the treatment itself can be represented by the sum of the expected value of the possible individual outcomes.

The benefit of the treatment is not the same as the outcome of the treatment, because the patient may recover even without treatment. So the *net benefit* of treatment is the difference between the expected outcome with and without treatment. The benefit of an intervention at the population level is the aggregate of net benefits to individual patients. So, if the expected benefit of an average patient is obtained, the aggregate benefit of the population programme can be derived by multiplying the individual benefit by the number of patients expected. Thus, the QALY algorithm is a combination of value of health states, durations, probabilities, and the number of patients. This is expressed more formally in Box 2.3. Some simple exercises to calculate QALYs are provided in Drummond *et al.* (2005).

Box 2.3 The QALY algorithm

In the simplest case, with no uncertainty, no temporal discounting and no changes in health over time, the value of a health gain from treatment for an individual, $QALY_G$, can be represented as:

$$QALY_G = T_1Q_1 - T_0Q_0,$$

where T is the number of years of survival, Q represents health state values, and the subscripts 1 and 0 represent health with and without treatment, respectively.

Alternatively, introducing uncertainty and temporal discounting, and assuming discrete time so that changes in health occur only when moving from one period to the next, the expected net gain of a treatment to any one individual can be expressed as:

$$QALY_G = \Sigma_h \Sigma_t\, p_{1ht}Q_{ht} - \Sigma_h \Sigma_t\, p_{0ht}Q_{ht},$$

where p_{1ht} and p_{0ht} represent the probabilties of an individual finding himself in health state h in time period t with and without treatment, respectively. Q_{ht} is the value of health state h at time t (the subscript t here allows for constant rate temporal discounting so that $Q_{ht} = Q_h / (1 + r)^t$ where r is the discount rate).

From: *Health Technology Assessment* 1999; 3(9) 'A Review of the use of Health Status Measures in Economic Evaluation' by Brazier, Deverill, Green, Harper and Booth. © Crown copyright material is reproduced with the permission of the Controller of HMSO and Queen's Printer for Scotland.

The QALY approach can be used at the *individual level* to compare the benefits of medical interventions in clinical trials (i.e. within diagnostic groups) and, through the calculation of cost per QALY ratios; or at the *social level* to determine priorities between interventions. Since the approach combines quality of life and length of life into a single number, it applies to interventions which extend life, only improve quality of life or which have consequences for both quality and quantity of life. The approach is therefore widely used in economic evaluations in the form of cost per QALY analyses.

2.5.2 Assumptions underlying the preference-based QALY

Health is experienced as a profile of states occurring at different points in time, lasting for different periods of time and occurring in different sequences. For the QALY to represent individual preferences over time, then a number of assumptions need to be made about the nature of people's preferences. At this point it is sufficient to observe that for QALYs to represent individual preferences over health profiles, then health state values must be independent of the duration of the states, when they occur and in what sequence, and in most applications it assumes that people are risk-neutral. These are very restrictive assumptions, but as mentioned earlier they would equally apply to the use of conventional health status measures. These assumptions of the QALY model are examined in detail in Chapters 3 and 11.

2.5.3 Putting the 'Q' into the QALY

To calculate QALYs, it is necessary to represent health on a scale where death and full health are assigned values of 0 and 1, respectively. Therefore, states rated as better than dead have values between 0 and 1, and states rated as worse than dead have negative scores which, in principle, are bounded by negative infinity. The key task is to estimate the value of the 'Q' in the QALY, and this forms the focus of the remainder of this book.

How this can be done will be demonstrated by presenting one of the most widely used instruments for estimating the value of 'Q', the generic preference-based measure of health the EQ-5D. This instrument has a structured health state descriptive system with five dimensions: mobility, self-care, usual activities, pain/discomfort and anxiety/depression. Each dimension has three levels of: no problem (level 1), moderate or some problem (level 2) and severe problem (level 3). Together these five dimensions define a total of 243 health states formed by different combinations of the levels (i.e. 3^5), and each state is described in the form of a five-digit code using the three levels (e.g. state 12321 means no problems in mobility, moderate problems in self-care, and so on).

Table 2.4 EQ-5D questionnaire (from the Euroqol Group)

Here are some simple questions about your health in general. By ticking one answer in each group below, please indicate which statements best describe your own health state TODAY.

Please tick one

1. **Mobility**
   I have no problems in walking about
   I have some problems in walking about
   I am confined to bed

2. **Self-care**
   I have no problems with self-care
   I have some problems washing or dressing myself
   I am unable to wash or dress myself

3. **Usual activities**
   I have no problems with performing my usual activities (e.g. work, study, housework, family or leisure activities)
   I have some problems with performing my usual activities
   I am unable to perform my usual activities

4. **Pain/discomfort**
   I have no pain or discomfort
   I have moderate pain or discomfort
   I have extreme pain or discomfort

5. **Anxiety/depression**
   I am not anxious or depressed
   I am moderately anxious or depressed
   I am extremely anxious or depressed

Reproduced from Dolan P, 'Modelling valuations for EuroQol Health States'. *Medical Care* 35(11):1095–1108 (1997) with permission from Lippincott, Williams and Wilkins.

It can be administered to patients or their proxy using a short one-page questionnaire with five questions (Table 2.4).

The EQ-5D can be scored in a number of ways depending on the method of valuation and source country, but the most widely used to date is the UK York TTO Tariff shown in Table 2.5. This 'population value set' provides an algorithm for the value of all 243 states calculated as a series of decrements from one (the value for full health, 11111). For all health states other than 11111, there is a constant decrement of 0.081, followed by the decrement associated with each level 2 or 3 that appears in the state and, finally, for those states with a level 3, there is an additional decrement (the 'N3' term). For example, the value for the state described by the profile 11223 is $1.0 - (0.081 + 0.036 + 0.123 + 0.236 + 0.269) = 0.255$.

This population value set was obtained by valuing a sample of 42 health states defined by the EQ-5D using the time trade-off (TTO) method with a sample of around 3000 members of the UK general population. This asks

Table 2.5 UK TTO EQ-5D tariff (from Dolan 1997)

Dimension	Level	Decrement
Constant		0.081
Mobility	2	0.069
	3	0.314
Self-care	2	0.104
	3	0.214
Usual activity	2	0.036
	3	0.094
Pain/discomfort	2	0.123
	3	0.386
Anxiety/depression	2	0.071
	3	0.236
N3		0.269

Application of tariff: the value of a health state is calculated as a series of decrements from one. For all health states other than 11111, there is a constant decrement of 0.081, followed by the decrement associated with each level 2 or 3 that appears in the state and finally for those states with a level 3, there is an additional decrement (the 'N3' term), e.g. 11223 = 1.0 − (0.081 + 0.036 + 0.123 + 0.236 + 0.269) = 0.255.

Reproduced from Dolan P. Modelling Valuations for EuroQol Health States. *Medical Care* 35(11):1095–1108 (1997) with permission from Lippincott, Williams and Wilkins.

people to imagine they will be an EQ-5D state for 10 years (t), and then asks them to consider a number of shorter periods in full health, i.e. at level 1 in each dimension. At the point where respondents are unable to choose between the 10 years in the state and a given duration in full health, x, the value of the state is given as x/t. Different valuation methods are reviewed in detail later in the book. These health state valuation data were then analysed by regression in order to estimate the decrements shown in Table 2.5. The different methods for modelling health state preference data are described in detail in Chapter 6.

The advantage of using generic preference-based measures like the EQ-5D is that they are easy to use and come off the shelf (though some have a charge). They can be incorporated into most clinical trial and routine data collection systems comparatively easily, with little additional burden for respondents. All are self-completed, though they can be administered to carers or other proxies. They are generic and so should be relevant to all patient groups. This last feature is important to those health economists seeking to standardize all aspects of methods in order to achieve comparison between patient groups. The arguments for and against this degree of standardization are reviewed in Chapter 4.

The aim of this book is not to promote one or other of the generic preference-based instruments, but to provide an in-depth understanding of what underpins them. This is in order to help the reader appreciate the technical and normative judgements involved in their construction. The field has been developing rapidly in recent years, and now does not seem to be the time to call a halt to such developments.

2.6 The questions addressed in this book

The EQ-5D provides a useful starting point for the rest of this book, since it demonstrates the key features of any method for measuring and valuing health. Underpinning this and similar instruments are a number of core questions: what is the measure of value, what is being valued, how is it valued, who values it and how should it be aggregated? (Box 2.4).

The first of these core questions is the unit of value. To be able to make cross-programme comparisons it is necessary to have a numeraire or some means of valuing benefits in a common currency. This can be money, as used in CBA. The QALY is another and forms the subject of this book. A unit of value must allow cross-programme comparisons, so a QALY estimated for an intervention in one group of patients is comparable with QALYs estimated for another intervention for a different medical condition in a different group of patients.

Having decided to use the QALY, the next question is what aspects of quality of life should be covered by the measure. Some cover quite narrowly defined aspects of impairment and symptomology associated with medical conditions, whilst others take a higher level and broader conception of quality of life. There are questions as to whether the measure should be generic like the EQ-5D or more specific, and indeed whether it should be based on a structured classification at all, or rather use a bespoke vignettes approach.

The valuation questions concern three things. The first is which technique of valuation should be used. The EQ-5D has been valued using TTO and VAS. Other generic preference-based measures such as the HUI3 and SF-6D used the standard gamble method, which some have argued should be the gold standard method of valuation in this field. A related issue is the variant of technique that should be used, since major differences have been found across variants for the same technique due to framing effects. The second question concerns the source of values, and whether they should be obtained from patients themselves, their carers and medical professionals, or members of the general population. The third issue is how to aggregate QALYs across populations. Can we assume that a QALY is a QALY regardless of who receives it, or does the value of a QALY depend on when it arises or on who receives it?

Box 2.4 Core questions to address in the measurement and valuation of health for use in economic evaluation

What should be the measure of value?

To be able to make cross-programme comparisons it is necessary to have a numeraire or some means of valuing benefits using a common currency. This can be money, and this is used in cost-benefit analysis. Another that has become widely used is the quality-adjusted life year (QALY).

How should it be described?

Having decided to use the QALY, a key question is what aspects of quality of life should be covered by the measure. Some cover quite narrowly defined aspects of impairment and symptomology associated with a medical condition, whilst others take a higher level and broader conception of quality of life.

How should it be valued?

There are a range of techniques for valuing health (such as standard gamble, time trade-off and visual analogue scales) and variants of them.

Who should provide the values?

A number of different people could provide the values, including patients themselves, their carers and medical professionals, or members of the general population.

How should QALYs be aggregated?

The value of a QALY may depend on when it arises or who receives it.

Adapted from Dolan (2000).

2.7 Concluding remarks

The impact of health care interventions on a person's perceived health is an important benefit. Many of the existing health status measures used in clinical trials and health services research in general are not suitable for use in economic evaluation. These instruments were not designed for this purpose and have little role in the assessment of cost-effectiveness in their current form. For this reason, preference-based measures have been developed in order to generate QALYs. These instruments directly incorporate preferences and values, and produce a measure that in principle enables cross-programme comparisons, at least within health care. Underpinning these instruments are a number of core questions: what should be the measure of benefits in health care, how is it to be described, how is it to be valued, who is to value it and how should the measure be aggregated? Addressing these questions forms the main focus of this book.

References

Billingham LJ, Abrams KR, Jones DR (1999). Methods for the analysis of quality of life and survival data in health technology assessment. *Health Technology Assessment* 3(10):1–152.

Bowling A. (1997). *Measuring health: a review of quality of life and measurement scales.* Open University Press, Milton Keynes, UK.

Brazier JE, Usherwood TP, Harper R, Jones N, MB, Thomas K (1998). Deriving a preference based single index measure for health from the SF-36 *Journal of Clinical Epidemiology* 51:1115–29.

Brazier JE, Deverill M, Green C, Harper R, Booth A (1999). A review of the use of health status measures in economic evaluation. *Health Technology Assessment* 3(9):1–164.

Brazier J, Roberts J, Deverill M (2002). The estimation of a preference-based single index measure for health from the SF-36. *Journal of Health Economics* 21:271–92.

Briggs AH, O'Brien B (2001). The death of cost-minimisation analysis? *Health Economics* 10:179–84.

Buxton M, Acheson R, Caine N, Gibson S, O'Brian B. (1985). *Costs and benefits of the heart transplant programmes at Harefield and Papworth hospitals.* DHSS Office of the Chief Scientist Research Report No. 12, HMSO, London.

Claxton K, Akehurst R, Brazier JE, Briggs A, Buxton M, McCabe C, Sculpher M (2006). Discounting and cost effectiveness–stepping back to sort out the confusion. *Health Economics* 15:1–5.

Coast J (2004). Is economic evaluation in touch with society's health values. *British Medical Journal* 329: 1233–6.

Commonwealth Department of Health, Housing and Community Service (2002). *Guidelines for the pharmaceutical industry on the submission to the Pharmaceutical Benefits Advisory Committee.* Australian Government Publishing Service, Canberra.

Dolan P (1997) Modelling Valuation for EuroQol Health States. *Medical Care,* 35(11):1095–1108.

Donaldson C, Gerard K (1993). *Economics of health care financing: the visible hand.* Macmillan, London.

Drummond MF, Sculpher M, O'Brien B, Stoddart GL, Torrance GW (2005). *Methods for the economic evaluation of health care programmes.* Oxford Medical Publications, Oxford.

Fitzpatrick R, Davey C, Buxton M, Jones DR (1998). Evaluating patient based outcome measures for use in clinical trials. *Health Technology Assessment* 2(14):1–74.

Gold MR, Siegel JE, Russell LB, Weinstein MC (1996). *Cost-effectiveness in health and medicine.* Oxford University Press, Oxford.

Guyatt GH, Berman LB, Townend M, Pugsley SO, Chambers LW (1987). A measure of quality of life for clinical trials in chronic lung disease. *Thorax* 42:773–8.

Health Insurance Council (1999). *Dutch Guidelines for Pharmacoeconomic research*. CVZ, Amstelveen, Netherlands.

Health Technology Board for Scotland (2002). *Guidance for manufacturers on submission of evidence relating to clinical and cost effectiveness in Health Technology Assessment*. Health Technology Board, Glasgow.

Hunt SM, McEwen J, McKenna SP (1986). *Measuring health status*. Croom Helm, London.

Jachuck SJ, Brierley H, Jachuck S, Willcox PM (1982). The effect of hypotensive drugs on quality of life. *Journal of the Royal College of General Practitioners* 32:103–5.

Jenkinson C (1991). Why are we weighting? A critical examination of the use of item weights in a health status measure. *Social Science and Medicine* 27:1413–6.

Karnofsky DA, Burchenal JH (1949). The clinical evaluation of chemotherapeutic agents against cancer. In: McLeod CM, ed. *Evaluation of chemotherapeutic agents*. Columbia University Press, New York, pp. 191–205.

Loomes G, McKenzie L (1989). The use of QALYs in health care decision making. *Social Science and Medicine* 28, 299–308.

Matthews JNS, Altman DG, Campbell MJ, Royston P (1990). Analysis of serial measurements in medical research. *British Medical Journal* 300:230–5.

Miller W, Robinson LA, Lawrence RS (2006). Valuing Health for Regulators Cost-Effectiveness Analysis. The National Academic Press. Washington.

Ministry of Health (Ontario) (1994). *Ontario guidelines for the economic evaluation of pharmaceutical products*. Ministry of Health, Toronto.

National Institute for Health and Clinical Excellence (2004) *NICE guide to the methods of technology appraisal*. NICE, UK.

Nicholl J, Brazier JE, Milner PC, Westlake L, Kohler B, Williams BT, Ross B, Frost E, Johnson AG (1992). Randomised controlled trial of cost-effectiveness of lithotripsy and open cholecystectomy as treatments for gallbladder stones. *Lancet* 340:801–7.

Raczek AE, Ware JE, Bjorner JB, Gandek B, Haley S, Aaronson NK, Apolone G, Bech P, Brazier JE, Bullinger M, Sullivan M (1997). Comparison of Rasch and summated rating scales constructed from the SF-36 physical functioning items in seven countries: results from the IQOLA project. *Journal of Clinical Epidemiology* 51:1203–14.

Spilker B, Molinek FR Jr, Johnston KA, Simpson RL Jr, Tilson HH, eds (1990). Quality of life bibliography and indexes. *Medical Care* 28, DS1–77.

Sugden R, Williams A (1978). *The principles of practical cost-benefit analysis*. Oxford University Press, Oxford.

Torrance GW, Thomas WH, Sackett DL (1972). A utility maximization model for evaluation of health care programs. *Health Services Research* 7:118–33.

Torrance GW (1986). Measurement of health state utilities for economic appraisal: a review. *Journal of Health Economics* 5:1–30.

Tsuchiya A, Dolan P (2005). The QALY model and individual preferences for health states and health profiles over time: a systematic review of the literature. *Medical Decision Making* 25(4):460–7.

Ware JE, Snow KK, Kolinski M, Gandeck B (1993). *SF-36 health survey manual and interpretation guide*. The Health Institute, New England Medical Centre, Boston, MA.

Weinstein, MC, Statson, WB (1977). Foundations of cost-effectiveness analysis for health and medical practices. *New England Journal of Medicine* 296:716–21.

Williams A (1985). Economics of coronary artery bypass grafting. *British Medical Journal* 291:326–9.

World Health Organization (1948) *Constitution of the World Health Organisation. Basic documents.* World Health Organization, Geneva.

Chapter 3

Foundations in welfare economics and utility theory: what should be valued?

This chapter examines the first of the questions identified in the last chapter (Box 2.3): what is to be valued? It starts by reviewing the theoretical underpinnings in economics for government intervention in health care. It then presents the alternative of resource allocation by planning and the implications this has for the use of economic evaluation and the measure of benefit. This is followed by a welfarist foundation for a measure of health, and finally some non-welfarist arguments are considered.

3.1 Economic theory and economic evaluation

3.1.1 Resource allocation through the market

Modern economics starts from a theory of competitive markets, between free sellers and buyers. The good in question can be raw materials, equipments, labour hours and skills, various services and final consumption goods. Economic theory explores the assumptions under which, without any external regulations and interventions from the government, market equilibria will be achieved. When 'market equilibrium' is achieved, supply and demand meet and the market 'clears'; in lay terms, it means that an exchange price for a good in question is reached, under which the total quantity the sellers want to supply and the total quantity the buyers want to purchase match, so that under this price there are no leftovers or shortages. Modern economic theory has demonstrated that free competitive market equilibria are Pareto efficient. 'Pareto efficiency' is satisfied when there is no wastage; more technically, this means that it is impossible to improve further the situation of anybody involved without making worse the situation of at least one other person. In a fully functioning market there would not be any need for government intervention, except perhaps to enforce property rights; there would be no need for economic evaluation or any other means of valuing benefits (apart from that implied by the exchange prices of goods and services).

A significant part of modern economic theory is about predicting what happens to different markets when the conditions for such perfect markets are not met, and/or about exploring ways to achieve Pareto efficiency in the absence of these conditions.

There are several conditions for a perfect market; the four most important ways in which the health care market fails are discussed below.

Lack of certainty

Health and health care have several layers of uncertainties associated with them. Although there are exceptions (e.g. stable and chronic illnesses), most of the time people do not know when they will become ill, and what treatment they will require. In addition, the link between health care and health is intrinsically probabilistic, and so, when individuals consume health care, it is not certain what degree of health improvement will be achieved, or how they might feel about the improved state of health. Of these different kinds of uncertainty, the first type, combined with 'risk aversion', means that there is scope for health care insurance (see Box 3.1).

However, insurance has its own side effects. The first of these is ex ante consumer moral hazard. '*Ex ante*' means that this happens before the illness incident. Once consumers are covered by insurance, this makes the risk of possible health care expenditure less of a concern to them. Therefore, individuals

---

Box 3.1 Actuarially fair premium and risk aversion

The *actuarially fair premium* is calculated as the product of the size of the possible health care expenditure and the probability of this need arising. So, for example, if the health care expenditure should it be required is £500, and if the chances of it being required is 1 per cent, then the actuarially fair premium is £5.

An individual who is *risk-averse* will prefer the prospect of paying this £5 insurance premium for certain and not have to pay the £500 medical bill should they fall ill to the alternative prospect of not purchasing the insurance coverage and instead having to pay the £500 medical bill out of their own pocket should they become ill. The degree of *risk aversion* will determine how much more than the actuarially fair premium the individual will be willing to pay as insurance premiums. A *risk-neutral* individual will be indifferent between having insurance coverage at an actuarially fair premium, and not purchasing the insurance.

will take less precaution and care to avoid illnesses, leading to increased level of risk, and thus the potential for higher premiums. The second is ex post consumer moral hazard. '*Ex post*' indicates that this concerns the stage after the incidence of illness. The effect of insurance on individual consumers is that they no longer have to pay for medical bills out of their own pocket at the point of health care consumption, while the actual cost required to produce that health care remains unaffected. So when rational individuals decide to consume health care, they overconsume relative to the socially optimal level. (This can also be understood as a problem in information asymmetry between the insurer and consumer; see below.)

Lack of symmetry of information between the insurer and consumer

Symmetry of information between two parties means that both parties have the same information. When individuals have different levels of risk of ill health, and there is an asymmetry of information in the health care insurance market so that individuals know their own risk level but the insurer only knows the whole distribution, this may lead to 'adverse selection'. One extreme case is the situation where whatever premium the insurer sets, those with lower risks relative to it will leave the risk pool. In such cases, the premium needs to be adjusted upwards continually in order to provide adequate cover for those with higher risks. Eventually, the premium for the higher risks will become too expensive, and the market itself collapses. This is a 'market failure' for the lower risks, since there is an insurer willing to insure them at a premium they are willing to pay, but the transaction does not take place because the insurer cannot tell the lower risks apart from the higher risks. This is not a market failure for the higher risks, since for them it simply means that the price of what they want is beyond their means. (However, there may be equity issues associated.) One way to counter this is to introduce a public compulsory insurance system that deliberately redistributes from the lower risks to the higher risks.

Lack of symmetry of information between the doctor and patient

In the health care market, the consumer is not independent from the supplier. Because the doctor (supplier) has more information than the patient (consumer) about the health problem and available health care interventions, he often acts as the agent for the patient who then becomes the principal. This imperfect or dual agency, where the doctor is both the supplier and the agent of the consumer at the same time, may lead to supplier-induced demand. This is the case where the supplier affects the preference of the consumer so that their demand is manipulated, causing overconsumption of health care. This is also called supplier moral hazard.

Existence of externalities

An externality is present when the effect of production activities or consumption behaviour goes beyond the direct parties. For instance, the effect of consumption may spill over to those beyond the consumer. A positive externality in consumption means that one individual's consumption not only makes the consumer herself happier, but makes others happier as well. There are two different kinds of externalities in health care. One kind is called selfish externality. This is when the health benefit of health care consumption is not restricted to the consumer herself, as with vaccinations. If one individual gets inoculated, not only is she protected from the infectious disease, it also means that those around her are exposed to one fewer possible source of infection. The other is called caring externality. This is when an individual's utility or happiness is directly affected by the well-being of others, not through reduced risk of her own ill health. For example, people may find it uplifting to know if those who previously could not purchase health care were provided for. The existence of such positive externalities will lead to underconsumption of health care in the market.

Whereas in reality most actual markets fail to satisfy some conditions for a perfect market, a special characteristic of the market for health care is that a whole series of these conditions are unmet. (For more detail on this topic, see Donaldson and Gerard 2005.)

However, it does not automatically follow that, just because a given free unregulated market will lead to highly inefficient outcomes, therefore there should be government regulations and public policy interventions. The beauty of the market mechanism is that it is a completely decentralized system: each individual player will make decisions for himself based on information that is locally and readily available to him. Compared with this, resource allocation by policy making implies centralization, which is a high-cost process requiring large amounts of information to be collected and analysed in order for collective decisions to be made. There are two things to consider before introducing major government regulations to the market: the size of the efficiency loss, and whether government interventions will do more good than harm.

On the other hand, government intervention may be justified independently of market mechanisms. Even where Pareto efficient outcomes are achieved by non-intervention, if the distribution of the commodity is regarded as important in terms of equity, then government may be required to intervene in order to achieve this aspect (provided intervention will do more good than harm). Indeed, most people would agree that health is a special commodity, unlike most other consumer goods, since being healthy is fundamental to individual well-being and flourishing. If this puts *health* on the policy agenda with equity implications, then, to the extent that *health care* contributes to the upkeep and improvement of health, this should also be regarded as an equity concern.

Thus, the market for health care resource allocation is one where it is likely to be highly distorted if not regulated, leading to very large inefficiencies, with potential to lead to inequities and injustice. Evidence-based planned resource allocation is expected to have more efficient and equitable results than leaving the process to an unregulated market.

3.1.2 Resource allocation by planning

Once the judgement has been made that health care resource allocation cannot be left to unregulated markets, and that the provision of health care services will be carried out by planned allocation, either by a publicly funded health care system or by some means such as health maintenance organizations, a need for decision criteria arises. The starting point may be to go back to the Pareto efficiency criterion, and to aim to design a resource allocation system that will achieve such efficiency. However, the Pareto efficiency criterion is not very practical in the planning context, when assessing alternative programmes, because it is not always the case that there is one programme that makes at least one person better off without making anybody else worse off. It is very likely that, for any programme, there will be at least one person who will be made worse off with the programme than without. If this happens, the Pareto criterion is inconclusive.

The Kaldor and the Hicks criteria solve this inconclusiveness. The Kaldor criterion claims that, if, after the change, the 'winners' (i.e. those whose situation improves due to the programme) could get together to 'compensate' all the 'losers' (i.e. those whose situation deteriorates) so that everybody would be better off with the change than without, then the programme improves total efficiency. The Hicks criterion is parallel to this, except that it asks whether, before the change, the losers-to-be could jointly 'bribe' all the winners-to-be, so that everybody would be better off without the change than with, and if so then dropping the programme improves total efficiency. There are two related things to note. One is that since the compensation or bribes are not required actually to be paid, improving efficiency will inevitably violate the Pareto criterion: in other words, there will always be actual losers. More specifically, the losers in the Kaldor scenario, who need compensation from the winners to be at least as well off as they were before the implementation of the programme, are made worse off with the change, because the compensation is not actually paid to them when the programme is implemented. Alternatively, the winners-to-be in the Hicks scenario, who need the bribe from the losers-to-be in order to be at least as well off without the programme as they would be with the programme, would be made worse off, because the bribe is not actually paid to them when the programme is withdrawn. The customary practice of referring to the Kaldor and Hicks criteria as 'potential Paretian' is highly misleading in this respect: in actuality it will always violate the Paretian criterion. The other, related, point to note is that the Kaldor–Hicks criteria only relate to efficiency, or the total good and wealth in an economy, and have no regard for distribution or fairness (and that is why it does not matter if the actual compensation or bribe are not actually paid out, because they are transfers and do not imply changes in the level of total efficiency).

What the winners in the above example gain from the decision can be called 'benefits' of the programme, and what the losers bear can be called 'costs'. Then, the CBA becomes the operationalization of the Kaldor criterion. The basic idea of CBA is to sum up all costs and benefits associated with a given programme and, if the 'net benefit' is positive (i.e. the sum of benefits is larger than the sum of costs), then the total gains to the winners are larger than the total losses to the losers. This can be interpreted to mean that should the winners be called upon to compensate the losers, their gains should be large enough to compensate the losers for their losses, and thus satisfy the Kaldor criterion. This is the welfare economic foundation of CBA. The obvious requirements to make such an analysis work are that benefits and costs are measured in a common unit, such as money, and that each unit of money has equal value for the winners and the losers. Also since CBA is founded on the Kaldor criterion, it has no regard for distribution or fairness. (For further details on this topic, see Boardway and Bruce 1984.)

There are two possible concerns regarding the use of CBA in the area of publicly funded health care resource allocation. First, there is strong resistance, both within the medical community and amongst the general public, towards attaching a monetary value to the health (and life) of a person. If economic evaluation can be carried out without representing health benefits directly in monetary terms, then policies based on such an analysis may become more acceptable beyond the health economics community. Secondly, CBA requires an individual level assessment of the benefits (and the costs) in monetary terms, which means that the way in which a unit of health benefit is reflected in the analysis is affected by whether it is a unit of health benefit to, for example, a rich person or to a poor person, because rich people can afford to pay more for the same health benefit. At one level, this is the correct thing to do; other things being the same, it is more efficient to improve the health of the rich rather than the poor. However, this may be unacceptable to some.

As was pointed out above, health (and by association health care) is often seen as a special good where distribution and equity are central policy concern, alongside efficiency. The conventional way in economics to deal with this is to include 'distributional weights' when the costs and benefits are aggregated, so that the differences in the 'marginal social welfare of individual income' between the rich and the poor are reflected in the calculations. Intuitively, imagine that the income of the rich or of the poor can be increased by a small amount: which would contribute more to improved overall social welfare? If increasing the income of the poor by a small amount is regarded as having a larger impact on social welfare, say twice as good, than increasing the income of the rich by the same amount, then this figure can be used as the weight to correct for the inequality in income between the rich and the poor. The difficulty of this approach is where from, or how, to get this figure, and application in actual CBAs is rare. These issues will be revisited in Chapter 10 on aggregation of health benefits across different individuals.

On the other hand, there are also three possible concerns regarding the use of CEA in public resource allocation. The first is that cost per QALY analysis struggles to capture 'non-health benefits', such as recovered productivity of both the patient and carers, the reassurance of having information, the value of being treated with respect, and so on. CEA is based on the intuitively attractive idea that efficiency is the ratio of inputs to outputs. However, whereas inputs can be converted to money terms, if outputs are to be represented in health terms, where do non-health benefits fit in? Non-health benefits, which cannot be converted to units of health gain, are often either ignored or converted into monetary terms and processed as negative costs; but either way, the analysis no longer represents the ratio of all inputs to all outputs. (Note that the ratio of health *and* non-health benefits to costs is not the same as the ratio of health benefits to costs *minus* non-health benefits.) In contrast, with CBA, since all inputs and all outputs are measured in the same unit, the results are reported in terms of net benefits, and there are no ambiguities about the treatment of non-health benefits: they can be treated as positive benefits, or as negative costs, and the results are not affected.

As a second concern, even when there are no benefits beyond health benefits to the patient, as was noted in Chapter 2, CEAs on their own cannot recommend whether or not a given health care intervention should be taken up, unless the analysis is combined with the concept of a threshold, introduced from outside the study. This means that whereas CBAs can be used to analyse allocative efficiency (the judgement regarding whether a treatment is worthwhile or not), CEAs can only be used to analyse technical or operational efficiency (the judgement regarding whether a treatment is more or less efficient relative to some reference such as the threshold), and not allocative efficiency.

The third concern surrounding cost per QALY analysis is that it is inefficient, because an efficient system needs to allocate resources according to 'effective demand' or, in other words, according to how much people are willing to pay for specific goods and services. If everybody's health is assumed to be of equal value, as measured in QALYs, when in fact the amount of money people are willing to pay for a QALY varies enormously, then allocating resources according to CEAs with QALYs will not achieve maximum efficiency. Indeed, if the objective of economic evaluations is to analyse the efficiency only of different competing resource uses with no regard for distribution and fairness, then CEAs are 'wrong'.

So, to recapitulate, concerns regarding CBA are that they monetize the value of health and life, and that they are insensitive to the impact of income inequality. On the other hand, the concerns over CEA with QALYs are that they cannot incorporate non-health benefits appropriately, that they cannot address allocative efficiency on their own and that they do not promote the most efficient use of limited resources.

How much weight one gives to these concerns is linked to two schools of thought regarding the relationship between CBA and cost per QALY analysis. One is often referred to as the 'welfarist' approach, and holds that CBA is the theoretically correct method of economic evaluation, and cost per QALY analysis is a poor substitute for it, merely tolerated because it avoids the thorny issue of monetary valuation of health. An important topic within this school is the identification of the conditions under which the two types of analysis will reach the same conclusion regarding the funding or otherwise of a given health care intervention (e.g. Johannesson 1995b; Garber and Phelps 1997; Bleichrodt and Quiggin 2003; see also Dolan and Edlin 2002; Hansen *et al.* 2004). The other school of thought, referred to as the 'extra-welfarist', 'non-welfarist' or 'decisionmaker's' approach, holds that cost per QALY analysis is the preferred type of analysis not because it is a practical second-best, but because it is the type of analysis that is more relevant to policy, where equity is a main concern alongside efficiency. Note then that the concern about the equivalence or otherwise of CBA and CEA with QALYs is no longer an issue. (Tsuchiya and Williams 2001). Furthermore, to the extent that it can be argued that the objective of publicly funded health care is to improve population health, it becomes appropriate to leave out non-health benefits.

3.2 **The measure of benefit**

The above description going from CBA to cost per QALY analysis involves not only the change in the way outcomes are presented, but also a possible change in the underlying philosophy regarding the measure of health benefits. CBA is typically embedded in the welfarist philosophy, which holds that what matters in the measurement of social welfare is the well-being of constituent individuals *as assessed by themselves*. Applied to the economic evaluation of health care interventions, it means that the assessment of the size of the benefit from a given medical intervention should be based on the extent to which individual patients are affected and how they, as consumers, value this impact. This is why CBAs are typically based on how people value changes in their own health, expressed in terms of out-of-pocket payments.

On the other hand, CEA with QALYs is usually seen as being based on a non-welfarist approach, where the measurement of social welfare is based on a more external assessment of the well-being of affected individuals. While the *description* of the relevant health states that happen come from the patients themselves, the *valuation* of these states come from elsewhere, typically from a representative sample of the wider tax-paying public (for further details, see Chapter 5).

However, it is important to note that there can also be welfarist CEAs with QALYs and there can be non-welfarist CBAs as well. Welfarist cost per QALY analysis builds on a literature that places the concept of the QALY upon utility theory; this is one of the approaches explained in this section. On the other hand, non-welfarist CBA relies on monetary valuation of benefits, but this valuation is drawn from a non-welfarist perspective. The methods of eliciting monetary preferences for health programmes is beyond the scope of this book, and the interested reader is referred to for example Johansson (1995), Johannesson (1996), Pauly (1996) or Drummond *et al.* (2005). However, to give a simplified explanation, people can be asked to specify how much additional tax could be payable in order to introduce a particular health programme. If the question stresses the probability of the respondents themselves needing this service and contrasts the expected benefit they will receive with the additional tax they will need to pay, then it can be interpreted as being equivalent to a private insurance scenario, which is welfarist.

However, it is also possible to frame non-welfarist questions, for example by asking respondents to consider themselves to be the local policy maker, by stipulating that the respondents themselves will not benefit from this programme and/or by stressing the number of people affected or the overall health impact on the community. Since CBAs based on such information are no longer underwritten by individual utility theory, rather than to call them CBAs that carry welfarist connotations it may perhaps be more appropriate to call them 'CEAs with monetized benefits'. An interesting issue for such an analysis is what the assumed policy objective is. Welfarist economic evaluation aims to maximize the sum of individual utility. Non-welfarist CEA with QALYs has population health as the desideratum. Since non-welfarist CEA with monetized benefits can include non-health benefits, it no longer makes sense to say population health is the desideratum. It needs some concept of the good, to be distributed across the population.

This section looks at welfarist foundations of the concept of the QALY, followed by non-welfarist foundations (3.1).

3.2 The welfarist theory of the QALY

The welfarist theory of the QALY assumes that the QALY represents individual utility concerning their own health. A simple case is where the level of health stays constant throughout the survival, so that there is only one health state between 'now' and 'death'. This is usually referred to as a 'chronic' state. If the utility associated with this constant state survival is to be represented by the number of QALYs, i.e. by the number of years of survival multiplied by the quality of life weight corresponding to that state, then 'mutual utility independence between quantity and quality of life', 'constant proportional time trade-off' and 'risk neutrality with respect to life years' need to be satisfied (Pliskin *et al.* 1980). The derivation of these conditions is based on theory of choice under uncertainty, or expected utility theory. Box 3.2 gives examples of what these conditions mean, and of subsequent developments. The interested reader is referred to the original papers cited in Box 3.2 for a more formal presentation.

In addition to these conditions, if more than one health state is involved in a 'health profile' followed by death, and if the number of QALYs associated with the health profile is to be equal to the sum of individual composite health states, then the 'additive separability' condition is also required. This condition is required because the number of QALYs associated with a given health profile is assumed to be the sum of QALYs associated with each of the composite health states, weighted by their duration. Additive separability assumes that the utility of a state is unaffected by states that precede it or follow it, which might be unrealistic. An alternative approach that does not require the additive separability condition is to treat health profiles themselves as the unit of valuation, and to value these directly. This will allow interactions between the value of health states and their duration. The obvious disadvantage is that the number of outcomes that need to be evaluated will multiply, making it impossible to have any kind of off-the-shelf quality of life instrument. The approach is associated with the healthy year equivalent explained in Box 3.3, and is revisited in Chapter 4.

At an empirical level, there are numerous studies demonstrating that expected utility theory does not have descriptive validity regarding individual choice under uncertainty. In the context of choice over health outcomes,

Table 3.1 CBA and CEA: welfarism and non-welfarism

	Welfarist		Non-welfarist	
	CBA	CEA with QALYs	CEA with monetized benefits	CEA with QALYs
Measure of health benefit	Monetary value	QALYs	Monetary value	QALYs
Perspective of valuation	The potential patient/ consumer/insurance policy holder	The potential patient/ consumer/insurance policy holder	The citizen/tax payer	The citizen/tax payer
Measure of efficiency	Net benefit	Cost per QALY	Net benefit	Cost per QALY
Concept of efficiency	Allocative efficiency	Technical efficiency	Allocative efficiency	Technical efficiency
Treatment of non-health benefits	Yes	No	Yes	No
Concern for equity	Low	Low	Mild	Moderate
The desideratum utility	Sum of individual	The 'good'		Population health

Box 3.2 When is a QALY a representation of individual utility over health?

The adjective 'mutual' in the first condition of Pliskin *et al.* (1980) implies that it can be broken down into two elements, namely: (1a) that utility over duration is independent of the quality of life associated with the survival; and (1b) that the utility, or the quality of life weight, associated with survival in a given health state, is independent of the duration. Suppose individuals are asked to make a choice over two alternatives:

> **alternative 1**: to live in health state h for *2 years for certain*
> **alternative 2**: a lottery with a 50–50 chance to live in health state h for *either 1 year or for 4 years.*

There are no right or wrong answers, and individuals can prefer either alternative. Condition (1a) means that the individual's choice over the two alternatives is not affected by what health state h is. So, if one prefers alternative 1 over alternative 2 when health state h is specified as 'in constant mild depression', then one should also prefer alternative 1 to 2 when state h is replaced with 'in constant severe depression'.

On the other hand, condition (1b) means that the individual's choice over alternatives 3 and 4 are not affected by the duration t, where the two alternatives are for instance:

> **alternative 3**: to live for t years for certain *in constant moderate pain*
> **alternative 4**: a lottery with a 50–50 chance to live for t years *either in constant mild pain or in constant severe pain.*

So, if one prefers alternative 3 over alternative 4 when duration t is given as 2 years, then one should continue to prefer alternative 3 over 4 when duration t is increased to 20 years, or reduced to 2 months.

The second condition, constant proportional time trade-off, means that, suppose an individual is indifferent between alternatives 5 and 6:

> **alternative 5**: to live for T years for certain *in constant severe depression*
> **alternative 6**: to live for t years for certain *in constant mild depression*
> $(t < T)$;

this indifference is not affected by changing the values of t and T proportionately. So, if one is indifferent between the two alternatives when $T = 3$ years and $t = 2$ years, then one should continue to be indifferent

Box 3.2 When is a QALY a representation of individual utility over health? *(continued)*

when these figures are changed to $T = 30$ and $t = 20$, or to $T = 3$ months and $t = 2$ months.

The third condition, risk neutrality over years of life, means that the individual is indifferent between:

> **alternative 7**: to live in health state h for *2 years for certain*
> **alternative 8**: a lottery with a 50–50 chance to live in health state h for *either 1 year or for 3 years*,

because the expected duration of alternative 8 (the sum of the years weighted by the respective probabilities: $0.5 \times 1 + 0.5 \times 3 = 2$) is the same as the expected duration of alternative 7: to live for 2 years in state h.

Subsequently, Bleichrodt *et al.* (1997) have demonstrated that the number of assumptions can be reduced to two: risk neutrality in life years and the 'zero condition'. The latter implies that where the duration of survival is zero life years, all health states have the same utility level.

For the case of risk aversion, Miyamoto *et al.* (1998) further demonstrated that the requirement becomes the zero condition and 'standard gamble invariance'. Suppose the individual is indifferent between:

> **alternative 7'**: to live in health state h for *2 years for certain*
> **alternative 8'**: a lottery with a 40–60 chance to live in health state h for *either 1 year or for 3 years*

then standard gamble invariance means that this 40–60 chance is not affected by the health state h, as long as it is a health state worth living in.

---

individual preferences are frequently found to violate the conditions above in a non-systematic way (for a review, see Tsuchiya and Dolan 2005). This has two implications: first, there is no systematic way to correct the violations at the individual level; but, secondly, the conditions tend to be satisfied at the aggregate level.

There are two approaches to this. One is to generalize or adapt utility theory so that it can accommodate individual behaviour that amounts to violations of the original theory (see Box 3.3). The aim of such research is to reconstruct the QALY concept based on relaxed utility foundations, and then to explore whether or not actual individual choice behaviour will satisfy the associated conditions for the new QALY concept to hold. The objective of this first

Box 3.3 Two proposals to make QALYs better reflect actual individual preferences

The first proposal is to define the measure of benefit as the number of years in full health that is equivalent to the expected health outcome (including health profiles). This number is defined as the healthy year equivalent (HYE; Mehrez and Gafni 1989). The concept does not rely on the QALY model (survival weighted by quality of life), and thus does not impose any conditions on individual preference between life years and quality of life. It was subsequently proposed that this concept can be operationalized through the use of a two-stage standard gamble (Mehrez and Gafni 1991), which led to a major theoretical debate (in chronological order: Buckingham 1993; Culyer and Wagstaff 1993; Gafni *et al.* 1993; Bleichrodt 1995; Johannesson 1995a; Loomes 1995; Culyer and Wagstaff 1995; Wakker 1996; Morrison 1997). The conclusion reached is that HYE measured by two-stage standard gambles is theoretically equivalent to a time trade-off exercise, but with a larger margin for error at the practical level. For a review of the HYE debate, see Towers *et al.* (2005).

A more recent proposal is to re-build the QALY model based on generalizations of expected utility theory developed in theoretical economics, for example rank-dependent expected utility theory (Wakker and Stiggelbout 1995: Miyamoto 1999; Doctor *et al.* 2004; Bleichrodt and Pinto 2005; Bleichrodt and Quiggin 2005). The essence of this proposal is to allow for the fact that people seem to overestimate very small and very large probabilities, and to underestimate mid-range probabilities. By introducing the notion that subjective probability (based on which people make choices) is not the same as objective probability, the theory has been found to be successful in providing a more accurate account of individual choice under uncertainty.

approach then is to identify a theory that successfully represents actual individual choice under uncertainty. The alternative approach is to accept that real individual choice under uncertainty violates axioms of expected utility theory, but to continue to use the theory as the normative basis on which to build policy decisions, since such violations do not diminish the normative validity of the theory. If individual choice in the real world is found to be irrational by whatever definition of rationality, it makes no sense for public policy to emulate such irrational choices, nor does it make sense to abandon the definition of rationality because of it (Tsuchiya and Dolan 2005). Alongside the exploration of theories of individual choice that have improved descriptive validity, there needs to be a normative discourse on what should be the basis on which to make policy decisions, and how this should be determined.

3.2.2 The non-welfarist theory of the QALY

An altogether different approach is a 'non-welfarist theory' of the QALY. Standard economic theory is 'welfarist', which means that it assumes individuals are the best judges of their own welfare, expressed in terms of individual utility, and that social welfare is the sum of individual utilities. Non-welfarism challenges this notion of the social good as a function of individual utility as assessed by the individuals themselves, and allows for the notion of the social good which is a function of, for example in the area of publicly funded health care resource allocation, total population health as assessed by the tax-paying citizenry at large. This leads to an alternative approach to the value of the QALY, which posits that the QALY is not a representation of individual utility, but a measure of health as a social desideratum. The line of argument here holds that the reason why producing 10 QALYs is twice as good as producing five QALYs at the same cost is not because it generates twice as much individual utility, but because it generates twice as much social good.

This approach can be traced back to the theory of capabilities and functionings, first proposed by Amartya Sen (1982, 1985; also see Sugden 1993), as an alternative to welfarist economics, which in effect assumes that judgements on social welfare, or social desirability of different states of the world, can be made on the basis of people's welfare information alone. In the narrowest sense, this means information on people's consumption behaviour or their 'revealed preference', but in the context of CBA this can include information on what people state for example in surveys, or their 'expressed preferences'. Sen's proposal is to involve a much wider information base concerning the set of opportunities the individuals have beyond the particular outcomes they choose for themselves. Note that the set of desirable basic opportunities to individuals does not necessarily come from the individuals themselves, because it is based on the notion of what everybody ought to have for social good to be achieved. The approach was adopted in the area of health care by Culyer (1989) under the banner of 'extra-welfarism' (also see Brouwer and Koopmanschap 2000; Cookson 2005).

The advantage of this approach is that the actual individual utility of those directly affected may or may not change proportionally to the size of QALY gains, but this is now irrelevant (Tsuchiya and Williams 2001). Note also that it will be awkward under this school to refer to cost per QALY analysis as cost 'utility' analysis. The difficulty of this approach on the other hand is that the process by which the social desideratum is determined is not clear, and possibly beyond the remit of economic analysis. However, note how similar this non-welfarist approach is in some respects to the argument above on the normative status of expected utility theory; and there, too, the difficulty would be the issue of who decides what constitutes rationality, and how.

3.3 Conclusion

The aim of this chapter was to examine what is to be valued for use in economic evaluation and specifically the place of the QALY measure. It started with a review of the theoretical foundations of public intervention and the role of economic evaluation. It then moved on to the economists' default position, the market mechanism. This failure leads to health care resource allocation by government intervention, followed by the distributional implications of using CBA, and the cost per QALY analysis as an alternative to CBA. The next section looked at two different theories of the QALY; one that interprets the QALY as a representation of individual utility, and another that interprets the QALY as a measure of social good in health policy. Finally, there was discussion of non-welfarist foundation for the QALY. This issue of welfarism and non-welfarism will be revisited in Chapter 10.

References

Bleichrodt H (1995). QALYs and HYEs—under what conditions are they equivalent? *Journal of Health Economics* 14:17–37.

Bleichrodt H, Pinto JL (2005). The validity of QALYs under non-expected utility. *The Economic Journal* 115:533–50.

Bleichrodt H, Quiggin J (2003). Life-cycle preferences over consumption and health: when is cost-effectiveness analysis equivalent to cost-benefit analysis? *Journal of Health Economics* 18:681–708.

Bleichrodt H, Quiggin J (2005). Characterizing QALYs under a general rank dependent utility model. *Journal of Risk and Uncertainty* 15:151–65.

Bleichrodt H, Wakker P, Johannesson M (1997). Characterizing QALYs by risk neutrality. *Journal of Risk and Uncertainty* 15:107–14.

Boardway R, Bruce N (1984). *Welfare economics*: Basil Blackwell, Oxford.

Brouwer W, Koopmanschap M (2000). On the economic foundations of CEA: ladies and gentlemen, take your positions! *Journal of Health Economics* 19:149–67.

Buckingham K (1993). A note on HYE (healthy years equivalent). *Journal of Health Economics* 12:301–9.

Cookson R (2005) QALYs and the capabilities approach. *Health Economics* 14:817–29.

Culyer AJ (1989). The normative economics of health care finance and provision. *Oxford Review of Economic Policy* 5: 34–58

Culyer AJ, Wagstaff A (1993). QALYs versus HYEs. *Journal of Health Economics* 12:311–23.

Culyer AJ, Wagstaff A (1995). QALYs versus HYEs—a reply to Gafni, Birch and Mehrez. *Journal of Health Economics* 14:39–45.

Doctor JN, Bleichrodt H, Miyamoto J, Temkin NR, Dikmen S (2004). A new and more robust test of QALYs. *Journal of Health Economics* 23:353–67.

Dolan P, Edlin R (2002). Is it really possible to build a bridge between cost-benefit analysis and cost-effectiveness analysis? *Journal of Health Economics* 21:827–43.

Donaldson C, Gerard K (2005). *Economics of health care financing: the visible hand*, 2nd edn. Palgrave McMillan, Basingstoke, UK.

Drummond MF, Sculpher MJ, Torrance GW, O'Brien B, Stoddart GL (2005). *Methods for the economic evaluation of health care programmes*, 3rd edn. Oxford University Press, Oxford.

Gafni A, Birch S, Mehrez A (1993). Economics, health and health economics—HYEs versus QALYs. *Journal of Health Economics* 12:325–39.

Garber AM, Phelps CE (1997). Economic foundations of cost-effectiveness analysis. *Journal of Health Economics* 16:1–31.

Hansen BO, Hougaard JL, Keiding H, Østerdal LP (2004). On the possibility of a bridge between CBA and CEA: comments on a paper by Dolan and Edlin. *Journal of Health Economics* 23:887–98.

Johannesson M (1995a). Quality-adjusted life-years versus healthy-years equivalents—a comment. *Journal of Health Economics* 14(1):9–16.

Johannesson M (1995b). The relationship between cost-effectiveness analysis and cost-benefit analysis. *Social Science and Medicine* 41:483–9.

Johannesson M (1996). *Theory and methods of economic evaluation of health care*. Kluwer Academic Publishers, Dordrecht.

Johansson P-O (1995). *Evaluating health risks: an economic approach*. Cambridge University Press, Cambridge.

Loomes G (1995). The myth of the HYE. *Journal of Health Economics* 14:1–7.

Mehrez A, Gafni A (1989). Quality-adjusted life years, utility-theory, and healthy-years equivalents. *Medical Decision Making* 9:142–9.

Mehrez A, Gafni A (1991). The healthy-years equivalents—how to measure them using the standard gamble approach. *Medical Decision Making* 11:140–6.

Miyamoto J (1999). Quality-adjusted life years (QALY) utility models under expected utility and rank dependent utility assumptions. *Journal of Mathematical Psychology* 43:201–37.

Miyamoto JM, Wakker PP, Bleichrodt H, Peters HJM (1998). The zero-condition: a simplifying assumption in QALY measurement and multiattribute utility. *Management Science* 44:839–49.

Morrison GC (1997). HYE and TTO: what is the difference? *Journal of Health Economics* 16:563–78.

Pauly MV (1996). Valuing health care benefits in money terms. In: Sloan FA, ed. *Valuing health care: costs, benefits, and effectiveness of pharmaceuticals and other medical technologies*. Cambridge University Press, Cambridge, pp. 99–124.

Pliskin JS, Shepard DS, Weinstein MC (1980). Utility functions for life years and health status. *Operations Research* 28:206–24.

Sen A (1982). *Choice, welfare, and measurement*. Basil Blackwell, Oxford.

Sen A (1985). *Commodities and capabilities*. North-Holland Publishing, Amsterdam.

Sugden R (1993). Welfare, resources, and capabilities: a review of inequality reexamined by Amartya Sen. *Journal of Economic Literature* 31:1947–62.

Towers I, Spencer A, Brazier J (2005). Healthy year equivalents versus quality-adjusted life years: the debate continues. *Expert Review of Pharmacoeconomics and Outcomes Research* 5:245–54.

Tsuchiya A, Dolan P (2005). The QALY model and individual preferences for health states and health profiles over time: a systematic review of the literature. *Medical Decision Making* 25:460–7.

Tsuchiya A, Williams A (2001). Welfare economics and economic evaluation. In: Drummond M, McGuire A, eds. *Theory and practice of economic evaluation in health care*. Oxford University Press, Oxford, pp. 22–45.

Wakker P (1996). Criticism of healthy-years equivalents. *Medical Decision Making* 16:207–14.

Wakker P, Stiggelbout A (1995). Explaining distortions in utility elicitation through the rank-dependent model for risky choices. *Medical Decision Making* 15:80–6.

Chapter 4

Describing health

The valuation of health, whether narrowly or broadly defined, requires some means of first describing it. The economic evaluation literature in health care (as elsewhere in economics) has tended to neglect the methodological issues around describing benefits and instead has focused on methods of valuation. This contrasts with the psychometric literature, where it has long been recognized that what you describe and the way you describe it will affect the values you obtain.

This chapter considers the description of health in two parts. The first part is more conceptual and considers what should be described, and the second part reviews the practical issues in developing and testing descriptive systems. This chapter does not consider the direct valuation of one's own health by a respondent, which potentially avoids the need to describe the states first (arguments for using direct valuations of states rather than asking others to value a hypothetical state is reviewed in Chapter 5).

4.1 What should be described?

There are a number of important conceptual issues to consider prior to looking at the more practical issues surrounding the construction of states of health, including the definition of health, the notion of a health spectrum (from impairment to participation) and scope (whether it should be limited to a condition, programme or generic health, or extend into non-health aspects of well-being).

4.1.1 What is health?

In Chapter 2 we presented the famous definition of health introduced by the Constitution of the World Health Organisation (1948) as: 'A state of complete physical, mental and social well-being, and not merely the absence of disease and infirmity'. This is a very broad definition that does not offer any clear guidance on the content of an instrument for measuring health. Indeed, there have been some researchers in the field who have not used this definition. There are those instrument developers who have taken a narrower definition that focuses on symptoms and impairments. Health may impact on social well-being, but some have questioned whether it can be regarded as a dimension of health in its own right. Those who take such a narrow definition of health have either nonetheless described the impact of health on these broader notions of well-being and quality of life in their instrument, e.g. AQoL by Hawthorne *et al.* (1997), or they have sought to exclude them altogether from their instrument, e.g. HUI3 (Feeny *et al.*, 2002). Such differences in the use of terminology are confusing, but in a sense do not matter. What matters for health policy is the specific content of the description of benefit. Whether or not social activities are counted as health, health-related quality of life or quality of life does not matter; the important question is whether impact on social activities should form the part of the description of the benefits of health care. This chapter is concerned with establishing the appropriate content descriptions of benefit for informing resource allocation decisions.

As a consequence, measures of health or health-related quality of life differ considerably in their content in terms of whether they focus on symptoms or impairments through to broad notions of impact on role and social functioning, whether they are concerned with capabilities or performance and their scope (condition specific, generic health or broader notions of well-being). These conceptual issues are addressed in some detail in this section.

Health as a spectrum

There is an important distinction to be made between the 'stimulus', such as a disease or its treatment, and an 'outcome' in terms of impairments, disabilities and participation in society. These can all be health, so for example a patient may have a medical condition, such as macular degeneration or rheumatism, that may have implications for a person's vision and dexterity respectively, and then these in turn may impact on a person's ability to read or walk, and these impacts may have consequences for a person's ability to function in society (in terms of work, household tasks, visiting friends and relatives, and so forth). Measures of health have tended to exist on this spectrum, starting with a narrow conception of health as the absence of disease through to its impact of a person's ability to function and ultimately to participate in society. This can be seen in the World Health Organization (WHO) 'International Classification of Impairments, Disabilities and Handicaps' (World Health Organization 1980) or the revised version renamed as the 'International Classification of Functioning, Disability and Health' (World Health Organization 2001). The WHO classification defines health in terms of impairment, disability and handicap, and links them together in a conceptual framework (Fig. 4.1). An important question in the design of a measure of health is how far along this spectrum its description should be located.

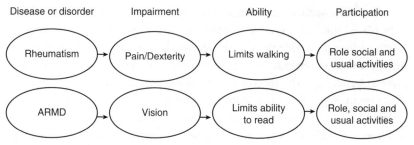

Fig. 4.1 WHO international classification of impairment, abilities and participation (with examples).

The difference between a comparatively objective description of the symptoms or physical impairment associated with a medical condition and its impact on social participation will be the preferences of the patient (who completes the descriptions) and the extent to which they are able to adapt to their medical condition. Someone who has a chronic impairment or disability is likely to change in a number of ways, both physically and emotionally. While initially a person may find that her participation in role and social activities, for example, is severely reduced by an impairment (such as a loss of vision or mobility), over time she may overcome some of these problems and indeed change her activities and so reduce the impact.

The developers of the HUI3 designed their instrument to assess aspects of impairment and disability (known as 'within-skin aspects' of health) and avoided the use of descriptions concerned with social participation (Feeny 2002; Feeny *et al.* 2002). The way an impairment or disability affects a person's participation is partly a matter of choice, and the developers of HUI3 wanted these considerations to be left to the respondents undertaking the valuation. Respondents to the valuation task should be using their preferences rather than those of the patients who completed the description of their health. The developers of the HUI3 wanted effectively 'pure' general population values that are not contaminated by patient preferences[1].

---

[1] A useful consequence of using descriptions of impairments and disabilities is that dimensions are more likely to be independent from one another. There will always be some correlation in prevalence between dimensions of health, but the correlation between dimensions of impairment are likely to be less than those for participation [e.g. the correlations between the dimensions of the HUI3 are considerably lower than for dimensions of the EQ-5D (Feeny 2002)]. This is extremely useful for the valuation survey, where some of the states chosen for valuation may prove to be infeasible if the dimensions are too highly correlated (such as being in severe pain but having no problems with social activities). The importance of this problem is discussed in Chapter 6.

On the other hand, it can be argued that general population values are likely to be biased precisely because they will not anticipate the degree of adaptation, so why not provide them with information on social participation that helps them to understand what it is like? There is evidence that we are very poor at predicting the degree to which we would adapt to a poor state (Kahneman 2000). Respondents to these surveys are usually members of the general population who have little or no experience of many impairments, and it may be helpful to give them a description of the resulting impact on their lives. The question of whether or not adaptation should be incorporated into the values used in economic evaluation is examined at some length in the section 'Who should value health' in Chapter 5. At this point, we hope we have demonstrated that the same issues arise in the way health is described.

There are more general arguments for wanting to use participation and concepts closer to notions of well-being and quality of life. Quality of life researchers have argued that the more narrow 'health'-focused descriptions fail to reflect what matters to patients (McGee *et al*. 1991; Bowling 1997; McKenna *et al*. 1999; Bradley 2001; Grewal *et al*. 2006). Health is merely a means to the ultimate end of improved quality of life. Measures focusing on the participation end of the spectrum lend themselves more to being generic, since the dimensions such as role functioning, social activities and personal attachment are not specific to a particular condition. These can be affected by a range of different diseases and impairments. However, it is not possible to generalize on this point since there are important exceptions. The HUI3, for example, is generic without extending 'beyond the skin', and there are examples of condition-specific measures that do locate themselves further along the spectrum towards well-being and quality of life (Bradley *et al*. 1999; McKenna *et al*. 1999).

Many preference-based generic measures (as well as non-preference-based ones) combine different points along the spectrum. The EQ-5D, for example, includes two dimensions for impairment (pain, and depression and anxiety), two for disability (mobility and self-care) and one for participation (usual activities). The SF-6D also has dimensions from all three. The problem with mixing up points along the spectrum is that there is a risk of double counting. Diseases that impact on pain are likely to impact on all three, and so respondents valuing an EQ-5D or SF-6D state may be valuing the impact of pain on quality of life three times over. More thought should be given to removing this double counting.

Capacity or performance

Another conceptual concern is whether to describe a person's capacity or their performance. The argument for choosing capability is that it separates what a person can do from what they choose to do, and thereby removes a person's preferences from the description. This overcomes the concerns that the developers of the HUI3 have with using social participation in a descriptive system. This has been the approach of Coast and colleagues in their index of capability for health and social policy evaluation for older people (Coast *et al.* 2006). In contrast, there has been a re-wording of the items of the original version of QWB from capacity to behaviour and actual performance (Kaplan *et al.* 1976; Kaplan and Anderson 1990). Kaplan *et al.* (1976) have argued that asking about behaviour and actual performance is better because it avoids the need for respondents to make difficult judgements about what he/she *could* do. SF-6D and EQ-5D also ask about performance rather than capacity.

4.1.2 Scope of measurement: condition-specific, generic health or overall well-being?

A description of benefits for economic evaluation, be it impairment or handicap, or indeed well-being beyond health, can be specific in some way, such as by disease group (e.g. asthma), a dimension of health (e.g. pain in back pain) or a particular care group (e.g. the elderly); or it can be generic to health (e.g. the EQ-5D or SF-36); or it can be a general measure of quality of life or well-being suitable for assessing more than health or health-related aspects of quality of life. This section focuses on two key questions arising from these choices: whether to use condition-specific or generic health descriptions, and whether to limit the description to health or extend it to other aspects of well-being.

Condition-specific versus generic descriptions

The argument for using *generic* preference-based measures of health in economic evaluation is to permit comparisons between health care programmes, even where they involve different medical conditions and treatments. They achieve this by using a standardized generic descriptive system, and a single preference-based algorithm for deriving an index value. The Natioanl Institute for Clinical Excellence (2004) has been one agency that accepts this argument and requires the use of a generic preference-based measure in the reference case economic analysis.

However, generic measures of health have been found to be inappropriate or insensitive for many medical conditions (e.g. Harper *et al.* 1997; Kobelt *et al.* 1999; Barton *et al.* 2004; Espallargues *et al.* 2005). An alternative is to use condition-specific descriptions that have been shown to be more sensitive to changes in the condition than generic measures and more relevant to the concerns of patients (Brazier and Fitzpatrick 2002; Guyatt 2002). This can be done using either a standard condition-specific descriptive system where health is described across a set of multilevel dimensions or vignettes (see below for discussion of how this might be done). Standardized preference-based condition-specific measures of health are starting to be developed and there are a number of examples now in the literature (e.g. Revicki *et al.* 1998; Brazier *et al.* 2005; Yang *et al.* 2006). The vignette approach to describing specific conditions and their treatment has been used for many years, and indeed was more prevalent before the emergence of the generic preference-based measures (e.g. Sackett and Torrance 1978; Bass *et al.* 1994; Cook *et al.* 1994).

The arguments for and against using condition-specific descriptions are summarised in Box 4.1. One argument for using condition-specific descriptions is that they are expected to be more sensitive to the consequences of the condition suffered by the patient because they focus on the most important dimensions pertinent to that condition (Fig. 4.1). Condition-specific descriptions may thereby achieve a greater degree of precision and so better reflect differences in severity of the conditions and changes over time. A cruder generic measure may miss more subtle changes or require a larger sample size to be able to pick them up. A more fundamental argument is that generic measures may not cover all dimensions of relevance to a condition. Generic measures are designed to cover the core dimensions of health, and what this means in practice is that they cover the more common dimensions of health (Ware and Sherbourne 1992; Brooks and the EuroQol Group 1996). No instrument is able to cover all health dimensions. Existing generic instruments have been found to cover little more than 50 per cent of health dimensions elicited from a survey of the general population (Williams 1995). This has been shown to be a problem with urinary incontinence, where the general health questionnaires do not cover some of the important consequences of bladder problems for quality of life (such as the impact on personal relationships and sleep) and have been found to be insensitive to improvement after treatment that was shown to be effective using other instruments (Sand *et al.* 1994).

An argument for generic measures is that condition-specific descriptions may fail to capture the impact on co-morbidities suffered by patients and the side effects of treatment. Patients commonly have co-morbidities, particularly in older age, and these conditions can be more important to the patient's health than the condition being treated (but may be affected by the treatment). Most health care interventions have side effects which have little to do with the conditions being treated, and indeed many new pharmaceutical products differ in terms of their side-effect profile rather than their consequences for the condition being treated. A condition-specific measure could therefore give a partial and potentially misleading view.

Box 4.1 The arguments for and against using (condition or programme) specific descriptions in economic evaluation

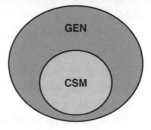

Fig. 1 CSM focuses.

There are two possible ways to perceive the relationship between generic (GEN) and condition-specific measures (CSMs). One is characterized in Figure 1 where CSMs are seen to focus more on the domains of interest, and the other in Figure 2, where CSMs are seen to cover different dimensions.

Arguments for specific measures:

- By focusing on the condition, they are able to be more sensitive for a given dimension (consistent with the view in Figure 1).

- By focusing on the condition, they cover important dimensions of the condition missed by generic measures (consistent with the view in Figure 2).

Arguments against specific measures:

- They may miss the impact on possible co-morbidities (consistent with the view in Figure 2).

- They may miss side effects (consistent with the view in Figure 2) (though some measures include side effects of common treatments).

- They will not be comparable across programmes (due to preference dependence between dimensions).

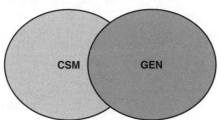

Fig. 2 CSM covers different dimensions.

The solution commonly advocated in health services research (outside of health economics) is to use a generic *and* condition-specific measure in the same study (Guyatt 2002). However, a decision must still be made as to which to use—economic evaluation needs to have one preference-based measure (Dowie 2002). Another would be to develop specific instruments that cover common side effects of treatments (e.g. the HIV Symptom Distress Module developed by Justice *et al.* 2001). A related solution would be to develop vignettes that incorporate condition and treatment effects, and this is discussed later. As new treatments come along, these could be modified.

A more fundamental concern with condition-specific instruments is whether they can be used to make comparisons between interventions for different conditions. The answer to this question depends on whether the method of valuation ensures comparability. It seems to have been an implicit assumption in the WTP literature and the early QALY literature of the 1970s and 1980s that this is the case, but more recently it has been argued that comparability needs a single generic descriptive system (Dowie 2002; National Institute for Health and Clinical Excellence 2004). A response to this position is that comparability can be achieved by the use of a common numeraire such as money or a year in full health. Provided the values were obtained using the same valuation technique (and variant of the technique) with common anchors (full health and death) and the values were obtained from the same type of respondents (such as a representative sample of the general population), it could be argued that a common measuring stick is being used and so comparisons can be made between QALYs estimated using different descriptive systems. In practice, however, studies have often used different valuation methods, so these requirements do not hold (Drummond *et al.* 1993).

For comparability to be achieved between specific instruments requires an additional assumption, namely that the impact of different dimensions on preferences is additive, whether or not they are included in the descriptive system. The impact of breathlessness on health state values, for example, must be the same whether or not the patient has other health problems not covered by the vignette or descriptive system, such as pain in joints. Then provided the intervention only alters the dimensions covered in the specific instrument, the estimated change in health state value would be correct. It assumes preference independence between dimensions included in the descriptive system of the specific measure and those dimensions not included (i.e. for a health state with six dimensions, where the level of each dimension is indicated by a digit, then the difference between state XXX111 and YYY111 should be the same as the difference between XXX333 and YYY333).

Preference interactions have been shown to exist in the published literature. Dimensions of health have been found to be largely complementary (Dolan 1997; Brazier *et al.* 2002; Feeny *et al*, 2002), with the impact of a problem on one dimension of health being reduced by the existence of a problem on another domain. When the different dimensions are included in the descriptive system, then such interactions can be modelled in various ways (see Chapter 6 on modelling). For dimensions outside a descriptive system, then clearly this is not possible. This is likely to create a bigger problem in specific measures that focus on a small subset of health dimensions compared with generic measures that cover a broader range of health dimensions (though the problem will also exist for generic health measures, since they too exclude many important dimensions). Furthermore, these problems apply to preference-based measures of health and WTP methods.

So what is the solution?

A perfect measure of health-related quality of life: '… would tap all aspects of HRQL, would be anchored to death and full health in a manner that allowed integration of quality and quantity of life, and would be able to detect any important differences in HRQL' (Guyatt 2002). The problem is that respondents undertaking a valuation task struggle with more than 5–9 pieces of information at once and so there is more of a practical constraint on the size of descriptive systems designed for valuing than for non-preference-based measures. Any descriptive system that is to be amenable to valuation will exclude many dimensions of health. For use in cross-programme comparison, it is ultimately a trade-off between having measures that are relevant and sensitive to those things that matter to patients (including side effects) and the potential size of the preference dependence between dimensions. Pragmatically, the importance of preference interactions will not be the same between conditions. Where most patients have one condition or where the condition concerned dominates, then the role of interactions is likely to be more modest. The relative importance of the different arguments in this trade-off will vary between conditions.

Population-specific measures

Specific measures can be aimed at entire groups, such as children, the elderly, mentally ill or institutionalized people, rather than just single individuals. The arguments are similar to those concerning condition-specific measures, namely that no measure can be suitable for all patient groups (Donaldson *et al.* 1988). This is clearly the case with children, where the measurement of disabilities or participation, for example, will be confounded by the child's cognitive and emotional development (Eiser and Morse 2001). A failure to take adequate account of development means that a measure may suggest that the health or quality of life of a child is improving when these changes are due to natural development. It could also be argued that the dimensions of health and quality of life that matter to a child or indeed a retired person may be substantially different from those that matter to a working adult. Users of services for the mentally ill may also experience very different types of health problem.

For this reason, instruments such as the EQ-5D and SF-6D are not recommended in children, although the position is less clear for the very elderly or people with, say, severe mental illness. Group-specific measures should not raise the same problems as condition-specific measures since they should cover a broader range of dimensions (although mental illness may raise these concerns if it excludes any dimensions for physical health). However, it does raise a problem for making cross-group comparisons necessary for informing resource allocation. This means that the same methods of valuation must be used along with the same anchors for the upper and lower states, such as being dead and in full health (or optimal quality of life). Equivalence across group-specific measures needs to be demonstrated. Similar issues are raised in using different language versions of existing instruments for those who do not speak the local majority language. (For the issue of across-language comparability for international studies, see Chapter 11.)

Of course, equity consideration may mean that a QALY to a child is worth more than a QALY to a member of the general population (see Chapter 10), but this still requires a health state value.

Health or well-being

There is no reason why the concept of a QALY needs to be limited strictly to health, and indeed its very name indicates a rather broader view of benefits. Neither is there any reason why the benefits of a health care intervention have to be restricted to health. The arguments for and against a broader scope that extends to other, non-health aspects of well-being in part mirror those surrounding the condition-specific versus generic measures of health debate (see above). A broader measure may be less sensitive and less likely to reflect dimensions of health important to patients. However, narrower health measures ignore important aspects of well-being that may be altered by health care interventions and, if the measure is intended to reflect the overall impact of health on well-being, then the preference interactions between health and other aspects of well-being may undermine the validity of the valuations.

In Chapter 3 we reviewed the welfarist and non-welfarist arguments for focusing on health, as opposed to 'utility' in general. It has been argued that the primary aim of many public health care systems has been to maximize health from a limited budget (allowing for equity concerns about the distribution of health), which needs a measure of health, and the QALY seems well suited to this end. This has been the view taken by NICE (2004) in its recommendations for methods of economic evaluation.

This raises the question of what is the distinction between health and quality of life. The broad WHO definition of health has been very influential in the development of health status measures (Ware 1987). However, it has been criticized for being indistinguishable from the concept of well-being itself (Evans and Wolfson 1980). Existing preference-based generic measures have dimensions such as role functioning (e.g. work) and social activities, that are arguably nearer to notions of overall well-being than health, and some measures even have items concerning happiness. Whilst the dimensions of these measures do not cover all aspects of well-being, they are broad and extend beyond what many would regard as health. Some instrument developers have used the concept of 'health-related quality of life', but 'related' is rather vague since role, social activities and happiness are all affected by far more than health alone. Equally, there are dimensions not in these generic measures, such as wealth and education, that might also be related to health.

The problems of distinguishing between health and well-being are largely semantic, but what is important is that the description covers those things thought to be important for influencing health policy (Richardson 1994).

4.2 Practical concerns in the description of health

There are two broad approaches to describing health with a view to deriving health state values. One is to construct a bespoke description of the condition and/or its treatment and the other is to use a standardized descriptive system (such as the EQ-5D). A bespoke description, sometimes referred to as a vignettes in the literature, can take the form of a text narrative (e.g. Sackett and Torrance 1978; Llewellyn-Thomas et al. 1984; Gerard et al. 1993) or a more structured description using a bullet point format (Bass et al. 1994). More recently, researchers have begun to explore alternative narrative formats, such as the use of videos or simulators (Lenert and Sturley 2001; Aballéa and Tsuchiya 2004).

The standardized descriptive system already takes a structured format with a set of multilevel dimensions. Any given health state is formed by combining one level from each of these dimensions. A well known example of this is the EQ-5D with five dimensions, each containing three levels that can be combined to form 243 states (i.e. 3^5).

The use of bespoke vignettes was more common in the early years of obtaining health state values (Torrance 1976), but there has been a steady rise of the standardized generic systems in recent years. Standardized descriptive systems raise an additional set of problems that are addressed in a separate section.

There has been surprisingly little written in the economics literature on the appropriate design of health state descriptions or the way in which they should be constructed (Smith and Dobson 1993). This section attempts to bring the literature and address key issues, such as the arguments for and against using standardized approaches rather than bespoke vignettes. It examines key debates in the construction of such descriptions, such as whether to use disease labels or not, whether to use first, second or third person, and how to generate the descriptions in the first place. Then it examines the more practical issues in the construction of descriptions, but it begins by considering the criteria for constructing and testing descriptions.

4.2.1 Criteria for constructing and testing descriptions

The criteria of practicality, reliability and validity are important concerns for assessing the performance of any measurement instrument. These are the psychometric criteria traditionally applied to non-preference-based measures of health and quality of life, but, until recently, rarely considered in relation to the construction of descriptive systems for valuation. However, they are starting to be applied to the standardized descriptive systems such as the EQ-5D and SF-6D (see Chapter 8).

It is easier to see how these criteria might be applied to standardized health state descriptions. The *practicality* of administering the descriptive system depends on its acceptability to patients and the cost of administration (e.g. in terms of time). This can be assessed in terms of method of administration, how long the instrument takes to administer and the proportion of completed questionnaires. *Reliability* is the ability of a measure to reproduce the same value on two separate administrations when there has been no change in health. This can be over time or between methods of administration, such as postal surveys and interviews using the same questionnaire.

The *overall validity* of a measure for deriving QALYs has a number of components, but an important part is the validity of the description of the states (Brazier and Deverill 1999). *Descriptive validity* can be assessed in terms of the content, face and construct validity of the descriptions of the health state (Bowling 1997; Streiner and Norman 1997). *Content validity* is defined as the extent to which the description comprehensively covers the different dimensions of health and is sufficiently sensitive to changes. *Face validity* considers whether the items of each domain are sensible and appropriate for the population.

These two forms of validity can apply to all types of vignettes and standardized health state classifications. They tend to be judged partly by the way the content was obtained. Where the developer based the content on well conducted qualitative interviews of patients or other well informed parties (such as carers) then this lends credibility to the descriptions. The validity of the content can also be tested using cognitive interview techniques to establish whether patients, for example, understand the descriptions in the way they are intended to be understood. Content might also be tested in focus group settings or through in-depth qualitative interviews to establish whether patients (or relevant others) believe the description to be realistic.

Construct validity is tested empirically in terms of the extent to which a measure agrees with other measures or indicators of health. There are two commonly used approaches in the psychometric literature to examining construct validity of a standardized descriptive system. One approach is to examine whether it is able to differentiate between groups thought to differ in terms of their health, and the other is the extent to which it correlates with another measure of health. Construct validation can never prove the descriptive validity of an instrument, since this also depends on the hypotheses. Furthermore, construct validation should be performed on descriptions and not the preference-based index derived from the measure (Brazier and Deverill 1999). Whether or not a difference in health translates into a change in the preference index depends on whether it is regarded as important to the respondent in the valuation exercise.

A related empirical test is *responsiveness*, which is the ability of an instrument to measure 'clinically significant changes' in health. It is regarded as the key property of a measure for evaluating the impact of health care interventions. It is also related to reliability since, other things being equal, the more narrowly distributed the scores of a measure when there is no change in health the more able it is to detect change. Responsiveness is usually assessed in the psychometric literature using measures such as the 'effect size', where the mean change in score is divided by either the standard deviation at baseline or the standard deviation of the change (Guyatt *et al.* 2000). The effect size indicates the relative size of the 'signal' in comparison with underlying 'noise' in the data. The effect sizes of different instruments are compared for groups of patients assumed to have experienced a health change, such as after an operation of known effectiveness (e.g. a knee operation) or where the patient's doctor reported a change in health.

A common assumption in the psychometric literature is that for a given health change, the measure with the larger effect size is the better measure (Fitzpatrick *et al.* 1993; Katz *et al.* 1994). Where the objective is to minimize the sample size, this makes sense. However, when the purpose is to compare the size of change between treatments as part of an economic evaluation, within or between conditions, it is the value of the change which matters. (See an example of its application to preference-based measures in Walters and Brazier 2005.) Effect sizes do not indicate the value or importance of a change. For an economic measure, responsiveness is simply whether or not the descriptive system reflects a change in health in order that it *could* be valued.

The validity of bespoke vignettes tends not to be tested empirically like its standardized counterpart. While the more qualitative examinations of focus group work and cognitive interviewing provide some evidence for the validity of the descriptions, they cannot be used to test the quantitative validity of the descriptions. A patient population follows a distribution of states (that are often changing over time), whereas a vignette only describes one of these states. Even within a given clinical state, patients may experience a distribution of symptoms, functionings and feelings of well-being. The extent to which a set of vignettes accurately represent this distribution of symptoms is a quantitative matter that is not usually examined. This feature is built into standardized descriptive systems and can be tested in terms of construct validity and responsiveness.

There is a small and emerging literature on how to test the practicality, reliability and validity of descriptions for valuation. This section has discussed the key concepts and how they might be tested. Later a description is given of how these can be applied in the construction of a standardized state classification. The next section considers the design choice issues in constructing the vignettes and states, some of which can be resolved using these criteria, but many as yet remain unresolved.

4.2.2 Constructing descriptions—the role of framing and naming

Prior to embarking on the construction of a standardized descriptive system or bespoke vignette, it is important to have a clear idea of what should be described. Instrument developers need to set out the scope and definition of the health concepts being described. They should decide, for example, whether they are using a narrow definition of health, such as the developers of the HUI3, or a broader definition (Coast *et al.* 2006). Then they need to decide the scope of the description, whether it is to be generic to all patient groups, or specific in some way (say by condition, programme or care group). Then developers can start the empirical work of generating dimensions and items.

The purpose is to describe the state accurately and be comprehensible to the respondents being asked to undertake the valuation (using one of the valuation techniques). As mentioned before, any description is partly the product of a trade-off between these two requirements. The construction of standardized descriptive systems and vignettes raises a host of questions about the precise framing of the content and has been shown to have significant implications for the health state values obtained (Smith and Dobson 1993).

Comprehension

The need for respondents to be able to understand the states limits the size of the system. Respondents often report little or no difficulty with the valuation task (e.g. Brazier *et al.* 2002; McCabe *et al.* 2005); nonetheless there is evidence of respondents adopting simplifying heuristics when undertaking preference elicitation tasks (Lloyd 2003). Larger and more complex descriptions are more likely to result in respondents adopting heuristics such as focusing on one of the dimensions. This may invalidate the valuation obtained since respondents are not valuing the entire content of the states, as is usually assumed by the investigator. The extent of this and related problems of comprehension need to be tested in a pilot study prior to embarking on a large valuation survey (see examples reported in the context DCE in Ryan and Gerard 2003).

Narrative versus structured format

A key choice is whether to use a narrative format in describing a state or whether to opt for a more structured approach using bullet points. The latter can be developed into an entire health state descriptive system that defines numerous standard health states (like the EQ-5D) or it can be specific to the few states being valued (Llewellyn-Thomas *et al.* 1984). The advantage of using a narrative format is that it offers a more natural portrayal of the state and often uses a richer description. It has recently been developed using videos of interviews with patients or actors being a patient (Lenert and Sturley 2001). These approaches may provide more realism to members of the general public trying to imagine what the states are like.

Llewellyn-Thomas and colleagues (1984) undertook a comparison of structured bullet style descriptions and narratives for five health states. They found that VAS and standard gamble (SG) values for the narrative format gave consistently lower values than the structured format. The authors acknowledge that this study does not just show the effect of format since the narrative format actually contained more symptoms and so this may have been why they were given lower values. It could be argued that the ability to incorporate more symptoms and problems is an advantage of the narrative format, but this has not been tested.

The disadvantage of narrative format is that it may contain subtle signals that divert the respondents away from the essence of the state. Later we consider the arguments for and against disease labelling, but often these narrative approaches use or allude to the nature of the condition. The structured format, which focuses on the key dimensions, can be used to construct a descriptive system that can define many states and. as described later in this book, with the use of modelling techniques it means that, based on a valuation of a sample of states, the value of hundreds and even thousands of states not directly valued can be estimated. This creates an instrument that can be administered to patients in clinical trials and other studies to obtain stochastic data on outcomes.

The valuation of a few narrative or structured vignettes (e.g. using bullet points) rather than a standardized classification like the EQ-5D is often used to populate decision analytic models (see Chapter 9). While this is a convenient way to obtain mean values for the set of states around which a model is structured, it does not produce the distribution of outcomes across the different dimensions of health and well-being. As argued earlier, this makes it difficult to validate the accuracy of the descriptions, and the uncertainty around the impact of the state on health and quality of life is lost. However, standard systems can be used to value clinical states in the model by administering the instruments on patients in the states and estimating mean health state values and associated variance.

The flexibility and statistical advantages of structured formats need to be weighed against the potential for greater richness offered by a narrative format (at least for the state being valued). Another consideration is whether the purpose is to value states or value health profiles. As mentioned in Chapter 3, due to the violation of additive separability there has been an interest in valuing time profiles of health, and even some interest in incorporating risk and uncertainty into the descriptions. The theoretical arguments for and against the valuation of profiles are discussed in Chapter 3, but one of the issues raised in the literature has been the practicality of this approach. Researchers have had some success in valuing profiles, but there is evidence that some of these exercises were too ambitious, and respondents had cognitive difficulty in understanding the content of the descriptions (Towers *et al.* 2006).

Labelling and naming

Another question is whether or not to name the disease or medical condition in the health state description. Sometimes the medical condition is obvious from the state due to the symptoms being described, or where the items actually say the problem has been caused by a condition. One concern with the latter approach is that, when patients are asked to use these descriptions to report their current state of health, it is arguable whether or not they would be able to isolate the effect of the target medical condition, particularly if it occurs alongside co-morbidities. A patient may report depression, for example, but have little idea of its cause without a thorough psychiatric examination.

There have been a number of studies that have looked at the effect of disease labels on health state values (Sackett and Torrance 1978; O'Connor 1989; Gerard *et al.* 1993; Rabin *et al.* 1993; Robinson and Bryan 2001). Rabin and colleagues found that the explicit labelling of mental conditions such as mental handicap, schizophrenia and dementia tended to lower the valuations given. Gerard and colleagues (1993) found, however, that the values of breast cancer states were not altered by naming and labelling, and O'Connor and her colleagues found no alteration in the context of alternative drug therapies for oncology. However, there are sufficient studies demonstrating an impact of labelling to conclude that it can be important (Sackett and Torrance 1978; Llewelyn-Thomas *et al.* 1984; Robinson and Bryan 2001).

Evidence suggests that where labels have an impact, it is usually to lower values. This could be a consequence of an inadequate description in the unnamed state. By naming the state it allows the respondents to use their own knowledge of the state and its impact. The downside is that respondents may bring their own poorly informed assumptions about the impact of the state and may actually be mistaken. This could be due to their misconceptions about the state, or respondents may bring their own fears about longer term prognosis that are inconsistent with the time frame set in the valuation exercise. Unlabelled descriptions, such as those using generic dimensions of handicap and participation (as opposed to impairment and disability), will incorporate a degree of adaptation to the state that a respondent would not appreciate from a description of the state. On the other hand, some generic (and so unlabelled) descriptions may miss out on important aspects of the condition and its context.

Conclusion

It has long been recognized in the psychological literature that the precise wording of a state can have important implications for the values obtained from respondents (Tversky and Kahneman 1974). Describing a mortality outcome in terms of chance of death gives a different value from that obtained when describing it in terms of chances of survival (McNeil *et al.* 1981). This section has reported evidence on the differences between narrative and standard format and the impact of disease labelling. Some research has also been undertaken on the effect of framing the states in terms of first, second and third person, but the findings are not conclusive. Gerard *et al.* (1993) found no effect, but further work needs to be undertaken on the impact of these differences in framing and, more importantly, research needs to be undertaken into the most appropriate framing to ensure accuracy and comprehensibility to respondents.

For some issues, such as narrative versus structured formats, it is a complex trade-off between qualitative realism compared with realism in capturing uncertainty and the advantages of having a standardized generic descriptive system (as discussed earlier). For the issue of labelling, it is important to investigate why disease labelling has affected the result (using qualitative and cognitive techniques). Whether or not labels should be used seems to depend on the extent to which we want respondents to bring their own understanding of the condition to bear on their valuation. For obtaining general population valuations of health states, there would seem to be more of a case for using unlabelled states and relying on the descriptions of the impact of the disease, whereas for patients and experts [such as was the case for DALYs (World Bank 1993)] there may be a case for using disease labels.

4.2.3 Constructing standardized systems

A key constraint in designing a descriptive system for economic evaluation is that the set of health states must be amenable to valuation by respondents. The more widely used generic preference-based measures have between five and nine dimensions with 3–6 levels each. The limits on the size of a descriptive system mean that the choice of content must be made with great care.

The aim is to provide the respondent with an accurate description of the health state being considered. The descriptive system can be developed *de novo*, as was done with the EQ-5D and HUI3, or developed from an existing measure, such as the derivation of the generic SF-6D from the SF-36 (Brazier *et al*. 2002) or the condition-specific preference-based instrument from the King's Health Questionnaire (Brazier *et al*. 2005).

Developing a new descriptive system

Claims for the 'content validity' of an instrument typically rest on the comprehensiveness of the instrument and the methods used to generate its dimensions and items. An 'expert' approach to generating dimensions and items could be criticized for not accurately reflecting the views of those concerned, such as the patients, their carers or the health professionals. Economists, being concerned with ensuring the measure correctly reflects the arguments of an individual's utility function, are likely to prefer this patient-based approach. However, it has not been widely used in developing preference-based measures until recently. One exception had been the development of HUI2 where parents, though not their children, were asked to rank statements describing the health of children, and this information was used to inform the final choice of dimensions (Cadman *et al.* 1986). More recently, a preference-based measure for atopic dermatitis was developed from an instrument that had been based on interviews with children having the condition and their parents (Stevens *et al.* 2005).

Alternatively, the views of lay people could be used, and the best example of this has been the development of a measure for older people (Coast *et al.* 2006). These authors used qualitative techniques to develop the dimensions and the wording in a quality of life descriptive system. In-depth interviews were conducted with respondents aged 65 and over to find out what they felt was important to their quality of life. Data were analysed, and along with expert judgement a final set of dimensions was derived. These types of qualitative techniques can be used alongside quantitative psychometric methods to develop and refine the measure. For the latter, different versions of the instrument can be administered, perhaps alongside other measures, in order to explore the reliability, validity and responsiveness of the content. The final selection of dimensions and items also benefits from the application of the statistical techniques described in the next section.

Developing a descriptive system from an existing measure

There are many reasons why a researcher may want to estimate a preference-based measure from an existing measure of health. One reason is that the measure may have been widely used in clinical trials, such as the SF-36, and so using it to derive a preference-based measure considerably extends the scope for undertaking economic evaluation in health care. Another case is where a condition-specific measure is regarded as more sensitive or relevant than the existing generics. This section describes the psychometric and statistical methods that can be used in helping to construct a standardized health state descriptive system from such instruments. It examines the approach taken in the development of the SF-6D from the SF-36 and a number of condition-specific preference-based measures (Brazier *et al.* 2005; Yang *et al.* 2006). Some of the methods described in this section are also relevant to the development of a new preference based measure.

The existing instrument may look like the SF-36, which has 35 multilevel items, many of which have no obvious ordinal relationship; hence many millions of health states can be defined from this classification. The valuation of such a large multidimensional system would present enormous practical problems. As indicated earlier, it has been claimed that individuals can only process between five and nine pieces of information at a time in a valuation task (Miller 1956; Dolan *et al.* 1996). The aim is to produce a health state classification or system amenable to valuation by respondents, with a minimum loss of descriptive information and subject to the constraint that responses to the original instrument can be unambiguously mapped onto it. This implies that the text of the items should be altered as little as possible. The task is to determine the dimensions, items and the levels of the descriptive system.

The process described below has been refined by a team of researchers at Sheffield using a combination of conventional psychometric tests along with factor and Rasch analysis on data sets using the original instrument, and analysis and collection of valuation data (e.g. Young *et al.* 2005).

Selecting dimensions It is desirable for a health state classification designed for valuation to have structural independence between dimensions to avoid nonsensical 'corner' states (Feeny 2002). In other words, there must be little correlation between the dimensions. One technique for identifying structurally independent dimensions is factor analysis. This can be helpful in confirming the dimension structure of a measure or show where dimensions are not sufficiently independent and suggest ways to reduce the number of dimensions (Young *et al.* 2005). It can also be used to suggest possible dimensional structure where none was proposed by the original instrument developer (Stevens *et al.* 2005). Factor analysis needs to be used with care, however, since the factors it suggests might not make much sense.

Where an existing measure (or draft version of a potential new instrument) has too many dimensions, then selection can be assisted by obtaining the values of a relevant population, such as the general public or patients (see 'Who should value health' in Chapter 5). Cadman *et al.* (1986) provide an example of this approach, where they had 15 domains based on existing measures. Members of the general population (parents of children) were asked to rate the importance of the dimensions in terms of their quality of life. The top six were then selected to form the HUI2 and its successor the HUI3 (Torrance *et al.* 1996; Feeny *et al.* 2002). However, there must be some doubt as to whether this has any meaning without also providing information on levels.

Items The dimensions of preference-based measures are each usually based on one or two items (e.g. EQ-5D and five dimensions of the SF-6D), though occasionally more have been used (e.g. AQoL). The selection of items can be undertaken using a combination of conventional psychometric criteria, Rasch analysis and valuation data. Conventional psychometric criteria were applied in two studies of condition-specific measures using the following tests (Young *et al.* 2005): the amount of missing data, correlation of item to own dimension; distribution of response across categories of response; discrimination between severity levels; and responsiveness to change over two points in time. These provide psychometric tests of the practicality and validity of the items as descriptions of health.

A technique that has proven extremely helpful in the process of item selection and in reducing the number of item responses (and hence levels in the health state classification) is Rasch analysis. This is a mathematical technique that converts qualitative (categorical) responses to a continuous (unmeasured) latent scale using a logit model (Tesio 2003). It does this by drawing on item response theory, where the probability of an affirmative response to each item (or each response to each item) is modelled as a probability, and this information is used to assess the severity of the item against the latent variable (i.e. the dimension of interest). It is usually undertaken after a dimensional structure has been established, but it can also test whether an item belongs to the dimension (goodness of fit). It provides data on the ranking of different items in terms of the latent variable.

This method was used to select items from the 10 physical functioning items of the SF-36. It found items that described the most severe physical functioning problem ('Limited a lot in bathing and dressing') and the least severe ('Limited in vigorous activities'), and then the remainder were found to cluster together, and so many were redundant from an informational point of view. Items can also be eliminated where the response categories produce a pattern that is not consistent with the latent variable. It also provides evidence of differential item functioning, where an item behaves differently between different groups of responders, say by age, or by sex.

For a descriptive system that is to be used to generate preference scores, it also makes sense to use preference data to inform its construction. There is a considerable premium on space in a descriptive system, so it is important to ensure that it uses items that are the most significant in terms of its likely impact on a preference score. This could be explored by asking groups of respondents to rank and/or rate sets of items in terms of their likely impact on their quality of life. To be meaningful, this would have to be undertaken for each response choice. This would complement the psychometric data.

Levels Rasch analysis can also be used to understand the relative position of item response choices (such as none, very mild, mild, moderate, severe and very severe). It does this by producing threshold probability curves that indicate the probability of each response choice or level being affirmed at each point along the latent variable. These curves should not cross and ideally will be apart for most of the scale. Curves that come close or cross would be candidates for merger (Young *et al.* 2005). It is also possible to use preferences to inform the process by identifying levels that respondents are unable to distinguish. This can be done by asking respondents to rate categories on a rating scale. Alternatively, it can be done by obtaining valuations for whole states and then using modelling techniques to estimate coefficients for each level. The Rasch approach can be used on existing patient data sets using the full instrument, but the preference-based approach requires valuation data.

Using cluster analysis to generate vignettes

An alternative approach to developing a health state value from a measure of health has been presented by Lenert, Sugar and colleagues (Sugar *et al*. 1998; Lenert *et al*. 2000). Their approach uses statistical efficiency to identify a set of states from the scores generated by a health status measure, such as the two dimensions of the SF-12. They applied *k*-means cluster analysis to break up the patterns of the physical and mental health summary scores of the SF-12 into models with varying numbers of discrete states. They selected six states from the SF-12 data from a sample of depressed patients (i.e. near normal, mild mental and physical health impairment, severe physical health impairment, severe mental health impairment, severe mental and moderate physical impairment, and severe mental and physical impairment). These are actually defined in terms of scores, so a process of turning the score distributions of each state into words taken from the original 12 items to define the states had to be developed based on expert judgement.

This approach is a potentially useful alternative approach to that described before, since it is less time consuming and requires substantially fewer states to be valued. It provides an interesting way to generate structured vignettes that is based on evidence. It can also use more items than a specially constructed standardized descriptive system, since none have to be excluded to form a system. On the other hand, it does result in quite lengthy states because it does not take advantage of the psychometric analysis to reduce the number of items and levels. Another concern would be the link between dimension scores and the wording on the states, since this is still partly based on judgement. A given dimension score can be derived in a number of different ways, and deciding which one may have implications for the final utility scores. This approach has important potential, but it needs to be subjected to a sensitivity analysis of the states selected and the results compared with other methods, such as those described above.

4.3 **Conclusions**

The way benefits of health care are described defines what is to be valued and what by implication is being given a value of zero. This chapter examined the conceptual basis of the descriptors and methods for constructing them.

The conceptual questions are concerned with what should be valued, including the definition of health, the notion of a health spectrum (from impairment to participation) and scope. For use in cross-programme comparison, the decision to use condition-specific measures is ultimately a trade-off between having measures that are relevant and sensitive to those things that matter to a specific condition against the consequences for side effects and co-morbidities, and the extent of preference interactions between those dimensions included and those excluded. The decision between health and broader measure of quality of life can be seen as a trade-off like this; it can also be seen as a political question about the objectives of the health care system.

The construction of a descriptive system for a preference-based measure operates within a different set of constraints from non-preference-based measures of health, since they need to be explicitly valued. It is therefore important to make the descriptions comprehensible to respondents who may be familiar with the health states presented to them and accurately reflect the impact of the condition and its treatment. This raises important questions around the precise framing of the vignettes and whether or not to name the disease, since these can affect respondent valuations. There needs to be more qualitative research into how these factors influence results. There is a choice between a narrative vignettes approach and more structured descriptions, with the latter including the standardized health state classifications such as the (generic) preference-based measures. The development of descriptive systems should involve qualitative methods to generate and initially test items for the standardized system, and then use psychometric methods to help refine and test them. This is an evolving field in health economics.

References

Aballéa S, Tsuchiya A (2004). *Seeing and doing: feasibility study towards valuing visual impairment using simulation spectacles.* Sheffield Health Economics Group Discussion Paper, University of Sheffield. www.shef.ac.uk/scharr/heds.

Barton GR, Bankart J, Davis AC, Summerfield QA (2004). Comparing utility scores before and after hearing-aid provision. *Applied Health and Economic Health Policy* 3:103–5.

Bass EB, Steinberg EP, Pitt HA, Griffiths RI, Lillemoe KD, Saba GP, Johns C (1994). Comparison of the rating scale and the standard gamble in measuring patient preferences for outcomes of gallstone disease. *Medical Decision Making* 14:307–14.

Bowling A (1997). Measuring health: a review of quality of life and measurement scales. Open University Press, Milton Keynes, UK.

Bradley C (2001). The importance of differentiating health status from quality of life. *Lancet* 357:7–8.

Bradley C, Todd C, Gorton T, Symonds E, Martin A, Plowright R (1999). The development of an individualised questionnaire measure of perceived impact of diabetes on quality of life: the ADDQoL. *Quality of Life Research* 8:79–91.

Brazier JE, Deverill M (1999). A checklist for judging preference-based measures of health related quality of life: learning from psychometrics. *Health Economics* 8:41–52.

Brazier JE, Fitzpatrick R (2002). Measures of health related quality of life in an imperfect world: a comment on Dowie. *Health Economics* 11:17–9.

Brazier JE, Roberts J, Deverill M (2002). The estimation of a preference-based single index measure for health from the SF-36. *Journal of Health Economics* 21:271–92.

Brazier JE, Murray C, Roberts J, Brown M, Symonds T. (2005). *Developing a preference-based index for health from a condition specific measure, the King's Health Questionnaire.* Health Economics and Decision Science DP 02/05. The University of Sheffield.

Brooks R, the EuroQol Group (1996). EuroQol: the current state of play. *Health Policy* 37:53–72.

Cadman D, Goldsmith C, Torrance G, Boyle M, Furlong W (1986). *Development of a health status index for Ontario children: final report to the Ontario Ministry of Health.* Grant Research DM648 (00633), McMaster University, Hamilton, Ontario.

Coast J, Flynn T, Grewal I *et al.* (2006). *Developing an index of capability for health and social policy evaluation for older people: theoretical and methodological challenges.* HESG, University of Sheffield.

Cook J, Richardson J, Street A (1994). A cost-utility analysis of treatment options for gallstone disease—methodological issues and results. *Health Economics* 3:157–68.

Dolan P (1997). Modelling valuation for Euroqol health states. *Medical Care* 35:351–63.

Dolan P, Gudex C, Kind P, Williams, A (1996). Valuing health states: a comparison of methods. *Journal of Health Economics* 2:209–32.

Donaldson C, Atkinson A, Bond J, Wright K (1988). QALYS and long-term care for elderly people in the UK: scales for assessment of quality of life. *Age and Ageing* 17:379–87.

Dowie J (2002). Decision validity should determine whether generic or condiiton-specific HRQOL measure is used in health care decisions. *Health Economics* 11:1–8.

Drummond M, Torrance G, Mason J (1993). Cost-effectiveness league tables: more harm than good? *Social Science and Medicine* 37:33–40.

Eiser C, Morse R (2001). Quality of life measures in chronic diseases of childhood. *Health Technology Assessment* 5(3):1–157.

Espallargues M, Czoski-Murray C, Bansback N, Carlton J, Lewis G, Hughes L, Brand C, Brazier J. (2006) The impact of age related macular degeneration on health state utility values. *Investigative Ophthalmology and Visual Science* 46: 4016–23.

Evans RG, Wolfson AD (1980). Faith, hope and charity: health care in the utility function. Department of Economics, University of British Columbia and Department of Health Administration, University of Toronto, unpublished paper.

Feeny DH, Furlong WJ, Torrance GW, Goldsmith CH, Zenglong Z, Depauw S, Denton M, Boyle M. (2002) Multiattribute and single-attribute utility function the health utility index mark 3 system. *Medical Care* 40:113–28.

Feeny D (2002) The utility approach to assessing population health. In: Murray C, Salomon J, Mathers C, Lopez A, Lozano R, eds. *Summary measures of population health: concepts, ethics, measurement and applications.* World Health Organization, Geneva. pp. 515–528.

Fitzpatrick R, Zeibland S, Jenkinson C, Mowat A (1993). A comparison of the sensitivity to change of several health status measures in rheumatoid arthritis. *Journal of Rheumatology* 20:429–36.

Gerard K, Dobson M, Hall K (1993). Framing and labelling effects in health descriptions: quality adjusted life years for treatment of breast cancer. *Journal of Clinical Epidemiology* 46:77–84.

Grewal I, Lewis J, Flynn T, Brown J, Bond J, Coast J (2006). Developing attributes for a generic quality of life measure for older people: preferences or capabilities? *Social Science and Medicine* 62:1891–901.

Guyatt G (2002). Commentary on Jack Dowie, 'Decision validity should determine whether a generic or condition-specific HRQOL measure is used in health care decisions'. *Health Economics* 11:9–12.

Guyatt GH, Osoba D, Wu AW, Wyrwich, Narman GR (2000). Clinical Significance Consensus Meeting Group: methods to explain the clinical signficance of health status measures. *Mayo Clinic Proceedings* 77:371–83.

Harper R, Brazier JE, Waterhouse JC, Walters SJ, Jones NMB, Howard P (1997). A comparison of outcome measures for patients with chronic obstructive pulmonary disease (COPD) in an outpatient setting. *Thorax* 52:879–87.

Hawthorne G, Richardson J. Osborne R. McNeil H (1997). *The Australian quality of life (AQoL) instrument.* Monash University Working Paper 66

Justice AC, Holmes W, Gifford AL, Rabeneck L, Zackin R, Sinclair G, Weissman S, Neidig J, Marcus C, Chesney M, Cohn SE, Wu AW (2001). Development and validation of a self completed HIV symptom index. *Journal of Clinical Epidemiology* 54:S77–90.

Kahneman D (2000). Experienced utility and objective happiness: a moment based approach. In: Kahneman D, Tversky A, eds. *Choices, values, and frames.* Cambridge University Press, Cambridge. pp. 673–692.

Kaplan RM, Anderson JP (1990). The general health policy model: an integrated approach. In: Anonymous. *Quality of life assessments in clinical trials.* Raven Press, New York, pp. 131–148.

Kaplan RM, Bush JW, Berry CC (1976). Health status: types of validity and the index of well-being. *Health Services Research* 11:478–507.

Katz JN, Phillips CB, Fossel AH, Liang MH (1994). Stability and responsiveness of utility measures. *Medical Care* 32:183–8.

Kobelt G, Kirchperger I, Malone-Lee J (1999). Quality of life aspects of the over active bladder and the effect of treatment with tolterodine. *British Journal of Urology* 83:583–90.

Lenert LA, Sturley AE (2001). Acceptability of computerised VAS, TTO and SG rating methods in patients and the public. In: *Proceedings of the AMIA symposium* pp. 364–368. Washington.

Lenert LA, Sherbourne CD, Sugar C, Wells KB (2000). Estimation of utilities for the effects of depression from the SF-12. *Medical Care* 38:763–70.

Llewellyn-Thomas H, Sutherland HJ, Tibshirani R, Ciampi A, Till JE, Boyd NF (1984). Describing health states: methodological issues in obtaining values for health states. *Medical Care* 22:543–52.

Lloyd A. (2003) Threats to the estimation of benefit: are preference estimation methods accurate? *Health Economics*; 12:393–402.

McCabe C, Stevens K, Brazier JE. (2005). Utility scores for the HUI2: an empirical comparison of alternative mapping functions. *Medical Care* 43:627–35.

McGee HM, O'Boyle CA, Hicky A, O'Malley K, Joyce CRB (1991). Assessing the quality of life of the individual: the SEIQoL with a healthy and a gastroenterological unit population. *Psychological Medicine* 21:749–59.

McKenna SD, Doward LC, Alonso J, Kohaman T, Neiro M, Prieto L, Wiren L (1999). The QoL-AGHDA: an instrument for the assessment of quality of life in adults with growth hormone deficiency. *Quality of Life Research* 8:373–83.

McNeil BJ, Weichselbaum R, Pauker SG (1981). Speech and survival: trade offs between quality and quantity of life in laryngeal cancer. *New England Journal of Medicine* 305:982–7.

Miller GA (1956). The magical number seven, plus or minus two: some limits on our capacity for processing information. *The Psychological Review* 63(2):81–97.

National Institute for Health and Clinical Excellence (2004). *NICE guide to the methods of technology appraisal.* NICE, London.

O'Connor A (1989). Effects of framing and level of probability on patient preferences for cancer chemotherapy. *Journal of Clinical Epidemiology* 42:119.

Rabin R, Rosser RM, Butler C (1993). Impact of diagnosis on utilities assigned to states of illness. *Journal of the Royal Society of Medicine* 86:444.

Revicki DA, Leidy NK, Brennan-Diemer F, Sorenson S, Togias A (1998). Integrating patients' preferences into health outcomes assessment: the multiattribute asthma symptom utility index. *Chest* 114:998–1007.

Richardson, J. (1994). Cost-utility analysis—what should be measured. *Social Science and Medicine* 39:7–21.

Robinson S, Bryan S (2001). 'Naming and framing': an investigation of the effect of disease labels on health state valuations. Health Economics Study Group Meeting, University of Oxford.

Ryan M, Gerard K (2003). Using discrete choice experiements to value health care programmes: current practice and future research reflections. *Applied Health Econmics and Health Policy* 2:55–64.

Sackett DL, Torrance GW (1978). The utility of different health states as perceived by the general public. *Journal of Chronic Diseases* 31:697–704.

Sand PK, Richardson DA, Staskin DR, Swift SE, Appell RA, Whitmore KE (1994). Pelvic floor stimulation in the treatment of genuine stress incontinence: a multi-centre placebo controlled trial. *Neurology and Urodynamics* 13:356–67.

Smith K, Dobson M (1993). Measuring utility values for QALYs: two methodological issues. *Health Economics* 2:349–55.

Stevens K, Brazier JE, McKenna SP, Doward LC, Cork M (2005). The development of a preference-based measure of health in children with atopic dermatitis. *British Journal of Dermatology* 153:372–7.

Streiner DL, Norman GR (1997). *Health measurement scales: a practical guide to their development and use.* Oxford University Press, Oxford.

Sugar CA, Sturm R, Lee TT, Sherbourne CD, Olshen RA, Wells KB, Lenert LA (1998). Empirically defined health states for depression from the SF-12. *Health Services Research* 33:911–28.

Tesio L (2003). Measuring behaviours and perceptions: Rasch analysis as a tool for rehabilitation research. *Journal of Rehabilitation Medicine* 35:105–15.

Torrance GW (1976). Social preferences for health states: an empirical evaluation of three measurement techniques. *Socio-Economic Planning Sciences* 10(3):129–36.

Torrance GW, Feeny DH, Furlong WJ, Barr RD, Zhang Y, Wang Q (1996). Multiattribute utlity function for a comprehensive health status classification system: Health Utility Index mark 2. *Medical Care* 34:702–22.

Towers I, Brazier JE, Dolan P, Karampela K (2006). Does the whole equal the sum of the parts? Patient assigned utility scores for IBS health states and profiles. *Health Economics* 15:543–552.

Tversky A, Kahneman D (1974) Judgement under uncertainty: heuristics and biases. *Science* 185:1124–31.

Walters S, Brazier JE (2005). Comparison of the minimally important difference for two health state measures: EQ-5D and SF-6D. *Quality in Life Research* 14:1523–32.

Ware JE (1987). Standards for validating health measures: definition and content. *Journal of Chronic Diseases* 40:473–80.

Ware JE, Sherbourne CD (1992). The MOS 36-item Short-Form Health Survey (SF-36): I. Conceptual framework and item selection. *Medical Care* 30:473–83.

Williams A (1992). Measuring functioning and well-being, by Stewart and Ware. Review article. *Health Economics* 1:255–8.

Williams A (1995). *The measurement and valuation of health: a chronicle.* Centre for Health Economics, Discussion Paper, University of York.

World Bank (1993). *World development report 1993: investing in health.* Oxford University Press, Oxford.

World Health Organization (1948). *Constitution of the World Health Organization. Basic documents.* WHO, Geneva.

World Health Organization (1980). International classification of impairments, disabilities and handicaps. WHO, Geneva.

World Health Organization (2001). International classification of functioning, disability and health. WHO, Geneva.

Yang Y, Tsuchiya A, Brazier J, Young Y (2006). *Deriving a preference-based measure for health from the AQLQ.* Paper presented at the Health Economists' Study Group meeting, London.

Young T, Yang Y, Brazier J, Tsuchiya A (2005). *Using Rasch analysis to aid the construction of preference based measures from existing quality of life instruments.* Paper presented at the Health Economists' Study Group meeting, Newcastle, UK.

Chapter 5

Valuing health

5.1 Introduction

The question of how to adjust life years to reflect health levels experienced during those years (i.e. putting the 'Q' into QALYs) is the key question addressed in this book. This chapter is about the methods for valuing health, sometimes known as preference elicitation techniques. It begins by describing and then reviewing the main cardinal techniques used in the health economics literature for valuing health states (i.e. those methods that produce responses that are already on some interval scale). Ordinal or ranking techniques are considered in Chapter 7. Different techniques can generate different values, and so this chapter also addresses the question of which technique should be used. It goes on to examine the variants of each technique and the implications of each of these for the values obtained. Finally, this chapter addresses the question of who should be asked to value health states, and considers whether values should be based on preferences (as is usually the case in economics) or experiences.

5.2 Valuation techniques: a description

There are three main techniques for valuing health states: these are the standard gamble (SG), time trade-off (TTO) and the visual analogue scale (VAS). These are often called preference elicitation techniques, although strictly speaking VAS is not preference based and so we will use the more general term of valuation. Other techniques that have been used to value health states include magnitude estimation (ME), the equivalence technique (person trade-off or PTO), ranking and discrete choice experiments (DCEs). However, these techniques have been applied less frequently than the three main techniques. The use of ranking and DCE to value health states is considered in Chapter 7, and ME and PTO are dealt with here, but rather more briefly than the three main techniques. This section describes how each technique can be used to value chronic states considered to be better than being dead, states worse than being dead and temporary states.

5.2.1 **The visual analogue scale**

The VAS, sometimes referred to in the literature as the category rating scale or just the rating scale, is simply a line, usually with well defined end-points, on which respondents are able to indicate their judgements, values or feelings (hence it is sometimes called a 'feeling' thermometer). The distances between intervals on a VAS should reflect a person's understanding of the relative differences between the concepts being measured. VAS is intended to have interval properties, so that the difference between 3 and 5 on a 10-point scale for example should equal the difference between 5 and 7.

Historically the technique came from the psychophysics literature where there was an interest in measuring people's perceptions of various objective phenomena, such as heat and sound (Brazier *et al.* 1999). Subsequently it has been used in psychometrics to measure attitudes and feelings towards a broad range of social and psychological constructs. VAS has also been used in the context of health as a measure of symptoms and various domains of health, and to provide a single index measure of health-related quality of life (McDowell and Newell 1996). It was first identified as a possible measure for use in economic evaluation over three decades ago (Patrick *et al.* 1973) and has become one of the most widely used measures for this purpose, whether directly with patients or as a means of valuing health state classifications including the Quality of Well-being Scale (QWB) (Kaplan and Anderson 1988), Health Utility Index (HUI) (Feeny *et al.* 2002), 15-D (Sintonen 1994) and the EQ-5D (Brooks *et al.* 2003).

To use VAS in economic evaluation, it is essential to ensure comparability between respondents. To achieve this requires clear and unambiguous end-points, such as 'full health' at the top end (in the case of a vertical scale) and 'dead' at the lower end. It is important to define 'full health' in order to minimize the risk of between-respondent variation (although inevitably there probably remains some variation in the interpretation of 'full health' even if it is defined by the researchers). The use of terms such as 'best imaginable' health state and 'worst imaginable' health state as end-points, such as used by the Euroqol group, leaves more scope for variation in meaning between respondents and hence reduces comparability between them (see Fig. 5.1). This source of bias is partly overcome by the Euroqol group and others by a transformation described below.

Visual analogue scale for states considered worse than dead

For use in economic evaluation it is desirable to ensure that health state valuations can be placed on a zero to one scale, where zero is for states regarded as equivalent to dead and one for a state of full health. It is necessary to allow for

To help people say how good or bad their health is, we have drawn a scale (rather like a thermometer) on which the best state you can imagine is marked by 100 and the worst state you can imagine is marked by 0.

We would like you to indicate on this scale how good or bad your own health is today, in your opinion. Please do this by drawing aline from the box below to which ever point on the scale indicates how good or bad your current health state is.

```
Your own health state
       today
```

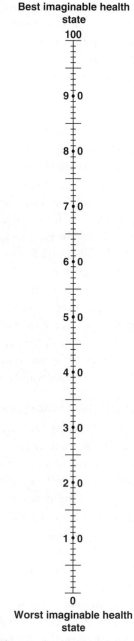

Best imaginable health state

100

9 0

8 0

7 0

6 0

5 0

4 0

3 0

2 0

1 0

0

Worst imaginable health state

Fig. 5.1 Example of a visual analogue scale (EQ-5D VAS)—own health. Copyright: Euroqol group www.euroqol.org. Reproduced with permission.

states that could be valued worse than being dead. For these reasons, it is important for respondents to be asked to value being dead on the same scale along with their own health or the various hypothetical states they are being asked to value. Having obtained a value for dead, then all health state valuations need to be transformed using the following formula:

$$A_i = R_i - R \text{ (dead)}/R \text{ (best)} - R \text{ (dead)}$$

where A_i = adjusted VAS rating for health state h_i; R (being dead) = raw rating given to being dead; R_i = raw rating given to health state h_i; R (best) = raw rating given to the best health state.

This transformation results in the value 1.0 for the best (or full) health state and zero for being dead. The value of A_i would lie within this range, or assume a negative value for states valued as worse than being dead. This adjustment is claimed to allow interpersonal comparisons (Torrance 1986; Measurement and Value of Health Froup 1994) and more arguably for putting the 'Q' into QALYs (Kaplan *et al.* 1979). It should be noted that this transformation is unbounded below zero.

There also needs to be a clear calibration on the scale, such as 0 to 10 or 0 to 100, though it is not clear whether the refinement of the latter really produces greater accuracy in the scale since respondents tend to opt for multiplies of 10 or 5 on a 100-point scale.

Figure 5.1 presents an example of the VAS developed by the Euroqol group.

Visual analogue scale for temporary health states

Temporary health states are defined as states lasting for a specified period of time after which there is a return to good health, whereas chronic health states last for the rest of a person's life (Torrance 1986). The duration of temporary health states may be specified in terms of weeks, months or even years, the only requirement being that the duration is less than life expectancy. Preferences for temporary health states can be measured using a VAS by instructing the respondent that the health states will last for a specified period of time after which the person will return to full health. The respondent is asked to place the best state (healthy) at one end of the scale and the worst temporary state at the other end. As with the valuation of chronic health states, the remaining temporary health states are then placed along the line such that their location reflects their relative ratings by the respondent. To encourage elicitation of interval scale values, respondents must be instructed to place the temporary health states on the line such that the relative distance between the locations reflects the differences they perceive between the health states.

Variants of the visual analogue scale

There are many variants of the VAS technique. The lines can vary in length, be vertical or horizontal, and may or may not have intervals marked out with different numbers. The QWB multiattribute utility scale (MAUS), for example, was valued by asking respondents to place health states into one of 15 numbered slots, where zero was dead and one was optimum health. The EQ-5D was valued using interval markings of 0–100, where 0 corresponds to the worst imaginable health and 100 corresponds to the best imaginable health (Fig. 5.1). Respondents may be asked initially to place the best and worst health states at the end points of the scale, or they may be asked to place the states on the scale in any order. Feeny and colleagues (2002) have also developed a feeling thermometer on which the respondent places cards describing different health states, whereas the EQ-5D asks respondents to indicate the position of a health state by drawing a line on a piece of paper from the health state description to the VAS instrument.

5.2.2 The standard gamble

The SG method gives the respondent a choice between a certain intermediate outcome and the uncertainty of a gamble with two possible outcomes, one of which is better than the certain intermediate outcome and one of which is worse. The SG task for eliciting the value attached to health states considered better than dead is displayed in Fig. 5.2 (based on Drummond *et al.* 2005). Essentially, the respondent is offered two alternatives. Alternative 1 is a treatment with two possible outcomes: either the patient is returned to normal health and lives for an additional t years (probability P), or the patient dies immediately (probability $1 - P$). Alternative 2 has the certain outcome of chronic state h_i for life (t years). The probability P of the best outcome is varied until the individual is indifferent between the certain intermediate outcome and the gamble. This probability P is the utility for the certain outcome, state h_i. This technique is then repeated for all intermediate outcomes. The SG

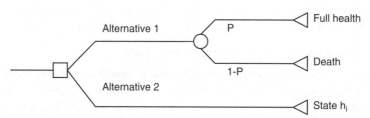

Fig. 5.2 Standard gamble for a chronic health state preferred to death.

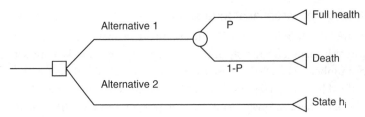

Fig. 5.3 Standard gamble for a chronic health state considered worse than death.

can also be applied to elicit the value attached to health states considered worse than death and temporary health states, and these are described below.

Standard gamble for states considered worse than dead

For chronic health states considered worse than dead, the standard gamble question has to be modified to that shown in Fig. 5.3. Again the respondent is offered two alternatives. Alternative 1 is a treatment with two possible outcomes: either the patient is returned to normal health and lives for an additional t years (probability P), or the patient remains in the chronic health state h_i for life (t years) (probability $1 - P$). Alternative 2 has the certain outcome of death. Torrance (1986) suggests that one way to present such a choice is to ask the respondent to imagine that they have a rapidly progressing terminal disease which will lead quickly to death if no intervention takes place. However, there is a treatment with a probability P of a complete cure and probability $1 - P$ of remaining in chronic state h_i. The probability P is varied until the individual is indifferent between the certain outcome of death and the gamble, at which the preference value for health state $h_i = -P/(1 - P)$.

This formula for translating SG responses to health state values results in a scale ranging from $-\infty$ to $+1$, which gives greater weight to negative values in the calculation of mean scores and presents problems for the statistical analysis. It has therefore been suggested in the literature that states valued worse than being dead should be simply the negative of the indifference probability of the best outcome (Patrick *et al.* 1994). This has the effect of bounding negative values at -1. This transformation has no theoretical support and is only one of a number of possible ways of dealing with the problem, but it is one that has become widely used elsewhere in the literature (Brazier *et al.* 2002; Feeny *et al.* 2002).

Standard gamble for temporary health states

There is a concern that temporary states also represent an unusual situation where the imminence of death in the task might distort respondents' valuation of the state. One solution suggested by Torrance (1986) is a two-stage process, where stage 1 involves an SG where all outcomes last for an additional *t* weeks, months or years followed by full health (though it could be another state). Alternative 1 is a treatment with two possible outcomes: either the patient is returned to normal health (probability *P*), or the patient lives for time period *t* in the worst temporary health state followed by full health (probability 1 − *P*). Alternative 2 has the certain outcome of the intermediate temporary health state h_i for an equivalent amount of time (*t* weeks, months or years) after which the patient is returned to full health. The probability *P* of the best outcome is varied until the individual is indifferent between the certain intermediate outcome and the gamble. If more than one temporary health state is being valued relative to the worst temporary health state, then this procedure is repeated for each health state.

Using this format, the formula for the utility of state h_i for time *t* is $h_i = P + (1 − P) h_j$ where h_i is the state being measured and h_j is the worst state. Here h_i is measured on a utility scale where full health for time period *t* is 1.0. In order to relate these utilities to the full health–death scale used to derive QALYs, there needs to be a second stage that involves valuing the worst temporary health state by redefining it as a short duration chronic state for time *t* followed by death, and valuing it relative to death and full health using the same technique as that described above for valuing chronic health states. This gives the value for h_j for time *t* which can then be inserted into the above formula to find the value for h_i for time *t* (see Fig. 5.4)

Some health economists have viewed the standard gamble as the 'gold standard' for the measurement of the 'utility' associated with particular health states, since it is based on the axioms of expected utility theory (EUT), which offers a normative framework for describing how individuals would make decisions under conditions of risk and uncertainty if they adhered to a set of basic axioms (Von Neumann and Morgenstern 1944). The SG has also been advocated on the basis that almost all decisions about health care are made under conditions of risk and uncertainty (Mehrez and Gafni 1993). The SG technique has been widely applied in the decision-making literature (Keeney and Raiffa 1976). It has also been extensively applied to medical decision

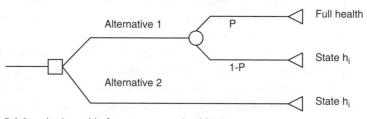

Fig. 5.4 Standard gamble for a temporary health state.

making, including the valuation of health states, where it has been used (indirectly via a transformation of VAS) to value the HUI2, HUI3 and SF-6D and also to value numerous condition-specific health state scenarios or vignettes.

Variants of the standard gamble

There are many variants of the SG technique. They differ in terms of the procedure used to identify the point of indifference, the use of props and the method of administration (e.g. by interviewer, computer or self-administered/paper questionnaire).

A widely used variant has been developed by Torrance and colleagues which addresses the problem of explaining probabilities to respondents through the use of a visual aid, known as the probability wheel (Torrance 1986; see Appendix 5.1 for an example of a probability wheel). This helps respondents to determine their point of indifference between the certain outcome and the gamble by iterating between values for the probability of success P (i.e. the 'ping–pong' method). The probability wheel is an adjustable disc with two sectors, each a different colour. It is constructed so that the relative size of the two sectors can be readily changed. The two alternatives are presented to the individual on cards and the two outcomes of the gamble alternatives are colour coded to match the two sectors of the probability wheel. The individual is informed that the probability of each outcome is proportional to the similarly coloured area of the disk. An example interview script for this variant of SG is reproduced in Appendix 5.2.

An alternative SG variant that does not require the use of a visual aid (titration method) has been developed by Jones-Lee and colleagues (1993). It uses a titration procedure in a questionnaire with a list of values for chances of success for treatment. The chances of success may be specified in terms of 'bottom-up' titration (i.e. 0, 5, 10 per cent, etc.) or 'top-down' titration (i.e. 100, 95, 90 per cent, etc.). Choosing from this list, respondents are asked to indicate all the values of P at which they are confident they would opt for treatment and all the values of P at which they would reject treatment. Finally, they are asked to indicate the value of P where they find it most difficult to choose between treatment and remaining in a hypothetical health state (see Appendix 5.3 for an example of the titration method for SG). This variant has been adapted for use on the computer by Stein et al. (2006a) and Lenert et al. (2002).

This process of 'chaining' described for temporary states can be used to value mild states where there is a concern that respondents might not be willing to trade risk of being dead for an improvement in health. The worst state h_j is some state better than being dead. The validity of such chaining is discussed below in the section which looks at the impact of different variants.

5.2.3 **The time trade-off**

The time trade-off technique (TTO) was developed specifically for use in health care by Torrance (1976) as a less complex alternative to the SG that overcomes the problems of explaining probabilities to respondents. In common with the SG, TTO presents the respondent with a choice. However, in TTO, the respondent is asked to choose between two alternatives of certainty rather than between a certain outcome and a gamble with two possible outcomes. The application of TTO to a chronic state considered better than dead is illustrated in Fig. 5.5.

The approach involves presenting individuals with a paired comparison. For a chronic health state preferred to death, alternative 1 involves living for period t in a specified but less than full health state (state h_i). Alternative 2 involves full health for time period x where $x < t$. Time x is varied until the respondent is indifferent between the two alternatives. The score given to the less than full health state is then x/t.

Time trade-off for states considered worse than dead

For a chronic health state considered worse than dead, the TTO task can be modified. In the Measurement and Valuation of Health (MVH) study, states considered worse than dead were valued using a procedure which involved respondents choosing between alternative 1, immediate death; and alternative 2, spending a length of time (y) in state h_i followed by x years in full health where $x + y = t$. Time x is varied until the respondent is indifferent between the two alternatives. The value for state h_i is then given by $h_i = -x/(t - x)$. Hence, the more time that is required in full health to compensate for the time spent in state h_i, the lower is the score for state h_i (see Fig. 5.6).

As for SG, one practical difficulty with this technique is that, although it imposes an upper limit of 1.0 on chronic health states preferred to death, it imposes no comparable lower limit on health states which are considered

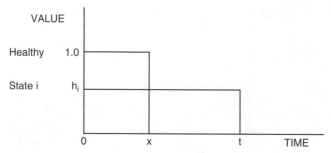

Fig. 5.5 Time trade-off for a chronic health state preferred to death.

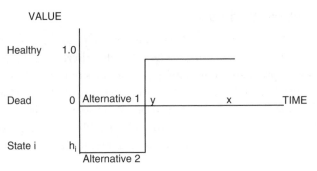

Fig. 5.6 Time trade-off for a chronic health state considered worse than death.

worse than death. This results in a scale ranging from minus infinity to +1.0, thereby giving greater weight to negative values in the calculation of mean scores and presenting problems for statistical analysis. It has therefore been recommended that the preference values of states considered worse than death are re-scaled such that the worst possible state is assigned a preference value of −1.0 (Torrance 1984).

Time trade-off for temporary health states

Figure 5.7 illustrates how temporary health states can be valued using the TTO method. As with the SG, intermediate states are measured relative to the best state (healthy) and the worst state (temporary state h_j). The respondent is offered a choice between two alternatives. Alternative 1 involves living in temporary health state h_i for time period t (the time period specified for the temporary health states) followed by a return to good health. Alternative 2 involves living in temporary health state h_j for time x where $x < t$, followed by full health. Time period x is varied until the respondent expresses indifference between the two alternatives, at which point the required preference value for

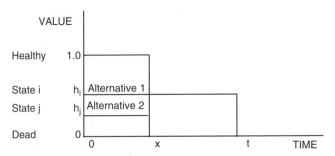

Fig. 5.7 Time trade-off for a temporary health state.

state $h_i = 1 - (1 - h_j)x/t$. If h_j is set to 0, this reduces to $h_i = 1 - x/t$. To transform the values onto the full health–death scale, the worst temporary health state must be redefined as a short duration chronic state (as for SG) and valued using the same TTO technique as that described above for valuing chronic health states.

Variants of the time trade-off

As there are for SG, there are numerous variants of TTO using different elicitation procedures, props (if any) and modes of administration. In common with SG, TTO values can be elicited using the ping–pong or titration search procedures. Visual aids have been developed to assist the respondent in the TTO elicitation task including props comprising a set of health state cards and a moving sliding scale to represent life years (see for example Torrance 1976; Dolan et al. 1996). The widely used variant developed by the York EQ-5D team for interviewer administration and using props is included in the appendix (Appendices 5.4–5.6). TTO was administered to value the first version of the HUI1 (Horsman et al. 2003), the EQ-5D (Dolan et al. 1996) and the AQoL (Hawthorne et al. 1999) as well as numerous condition-specific health states.

The person trade-off

The PTO technique is a technique for estimating the social value of different health states promoted most recently by Nord and others (Nord et al. 1999; Schwarzinger et al. 2004). As with TTO and SG, the PTO technique asks the respondent to make a choice between alternatives. The respondent is asked to make a choice in the context of social decision making involving groups of other people rather than asking the respondent to value her own state or imagine being in the state herself. The PTO is an adaptation of the method of adjustment or equivalent stimuli described in the psychometrics literature (Patrick et al. 1973). It was first applied within the health care field by Patrick and Erickson (1973), in the valuation of levels of well-being for a health status index.

Using this technique, the respondent is asked to indicate how many people in health state B are equivalent to a specified number of people in health state A by asking the following kind of question (Nord 1992): 'If there are x people in adverse health situation A and y people in adverse health situation B, and you can only help (cure) one group, which group would you choose?' (Nord 1992, p. 569). The number of people in health state B (y) is then varied until the respondent finds the two groups equivalent in terms of needing help. The undesirability of health state B is then x/y times as great as that of health state A. This process is then repeated for all other health states to be valued.

PTO has attracted the interest of those researchers who regard this approach as more relevant for social choice contexts than the conventional individual perspective of the other methods of preference elicitation.

Magnitude estimation

The technique of ME has its origins in psychometrics. It was originally developed to measure sensory and non-sensory perception as an alternative to the VAS (Stevens 1960). Using ME, respondents are asked to provide the ratio of undesirability of pairs of health states, e.g. is one health state twice as bad, three times worse, etc. than a comparative health state? If health state B is judged to be x times worse than health state A, the undesirability (disutility) of health state B is x times as great as that of health state A. By asking a series of such questions, all health states for valuation can be related to each other on the undesirability scale. The phrasing of the question was intended to generate data with ratio properties (i.e. one state is so much better or worse than another) and therefore it is often referred to in the psychometric literature as ratio scaling.

The technique of ME was used in the original valuation of the Rosser disability/distress classification. Respondents were asked to rank and value six marker states, and then to value five of these against the least ill state (Kind *et al.* 1982). All the remaining 23 states were valued against the marker states, including death. It was then possible to transform the value of all states onto a full health and death scale. There have been important variations in the versions of ME used to value health states. Rosser and Kind (1978) report asking respondents to indicate how undesirable one state was compared with another, whereas Kaplan and colleagues (1979) asked how many times more desirable one state was compared with another. The version used by Sintonen (1981) provides the respondent with a scale from 0 to 100 for answering the question.

The main applications of ME to the valuation of health states includes the Rosser classification and the 15D. It is rarely used now.

5.3 **Review of valuation techniques**

In an extensive review of outcome measures for use in economic evaluation, Brazier and colleagues advocated the three basic concepts of practicality, reliability and validity as the criteria that should be used to compare the performance of alternative methods of preference elicitation (Brazier *et al.* 1999). The practicality of a method is dependent upon its acceptability to respondents, which is a function of the length and complexity of the task, as well as its ability to keep the respondents' interest. It may be the case that some tasks cause distress to respondents (e.g. where there is reference to an early death).

These aspects of practicality can be assessed by examining the proportion of those individuals approached who agree to participate (i.e. the response rate) and the level of missing data (i.e. completeness). Reliability is the ability of a measure to reproduce the same quality adjustment values on two separate administrations, over which there is no difference in true health (or in whichever quantity is being measured, which may be the value placed on a hypothetical health state). The two measurements can be elicited from the same respondents at two points in time, known as test–re-test reliability, or from different respondents, known as inter-rater reliability.

The basis of the techniques in economic theory or 'theoretical validity' has been argued by some health economists to be the most important criterion in the assessment of the validity of a measure to be used in economic evaluation (Gafni 1996). The assessment of the theoretical basis of the techniques also helps identify the testable assumptions which underpin them. These provide a means of testing the empirical validity of the techniques. Tests of empirical validity also include consistency with other measures of stated preferences, such as ranking of states or other cardinal valuation techniques (though this does not really help distinguish between them).

5.3.1 Visual analogue scales

There is general agreement that VAS represents the most feasible of the health state valuation techniques, demonstrating high response rates and high levels of completion (Froberg and Kane 1989; Drummond *et al.* 2005). Green *et al.* (2000) reported that completion rates for VAS-based surveys were typically in excess of 90 per cent. VAS methods tend to be less expensive to administer than other methods because of their relative simplicity and ease of completion. This practicality has contributed to the wide utilization of VAS. There is also a significant amount of empirical evidence to demonstrate the reliability of VAS methods in terms of inter-rater reliability and test–re-test reliability (see for example O'Brien and Viramontes 1994; Gloth *et al.* 2001; Mannion *et al.* 2006). These studies cite test–re-test correlation coefficients (intraclass correlation or Pearson correlation) ranging from $r = 0.61$ (O'Brien and Viramontes 1994) to $r = 0.95$ (Mannion *et al.* 2006).

The direct and choice-less nature of the VAS tasks has given rise to concerns over the ability of this technique to reflect preferences on an interval scale (Bleichrodt and Johannesson 1997). A theoretical argument for VAS has been provided by Dyer and Sarin (1982), who argue that VAS represents a measurable value function that represents preferences under conditions of certainty, whereas utilities represent preferences under uncertainty. This enables a link to be made between the value and uncertainty in terms of an individual's relative risk attitude (Torrance *et al.* 1996). Dyer and Sarin suggest that this offers a stable relationship between SG and VAS, and hence a means of estimating SG values from VAS responses. Recent research into the existence of a stable value function is inconclusive. Bleichrodt and Johanneson (1997) did not find evidence of a stable value function, although a re-analysis of their data by Schwartz (1998) found that after adjustment for range–frequency bias in the VAS data, the results were consistent with the existence of a stable value function. Robinson and colleagues (2001) also found that adjusted VAS data were consistent with a stable value function, whereas unadjusted data were not. Schwartz, and Robinson and colleagues both used the Parducci–Weddell (PW) range–frequency model to adjust the VAS data (Parducci and Wedell 1986), and Torrance and others have recommended that this model be routinely used for VAS data which are to be applied in economic evaluation (Torrance *et al.* 2001). More recently, McCabe and colleagues demonstrated that the application of the PW model may produce data that are not on the 0–1 scale required for estimating utility weights in the QALY model and cannot be translated on to this scale using a linear transformation because the true adjusted value of the upper anchor is unknown (McCabe *et al.* 2004). Obviously data of this nature cannot readily be incorporated into economic evaluation.

There is also a concern that VAS methods are susceptible to response spreading, whereby respondents use all areas on the valuation scale when responding, especially where multiple health states are valued on the same scale. Response spreading can lead to health states that are very much alike being placed at some distance from one another on a valuation scale and health states that are essentially vastly different being placed very close to one another, as the respondent seeks to place responses across the whole (or a specific portion) of the available scale. If response spreading does occur, then this implies that VAS techniques do not generate an interval scale and the numbers obtained may not be meaningful (in the cardinal sense).

More generally, VAS is prone to context effects where the average rating for items is influenced by the level of other items being valued. Robinson *et al.* (2001) found that a series of core health states were given lower values when placed in a wider set of more severe health states than when placed in a wider set of milder health states. In addition, Torrance and colleagues (2001) found evidence of an end-point bias whereby health states at the top and bottom of the scale are placed further apart on the scale than would be suggested by a direct comparison of differences. It is not clear what, if any, interaction there might be between range frequency and end-point bias, or whether a simple adjustment for end-point bias followed by the application of the PW model would adequately remove bias from the data.

One economist, Broome (1993), has argued that VAS can be seen as better than SG and TTO because it is not contaminated by risk and time preference, respectively (discussed below). Broome is concerned with measuring some notion of 'good' rather than individual preferences that do not fall within the conventional welfarist framework. However, Broome's arguments may be viewed as consistent with a non-welfarist approach.

Historically, the ordinal properties of VAS methods have been largely accepted, given their origins within psychometrics and psychophysics. Although they often correlate well with measures of health status (e.g. pain, functioning and clinical symptoms), VAS techniques have generally been found to have only a weak correlation with SG and TTO (Jansen *et al.* 2000; Bryce *et al.* 2004;).

In summary, VAS techniques appear to measure aspects of health status changes rather than the satisfaction or benefit conveyed by such changes. Qualitative evidence of respondents seeing VAS methods as an expression of numbers in terms of 'percentages of the best imaginable state' (Nord 1991), or a 'percentage of functioning scale' (Robinson *et al.* 1997) rather than eliciting information about their preferences for health states provides support for this hypothesis. There is a large body of evidence to suggest that unadjusted VAS scores do not provide a valid measure of the strength of preference that can be used in economic evaluation. The evidence relating to the validity of VAS scores submitted to various types of transformations is presented below.

Mapping from VAS to SG and TTO

VAS to SG   Given the evidence that VAS may not produce health state utilities that can be used directly in the calculation of QALYs, there has been interest in mapping VAS values to SG or TTO utility values. For example, Torrance *et al.* (1996) and Feeny *et al.* (2002) used VAS to elicit preferences for the single and multiattribute health states defined by the HUI2 and HUI3 instruments and transformed these values into SG utilities using a specially estimated power function. Torrance and colleagues suggested that this has the advantage of retaining the ease of use of VAS with the theoretical advantages of a choice-based measure of health.

The main theoretical argument for the relationship between VAS and SG is based upon the Dyer and Sarin (1982) argument that utilities are made up of a combination of the measurable value function and relative risk attitude. VAS can be regarded as a technique for eliciting the measurable value function and SG as a technique for eliciting utilities. According to this theory, for individuals who are risk-neutral, SG and VAS values will be the same. A risk-averse person would exhibit a concave relationship between VAS and SG, indicating that he/she would prefer a certain health state with value x to an expected equivalent value (calculated by summing two or more health state values by their probability). In contrast, a risk-loving person would exhibit a convex relationship between VAS and SG. Given that the majority of people have been found to be risk-averse over uncertain prospects involving health, this provides an explanation for the relationship presented in Fig. 5.1.

A power function has been proposed to estimate this relationship represented by the following equation:

$$U = 1 - (1 - V)^b \text{ or } U = V^b$$

where the power term b represents an individual's constant relative risk attitude, with b greater than 1 implying risk aversion and b equal to one implying risk neutrality. U is the SG utility and V is the VAS value for the health state in question.

Bombardier and colleagues (1982) have offered an alternative theoretical explanation for the relationship between VAS and SG based upon a general aversion to gambling with one's own health. This general aversion is fixed regardless of the level of risk and hence can be represented by a constant term for the difference between SG and VAS values. Bombardier and colleagues estimated a linear relationship between 35 VAS and SG mean health state values which explained 76 per cent of the variation. Torrance and colleagues as well as Loomes have subsequently fitted a power function to the same data with an estimated value for the power term of 2.16 and 2.27 (and explaining 80 per cent of the variation), respectively (Loomes 1993; Torrance *et al.* 1996). Torrance and colleagues estimated weights for the HUI2 using the relationship between mean SG and VAS values for four health states. They fitted a power function to the data, which explained 97 per cent of the variation and had a value of 2.29 for the power term. More recently, Stevens *et al.* (2006), in an examination of the relationship between SG and VAS values in a UK valuation study of the HUI2, question the reliance on the assumption of a power curve relationship between VAS and SG data in the Health Utilities Index valuation framework. They found that the power function was not the best fitting model. It was outperformed by all other specifications in predictive performance (linear, quadratic and cubic functions), with the restricted cubic function demonstrating overall superiority.

VAS to TTO   The expected theoretical relationship between TTO and VAS has been the subject of rather less discussion in the literature, although an obvious source of any difference is time preference. For any rate of time preference other than zero, the time difference between the period in full health and the longer period in chronic health would influence the results. A constant positive time preference rate would reduce the value of time spent in the chronic state by a greater proportion than the time spent in full health, and hence the corresponding TTO values would increase. A negative time preference rate would have the opposite effect. The duration of time spent in a health state may also impact upon TTO values. There is evidence to suggest that the prospect of longer periods of time spent in chronic health states may be considered worse than shorter durations (Sutherland *et al.* 1982), indicating that TTO values decline with time, the opposite effect of a positive time preference rate.

Studies mapping the relationship between VAS and TTO include work by Torrance who estimated a power function between VAS and TTO from 18 pairs of health state values which explained 79 per cent of the variation and had a power term of 1.61 (Torrance 1976). Bombardier *et al.* (1982) estimated a linear model for the relationship between VAS and TTO for the 35 pairs of mean values, explaining 89 per cent of the variation. Similarly, Loomes estimated a power function of 1.82 explaining 88 per cent of the variation (Loomes 1993). Stiggelbout *et al.* (1994) have claimed to replicate Torrance's original findings on 183 cancer patients rating their own health. Unfortunately, none of these studies has presented standard econometric diagnostic information on the specification of the models, which means that it is not possible to compare the models or judge how well they actually fit the data.

Neither Torrance nor Stiggelbout *et al.* were able to fit satisfactory power functions to data at the individual level. Only Dolan and Sutton (1997) appear to have done this successfully. However, once again, the linear models outperformed the power models, and the power models suffered from heterogeneity and misspecification. The mapping functions were also found to differ substantially between the two variants of TTO.

In conclusion, although there would be significant practical advantages to being able to map from VAS to one of these choice-based techniques, the evidence suggests that the relationships between studies are not stable in terms of the form of the relationship and size of the model parameters.

5.3.2 **Standard gamble**

The SG appears to be acceptable in terms of its practicality, since large numbers of empirical studies have reported good response and completion rates. Many studies, across different respondent groups, have reported completion rates in excess of 80 per cent, with some studies reporting completion rates as high as 95–100 per cent (see for example recently published studies by Stewart *et al.* 2005 and Gerson *et al.* 2005). The SG has also been found to be feasible and acceptable amongst varied types of patient groups and clinical areas, including cancer, transplantation, vascular surgery and spinal problems. Several studies have provided support for the reliability of the SG (Ross *et al.* 2003; Wasserman 2005).

SG is rooted in expected utility theory (EUT). EUT has been the dominant theory of decision making under uncertainty for over half a century. Although there are now numerous alternative contenders, its simplicity and usefulness in constructing decision analytical models for use in economic evaluation have ensured its continued survival in applied work. Furthermore, the main preference-based QALY model is based in EUT (Chapter 3).

To recap, EUT theory postulates that individuals choose between prospects (such as different ways of managing a medical condition) in such a way as to maximize their 'expected' utility (Von Neumann and Morgenstern 1944). Under this theory, for a given prospect such as having a surgical operation, a utility value is estimated for each possible outcome, good or bad. These values are multiplied by their probability of occurring and the result summed to calculate the expected utility of the prospect. This procedure is undertaken for each prospect being considered. The key assumption made by EUT over and above conventional consumer theory is independence, which means that the value of a given outcome is independent of how it was arrived at or its context. In decision tree analysis, this is the equivalent of saying that the value of one branch of the tree is unaffected by the other branches.

Due to its theoretical basis, the SG is often portrayed as the classical method of decision making under uncertainty, and due to the uncertain nature of medical decision making the SG is often classed as the 'gold standard' (Drummond *et al.* 2005). As medical decisions usually involve uncertainty, the use of the SG method would seem to have great appeal. However, Richardson (1994) notes that the type of uncertain prospect embodied in the SG may bear little resemblance to the uncertainties in various medical decisions, so this feature may be less relevant than others have suggested.

The status of SG as the gold standard has been criticized given the existence of ample evidence that the axioms of EUT are violated in practice (Hershey *et al.* 1981; Schoemaker 1982). One response in health economics (as elsewhere) has been that EUT should be seen as a normative rather than a descriptive theory, i.e. it suggests how decisions should be made under conditions of uncertainty (Drummond *et al.* 2005). However, this still does not alter the concern that the values generated by SG do not necessarily represent people's valuation of a given health state, but incorporate other factors, such as risk attitude, gambling effects and loss aversion (Broome 1993; Richardson 1994). A respondent's attitude to risk, for example, may be risk-averse, risk-neutral or risk-seeking, and at times may be a mixture of all three (Loomes and McKenzie 1989). Kahneman and Tversky (1979) have argued that respondents generally act as if they are risk-averse when choices are framed in terms of potential gains and as risk-seeking when choices are framed in terms of potential losses. Kahneman and Tversky also found that individuals tend to overestimate small probabilities and underestimate large probabilities, and suggest that probabilities of less than 0.1 and greater than 0.9 present individuals with difficulties, which raises concerns in the context of health state valuation tasks. All these factors will 'contaminate' SG values in some way.

Empirical evidence relating to the consistency of SG responses with expected rankings is more promising. In a general population sample of 335 respondents, Dolan *et al.* (1996) examined the performance of the SG and TTO against 12 logically consistent comparisons (EQ-5D health states) and reported that SG produced high levels of consistency. Rutten van Molken *et al.* (1995*a*) compared SG responses with hypothesized preferences based on the natural underlying order of health state descriptions used (fibromyalgia patients $n = 85$, anklyosing spondylitis patients $n = 144$) and found a high level of consistency. Llewellyn-Thomas *et al.* (1982) reported that the SG provided a high level of consistency against an expected rank ordering of health states (cancer patients, $n = 64$). They found that 54 (84 per cent) of 64 respondents ranked five health states via SG in accordance with *a priori* expectations; with nine of the remaining respondents providing a rank order with only one inconsistent pairing.

5.3.3 Time trade-off

A wide variety of empirical studies have demonstrated that the TTO technique is a practical, reliable and acceptable method of health state valuation (Green *et al.* 2000). The TTO has been used in a self-administered format (Stavem 1999), and Lenert and Sturley (2001) have shown that computer-based applications of TTO are practical and acceptable.

The applicability of the TTO in medical decision making has been questioned by some commentators (e.g. Mehrez and Gafni 1991) due to the fact that the technique asks respondents to make a choice between two certain outcomes, when health care is characterized by conditions of uncertainty. Others have argued that it is possible to adjust TTO values to incorporate individuals' attitudes to risk and uncertainty (Stiggelbout *et al.* 1994; Cher *et al.* 1997), though this is rarely done. Furthermore, adjusting for risk attitude is difficult when there are strong theoretical and empirical grounds for arguing that there is not a constant attitude to risk.

An underlying assumption of the TTO method is that individuals are prepared to trade-off a constant proportion of their remaining life years to improve their health status, irrespective of the number of years that remain. However, it seems reasonable to postulate that the valuation of a health state may be influenced by a duration effect relating to the time an individual spends in that state (Sackett and Torrance 1981). A study by Sutherland *et al.* (1982) identified a maximal endurable time for some severe health states beyond which they yielded negative utility. Furthermore, for short survival periods, it was observed that individuals were not willing to trade any survival time (measured in life years) for an improvement in quality of life, apparently suggesting that individuals' preferences are lexicographic for short time durations. Further work by Dolan (1996) found that poor states of health generated from the EQ-5D valuation system became more intolerable to a sample of the general population the longer their duration. If individuals do not trade-off a constant proportion of their remaining life expectancy in the valuation of health states, then values elicited using specific time durations (e.g. 10 years) cannot be assumed to hold for states lasting for different time periods.

The impact of *time preference* on valuations is another issue that causes theoretical concerns with the TTO. If individuals have a positive rate of time preference, they will give greater value to years of life in the near future than to those in the distant future. Alternatively respondents may prefer to experience an episode of ill health immediately in order to eliminate 'dread' and move on. For instance, this hypothesis may explain why some women with a family history of breast cancer opt for mastectomy before any breast cancer is detected. In practice, however, the evidence suggests that the majority of individuals exhibit positive time preferences for health (Van der Pol and Cairns 2000), although empirically the validity of the traditional (constant) discounting model in health has been challenged in favour of a model which allows for decreasing time aversion (Cairns and Van der Pol 1997) (implying that the longer the period of delay for the onset of ill health, the lower the discount rate). TTO values are rarely corrected for time preference.

Empirical evidence again offers some support for TTO. In terms of stated preferences, Ashby *et al.* (1994) compared TTO scores with the rank ordering of states given by respondents. They elicited health state valuations for health states of women after treatment for breast cancer, from a number of groups consisting of nurses, hospital doctors, general practitioners, University staff and breast cancer patients (total $n = 138$). Respondents ranked and valued five health states, presented with a health state baseline, and the authors report results that show a considerable degree of consistency in ranking and that rank ordering was consistently reflected in the mean TTO values.

One concerning aspect of the empirical findings of TTO studies is the extent to which respondents have been unwilling to trade or sacrifice any of their remaining life expectancy for improvements in health in some studies. Robinson *et al.* (1997) refer to a 'threshold of tolerability' below which health states would have to fall before respondents would be willing to sacrifice even a few days. In a general population study based upon the EQ-5D, Dolan *et al.* (1996), found that approximately 5 per cent of subjects were unwilling to sacrifice any life expectancy in order to avoid more than half of the states they valued.

5.3.4 **Person trade-off**

To date, the PTO technique has not been widely used to value health states and hence the feasibility and acceptability of the PTO is relatively unknown. In an early examination of the technique Patrick *et al.* (1973) report that it 'is too complex for use outside of a laboratory-like individual interview'. Nord (1995) reports that the PTO can be quite demanding, warns of possible framing effects and advises the use of multistep procedures to introduce individuals to the issues involved. Nord suggests that self administered formats may not be suitable, and also advocates the use of a reflective element within PTO to allow individuals to consider their responses. Pinto Prades (1997) found the PTO acceptable and feasible in a pilot study involving interviews with 30 undergraduate students. Murray and Lopez (1997) report the use of the PTO technique to elicit health state preferences for the assessment of the severity of disability as part of large multinational study. Although Murray and Lopez do not present information on the performance of the PTO technique, they report that the PTO protocol was a group exercise (nine groups) for between eight and 12 participants lasting 10 hours, where discussion was an important element of the process and other health state valuation methods were used to encourage respondents to think carefully about the process.

Given that the PTO asks individuals to consider choices concerning the treatment of others, it is thought that subjects may find it difficult and unpleasant to make such direct decisions (Nord 1995). In a pilot study involving 53 Norwegian politicians, Nord (1995) found that there was a willingness to respond to PTO tasks (36 respondents); however, Nord also found evidence that there was some reluctance to participate (17 respondents). Further evidence is required from empirical studies to demonstrate the practicality of the PTO.

As with practicality, the reliability of the PTO is yet to be demonstrated. Nord (1993, 1995) found a strong random element in individual PTO responses, but suggests that responses may be reliable at an aggregate or group level. However, there is very little evidence on reliability in relation to PTO, and Nord himself advocates further research in this area. In addition, whilst the technique is seen as intuitively appealing (Nord 1995), there are no theoretical underpinnings advocated in the current literature, other than psychometric qualities surrounding adjustment or equivalent stimuli (Patrick *et al.* 1973). Although the PTO technique is choice based, the choice is made in a 'social' context with outcomes relating to the welfare of others, therefore standard consumer theory cannot be applied to the decision task. It may be that the PTO, due to its social preference perspective, can be linked to the economics literature surrounding the valuation of externalities, yet this link has not been established so far.

Richardson (1994) supports the potential interval scale properties of the PTO due to the fact that there is a clear and comprehensible meaning to the PTO (where the numbers are specified). Pinto Prades (1997) also comments that one of the hypothetical advantages of the PTO in the context of economic evaluation for health care is that it asks the right questions (i.e. trade-offs between people).

With respect to hypothesized preferences, Pinto Prades (1997) compared the performance of PTO, SG and VAS on the basis of predictive power, measuring the degree of ordinal agreement between an expected ordering (given by the respondents) and an ordering directly obtained using the three methods at an individual level (the degree of agreement was measured using Kendall's measure of association—where 0 reflects independence between orderings). VAS was found to have a poor association (−0.06), whilst SG and two of the three variants of the PTO used were found to have a better association, having similar results (0.34–0.393), One of the variants of the PTO used (PTO-3) was found to have a greater level of association (0.621) than the other methods used. Pinto Prades (1997) also assessed the techniques on the basis of strength of preference (cardinal) using a hypothetical voting exercise reflecting the treatment intervals of paired comparisons, finding that the PTO (variant 3 used) was a better reflection of social preferences than other techniques used. The study by Pinto Prades is a pilot study within a convenience sample, yet it may suggest that the PTO is better able to reflect social preferences than are SG and VAS methods. However, some would argue that these latter methods do not set out to measure social preferences.

5.4 **Overview and comparison of techniques**

In the context of cost per QALY analysis, health economists have tended to favour the choice-based scaling methods of SG and TTO (Dolan *et al.* 1996; Sculpher 1996; Brazier *et al.* 2005; Drummond *et al.* 2005) and a choice-based method is also recommended by the National Institute for Health and Clinical Excellence (NICE) in its guide to the conduct of technology appraisals (2004). Each of the SG and TTO methods starts with the premise that health is an important argument in an individual's utility function. The welfare change associated with a change in health status can then be determined by the compensating change required in one of the remaining arguments in the individual's utility function that leaves overall utility unchanged (Dolan *et al.* 1996). In the SG, the compensating change is valued in terms of the risk of immediate death. In the TTO, the compensating change is valued in terms of the amount of life expectancy an individual is prepared to sacrifice.

SG has the most rigorous foundation in theory in the form of EUT theory of decision making under uncertainty. However, there are theoretical arguments against the use of SG in health state valuation and there is little empirical support for EUT. There are also concerns about the empirical basis of the TTO technique. There is evidence to suggest that duration effects and time preference effects can have an impact on the elicitation of TTO values (Sutherland *et al.* 1982; Dolan and Gudex 1995).

In reality, SG and TTO valuations can both be seen as containing biases as measures of preference. A key review by Bleichtrodt (2002) summarized each of these techniques in terms of four key possible sources of bias relating to utility curvature, probability weighting, loss aversion and scale compatibility.

In terms of *utility curvature*, SG imposes no restriction on the utility function for the duration of the health state, whereas the TTO assumes that utility is linear in duration. If, as expected, the majority of individuals exhibit positive time preference for health, then this will result in TTO values being biased upwards. However, because SG imposes no restriction on the utility function for the duration of the health state, the existence of utility curvature does not lead to a bias in the SG utilities.

Probability weighting affects SG values but not TTO values, since these are elicited under conditions of certainty and no probabilities are involved. Empirical evidence suggests that the probability weighting function is most typically inverse S shaped, implying that individuals tend to overweight small probabilities and underweight large probabilities. According to Bleichrodt (2002), the point where the function changes from overweighting probabilities to underweighting probabilities lies approximately at 0.35 and, given that the probabilities reported in SG elicitations tend to be over 0.35, this implies that SG values are generally biased upwards by probability weighting.

Loss aversion implies that individuals tend to be more sensitive to losses than to gains. If loss aversion holds, then this will make individuals more reluctant to give up healthy life years in the TTO, leading to an upward bias in TTO utilities. In the case of SG, loss aversion will tend to cause individuals to weight the certain outcome more highly than the gamble. Hence they will tend to state a higher value of *P* at which they would be indifferent between the gamble and the certain outcome, again leading to upward biases in SG values.

Scale compatibility means that an individual assigns more weight to an attribute the higher its compatibility with the response scale used. In the TTO, the individual is asked how many years in full health are equivalent to a longer period of time in some intermediate state of health, so the response scale is duration. If an individual exhibits scale compatibility in responding to TTO questions, this implies that they give more weight to duration than to health status. As a consequence, the individual will be less willing to give up life years for an improvement in health status, leading to an upward bias in TTO values. In SG, probability is used as the response scale. Therefore, scale compatibility predicts that an individual will focus upon probability in the evaluation of the SG question. Three probabilities are involved in the SG question and so scale compatibility may lead to either downward or upward biases in the SG values, the overall effect being ambiguous.

Table 5.1 summarizes the arguments made by Bleichrodt in relation to the biases in SG and TTO values. Salomon and Murray (2004) compared the VAS, SG, TTO and PTO for a range of health states on the premise that none of the available methods gives the exact quantity of interest, i.e. directly interpretable strength of preference values for health states, but each of them produces responses from which this may be imputed. For each technique, one auxiliary parameter was also used to describe the relationship between strength of preference and responses on that type of question. The VAS model was based upon a power function transformation of the true intensity levels (Stevens 1960). The TTO model allowed for time preference in individual choices over health and longevity (Dolan and Gudex 1995). The SG responses were modelled as a function of the underlying health state value and a risk aversion parameter, and the PTO responses were modelled using similar functions to those used for the SG but allowing for a distinct parameter to capture

Table 5.1 Overview of the biases in SG and TTO values (Bleichrodt 2002)

Effect	Bias in SG values	Bias in TTO values
Utility curvature	None	Downward
Probability weighting	Generally upward	None
Loss aversion	Upward	Upward
Scale compatibility	Ambiguous	Upward

Copyright John Wiley & Sons Limited. Reproduced with permission from: Bleichrodt H (2002). A new explanation for the difference between time trade off utilities and standard gamble utilities. *Health Economics* 11:447–56.

distributional concerns. They found considerable agreement in the rank ordering of the health states implied by the different methods at both the individual and aggregate levels, supporting the hypothesis that each different method may be related monotonically to a common set of core values. However, even these partial adjustments did not ensure they produced the same results.

In conclusion, there are theoretical concerns with all these techniques. We argue that unadjusted VAS values do not provide a valid basis for estimating preferences over health states, and satisfactory adjustments remain elusive. For trade-off-based valuations from an individual perspective, the current choice is between SG and TTO, but for the reasons outlined above the values they generate are distorted by factors apart from preferences over health states, and currently there is no compelling basis on which to select one or the other. This is one reason why researchers in the field have begun to examine the potential role of ordinal techniques such as ranking and discrete choice experiments, as we will discuss in Chapter 7. PTO continues to offer an interesting alternative for those wishing to adopt a social perspective to valuing health states, but there are other approaches to incorporating social concerns in QALYs (see Chapter 11).

5.5 The impact of different variants of the valuation techniques—evidence for preference construction?

The debate around the appropriate technique for valuation has tended to be the focus of the academic literature; however, there are many variants of each technique and these too may have important implications. Techniques vary in terms of their mode of administration (interview or self-completion, computer or paper administration), search procedures (e.g. iteration, titration or open ended), the use of props and diagrams, time allowed for reflection and individual versus group interviews. There have been few publications in the health economics literature comparing these alternatives, but what evidence there is suggests that health state values vary considerably between variants of the same technique.

5.5.1 Format

Dolan and Sutton (1997) compared two variants of the SG and TTO, one using props and the other no props. These two variants differed not only in terms of the materials used (props versus no props), but also their mode of administration (props is interviewer administered and no props is designed for self-completion) and their procedure for finding the indifference value.

The props variant used a 'ping–pong' search procedure and the no props used titration. Dolan and Sutton (1997) found that differences between variants were more pronounced than differences between techniques. In particular, they found that TTO props valuations tended to be higher than VAS responses for mild states and lower for more severe states. SG props valuations were broadly similar to VAS scores over a wide range, and titration method valuations were consistently higher than VAS valuations, especially for more severe states. In another study comparing titration versus ping–pong search procedures using a common mode of administration (a standardized computer program), Lenert *et al.* (1998) found that health state values were between 0.10 and 0.15 higher with the titration search procedure than with the ping–pong search procedure for both SG and TTO methods. Differences due to search procedures were found to be similar in magnitude to the differences between SG and TTO methods using the same search procedure, with SG values being, on average, higher than TTO values for the same health state.

A further study by Brazier and Dolan (2005) compared SG props (ping–pong with interviewer administration) to no props (titration with self-completion) and found that the mean titration values were significantly higher on average for the first four of the seven health states valued. Brazier and Dolan suggested that this result could be explained by anchoring, since titration typically starts eliciting preferences at the upper end of the scale, whereas the ping–pong iterates respondents between the upper and lower ends, thereby reducing any anchor point bias. Brazier and Dolan argue that this hypothesis is supported by the finding that a significantly lower proportion of respondents chose a probability of success of 1.0 with ping–pong compared with titration. A view expressed by some of the respondents in their study was that the ping–pong procedure actually confuses people and encourages them to take risks. This was a crossover study, and the last three states had values that were found to be contaminated by what went before.

5.5.2 Chaining of health state values

It has been suggested in the literature that for valuing milder health states, where respondents may be less willing to risk death, an alternative variant is to value such states (h_i) against an uncertain prospect of full health or another state worse than the one being valued (h_j), but not as bad as being dead (Drummond *et al.* 2005). This is essentially the approach suggested for valuing temporary states (Fig. 5.4). The lower state is then valued in an SG as the intermediate state against the gamble of full health or being dead. By a simple 'chaining' process, it is possible to transform the indifference probability value from the first gamble (P_x) using the indifference probability value from the second gamble (P_y) onto the full health–death scale [i.e. $h_i = P_x + (1 - P_y) \times P_x$]. According to the axioms of EUT, the chained value for health state h_i should be the same as the value obtained from a single gamble involving full health and being dead as lower anchor (or the equivalent gamble for states worse than being dead).

A number of studies have found that values chained via the worst state are consistently higher than the values obtained directly (Llewellyn-Thomas *et al.* 1982; Jones-Lee *et al.* 1993; Rutten van Molken *et al.* 1995b). As observed by Jones-Lee *et al.* (1993) in their studies of injury state valuation '… Varying the severity of the consequence of failure in the risky treatment requires a conceptually more difficult adjustment than keeping the risky treatment the same and varying the severity of the injury description' (p. 62). There are a number of theoretical explanations of this phenomenon, including the existence of a gambling effect (Richardson, 1994) and loss aversion due to a reference point effect (Oliver 2003).

5.5.3 Implications

The evidence that the way people are asked preference elicitation techniques has a major impact on the results has a number of implications. First, it demonstrates the importance of using a common variant to ensure comparability between studies. It is not enough to claim two studies used the same methods simply because they both claim to have used TTO or SG. It is necessary to demonstrate that the two studies used the same variant and the same technique (and respondents with the same characteristics). Secondly, there might be scope for correcting for some of these differences if they prove to be systematic. This approach has been applied by Oliver (2003) and Morrison (1994) with some success, but there has been little of this work to date. There is a need for utilizing cognitive techniques to understand better the reasons for the differences between variants.

More fundamentally, this evidence suggests that people do not have well defined preferences over health prior to the interview, but rather their preferences are constructed during the interview. This would account for the apparent willingness of respondents to be influenced by the precise framing of the question. This may be a consequence of the cognitive complexity of the task. Respondents are typically asked to consider variations in up to eight health dimensions alongside a life and death scenario involving probabilities or survival. Evidence from the psychology literature suggests that respondents faced with such complex problems tend to adopt simple decision heuristic strategies (Lloyd 2003). This may be particularly true where the respondents have little time to consider their real underlying values. Also much of the interview work has been done using 'cold calling' techniques, i.e. the respondents are members of the general public who have not been prepared in any way for the interviews. A well conducted preference elicitation study should provide a full explanation of the task to the respondent and undertake a practice question, but typically respondents are then expected to generate health state values in one sitting with little time given for reflection.

These arguments suggest that respondents need to be given more time and support to reflect on their values in order to process such complex information. There is a case for allowing respondents more time to learn the techniques, to ensure they understand them fully and to allow them more time to reflect on their health state valuations. It has been suggested that respondents could be re-interviewed after they have had time to reflect and deliberate on the health state in question, and that this process may be helpful in encouraging the development of 'well formed' preferences (Shiell *et al.* 2000) see Box. 5.1). An implication may be to move away from the current large-scale surveys of members of the general public involving one-off interviews, to smaller scale studies of panels of members of the general public who are better trained and more experienced in the techniques and who are given time to fully reflect on their valuations (Stein *et al.* 2006*b*).

Box 5.1 Preferences for health states: elicited or constructed?

In a study of health preferences in a sample of 62 members of staff and students from the Department of Community Medicine at the University of Sydney and Westmead Hospital (Shiell *et al.* 2000), participants were asked to value a set of states at three points in time (initial interview and repeat interviews 1 and 8 weeks after the initial interview). A standard format was followed at each interview in which participants were asked to value two chronic health states: first using VAS and secondly using SG. At the end of the second and third interviews, all of the participants were asked whether they had given any thought to the issues raised in the previous interview and whether anything of significance had happened to them since the last interview which may have influenced their responses in the repeat interview. In order to control for unstable preferences, the analysis was repeated both with and without those respondents who reported a significant event between interviews. For the majority of participants, values were stable

Box 5.1 Preferences for health states: elicited or constructed? *(continued)*

over repeat administrations. However, one-third of participants deliberately changed their answers and suggested that the interview process had forced them to think about their answers more deeply. The omission of those who experienced a significant event did not change the results. The key finding of this work is that while it is not possible to draw definitive conclusions from such a small sample, it does suggest that the assumption of completeness of preferences should not be taken for granted and a process of reflection and deliberation may be necessary before it is possible to elicit valid and reliable estimates of preference.

5.6 Aggregation of health state values

Once health state values have been obtained, individual responses have to be aggregated in some way. The choice includes the mean, the median or some modal response. Economists have generally advocated the mean average as representing the theoretically correct way to aggregate individual values, irrespective of the nature of the distribution. This is because the mean reflects people's intensity of preference and follows conventional welfare concerns with addressing whether the total benefits to those who gain are greater than the sum of the benefits to those who lose from a policy change. However, in the area of public policy, it may be argued that group preferences should be expressed in terms of the median value. The median treats each person's valuations as equal in a voting context. A comparison of an EQ-5D population value set based upon mean values with a value set based upon median values revealed differences, in that the median based value set exhibited higher values for less severe states and lower values for more severe states (Dolan 1997). Dolan suggests that the choice of population value set is a matter of judgement: 'without a gold standard by which to compare the two tariffs, this choice should ultimately be based upon a prior philosophical position on how preferences should be aggregated rather than on intuition about which set of valuations seem to produce better answers' (Dolan 1997).

The general consensus within health economics to date has been to adopt mean health state values as the most appropriate aggregation measure for informing decision making within the methodology of economic evaluation, and whilst this would seem to follow from a conventional welfarist view, under the non-welfarist view there is scope to conceive and develop alternative value sets that reflect the population median or modal preference.

5.7 **Who should value health?**

Historically, it was recognized that values for health could be obtained from a number of different sources including patients, their carers, health profession-als and the community. Currently health state values are usually obtained from members of the general public trying to imagine what the state would be like, but in recent years the main criticism has come from those who believe values should be obtained from patients (Ubel *et al.* 2003). This section con-centrates on the general population versus patients' values or, as it has been most recently characterized, as the choice between using health state values based on preferences versus experiences (Brazier *et al.* 2005; Dolan and Kahneman 2006).

5.7.1 **Why does it matter?**

The choice of whose values to elicit is important, as it may influence the resulting values. A number of empirical studies have been conducted which indicate that patients with first hand experience tend to place higher values on dysfunctional health states than do members of the general population who do not have similar experience, and the extent of this discrepancy tends to be much stronger when patients value their own health state (Hurst 1996; Tengs and Wallace 2000; Ratcliffe *et al.* 2004). The potential importance of this dif-ference can be seen in the example of colostomies, where patients with colostomies valued the health-related quality of life of living with them as 0.92 compared with a value of 0.80 from a sample of the general population (Boyd *et al.* 1990). This implies that the incremental gain from removing colostomies and restoring patients to full health would be more than twice as large using the general population value compared with the patient value. Clearly this dif-ference would have a substantial effect on the cost per QALY estimates for treatments to eradicate colostomies.

5.7.2 **Why do these discrepancies exist?**

There are a number of possible contributing factors for observed differences between patient and general population values including poor descriptions of health states (for the general population), use of different internal standards, or response shift and adaptation (Ubel *et al.* 2003).

Poor descriptions of health states

An important potential source of discrepancy is that descriptions provided to the general population may not accurately describe the health state. Most health state descriptive systems contain a limited number of attributes and tend to focus upon the negative aspects of a health state. As such, individuals tend to bring their own information to the valuation exercise by drawing upon their own personal experiences or stereotypes. Given that the personal experiences of patients and members of the general public are unlikely to be the same, it may mean that, in effect, they are evaluating different health states even when provided with identical descriptions of the health state to be valued. It has also been suggested that general population respondents focus too much on ill health and ignore the remaining positive aspects of a person's life (Ubel *et al.* 2003). It is possible that this problem could be reduced by more accurate health state descriptions (see Chapter 4 for a discussion of this issue).

Changing standards

A well known phenomenon in the psychometric literature is 'response shift', which refers to the possibility that individuals will change their own internal standards for evaluating their own health in response to changes in their health (Sprangers and Schwartz 1999). Response shift occurs due to changes in expectations. For example, an elderly individual may rate his or her health according to their expectations of the best possible health for a person of their age rather than best possible health *per se*. Similarly a patient may rate his or her health by comparing themselves with other patients rather than with healthy individuals. In either instance, response shift will contribute to discrepancies between patient and general population values for the same health states and, unlike the problem of incomplete or inaccurate health state descriptions, it is difficult to see how, in practice, response shifts can be reduced or eliminated. Indeed it can be argued that response shift effects in health state valuation tasks conducted with patients should not be of concern, since these reflect the entirely laudable concepts of adaptation and coping.

5.7.3 **Adaptation to the state**

Someone in an ill health state is likely to adapt over time, both physically and emotionally. Physical changes include the acquisition of new skills to help cope with a disability, such as learning to use a walking stick. A person may also change the things they do in order to limit the impact of their disability or illness. For example, someone who once played football may take up a sport that has a lower impact on his or her knees. There are also psychological adaptations that include a shift in the weight people place on different aspects of health and quality of life and, more fundamentally, a change in their view of what matters in life. People may also lower their expectations of what they can achieve.

It is well established in the literature that people tend to underpredict their ability to adapt (Kahneman 2000). When general population respondents read the description of a state, their valuation may reflect an initial response to say, going blind, rather than what it would be like for an extended period. In other words, they focus on the transition to the state rather than the longer term consequences. This focus results in the general population giving lower values compared with patient self-reported values for chronic states of health.

5.7.4 How do generic preference-based measures currently take patient views into account?

The impact of response shift and adaptation on the size of the discrepancy between patient and general population valuations will depend on the descriptive system being used. A degree of adaptation to physical disability is already incorporated into those descriptive systems that have dimensions such as role and social functioning, such as the SF-6D or usual activities in the EQ-5D (see Chapter 8 for a description of these instruments). The developers of the HUI3, however, excluded these social dimensions of health in part to remove adaptation. Nonetheless, all the generic descriptive systems take some account of psychological adaptation through dimensions concerned with mood (such as anxiety, positive affect and depression). Indeed, it could be argued that the wording of other dimensions, such as those concerned with physical functioning and pain, contain a significant element of self-evaluation and so also incorporate a degree of adaptation. For example, does a 90-year-old person reporting 'some problems with mobility' on the EQ-5D really mean the same as a 25-year-old reporting this level? Whether or not it is appropriate from a normative point of view to take any account of adaptation (as explored in the next section), it would seem that existing preference-based measures do take some account of adaptation.

5.7.5 Why use general population values?

A highly influential body who advocated the use of general population values was the Washington Panel on the Cost Effectiveness in Health and Medicine who argued that: '… the best articulation of society's preferences for a particular state would be gathered from a representative sample of fully informed members of the community'. The Panel went on to use the notion of the 'veil of ignorance' to support the use of community values, where 'a rational public decides what is the best course of action when blind to its own self-interest, aggregating the utilities of persons who have no vested interest in particular health states seems most appropriate' (Gold *et al.* 1996). This reflects a concern that patients will only think of their own health state and not appreciate how it compares with those of other patients. They argue that the values of different patient groups are not comparable, whereas a general population sample provides a coherent set of values.

The main arguments for and against general population values are summarized in Box 5.2. A key argument is that the general population pays for

---

Box 5.2 Preferences versus experience

Using patient values based upon experience

For:

- Patients know their own health state better than anyone trying to imagine it.
- It is the well-being of the patient that we are interested in since ultimately it is the patients who will be the losers and gainers from a public programme.

Against:

- It is possible that patients may behave strategically, e.g. in overemphasizing the benefits of a new treatment in terms of the health improvement experienced in order to try to ensure that they will have access to it.
- Patient may be unable or unwilling to provide values (or indeed it may be unethical).
- Adaptation to a particular health state may work against the patient's best interests because it may result in them assigning higher health state values to a dysfunctional health state, thereby lessening the value of quality of life improvements due to new health care technologies, and some of this may be regarded as undesirable (e.g. low expectations).

Using general population values based upon preferences

For:

- The 'veil of ignorance' argument was advocated by the Washington Panel on Cost-effectiveness in Health and Medicine to support the use of general population values where the utilities of individuals who have no vested interest in particular health states are aggregated to generate summary health state values.
- Public funding (in the form of taxation, for example) can essentially be seen as public insurance and so it is the ex ante public preferences that should be used to value health states.

> **Box 5.2 Preferences versus experience** *(continued)*
>
> Against:
>
> ♦ Members of the general population generally have little or no first hand experience of the health states being valued.
>
> ♦ Whilst members of the general population want to be involved in health care decision making, it is not clear that they want to be asked to value health states specifically (see for example Litva et al. 2002; Richardson et al. 2003

the service. Whilst members of the general population want to be involved in health care decision making, it is not clear that they want to be asked to value health states specifically (see for example Litva *et al.* 2002). At the very least, it does not necessarily imply the current practice of using relatively uninformed general population values.

5.7.6 Why use patient values?

A common argument for using patient values is the fact that patients understand the impact of their health on their well-being better than someone trying to imagine it. As Buckingham has pointed out: 'To ask a person of 20 how s/he will value health at the age of 70 is to ask an enormous amount of their imagination. To ask a 70 year old how important their health is to them is likely to result in far more valuable information' (Buckingham 1993). However, this fact does not imply that raw patient values should be used on their own to inform resource allocation decisions. This requires a value judgement that society wants to incorporate all the changes and adaptations that occur in patients who experience states of ill health over long periods of time. Some adaptation may be regarded as 'laudable', such as skill enhancement and activity adjustment, whereas cognitive denial of functional health, suppressed recognition of full health and lowered expectations may be seen as less desirable (Menzel *et al.* 2002). Furthermore, there may be a concern that patient values are context based, reflecting their recent experiences of ill health and the health of their immediate peers (Ubel *et al.* 2003).

Putting normative concerns to one side, asking patients to value their own health, and to do so sufficiently frequently, raises some major practical problems. Many patients by definition are quite unwell and maybe be unable or unwilling to undertake complex and quite intrusive valuation tasks. In addition, there may also be ethical concerns with asking patients in terminal conditions to imagine scenarios involving either the risk of death or shorter life expectancies.

The psychological work on 'experienced' utility mainly uses rating scales, which are criticized by health economists for lacking the choice context required to obtain a preference value, such as achieved in SG, TTO or WTP. However, the use of choice-based methods presents a paradox. The accepted choice-based techniques for valuing health states, such as SG or TTO, require a patient to value their existing state by imagining what it would be like to be in full health, which they may not have experienced for many years. For patients who have lived in a chronic health state such as chronic obstructive pulmonary disease or osteoarthritis, for example, the task of imagining full health is as difficult as a healthy member of the general population trying to imagine a poor health state.

5.7.7 A middle way—further research

One conclusion from the above is that it seems difficult to justify the exclusive use of patient values or the current practice of using values from relatively uninformed members of the general population. It has already been argued that existing generic preference-based measures already take some account of adaptation and response shift, but whether this is sufficient is ultimately a normative judgement. If it is accepted that ultimately it is the values of the general population that are required to inform resource allocation in a public system, it might be argued that respondents should be provided with more information on what the states are like for patients experiencing them. This position has been proposed by a number of commentators on the subject (Menzel et al. 2002; Fryback, 2003; Ubel et al. 2003). This would require the development of explicit methods for providing better ways of conveying information about the states to the general population respondents (Brazier et al. 2005). These could include improvements in the health state descriptions and providing more information on the size and nature of the adaptation experienced by patients over time. It could involve providing patient values to the general population sample prior to their valuation of the states.

5.8 Conclusions

This chapter has considered the issue of how to value the quality adjustment weight component of QALYs for use within the methodology of economic evaluation. The reader may feel somewhat overwhelmed by the large array of valuation techniques and variants on offer and the choice of sources of value. Indeed, there are further choices offered in the chapter on ordinal techniques (Chapter 7). Some of the decisions can be made on theoretical grounds (such as the use of a choice-based method for deriving preferences) or empirical grounds (some variants generate more consistent values than others), but often the analyst is left with either a trade-off between different types of distortion (e.g. the SG versus TTO) or a need to make normative choices (e.g. the extent to which adaptation should be incorporated).

The vastness of the array is not surprising. The mistake is to assume that there is a single set of 'true' values for health states or profiles. However, a decision maker needs a common and consistent set of methods for informing decisions and so choices need to be made about technique, variant and source of values. Such choices are made for reasons of expediency for assisting decision making (e.g. National Institute for Health and Clinical Excellence 2004), but it is important to continue research into major outstanding issues such as the theoretical basis of different techniques, ways to improve their reliability and validity (for a given concept), lengthier elicitation processes, and so forth.

References

Ashby J, O'Hanlon M, Buxton MJ (1994). The time trade-off technique: how do the valuations of breast cancer patients compare to those of other groups? *Quality of Life Research* 3:257–65.

Bleichrodt H (2002). A new explanation for the difference between time trade off utilities and standard gamble utilities. *Health Economics* 11:447–56.

Bleichrodt H, Johannesson M (1997). An experimental test of a theoretical foundation for rating-scale valuations. *Medical Decision Making* 17:208–16.

Bombardier C, Wolfson A, Sinclair A, McGreer A (1982). Comparison of three measurement methodologies in the evaluation of functional status index. In: Deber R, Thompson G, eds. *Choices in health care: decision making and evaluation of effectiveness*. University of Toronto, Toronto, Canada, pp. 298–322.

Boyd NF, Sutherland HJ, Heasman ZK, Trichtler DL, Cummings BJ (1990). Whose values for decision making? *Medical Decision Making* 10:58–67.

Brazier J, Dolan P (2005). *Evidence of preference construction in a comparison of variants of the standard gamble method*. Health Economics and Decision Science Section Discussion Paper no 05/04, University of Sheffield.

Brazier J, Deverill M, Green C, Harper R, Booth A (1999). A review of the use of health status measures in economic evaluation. *Health Technology Assessment* 3(9):1–164.

Brazier J, Roberts J, Deverill M (2002). The estimation of a preference-based single index measure for health from the SF-36. *Journal of Health Economics* 21:271–92.

Brazier J, Akehurst R, Brennan A, Dolan P, Claxton K, McCabe C, Sculpher M, Tsuchiya A (2005). Should patients have a greater role in valuing health states? *Applied Health Economics and Health Policy* 4:201–8.

Brooks R, Rabin RE, de Charro FTH, eds (2003). The measurement and valuation of health status using EQ-5D: a European perspective. Kluwer Academic Press, Dordrecht.

Broome J.(1993). QALYs. *Journal of Public Economics* 50:149–67.

Bryce CL, Angus DC, Switala J, Roberts MS, Tsevat J (2004). Health status versus utilities of patients with end-stage liver disease. *Quality of Life Research* 13:773–82.

Buckingham, K (1993). A note on HYE (healthy years equivalent). *Journal of Health Economics* 12:301–9.

Cairns JA, Van der Pol MM (1997). Saving future lives: a comparison of three discounting models. *Health Economics* 6:341–50.

Cher DJ, Miyamoto J, Lenert LA (1997). Incorporating risk attitude into Markov-process decision odels: importance for individual decision making. *Medical Decision Making* 17:340–50.

Dolan P (1996). Modelling valuations for health states: the effect of duration. *Health Policy* 38:189–203.

Dolan P (1997). Aggregating health state valuations. *Journal of Health Services Research and Policy* 2:160–7.

Dolan P, Gudex C (1995). Time preference, duration and health state valuations. *Health Economics* 4:289–99.

Dolan P, Kahneman D (2006). *Interpretations of utility and their implications for the valuation of health*. Princeton University Working Paper, USA Princeton.

Dolan P, Sutton M (1997). Mapping visual analogue scale health state valuations on to standard gamble and time trade-off values. *Social Science and Medicine* 44:1519–30.

Dolan P, Gudex C, Kind P and Williams A (1996).Valuing health states: a comparison of methods. *Journal of Health Economics* 15:209–31.

Drummond MF, Sculpher MJ, Torrance GW, O'Brien BJ, Stoddart GL (2005). *Methods for the economic evaluation of health care programmes*, 3rd edn. Oxford University Press, Oxford.

Dyer JS, Sarin RK (1982). Relative risk aversion. *Management Science* 28:875–86.

Feeny D, Furlong W, Torrance G, Goldsmith C, Zenglong Z, DePauw S, Denton M, Boyle M (2002). Multiattribute and single attribute utility functions for the Health Utilities Index Mark 3 system. *Medical Care* 40:113–28.

Froberg DG, Kane RL (1989). Methodology for measuring health-state preferences—II: Scaling methods. *Journal of Clinical Epidemiology* 42:459–71.

Fryback DG (2003). Whose quality of life? Or whose decision? *Quality of Life Research* 12:609–10.

Gafni A (1996). HYEs: do we need them and can they fulfil their promise? (comment). *Medical Decision Making* 16:215–6.

Gerson LB, Ullah N, Hastie T, Triadafilopoulos G, Goldstein M (2005). Patient derived health state utilities for gastro-oesophageal reflux disease. *American Journal of Gastroenterology* 100:524–33.

Gloth FM, 3rd, Scheve AA, Stober CV, Chow S, Prosser J (2001). The Functional Pain Scale: reliability, validity, and responsiveness in an elderly population. *Americal Medical Directors Association* 2(3):110–4.

Gold MR, Siegel JE, Russell LB, Weinstein MC (1996). *Cost-effectiveness in health and medicine*. Oxford University Press, Oxford.

Green C, Brazier J, Deverill M (2000). Valuing health-related quality of life. A review of health state valuation techniques. *Pharmacoeconomics* 17:151–65.

Hawthorne G, Richardson J, Osbourne R (1999). The assessment of quality of life (AQoL) instrument: a psychometric measure of health related quality of life. *Quality of Life Research* 8:209–24.

Horsman J, Furlong W, Feeny D, Torrance G (2003). The Health Utilities Index (HUI(R)): concepts, measurement properties and applications. *Health and Quality of Life Outcomes* 1:54.

Hershey JC, Kunrather HG, Schoemaker PJH (1981). Sources of bias in assessment procedures for utility functions. *Management Science* 28:936–54.

Hurst NP (1996). A longitudinal study of patients with rheumatoid arthritis. Presentation to a Clinical Users Group of the EQ-5D, York, UK.

Jansen SJ, Stiggelbout AM, Nooij MA, Kievit J (2000). The effect of individually assessed preference weights on the relationship between holistic utilities and non preference-based assessment. *Quality of Life Research* 9:541–57.

Jones-Lee M, Loomes G, O'Reilly D, Phillips P (1993). *The value of preventing non fatal road injuries: findings of a willingness to pay national sample survey*. Transport Research Laboratory, UK.

Kahneman D, Tversky A (1979). Prospect theory: an analysis of decision under risk. *Econometrica* 47:263–91.

Kahneman D (2000). Evaluation by moments: past and future. In: Kahneman D, Tversky AS, eds. *Choices, values and frames*. Cambridge University Press and the Russell Sage Foundation, New York, pp. 693–708.

Kaplan RM, Anderson JP (1988) A general health policy model: update and applications. *Health Services Research* 23:203–35.

Kaplan RM, Bush JW, Berry CC (1979). Health status indices: category rating versus magnitude estimation for measuring level of well being. *Medical Care* 17:501–25.

Keeney RL, Raiffa H (1976). *Decisions with multiple objectives: preferences and value trade-offs*, John Wiley and Sons, New York.

Kind P, Rosser R, Williams A (1982). A valuation of quality of life: some psychometric evidence. In: Jones-Lee MW, ed. *The value of life and safety*. North-Holland, Amsterdam, pp. 159–70.

Lenert LA, Sturley AE (2001). Acceptability of computerised VAS, TTO and SG rating methods in patients and the public. In: *Proceedings of the AMIA symposium* pp. 364–368. Washington DC.

Lenert LA, Cher DJ, Goldstein MK, Bergen MR, Garber A (1998). The effect of search procedures on utility elicitations. *Medical Decision Making* 18:76–83.

Lenert LA, Sturley A, Watson ME (2002). iMPACT3: Internet based development and administration of utility elicitation protocols. *Medical Decision Making* 22:522–5.

Litva A, Coast J, Donovan J, Eyles J, Shepherd M, Tacchi J, Abelson J, Morgan K (2002). 'The public is too subjective': public involvement at different levels of health-care decision making. *Social Science and Medicine* 54:1825–37.

Llewellyn-Thomas H, Sutherland HJ, Tibshirani R, Ciampi A, Till JE, Boyd NF (1982). The measurement of patients' values in medicine. *Medical Decision Making* 2:449–62.

Lloyd AJ (2003) Threats to the estimation of benefit: are preference elicitation methods accurate? *Health Economics* 12:393–402.

Loomes G (1993). Disparities between health state measures: is there a rational explanation? In: Gerrard W, ed. *The economics of rationality*. Routledge, London. pp. 149–178.

Loomes G, McKenzie L (1989). The use of QALYs in health care decison making. *Social Science and Medicine* 28:299–308.

Mannion AF, Junge A, Fairbank JC, Dvorak J, Grob D (2006). Development of a German version of the Oswestry Disability Index. Part 1: cross-cultural adaptation, reliability, and validity. *European Spine Journal* 15:55–65.

McCabe C, Stevens K, Brazier J (2004). *Utility values for the Health Utility Index Mark 2: an empirical assessment of alternative mapping functions.* Health Economics and Decision Science Section Discussion Paper no 01/04, University of Sheffield.

McDowell I, Newell C (1996). *Measuring health: a guide to rating scales and questionnaires,* 2nd edn. Oxford University Press, New York.

Measurement and Valuation of Health Group (1994). *Time trade-off user manual: props and self completion methods.* Centre for Health Economics, University of York.

Mehrez A, Gafni A (1991). The healthy-years equivalents: how to measure them using the standard gamble approach. *Medical Decision Making* 11:140–6.

Mehrez A, Gafni A (1993). HYEs versus QALYs: in pursuit of progress. *Medical Decision Making* 13:287–92.

Menzel P, Dolan P, Richardson J, Olsen A (2002). The role of adaptation to disability and disease in health state valuation: a preliminary normative analysis. *Social Science and Medicine* 55:2149–58.

Morrison GC (1994). *Consistency within and between methods of eliciting preferences from the public. Willingness to pay versus standard gamble.* Department of Economics and CRIEFF Discussion Paper 9407, University of St Andrews, UK.

Murray CJ, Lopez AD (1997). Regional patterns of disability free life expectancy and disability adjusted life expectancy: Global Burden of Disease Study. *Lancet* 349:1347–52.

National Institute for Health and Clinical Excellence (2004). *Guide to the methods of technology appraisal.* NICE, London.

Nord E (1991). The validity of a visual analogue scale in determining social utility weights for health states. *International Journal of Health Planning and Management* 6:234–42.

Nord E (1992). Methods for quality adjustment of life years. *Social Science and Medicine* 34:559–64.

Nord E (1993). The trade off between severity of illness and treatment effect in cost value analysis of health care. *Health Policy* 24:227–38.

Nord E (1995). The person-trade-off approach to valuing health care programs *Medical Decision Making* 15:201–8.

Nord E, Pinto JL, Richardson J, Menzel P, Ubel P (1999). Incorporating societal concerns for fairness in numerical valuations of health programmes. *Health Economics* 8(1):25–39.

O'Brien B and Viramontes JL (1994). Willingness to pay: a valid and reliable measure of health state preference? *Medical Decision Making* 14:289–97.

Oliver A (2003). The internal consistency of the standard gamble: tests after adjusting for prospect theory. *Journal of Health Economics* 22:659–74.

Parducci A Wedell DH (1986). The category effect with rating scales: number of categories, number of stimuli and method of presentation. *Journal of Experimental Psychology* 12:496–516.

Patrick DL, Erickson P (1973). *Health status and health policy. Quality of life in health care evaluation and resource allocation.* Oxford University Press, New York.

Patrick DL, Bush JW, Chen M.M (1973). Methods for measuring levels of well-being for a health status index. *Health Services Research* 8:228–45.

Patrick DL, Starks HE, Cain KC, Uhlmann RF, Pearlman RA (1994). Measuring preferences for health states worse than death. *Medical Decision Making* 14:9–18.

Pinto Prades JL (1997). Is the person trade-off a valid method for allocating health care resources? *Health Economics* 6:71–81.

Ratcliffe J, Brazier JE, Palfreyman S, Michaels JA. (2004) A comparison of patient and population values for health states. Presentation to the Health Economists Study Group, University of Glasgow, June.

Richardson J (1994) Cost utility analysis: what should be measured? *Social Science and Medicine* 39:7–21.

Robinson A, Dolan P, Williams A (1997). Valuing health states using VAS snd TTO: what lies behind the numbers? *Social Science and Medicine* 45:1289–97.

Robinson A, Loomes G, Jones-Lee M (2001). Visual analogue scales, standard gambles and relative risk aversion. *Medical Decision Making* 21:17–27.

Ross PC, Litterby B, Fearn P (2003). Paper standard gamble, a paper based measure of SG utility for current health. *International Journal of Technology Assessment in Health Care* 19: 135–47.

Rosser R, Kind P (1978). A scale of valuations of states of illness: is there a social consensus? *International Journal of Epidemiology* 7:347–58.

Rutten van Molken MP, Bakker CH, van Doorslaer EK, van der Linden S (1995a). Methodological issues of patient utility measurement. Experience from two clinical trials. *Medical Care* 33:922–37.

Rutten van Molken MP, Custers F, van Doorslaer EK, Jansen CC, Heurman L, Maesen FP, Smeets JJ, Bommer AA, Raaijmakers JA (1995b). Comparison of performance of four instruments in evaluating the effects of salmeterol on asthma quality of life. *European Respiratory Journal* 8:888–98.

Sackett DL, Torrance GW (1981). The utility of different health states as perceived by the general public. *Journal of Chronic Diseases* 31:697–704.

Salomon JA, Murray CJL (2004). A multi-method approach to measuring health state valuations. *Health Economics* 13:281–90.

Schoemaker PJH (1982).The expected utility model: its variants, purposes, evidence and limitations. *Journal of Economic Literature* 20:529–63.

Schwartz A (1998). Rating scales in context. *Medical Decision Making* 18:236.

Sculpher M (1996). Economic evaluation of minimal access surgery: the case of surgical treatment for menorrhagia. HERG PhD thesis, Brunel University.

Schwarzinger M, Lanoe J, Nord E, Durand-Zaleski I (2004). Lack of multiplicative transitivity in person trade-off responses. *Health Economics* 13:171–81.

Shiell A, Seymour J, Hawe P, Cameron S (2000). Are preferences over health states complete? *Health Economics* 9:47–55.

Sintonen, H (1981). An approach to measuring and valuing health states. *Social Science and Medicine* 15C:55–65.

Sintonen H (1994). *The 15D-measure of health-related quality of life. I. Reliability, validity and sensitivity of its health state descriptive system*. National Centre for Health Program Evaluation, Working Paper 41, Melbourne.

Sprangers MA, Schwartz CE (1999). The challenge of response shift for quality-of-life-based clinical oncology research. *Annals of Oncology* 10:747–9.

Stavem K (1999). Reliabilty, validity and responsiveness of two multiattribute utility measures in patients with COPD. *Quality of Life Research* 8:45–54.

Stein K, Dyer M, Crabb T, Milne R, Round A, Ratcliffe J, Brazier J (2006a). *An Internet 'Value of Health' Panel: recruitment, participation and compliance.* Health Economics and Decision Science Discussion Paper 08/06, ScHARR, University of Sheffield, UK. http://www.sheffield.ac.uk/scharr/sections/heds/discussion.html.

Stein K, Ratcliffe J, Round A, Milne R, Brazier J (2006b). Impact of discussion on preferences elicited in a group setting. *Health and Quality of Life Outcomes* 4:22.

Stevens K, McCabe C, Brazier J (2006). Mapping between visual analogue scale and standard gamble data; results from the UK Health Utilities Index 2 valuation survey. *Health Economics* 15:527–33.

Stevens SS (1960). Ratio partition and confusion scales In: Gulliksen H, Messick S, eds. *Psychological scaling theory and applications.* John Wiley and Sons, New York.

Stewart ST, Lenert L, Bhatnager V, Kaplan RM (2005). Utilities for prostate cancer health states in men aged 60 years and older. *Medical Care* 43:347–55.

Stiggelbout AM, Kiebert GM, Kievit J, Leer JW, Stoter G, de Haes JC (1994). Utility assessment in cancer patients: adjustment of time trade off scores for the utility of life years and comparison with standard gamble scores. *Medical Decision Making* 14: 82–90.

Sutherland HJ, Llewellyn Thomas H, Boyd D and Till JE (1982). Attitudes towards quality of survival: The concept of maximum endurable time. *Medical Decision Making* 2:299–309.

Tengs TO, Wallace A (2000). One thousand health related quality of life estimates. *Medical Care* 38:583–637.

Torrance GW (1976). Social preferences for health states: an empirical evaluation of three measurement techniques. *Socio-Economic Planning Science* 10:129–36.

Torrance G (1984). Health states worse than death, In: van Eimeren W, Englebrecht R, Flagle CD, eds. *Third International Conference on System Science in Health Care.* Springer, Berlin, pp. 1085–1089.

Torrance G (1986). Measurement of health state utilities for economic appraisal. *Journal of Health Economics* 5:1–30.

Torrance G, Feeny D, Furlong W, Barr R, Zhang Y, Wang Q (1996). Multiattribute utility function for a comprehensive health status classification system. Health Utilities Index Mark 2. *Medical Care* 34:702–22.

Torrance GW, Fenny D, Furlong W (2001). Visual analogue scales: do they have a role in the measurement of preferences for health states? *Medical Decision Making* 21:329–34.

Ubel PA, Loewenstein G, Jepson C (2003). Whose quality of life? A commentary exploring discrepancies between health state evaluations of patients and the general public. *Quality of Life Research* 12:599–607.

Van der Pol MM, Cairns JA (2000). The estimation of marginal time performance in a UK wide sample (TEMPUS) project. *Health Technology Assessment* 4(1).

Von Neumann J, Morgenstern O (1944). *Theory of games and economic behaviour.* Oxford University Press, New York.

Wasserman J, Aday LA, Begley CE (2005). Measuring health state preferences for haemophilia, development of a disease specific utility instrument. *Haemophilia* 11(1):49–57.

Appendix 5.1 Probability wheel for the standard gamble

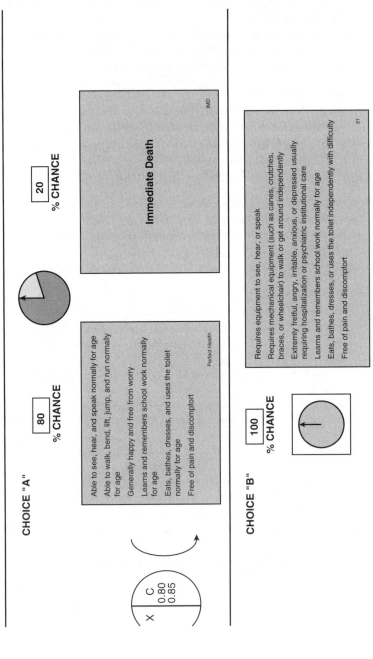

CHANCE BOARD

CHOICE "A"

| 80 |
| % CHANCE |

Able to see, hear, and speak normally for age

Able to walk, bend, lift, jump, and run normally for age

Generally happy and free from worry

Learns and remembers school work normally for age

Eats, bathes, dresses, and uses the toilet normally for age

Free of pain and discomfort

Perfect Health

| 20 |
| % CHANCE |

Immediate Death

IMD

CHOICE "B"

| 100 |
| % CHANCE |

Requires equipment to see, hear, or speak

Requires mechanical equipment (such as canes, crutches, braces, or wheelchair) to walk or get around independently

Extremly fretful, angry, irritable, anxious, or depressed usually requiring hospitalization or psychiatric institutional care

Learns and remembers school work normally for age

Eats, bathes, dresses, or uses the toilet independently with difficulty

Free of pain and discomfort

31

C
0.80
0.85

X

Appendix 5.2 Example extract from a script for eliciting health state valuations using the standard gamble probability wheel

In this part of the interview we are interested in your views about different health states. However, the questions are going to be different from those using the feeling thermometer.

For the example, I will show you three different descriptions of health. I will describe two choices; one choice will involve taking a risk, the other choice will not. I want you to decide between the two choices. If you think the two choices are equal, tell me. The amount of risk will be changed until we find out how much risk you will take to avoid the certain choice. In order to make the task easier to understand we will use an aid similar to a game board.

Description of the 'Chance Board'

> Place the chance board on the table with the wheel set to 90/10. Open Standard Gamble Health State Description Card Envelope 1.

We call this a chance board because it indicates the chance or probability of a certain event occurring. As you can see, the top part of the board is labelled Choice A and the bottom part of the board is labelled Choice B.

You will be asked to choose between A

> (point to choice A)

and B

> (point to choice B)

Choice B, at the bottom of the board, will describe a state of health, here is an example:

> (place example card in pocket of choice B).

If you choose B you are 100% certain to be in that state of health for the *rest of your life*

> (point to example card).

Choice A is a little more complex as it is a treatment which does not always work. If the treatment DOES work, you will be in the health state shown on this pink card for the rest of your life

(Place the perfect health card in the left pocket of choice A).

However, if the treatment DOES NOT work, you will be in the health state shown on this blue card

(Place the immediate death card in the right hand pocket of choice A).

Therefore, if you choose A, there are *two* possible results.

The chances of each of these results occurring are shown by numbers appearing in the windows above each pocket

(point to the windows),

and by the amount of blue and pink inside the circle

(point to the circle).

Another way of explaining the chance aspect of Choice A is that for every 100 patients who choose Choice A, 90 will experience the health state on the left following treatment,

(point to 90),

but 10 will experience the health state on the right

(point to 10).

No one will know before choosing whether they will be one of the 90 or one of the 10. That is the chance they take.

During the interview, these chances will change and I will ask you to choose Choice A or Choice B each time I change the chances.

DEMONSTRATE BY TURNING THE WHEEL ON THE CHANCE BOARD TO 20/80

Now before we start looking at other health states, would you like me to explain how the Chance Board works again?

If they answer yes, repeat the description of the chance board above. If they answer no, go to instruction 2.

Instruction 2

Let's work through the first question carefully together. In Choice A, the description will stay the same each time and is described by the pink card, Perfect Health, in the left-hand top pocket, and the blue card, Immediate Death, in the right-hand pocket. The health state of Choice B is one described by a green card.

There are no right or wrong answers, only what *you* think.

> Place the Perfect Health card in the left hand pocket of Choice A and the Immediate Death card in the right hand pocket of Choice A. Hand green card to the respondent.

Please read over the description and when you are finished I will put it in pocket B at the bottom of the board.

> Place Green card in the Choice B pocket and set wheel to 100/0.

C1.1. The first health state I would like you to decide on is the one described by this green card.

You have already seen this card but could you please read over the description again.

> **SET THE WHEEL TO 100 ON THE LEFT AND 0 ON THE RIGHT. WHEN RESPONDENT HAS FINISHED READING, SAY**

As you can see Choice A is a 100 per cent chance of being in the health state described on the pink card, with zero chance of immediate death.

Choice B is a 100 per cent chance of being in the health state described on the green card.

Remember whichever choice you make you will be in the health state you end up in for the *rest of your life*. Would you prefer Choice A or Choice B now?

A	1 Go to C1.2
B	2 Go to C1.13
Can't decide	3 Go to instruction 3

> **C1.2. SET THE WHEEL TO 10 ON THE LEFT AND 90 ON THE RIGHT.**

Choice A is now a 10 per cent chance of the health state described on the pink card, with a 90 per cent chance of immediate death. Choice B is still a

100 per cent chance of the health state described on the green card. Would you prefer Choice A or Choice B now?

A	1 Go to C1.3
B	2 Go to C1.4
Can't decide	3 Go to instruction 3

C1.3. PLACE COVER 1 OVER CHOICE A OF THE CHOICE BOARD.

Suppose now that Choice A was a zero chance of the health state described on the pink card, with a 100 per cent chance of immediate death. Choice B is still a 100 per cent chance of the health state described on the green card.

Would you prefer Choice A or Choice B now?

A	1 Go to C1.14
B.	2 Go to C1.4
Can't decide	3 Go to instruction 3

C1.4. SET THE WHEEL TO 90 ON THE LEFT AND 10 ON THE RIGHT

Choice A is now a 90 per cent chance of the health state described on the pink card, with a 10 per cent chance of immediate death. Choice B is still a 100 per cent chance of the health state described on the green card.

Would you prefer Choice A or Choice B now?

A	1 Go to C1.6
B	2 Go toC1.5
Can't decide	3 Go to instruction 3

C1.5. PLACE COVER 2 OVER CHOICE A OF THE CHOICE BOARD.

Suppose now that Choice A was a 95 per cent chance of the health state described on the pink card, with a 5 per cent chance of immediate death. Choice B is still a 100 per cent chance of the health state described on the green card. Would you prefer Choice A or Choice B now?

A	1 Go to instruction 3
B	2 Go to instruction 3
Can't decide	3 Go to instruction 3

C1.6. SET THE WHEEL TO 20 ON THE LEFT AND 80 ON THE RIGHT

Choice A is now a 20 per cent chance of the health state described on the pink card, with an 80 per cent chance of immediate death.

Choice B is still a 100 per cent chance of the health state described on the green card.

Would you prefer Choice A or Choice B now?

A	1 Go to instruction 3
B	2 Go to C1.7
Can't decide	3 Go to instruction 3

C1.7. SET THE WHEEL TO 80 ON THE LEFT AND 20 ON THE RIGHT

Choice A is now an 80 per cent chance of the health state described on the pink card, with a 20 per cent chance of immediate death. Choice B is still a 100 per cent chance of the health state described on the green card.

Would you prefer Choice A or Choice B now?

A	1 Go to C1.8
B	2 Go to instruction 3
Can't decide	3 Go to instruction 3

C1.8. SET THE WHEEL TO 30 ON THE LEFT AND 70 ON THE RIGHT

Choice A is now a 30 per cent chance of the health state described on the pink card, with a 70 per cent chance of immediate death.

Choice B is still a 100 per cent chance of the health state described on the green card.

Would you prefer Choice A or Choice B now?

A	1 Go to instruction 3
B	2 Go to C1.9
Can't decide	3 Go to instruction 3

C1.9. SET THE WHEEL TO 70 ON THE LEFT AND 30 ON THE RIGHT

Choice A is now a 70 per cent chance of the health state described on the pink card, with a 30 per cent chance of immediate death.

Choice B is still a 100 per cent chance of the health state described on the green card.

Would you prefer Choice A or Choice B now?

A	1 Go to C1.10
B	2 Go to instruction 3
Can't decide	3 Go to instruction 3

C1.10. SET THE WHEEL TO 40 ON THE LEFT AND 60 ON THE RIGHT

Choice A is now a 40 per cent chance of the health state described on the pink card, with a 60 per cent chance of immediate death.

Choice B is still a 100 per cent chance of the health state described on the green card.

Would you prefer Choice A or Choice B now?

A	1 Go to instruction 3
B	2 Go to C1.11
Can't decide	3 Go to instruction 3

C1.11. SET THE WHEEL TO 60 ON THE LEFT AND 40 ON THE RIGHT

Choice A is now a 60 per cent chance of the health state described on the pink card, with a 40 per cent chance of immediate death.

Choice B is still a 100 per cent chance of the health state described on the green card.

Would you prefer Choice A or Choice B now?

A	1 Go to C1.12
B	2 Go to instruction 3
Can't decide	3 Go to instruction 3

C1.12. SET THE WHEEL TO 50 ON THE LEFT AND 50 ON THE RIGHT

Choice A is now a 50 per cent chance of the health state described on the pink card, with a 50 per cent chance of immediate death.

Choice B is still a 100 per cent chance of the health state described on the green card.

Would you prefer Choice A or Choice B now?

A	1 Go to instruction 3
B	2 Go to instruction 3
Can't decide	3 Go to instruction 3

C1.13.

Why did you choose a 100 per cent chance of the health state on the green card rather than a 100 per cent chance of the health state on the pink card?

RECORD VERBATIM RESPONSE

Go to instuction 3

C1.14.

Why did you choose a 100 per cent chance of immediate death rather than a 100 per cent chance of the health state on the green card?

RECORD VERBATIM RESPONSE

Appendix 5.3 Example of the titration method for the standard gamble

In the following exercises, the states of health in the upper boxes show the CERTAIN outcome of NOT having treatment (Choice A), but differ in every exercise. The states of health in the lower two boxes show the UNCERTAIN outcomes of having treatment (Choice B). One of these boxes shows the outcome for success, and the other shows the outcome for failure. These differ between exercises. For each choice there are a range of chances of a successful outcome and corresponding chances of failure. From now on, imagine that you yourself are in these states, and that they would last for the rest of your life without change.

N.B. Remember, there are no right or wrong answers—we are asking you to make value judgements.

Please put a ✓ against all cases where you are CONFIDENT that you would CHOOSE the
risky treatment (Choice B).

Please put an X against all cases where you are CONFIDENT that you would REJECT the treatment (Choice B) and accept the certain health state (Choice A).

Please put an = against all cases where you think it would be most difficult to choose between the treatment (Choice B) and accept the certain health state (Choice A).

Outcome of treatment

Chances of success	Chances of failure
100 in 100*	0 in 100*
95 in 100*	5 in 100
90 in 100	10 in 100
85 in 100	15 in 100
80 in 100	20 in 100
75 in 100	25 in 100
70 in 100	30 in 100
65 in 100	35 in 100
60 in 100	40 in 100
55 in 100	45 in 100
50 in 100	50 in 100
45 in 100	55 in 100
40 in 100	60 in 100
35 in 100	65 in 100
30 in 100	70 in 100
25 in 100	75 in 100
20 in 100	80 in 100
15 in 100	85 in 100
10 in 100	90 in 100
5 in 100	95 in 100
0 in 100	100 in 100

*You may be willing to accept the treatment but *only* if it has a chance of success of *higher* than 95 in 100 (i.e. a chance of failure which is less than 5 in 100). If so, at what level of success would you accept treatment?

Appendix 5.4 Example of a Time Trade-off Board

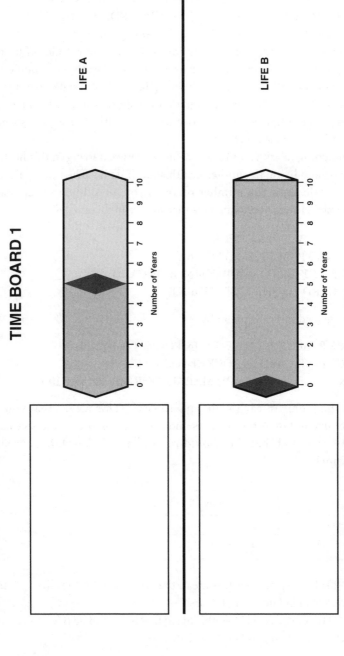

Source: © Centre for Health Economics, University of York, UK.

Appendix 5.5 Example extract from a script for eliciting health state valuations using the TTO board

PICK UP PINK AND BLUE CARD AND FIRST GREEN CARD
HAVE TTO BOARD SIDE '1' FACING UPWARDS.
SET BOARD MARKER FOR LIFE A TO 10 YEARS.

Now we are going to use a technique called the time trade-off to find out how good or bad you think living in some of the health states would be. The time trade-off asks you to compare living in two health states for a maximum period of 10 years. After this time period you must assume that you would die.

I'm going to start with a practice using a health state which is similar to those which you have just ranked.

I am going to ask you to make a choice between living in this health state (Life B) and living in another health state (Life A). The pink scale and the green scale show the number of years you would be in each state for. Remember, I want you to imagine that *you* are in these states.

C2a. INTERVIEWER CHECK:
PICK OUT PRACTICE TTO CARD.
ENTER LETTERS ON TOP CORNER OF CARD: _____
PASS CARD TO THE RESPONDENT.

Please read this card carefully.

PLACE PRACTICE TTO CARD IN POCKET FOR LIFE B.
PLACE PINK CARD IN POCKET FOR LIFE A
MAKE SURE THAT BOARD MARKER FOR LIFE A IS AT 10 YEARS.

At the moment, each scale says 10 years. This means that you would either live in Life A for 10 years and then die, or you would live in Life B for 10 years and then die. Would you prefer Life A or Life B, or are they the same?

Life A	1.	Go to C3
Life B	2.	
The same	3.	Ask c.

c. IF 'LIFE B' AT b. Does this mean that you would rather live in Life B for 10 years than in Life A for 10 years?

IF 'THE SAME' AT b. Does this mean that living in Life B for 10 years would be the same as living in Life A for 10 years?

Yes	1.	Go to C3
No (first time)	2.	Repeat b
No (second time)	3.	Go to C3

C3a. CONTINUE WORKING WITH CARD 'PRACTICE TTO'.
ENTER LETTERS ON REVERSE OF CARD: _____
   b. MOVE BOARD MARKER FOR LIFE A TO 0 YEARS.
   Now you would either die immediately, or you would live in Life B for 10 years and then die. Would you prefer to die immediately or to have Life B, or are they the same?

Life A	1.	Go to h. (state worse than death)
Life B	2.	Go to c. (state better than death)
The same	3.	Go to next health state

ASK IF 'LIFE B' (code 2) AT b.
c. STATE BETTER THAN DEATH
MARK 'X' UNDER 0 ON THE SCALE BELOW.

BETTER THAN DEATH SCALE	0	1	2	3	4	5	6	7	8	9	10

CONTINUE TO USE TIME BOARD WITH SIDE '1' UPWARDS

SET BOARD MARKER FOR LIFE A TO 5 YEARS ($t = 5$).
   d. Now you would either live in Life A for 't' years and then die, or you would live in Life B for 10 years and then die. Would you prefer Life A or Life B, or are they the same?

CONTINUE TO WRITE ON SCALE *ABOVE ON THIS PAGE*.

IF A: ✓ UNDER 't' MOVE MARKER 1 YEAR TO THE LEFT.
               REPEAT d. WITH 't' 1 LESS THAN LAST TIME.
IF B: X UNDER 't' MOVE MARKER 1 YEAR TO THE RIGHT.
               REPEAT d. WITH 't' 1 MORE THAN LAST TIME.
IF SAME: = UNDER 't' GO TO next health state

REPEAT d. UNTIL:	
A) YOU ENTER '='	Go to next health state
B) 'X' AND '✓' APPEAR NEXT TO EACH OTHER	*OR* Go to e.

ASK IF d. ENDED WITH 'X' AND '✓' NEXT TO EACH OTHER
e. LET 't' NOW BE HALFWAY BETWEEN THE ADJACENT CROSS AND TICK, I.E. 'SOMETHING AND 6 MONTHS'

What if you would either live in Life A for 't' and then die, or you would live in Life B for 10 years and then die. Would you prefer Life A or Life B, or are they the same?

Life A	1. Go to C4
Life B	2. Go to f.
The same	3. Go to next health state

IF 'LIFE B' (code 2) AT e.

IF THERE IS A X UNDER 9	1. Go to g.
IF THERE IS NOT A X UNDER 9	2. Go to next health state

f. INTERVIEWER CHECK:
ASK IF THERE IS 'X' UNDER 9 AND '✓' UNDER 10

Yes	1. Go to next
No	2. health state

g. Would you be prepared to sacrifice any time in order to avoid Life B?
IF YES: How many weeks?
ENTER WEEKS: _____
ASK IF 'LIFE A' (code 1) AT b.
h. STATE WORSE THAN DEATH
MARK '✓' UNDER 0 ON SCALE BELOW.

WORSE THAN DEATH SCALE	0	1	2	3	4	5	6	7	8	9	10

TURN TTO BOARD SIDE '2' UPWARDS.
MOVE GREEN CARD TO TOP LEFT POCKET ON SIDE '2'.
PLACE PINK CARD IN TOP RIGHT POCKET ON SIDE '2'.
PLACE BLUE CARD IN BOTTOM POCKET ON SIDE '2'.
SET BOARD MARKER FOR LIFE A TO 5 YEARS (t = 5).

Now here is a different choice.

i. Life A is now 't' years of this state (POINT TO THE GREEN CARD) followed by '$10 - t$' years in this other state (POINT TO THE PINK CARD). Or instead of that you could choose to die immediately (POINT TO LIFE B). Would you prefer Life A, or to die immediately, or are they the same?

WRITE ON SCALE ABOVE ON THIS PAGE.

IF A: ✓ UNDER 't' MOVE MARKER 1 YEAR TO THE RIGHT.
                         REPEAT i. WITH 't' 1 MORE THAN LAST TIME.

IF B: X UNDER 't' MOVE MARKER 1 YEAR TO THE LEFT.
                         REPEAT i. WITH 't' 1 LESS THAN LAST TIME.

IF SAME: = UNDER 't' GO TO D4

REPEAT i. UNTIL:	
A) YOU ENTER '='	GO TO next health state
B) '' AND 'X' APPEAR NEXT TO EACH OTHER	*OR* GO TO j.

ASK IF i. ENDED WITH '✓' AND 'X' NEXT TO EACH OTHER
j. LET 't' NOW BE HALFWAY BETWEEN THE ADJACENT TICK AND CROSS, I.E. 'SOMETHING AND 6 MONTHS'.

What if Life A was 't' of this state (POINT TO THE GREEN CARD) followed by '$10 - t$' in this other state (POINT TO THE PINK CARD). Or instead of that you could choose to die immediately (POINT TO LIFE B). Would you prefer Life A, or to die immediately, or are they the same?

Life A	1. Go to next health state
Life B	2.
The same	3.

Appendix 5.6 Example of titration method for the time trade-off

Choice A	Choice B
25 years	25 years
25 years	24 years
25 years	23 years
25 years	22 years
25 years	21 years
25 years	20 years
25 years	19 years
25 years	18 years
25 years	17 years
25 years	16 years
25 years	15 years
25 years	14 years
25 years	13 years
25 years	12 years
25 years	11 years
25 years	10 years
25 years	9 years
25 years	8 years
25 years	7 years
25 years	6 years
25 years	5 years
25 years	4 years
25 years	3 years
25 years	2 years
25 years	1 years
25 years	0 years

Please put an 'A' against all cases where you are CONFIDENT that you would choose **Choice A**. Please put a 'B' against all cases where you are CONFIDENT that you would choose **Choice B**. Please put an '=' against *the case* where you <u>cannot choose</u> between Choice A and Choice B

Chapter 6

Modelling health state valuation data

Preference-based measures of health have standardized multidimensional descriptive systems that generate hundreds and often thousands of health states (Kaplan and Anderson 1988; Sintonen 1994; Dolan 1997; Brazier *et al.* 2002*a*; Feeny *et al.* 2002; Hawthorne *et al.* 2001). It is simply not practical to elicit direct valuations for all health states described by most of these measures. The solution has been to value a subset of their health states and to estimate a function for predicting the values of all the states they define.

There have been two approaches to estimating a function for valuing states for a health state descriptive system: the decomposed and composite approaches (Froberg and Kane 1989). The decomposed approach employs multiattribute utility theory (MAUT) to determine the functional form and the sample of states to be valued. MAUT reduces the valuation task by making simplifying assumptions about the relationships between dimensions. The most commonly used specifications are the additive and multiplicative functional forms. The application of MAUT decomposes the valuation task into three parts. First, each dimension is valued separately to estimate single-attribute utility functions. Secondly, 'corner states' are valued; these are states in which one dimension is at one extreme (usually the worst level) and the rest are set at the other extreme (usually the best level). Third, a set of multiattribute states determined by the model specification is valued. Then by applying MAUT it is possible to solve a system of equations to calculate weights for each dimension and any parameter for preference interactions specified in the model. This approach has been used to value the various versions of the HUI (Torrance 1982; Torrance *et al.* 1996; Feeny *et al.* 2002), the AQOL (Hawthorne *et al.* 2001) and a condition-specific measure (Revicki *et al.* 1998).

The composite approach uses statistical modelling to estimate a function for valuing health states defined by the classification. A sample of states for valuation is selected using a statistical design such as an orthogonal array. A range of models can then be fitted to the data. Health state values present a significant challenge for conventional statistical modelling procedures since the distribution is commonly skewed, truncated, non-continuous and hierarchical (Brazier *et al.* 2002*b*). Attempts to model these data statistically have met with some success for the QWB, EQ-5D and SF-6D (Kaplan and Anderson 1988; Dolan 1997; Brazier *et al.* 2002*a*). More recently a non-parametric approach using Bayesian methods to model these data has been developed (Kharroubi *et al.* 2005)

This chapter describes the decomposed and composite approaches to analysing cardinal valuation data, how they have been applied and how to assess their performance. It addresses the debate concerning which approach is the best way to predict health state values. It aims to provide the reader with sufficient knowledge to undertake this type of modelling and to understand some of the controversies in the field. Chapter 7 considers the modelling of ordinal preference data.

6.1 **Statistical modelling**

This section draws heavily on the paper by Brazier *et al.* (2002*a*) and subsequent experience with the SF-6D and condition-specific instruments (e.g. Brazier *et al.* 2006; Yang *et al.* 2006). This work built on the pioneering work to value the QWB (Kaplan and Andersen 1988) and EQ-5D (Dolan 1997; Busschbach *et al.* 1999).

6.1.1 **Selection of health states**

To describe the problem, we consider the example of the SF-6D. As described elsewhere, the SF-6D is composed of six multilevel dimensions of health: *physical functioning, role limitation, social functioning, bodily pain, mental health* and *vitality* (Table 6.1). An SF-6D health state is defined by selecting a level from each dimension, starting with *physical functioning* and ending with *vitality*. Level 1 in each dimension represents no loss of health or functioning in that dimension, so that state 111111 denotes perfect health. The worst possible state is 645655, known as 'the pits'. A total of 18 000 health states can be defined in this way. The other main preference-based measures, including the EQ-5D and HUI3, are similar in construction.

There is little guidance on selecting which health states from a system such as the SF-6D to value for statistical modelling. One approach has been to use an orthogonal array to select the states required to estimate an additive model (e.g. by applying the Orthoplan procedure of SPSSwin). This was supplemented in the SF-6D valuation by selecting additional states randomly to enable the estimation of more sophisticated models (e.g. including additional terms for capturing interaction between dimensions) and to provide states to test the predictive properties of the model. An alternative is the balanced

Table 6.1 The SF-6D (from Brazier et al. 2002a)

Level	Level	Pain
Physical functioning		**Pain**
1	1	You have *no pain*
2	2	You have pain but it does not interfere with your normal work (both outside the home and housework)
3	3	You have pain that interferes with your normal work (both outside the home and housework) *a little bit*
4	4	You have pain that interferes with your normal work (both outside the home and housework) *moderately*
5	5	You have pain that interferes with your normal work (both outside the home and housework) *quite a bit*
6	6	You have pain that interferes with your normal work (both outside the home and housework) *extremely*
1	Your health does not limit you in *vigorous activities*	**Mental health**
2	Your health limits you a little in *vigorous activities*	1 — You feel tense or downhearted and low *none of the time*
3	Your health limits you a little in *moderate activities*	2 — You feel tense or downhearted and low a *little of the time*
4	Your health limits you a lot in *moderate activities*	3 — You feel tense or downhearted and low *some of the time*
5	Your health limits you *a little in bathing and dressing*	
6	Your health limits you *a lot in bathing and dressing*	
Role limitations		
1	You have *no* problems with your work or other regular daily activities as a result of your physical health or any emotional problems	
2	You are limited in the kind of work or other activities as a result of your physical health	
3	You accomplish less than you would like as a result of emotional problems	

Table 6.1 (Continued) The SF-6D (from Brazier *et al.* 2002a)

Level	
4	You are limited in the kind of work or other activities as a result of your physical health and accomplish less than you would like as a result of emotional problems
	You feel tense or downhearted and low *most of the time*
5	You feel tense or downhearted and low *all of the time*
Social functioning	**Vitality**
1	Your health limits your social activities *none of the time*
	You have a lot of energy *all of the time*
2	Your health limits your social activities *a little of the time*
	You have a lot of energy *most of the time*
3	Your health limits your social activities *some of the time*
	You have a lot of energy *some of the time*
4	Your health limits your social activities *most of the time*
	You have a lot of energy *a little of the time*
5	Your health limits your social activities *all of the time*
	You have a lot of energy *none of the time*

The SF-36 items used to construct the SF-6D are as follows: physical functioning, items 1, 2 and 10; role limitation due to physical problems, item 3; role limitation due to emotional problems, item 2; social functioning, item 2; both bodily pain items; mental health items, 1 (alternative version) and 4; and vitality, item 2.

[1]Most severe is defined as levels 4–6 for physical functioning, levels 3 and 4 for role limitation, 4 and 5 for social functioning, mental health and vitality, and 5 and 6 for pain.

Source: Reprinted from the *Journal of Health Economics*, 21, 271(292). Brazier JE, Roberts J, Deverill M, 'The estimation of a preference-based measure of health from SF-6D (2002), with permission from Elsevier.

design that ensures that any dimension level has an equal chance of being combined with the levels of other dimensions (see the example in Yang *et al.* 2006). State selection issues are largely unresolved and should be a priority for future research.

The subsamples of states chosen in this way are typically still too large for a respondent to value at a single sitting. Previous surveys have therefore further divided the subset of states into smaller sets for each respondent to value. These smaller sets must be chosen to ensure that respondents face a balance of severe, moderate and mild health states in order to minimize the risk of bias.

6.1.2 Data preparation

The data from valuation surveys must be prepared for statistical modelling. This may include making various adjustments to raw responses to the SG questions. Some health states defined by instruments such as the EQ-5D and SF-6D, for example, have been regarded by some members of the general population as worse than being dead. For states regarded as being worse than dead using standard gamble (SG), expected utility theory (EUT) would suggest that the health state value can be calculated to be $-P/(1 - P)$; where P is the indifference value for the state elicited from the SG task (see Chapter 5 for a full explanation). However, this results in a scale ranging from $-\infty$ to $+1$, which gives greater weight to negative values in the calculation of mean scores and presents problems for the statistical analysis. One solution has been to value the health state as the negative of the indifference probability value P (Patrick *et al.* 1994). This has the effect of bounding negative values at minus one. This has no theoretical support and is only one of a number of possible solutions. A similar solution to states worse than dead has been proposed for the time trade-off valuation technique (Chapter 5).

The SF-6D valuation survey asked respondents to value states against full health and the worst state (i.e. the 'pits') defined by the descriptive system. In order to estimate health state values on the conventional full health–dead scale, these values had to be transformed using the valuation of the 'pits' state also obtained from each respondent. The health state values used in the modelling for the SF-6D were therefore computed as: $U_x = P + (I - P) (U_y)$, where P is the unadjusted SG value for each state and U_y is the value of the 'pits' state against full health and death.

Previous studies have 'cleaned' health state valuation data by eliminating respondents who were thought to have been confused by the valuation task (Kaplan *et al.* 1979; Torrance *et al.* 1996; Brazier *et al.* 2002a), where confusion is generally defined as major inconsistencies in the values obtained. Excluding such cases has the advantage of improving the precision of the estimates; however, it reduces the size and the representativeness of the data set. In addition, care must be taken when interpreting inconsistencies as evidence of confusion. Some inconsistencies may represent simple one-off mistakes or may reflect departures from the axioms of EUT or even consumer choice theory more generally. Views vary on how to handle such departures from theory (Kaplan *et al.* 1979; Loomes 1993).

6.1.3 Features of health state valuation data

Two hundred and forty-nine health states defined by the SF-6D were valued by a representative sample of the UK general population using the SG valuation technique. From the 611 respondents in the sample there were 148 missing values from 117 individuals, resulting in 3518 observed SG valuations across 249 health states. Each health state was valued an average of 15 times. Mean health state values ranged from 0.10 to 0.99, and generally had large standard deviations (up to 0.5). A histogram and descriptive statistics for the 3518 individual adjusted health state valuations are presented in Fig. 6.1. Median health state values usually exceeded mean values, reflecting the negative skewness of the data. Negative observations (suggesting states worse than dead) were comparatively rare (245/3518) and over 23 per cent of observations lay between 0.9 and 1.0.

The distribution of observed health state values usually diverges substantially from normality (e.g. Fig. 6.1). Left skew and bimodality are common, depending on the valuation technique employed. Other instruments, such as the EQ-5D, produce valuation data that show somewhat less skew (though it still exists to some extent). While non-normality is a technical problem, skewness also raises questions about the appropriate measure of central tendency, which essentially determines whose values are given greatest weight. In the case of highly skewed distributions, the mean gives a higher weight to extreme responses, while the median weights all responses equally. The conventional welfare economics argument is that the mean should be used since this reflects strength of preference, whereas a more democratic solution is arguably to use the median (Williams 1995). Published algorithms for the preference-based measures generate mean health state values.

A further complexity is that the distribution of health state values is generally truncated and non-continuous. For example, SG scores are truncated at an upper limit since the chance of treatment success cannot be greater than one. Additionally the design of most surveys means that respondents can only specify values in discrete ranges. These departures from normality and continuity may warrant transformations of the data for statistical modelling (Brazier *et al.* 2002*a*, *b*).

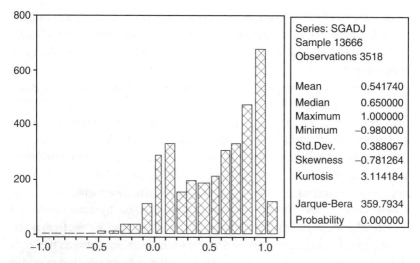

Fig. 6.1 Histogram and descriptive statistics for SG values of SF-6D health states (from Brazier *et al.* 2002a)
Source: Reprinted from Brazier JE, Deverill M, (2002). The estimation of a preference-based measure of health from the SF-6D. *Journal of Health Economics* 21, 271(292), with permission from Elsevier.

6.1.4 Specifying the model

The aim of statistical modelling is to estimate health state values for all states defined by descriptive systems such as the SF-6D. The value associated with a health state is assumed to be a function of that state; hence by estimating a relationship between the descriptive system and the observed values we can infer values for all states. Any model specification should deal with the complexities described above and the fact that the data are likely to be clustered by respondent. Respondents do not value the same set of states, and although allocation of states to respondents should be stratified in such a way as to remove any anchoring effects, random differences between health state values may be partly due to differences in the preferences of the respondents, rather than the attributes of those states.

A number of alternative models have been proposed for estimating functions from health state value data (Busschbach *et al.* 1999; Brazier *et al.* 2002a). The general model defined in Brazier *et al.* (2002a) is as follows:

$$y_{ij} = g\left(\beta' \mathbf{x}_{ij} + \theta' \mathbf{r}_{ij} + \delta' \mathbf{z}_j\right) + \varepsilon_{ij} \qquad (6.1)$$

where $i = 1, 2, ..., n$ represents individual health states and $j = 1, 2, ..., m$ represents respondents. The dependent variable, y_{ij}, is the value for health state i valued by respondent j. $\mathbf{x}$ is a vector of binary dummy variables ($\mathbf{x}\delta\lambda$)

for each level λ of dimension δ of the classification. Level $\lambda = 1$ acts as a baseline for each dimension, so in a simple linear model, the intercept represents state 1111111, and summing the coefficients of the 'on' dummies derives the value of all other states.

The intercept has an expected value of one. However, this estimate has been found to be significantly lower than one in a number of empirical studies (Dolan 1997; Brazier *et al.* 2002*a*). There are strong theoretical arguments for restricting the intercept to unity where the best state defined by the health classification (i.e. 111111 in the SF-6D) is the upper anchor in the SG or TTO task, since by definition this should be one. Incorporating this into the method of estimation is an important constraint. However, there may be situations where the upper anchor is not defined by the health state classification, but by states such as full or perfect health. In this case, it is possible for the intercept to diverge from unity.

The **r** term is a vector of terms to account for interactions between the levels of different attributes. **z** is a vector of personal characteristics that may also affect the value an individual gives to a health state, for example age, sex and education. The role of personal characteristics is not discussed in this chapter. *g* is a function specifying the appropriate functional form. ε_{ij} is an error term whose autocorrelation structure and distributional properties depend on the assumptions underlying the particular model used.

This simple additive model imposes no further restrictions on the relationship between dimension levels of the descriptive system. It does not, for example, impose an interval scale between the levels of each dimension, nor does it insist on a particular ordering of levels (indeed for the SF-6D the expected ordering of states was contradicted by the model results).

An ordinary least squares (OLS) model would ignore the clustering in the data since it assumes that each individual health state value is an independent observation, regardless of whether or not it was valued by the same respondent. A more valid specification, which takes account of variation both within and between respondents, is the one-way error components random effects (RE) model. This model divides the error between respondent-specific variation (assumed to be random across individuals) and an error term for the health state being valued by the respondent. Estimation is via generalized least squares (GLS) or maximum likelihood (MLE). A fixed effects model could also deal with clustering, but the RE model has been found to be more appropriate using the Hausman test (Brazier *et al.* 2002*a*; McCabe *et al.* 2005*a*).

Another way to handle the clustering of data is to aggregate the data prior to analysis. This was undertaken in the analysis of the SF-6D data, where an OLS model was estimated using mean health state values. RE models use individual level data (i.e. y_{ij} in equation 1) and this has the advantage of greatly increasing the number of degrees of freedom available for the analysis (for the SF-6D model by increasing the number of observations to model from 249 mean health state values to over 3500 individual level observations) and enabling the analysis of respondent background characteristics on health state valuations. Despite these apparent advantages, it is not clear whether one is necessarily superior for the purposes of predicting mean health state values (Gravelle 1995). Indeed, mean models were found to perform better than the RE models in the SF-6D valuation (Brazier *et al.* 2002*a*).

Analysis of first order interactions alone is problematic, since the large number of possible interactions means there is the potential of collinearity and a risk of finding that some are significant purely by chance. The approach adopted for a number of preference-based measures has been to use composite terms for describing interactions (Dolan 1997; Brazier *et al.* 2002*a*). The model used to value the SF-6D had one example of this called MOST which takes a value of 1 if any dimension in the health state is at one of the most severe level, and 0 otherwise[1].

The literature has examined a number of alternative functional forms to account for the skewed distribution of health state valuations. These have included a logit transformation and two complementary log–log transformations suggested by Abdalla and Russell (1995). These are chosen to map the data from the range $(-1,1)$ to the range $(-\infty,\infty)$. Secondly, left skew in these data, whereby 25 per cent of the values lie between 0.9 and 1, can be accounted for in a Tobit model with upper censoring, which treats the data as if they arise from a censored observation mechanism through which observations with true values greater than 1 are observed as 1. However, these transformations have not been found to improve the fit of models (Brazier *et al.* 2002*a, b*).

A new Bayesian 'non-parametric' approach has been developed that has the potential to offer a more flexible solution to some of the problems with modelling health state valuation data (Kharroubi *et al.* 2005). It has been applied to SF-6D data and demonstrated a number of improvements in performance relative to the RE model. It has the potential to utilize prior information and reduce the scale of surveys, such as in cross-country valuation work. It also offers a more complex way to examine the impact of background characteristics. This is a novel approach, and those interested in its application can obtain software available at http://www.shef.ac.uk/chebs.

The impact of background characteristics on health state values can be explored using an RE model for assessing their impact on intercept terms (e.g. Dolan and Roberts 2002 for the EQ-5D) or using a non-parametric Bayesian specification for assessing a multiplicative impact across all dimensions (Kharroubi *et al.* 2005).

6.1.5 **Model performance**

The performance of models has been assessed in a number of ways in the literature. It is common to report a model's explanatory power in terms of its adjusted R-squared, but this has limited value for comparing models estimated using different specifications such as RE and OLS, and for models without a constant it has no meaning. Models have also been assessed in terms of the sign, significance and consistency of the estimated coefficients of the dimension levels ($x\delta\lambda$) with any prior assumptions about the ordinality of the descriptive system. On the natural scale for valuations, with higher values indicating preferred health states, coefficients should be negative and the more severe the health problem, the larger should be the negative coefficient. However, for some descriptive systems, there might be some ambiguity regarding the ordering of statements (e.g. between 'your health limits you a little in bathing and dressing' versus 'your health limits you a lot in moderate activities' in the SF-6D). Furthermore, interaction terms would interfere with these orderings.

Ultimately the purpose of modelling these data is to predict mean health state values. Thus one way to evaluate models has been to examine the average absolute difference between predicted and observed mean health state values. This has been done by calculating the mean absolute error (MAE) and the root mean squared error. Models are sometimes also compared in terms of the numbers of errors greater than 0.05 and 0.10 in absolute value. Bias in predictions has been assessed using a t-test and the normality of prediction errors (e.g. the Jarque–Bera test). The pattern of errors can be observed by plotting observed against predicted mean health state values. Models have been estimated for the SF-6D, for example, that were found to underpredict values at the top end of the scale (see Fig. 6.2).

6.2 **Multiattribute utility theory**

6.2.1 **Specification of functional form**

The decomposed approach uses MAUT to specify a functional form in advance of undertaking the valuation survey. It is based on decision theory and is consistent with expected utility theory (Keeney and Raiffa 1976). MAUT reduces the valuation task by making simplifying assumptions about the relationship between dimensions. These simplifying assumptions place stringent restrictions on the way in which dimensions and dimension levels can interact with each other.

There are three functional forms used in practice: additive, multiplicative and multilinear (Box 6.1). The most restrictive is the additive functional form

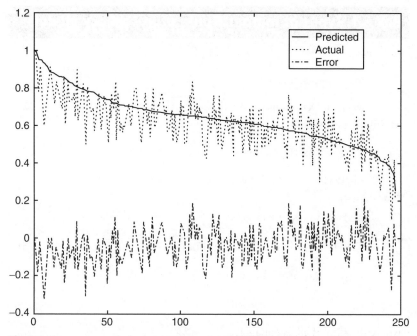

Fig. 6.2 Comparison of observed and predicted SF-6D health state values.

which assumes that dimensions are independent. It permits no interactions and simply adds up the decrements associated with each dimension. The multiplicative function permits a very limited form of interaction between dimensions. It assumes preference dependence to be the same between dimensions. The combined decrement of any pair of dimensions is assumed to be either: (1) more than the sum of the individual effects of the two dimensions (in which case they are substitutes); or (2) less than the sum of the individual effects of the two dimensions (in which case the dimensions are complements). The multilinear form is the least restrictive since it allows pairs of states and indeed higher order interactions to be estimated separately and so does not impose a limitation on the direction of the preference dependence. It is far more demanding in terms of the amount of valuation work required to parameterize such a model.

Evidence from work on the HUI (Torrance 1982; Torrance *et al.* 1996; Feeny *et al.* 2002) found that the assumptions of additivity did not hold (i.e. the k_js in equation 2 in Box 6.1 do not sum to unity). They found that dimensions were complements in preference terms, and this has been confirmed for the EQ-5D and SF-6D (Dolan 1997; Brazier *et al.* 2002*a*). The developers of the

Box 6.1 Types of multiattribute utility theory models

Additive:

$$u (X) = \text{<Insert equation>} \tag{1}$$

$$\text{where: } u (X) = \text{<Insert equation>} \tag{2}$$

Multiplicative (see note):

$$U (x) = \text{<Insert equation>} \tag{3}$$

$$\text{where } (1 + k) = \text{<Insert equation>} \tag{4}$$

Multilinear:

$$u(x) = k_1 u_1 (x_1) + k_2 u_2 (x_2) + \dots$$

$$+ k_{12} u_1 (x_1) u_2 (x_2) + k_{13} u_1 (x_1) u_3 (x_3) + \dots \tag{5}$$

$$+ k_{123} u_1 (x_1) u_2 (x_2) u_3 (x_3) + \dots$$

$$+ ..$$

where the sum of all ks equals 1.

Notation : $u_j(x^j)$ is the signal attribute utility function for attribute j.

$u(x)$ is the utility for health state x, represented by an n-element vector.

k and k_j are the model parameters

Note: The multiplicative model contains the additive model as a special case. In fitting the multiplicative model, if the measured k_j sum to 1, then $k = 0$ and the additive model holds.

Source: Torrance *et al.* (1995)

HUI3 have examined a limited form of the multilinear equation. Health states were selected for valuation in an independent sample in order to estimate 26 of the 28 first order interactions and four of the 56 second order interactions (Feeny *et al.* 2002). Some of these were found to be potentially important (i.e. >0.025), but their sign was always the same (i.e. preference complements). Feeny *et al.* (2002) conclude that although the multilinear form is less restrictive, the multiplicative form seems to capture the important interactions, and indeed it outperformed their version of the multilinear model. The estimation of a full multilinear equation for a descriptive system such as the HUI3 would require too many states to be valued, given the resources usually at the disposal of researchers in this field.

6.2.2 Design of valuation survey

The application of MAUT decomposes the valuation task into three parts: valuing single dimension states, 'corner' states and other multidimensional states. Below we describe the procedure used for the HUI3.

Single dimension states

The aim is to estimate single dimension utility functions. A single dimensional state is defined as a level of functioning on one dimension of the descriptive system, such as being 'Able to walk around the neighbourhood with walking equipment, but without the help of another person' (a single dimensional health state on the ambulation dimension). The respondent is asked to assume that all other dimensions are at level 1, the highest level of functioning. For the HUI3, a VAS is used in the valuations, though TTO or SG could have been used. The VAS is anchored by the highest level of functioning, e.g. 'Able to walk around the neighbourhood without difficulty and without walking equipment' and the lowest level of functioning, e.g. 'cannot walk', which are set to one and zero, respectively. The descriptive system of the HUI3 has 37 such single dimension health states to value.

Corner states

Secondly, 'corner states' are valued; these are multidimensional states where one dimension is at one extreme (usually the worst level of functioning) and the rest are set at the other extreme (usually the highest level of functioning). This requires the dimensions to be structurally independent, which implies that they are not correlated. Otherwise the respondent may have difficulty imagining the state. For example, it may be difficult to imagine a state with very severe pain but with no impact on social or role activities. This problem occurred for the HUI2 and so the developers used states 'backed off' from the corner, whereby the extreme levels are moderated and then additional calculations performed to extrapolate for the missing values (Torrance *et al.* 1996).

Multiattribute utility states

Thirdly, a set of multiattribute states are valued. These are determined by the exact specification of the multiattribute utility function (MAUF). A simple additive model only needs two multidimensional states to be valued, whereas multiplicative models require an extra state in order to calculate a value for the k parameter in equation 3 (Box 6.1).

6.2.3 **Analysis of data**

Using the chosen functional form, it is possible to solve a system of equations to calculate weights for each dimension and any parameter for preference interactions specified in the model.

The MAUFs for the HUI2 and HUI3 have been constructed in a number of stages (Torrance *et al.* 1996; Feeny *et al.* 2002; McCabe *et al.* 2005*a*). The first stage is to estimate the mean VAS value for each single and multidimensional state. [The MAUFs are often constructed to predict the disutility of a health state (i.e. one minus the utility) to make the valuation task easier for respondents.]

A VAS–SG mapping function is then estimated in order to convert the VAS into SG. This is done by asking respondents to value three states by SG as well as VAS, and estimating a power function between the two and applying this to all the other states they valued (details of this procedure and a critique are provided in Chapter 5 and Stevens *et al.* 2006). The final stage in the construction of the valuation tariff is to solve for one of the MAUFs presented in Box 6.1. Past work in health has tended to use the multiplicative form.

As for statistical modelling, there is a choice in the level of analysis. MAUFs can be calculated for each individual (provided each respondent undertook all the necessary valuations) or at an aggregate level. Individual MAUFs can be aggregated to give population mean estimates, but an aggregate analysis means it is not possible to estimate respondent-specific effects. Whether or not it is important to explore the impact of covariates on health state values depends on the policy context. For economic evaluation, it can be argued that it is the population that is important and, since the developers of the HUI2 found that the two approaches yield virtually identical results, there seems little reason to pursue the more laborious process of estimating individual level functions (Torrance 1986). For some policy makers, however, it may be relevant to understand how values vary by key background characteristics.

6.3 **Comparison of statistical modelling and MAUT**

There is a choice between using statistical modelling and MAUT to predict health state values, and there have been arguments on both sides (Dolan 2002; Feeny 2002; McCabe *et al.* 2005*a*). This section will attempt to summarize the debate.

MAUT provides a stronger and more explicit theoretical foundation for the design of valuation studies based in decision theory. However, it could be argued that this theoretical advantage counts for little unless it is better able to predict health state values. Furthermore, it could be argued that the statistical approach draws on a theoretical framework, but one based on statistical, rather than economic, theory.

MAUT seems to require direct valuation of a smaller set of states than the number that must be valued directly for estimating a statistical model. The HUI2 valuation function was estimated on the direct valuation of 29 states, and HUI3 used 40 states compared with 249 for the SF-6D. The EQ-5D was valued using just 43 states, but this is a much smaller descriptive system. This advantage has been exploited by the AQoL that has a 15-item descriptive system that would define many billions of states and uses a two-stage procedure to estimate a function (Hawthorne *et al.* 2001). The extent of this advantage is difficult to gauge since little is known about the optimal number of states for statistical modelling. Using a simple additive design, the SPSS 'orthoplan procedure' selected 49 states for the SF-6D, but this was felt to be inadequate to model possible interactions and so a further 200 were selected at random. More recently, valuation of condition-specific descriptive systems with five dimensions with five levels has been done successfully with 100 states using a balanced statistical design (Yang *et al.* 2006). Further work is required to determine the optimal statistical design, but current evidence suggests that MAUT requires fewer states to be valued and that this advantage is likely to increase with larger descriptive systems.

There is a question surrounding the plausibility of some of the MAUT valuation tasks, particularly the valuation of corner states. The developers had to undertake a 'backing off' procedure to reduce this problem with the HUI2, but designed the descriptive system of the HUI3 to be orthogonal and so avoided this problem. However, with those descriptive systems with dimensions that are more correlated, this may cause a problem. This is also a potential problem with the statistical approach, since some of the states selected to achieve an orthogonal array or balanced design may be implausible, though these states are usually less extreme in nature than the corner states required for MAUT.

Predictive validity can be compared for these two approaches. The EQ-5D was able to achieve mean absolute error of around 0.04 and SF-6D 0.08 compared to 0.087 for the HUI3 in an 'out of sample' set of states. These types of comparisons are contaminated by other differences in the descriptive systems, valuation technique and the source of values. A more rigorous test would be to compare the predictive abilities of these estimation methods using the same descriptive system, valuation technique and sample of respondents on an 'out of sample' set of states. This has been done by McCabe and colleagues (2005*b*) in a comparison of the predictions of a multiplicative

MAUF and a statistical method estimated on an independent random sample of the general population who valued 14 health states. The additive model was found to outperform the MAUF in terms of mean absolute error, root mean square error and proportion of predictions plus or minus 3 per cent from the actual mean value. A similar result was found by Currim and Sarin (1984) in a study of job choice in 100 MBA graduates in the USA using a self-administered questionnaire.

This is far from being conclusive evidence on the relative performance of these approaches. The McCabe *et al.* (2005*b*) study used the HUI2 methodology, so health state valuations were elicited using VAS and then mapped onto SG. There are numerous criticisms of using VAS to derive preference data, and the specific mapping function they employed could confound the result. However, the result may be genuine and reflect the problems with using a methodology that relies heavily on the valuation of corner states that rarely exist in practice, rather than the general mix of states used by the statistical approach. To resolve this important debate, there need to be more studies comparing these two approaches that use the same descriptive system and the same valuation method (preferably using a choice-based technique throughout) on independent samples.

It has also been argued that the relative advantages of each approach depend on the descriptive system (Dolan 2002). MAUT requires a greater degree of structural independence than statistical modelling since it depends on being able to value extreme corner states, whereas statistical modelling is more flexible in this regard. At the same time, Dolan (2002) has argued that '*Ceteris paribus*, as the total number of states (generated by the descriptive systems) increases, the robustness of the parameter estimates from the composite approach decreases, and so the axiomatic basis of the decomposed approach might become more attractive' (parenthesis added). However, whether a larger sized descriptive system with its finer gradations yields any demonstrable benefits in terms of changing decisions depends on the policy context. More empirical comparisons are needed to resolve this debate.

6.4 **The role of background variables**

This section examines the extent to which there is any systematic variation in health state values between subgroups of the population. Early research in this field suggested that there was little or no relationship between the background characteristics of respondents and health state values, but these tended to be either small-scale studies with fewer than 200 respondents (Llewellyn-Thomas *et al.* 1984; Balaban *et al.* 1986;Froberg and Kane 1989) or used rating scales and simple pairwise choices (Badia *et al.* 1995; Hadorn and Uebersax 1995) rather than one of the established cardinal preference-based methods for valuing health states, such as TTO or SG. Furthermore, these were mainly univariate studies.

The impact of covariates is better explored using a multivariate approach with a comparatively large valuation data set over many health states. One such study analysed a UK EQ-5D TTO valuation data set and found some evidence for a systematic variation of TTO values by age, sex and marital status (Dolan and Roberts 2002). The most important of these was age, but this finding may have been partly the result of an artefact of the TTO variant used for states worse than death, since 50 per cent of respondents over 60 regarded the scenario as implausible. Another study examined the SG health state valuations produced from the UK SF-6D survey (as described earlier in this chapter) using a non-parametric Bayesian approach (Kharroubi *et al.* 2007). It found 11 covariates had a reasonable probability of impacting on health state values. Age was found to have the strongest association, with a quadratic relationship where health state values initially increase from 18 to around 60, and then fall slowly until around 70, followed by a more rapid decline. The largest difference was between those under 40s and the over 65s for the worst state of 0.14, but this difference declined as states became milder. Own physical functioning was also found to have a strong relationship, with lower own physical functioning being associated with higher health state values. A weaker relationship was found with social functioning. Relationships were also found for sex, having a degree, employment, retirement, being a student, and degree of difficultly and understanding of the SG task.

There are a number of explanations for these relationships. The findings regarding own physical and social functioning support the arguments reviewed in Chapter 5 that people learn to adapt or cope to some extent with disability (Menzel *et al.* 1999; Ubel *et al.* 2003). As a consequence, they would regard the states described to them as having less of an impact than those not currently experiencing ill health. It might also be the case that people in ill health may be operating from a different reference point (Lenert *et al.* 2001). The findings about age may also reflect an adaptation effect or at least the consequences of experiencing many of the states in the past or the context of mixing with older, less on average healthy individuals. It also may be to do with a person's changing living circumstances, with respondents in middle age being less willing to risk their life due to having greater responsibilities than the young and old. However, the underlying reasons for this finding are not fully understood (Robertson *et al.* 1997). The reasons for sex, class, marital status, education and employment are also unclear.

Whilst these background variables are significant, their overall impact on the mean health state values tends to be quite modest (usually 0.05 or less). The descriptive content of the SF-6D and EQ-5D was far more important than any of these covariates (Dolan and Roberts 2002; Kharroubi *et al.* 2007). However, age has the potential to be important by grouping, with differences between the under 40s and the two older groups of up to 0.14 for the most severe ill health states (Kharroubi *et al.* 2005). This research raises the policy question of whether health state values should be adjusted to allow for the background characteristics of the recipient population, particularly one that is readily measurable such as age. The debate surrounding whose values should be used to estimate health state values has been reviewed in Chapter 5, but one limitation with age-specific QALYs is the difficulties of making cross-age group comparisons necessary to inform resource allocation.

6.5 **Conclusion**

Modelling health state values is an important task in the valuation of health state descriptive systems. It has become a very technical area using a range of different mathematical and statistical techniques. This chapter described in some detail the different techniques that can be used and their pros and cons. Research is likely to continue in this field in developing better methods for estimating models and in comparing the performance of different methods.

References

Abdalla M, Russell I (1995). Tariffs for the Euroqol health states based on modelling individual VAS and TTO data of the York Survey In: MVH Group, eds *Final report on the modelling of valuation tariffs*. Centre for Health Economics, University of York, UK. pp. 3–21.

Badia X, Fernandez E, Segura A (1995). Influence of socio-demograpjhic and health status variables on evaluation of health states in a Spanish population. *European Journal of Public Health* 5:87–93.

Balaban DJ, Sagi PC, Goldfarb NI, Nettler S (1986). Weights for scoring the quality of well-being instrument among rheumatoid arthritics: a comparison to the general population. *Medical Care* 24:973–80.

Brazier JE, Roberts J, Deverill M (2002a). The estimation of a preference-based measure of health from the SF-36. *Journal of Health Economics* 21:271–92.

Brazier JE, Rice N, Roberts J (2002b). Modelling health state valuation data. In: Murray C, Salomon J, Mathers C, Lopez A, Lozano R, eds. *Summary measures of population health: concepts, ethics, measurement and applications*. World Health Organization, Geneva. pp. 529–548.

Brazier JE, Fukahara S, Roberts J, Kharroubi S, Ikeda S (2006). *Estimating a preference-based index from the SF-36: the case of Japan*. HEDS 06 Discussion Paper, University of Sheffield.

Busschbach JV, McDonnell J, Essink-Bot M-L, van Hout BA (1999). Estimating parametric relationships between health state description and health valuation with an application to the EuroQol EQ-5D. *Journal of Health Economics* 18:551–71.

Currim IS, Sarin RK (1984). A comparative evaluation of multi-attribute consumer preference models. *Management Science* 30:543–61.

Dolan P (1997). Modeling valuation for Euroqol health states. *Medical Care* 35:351–63.

Dolan P (2002). Modelling the relationship between the description and valuation of health states. In: Murray C, Salomon J, Mathers C, Lopez A, eds. *Summary measures of population health: concepts, ethics, measurment and applications.* World Health Organization, Geneva. pp. 501–514.

Dolan P, Roberts J (2002). To what extent can we explain time trade-off values from other information about respondents? *Social Science and Medicine* 54:919–29.

Feeny D (2002). The utility approach to assessing population health. In: Murray C, Salomon J, Mathers C, Lopez A, eds. *Summary measures of population health: concepts, ethics, measurment and applications.* World Health Organization, Geneva.

Feeny DH, Furlong WJ, Torrance GW, Goldsmith CH, Zenglong Z, Depauw S, Denton M, Boyle M (2002). Multi-attribute and single-attribute utility function for the Health Utility Index Mark 3 system. *Medical Care* 40:113–28.

Froberg DG, Kane RL (1989). Methodology for measuring health-state preferences—I: measurement strategies. *Journal of Clinical Epidemiology* 42:345–54.

Gravelle H (1995). Valuations of Euroqol health states: comments and suggestions. Paper presented at the ESRC/SHHD Workshop on Quality of Life, Edinburgh, unpublished.

Hadorn DC, Uebersax J (1995). Large-scale health outcomes evaluation: how should quality of life be measured? 1—Calibration of a brief questionnaire and search for preference subgroups. *Journal of Clinical Epidemiology* 48:607–18.

Hawthorne G, Richardson G, Atherton-Day N (2001). A comparison of the Assessment of Quality of Life (AQoL) with four other generic utility instruments. *Annals of Medicine* 33:358–70.

Kaplan RM, Anderson JP (1988). A general health policy model: update and application. *Health Services Research* 23:203–35.

Kaplan RM, Bush JW, Berry CC (1979). Health status index: category rating versus magnitude estimation for measuring levels of well-being. *Medical Care* 17:501–25.

Keeney RL, Raiffa H (1976). *Decisions with multiple objectives: preferences and value trade-offs.* John Wiley and Sons, New York.

Kharroubi SA, O'Hagan A, Brazier JE (2005). Estimating utilities from individual health state preference data: a nonparametric Bayesian approach. *Applied Statistics* (in press).

Kharroubi SA, O'Hagan A, Brazier JE, (2007b). *Modelling covariates for the SF-6D standard gamble health state preference data using a nonparametric Bayesian method.* Social Science and Medicine (in press).

Lenert LA, Treadwell JR, Schwartz CE (2001). Associations between health status and utlities: implications for policy. *Medical Care* 37:470–89

Llewellyn-Thomas H, Sutherland HJ, Tibshirani R, Ciampi A, Till JE, Boyd NF (1984). Describing health states: methodological issues in obtaining values for health states. *Medical Care* 22:543–52.

Loomes G (1993). Disparities between health state measures: is there a rational explanation? In: Gerrard W, ed. *The economics of rationality.* Routledge, London. pp. 106–121.

McCabe C, Stevens K, Roberts J, Brazier JE (2005a). Health state values from the HUI-2 descriptive system: results from a UK survey *Health Economics* 14:231–44.

McCabe C, Stevens K, Brazier J, Roberts J (2005*b*). *Multi-attribute utility function or statistical inference models: a comparison of health state valuation models using the HUI2 health state classification system*. Presentation at iHEA 5th World Congress, Barcelona, Spain, July 2005. www.shef.ac.uk/scharr/section/heds/ihea2005.

Menzel P, Dolan O, Richardson J, Olsen JA (2002). The role of adaptation to disability and disease in health state valuation: a preliminary normative analysis. *Social Science and Medicine* 55:2149–58.

Patrick DL, Starks HE, Cain KC, Uhlmann RF, Pearlman RA (1994). Measuring preferences for health states worse than death. *Medical Decision Making* 14:9–18.

Revicki DA, Leidy NK, Kline N, Brennen-Diema F, Sorensen S, Togian A (1998). Integrating patient preferences into health outcomes assessment: the multiattribute Asthma Symptom Utility Index. *Chest* 114:998–1007.

Robertson A, Dolan P, Williams A (1997). Valuing health status using VAS and TTO: what lies behind the numbers? *Social Science and Medicine* 45:1289–97.

Sintonen H (1994). *The 15D-measure of health-related quality of life. I. Reliability, validity and sensitivity of its health state descriptive system*. National Centre for Health Program Evaluation, Working Paper 41, Melbourne.

Stevens KJ, McCabe CJ, Brazier JE (2006). Mapping between visual analogue and standard gamble data; results from the UK Health Utilities Index 2 valuation. *Health Economics* 15:527–34.

Torrance GW (1982). Multi attribute utility theory as a method of measuring social preferences for health states in long-term care. In: Kane RL, Kane RA, eds. *Values in long-term care*. Lovington Books, DC Heath & Co., pp. 127–156.

Torrance GW (1986). Measurement of health state utilities for economic appraisal: a review. *Journal of Health Economics* 5:1–30.

Torrance GW, Furlong W, Feeny D, Boyle M (1995). Multi-attribute preference functions. Health Utilities Index. *Pharmaco Economics* 7:503–20.

Torrance GW, Feeny DH, Furlong WJ, Barr RD, Zhang Y, Wang Q (1996). Multiattribute utility function for a comprehensive health status classification system: Health Utility Index mark 2. *Medical Care* 34:702–22.

Ubel PA, Loewenstein G, Jepson C (2002). Whose quality of life? A commentary exploring discrepancies between health state evaluations of patients and the general public. *Quality of Life Research* 12:599–607.

Williams, A. (1995). *The measurement and valuation of health: a chronicle*. Centre for Health Economics, Discussion Paper, University of York.

Yang Y, Tsuchiya A, Brazier J, Young Y (2006). *Deriving a preference-based measure for health from the Asthma Quality of Life Questionnaire (AQLQ)*. Health Economics Study Group, Newcastle, UK.

Chapter 7

Using ordinal data to estimate cardinal valuations

In Chapter 5, we reviewed the range of different methods that are most commonly used to elicit cardinal valuations of health states. Chapter 6 introduced approaches to modelling health state valuations using scoring functions estimated for generic health state descriptive systems. In this chapter, we consider the potential role of ordinal data collection methods as an alternative to the more widely used valuation elicitation techniques highlighted in Chapter 5. We review the variety of techniques for eliciting ordinal information on health state valuations, with an emphasis on discrete choice and ranking methods, and we describe methods for modelling these ordinal data in a way that produces results analogous to the valuation models estimated from cardinal responses.

7.1 Why consider ordinal ranking methods?

Although ordinal ranking tasks have been included in several major health valuation studies (Fryback *et al.* 1993; Brazier *et al.* 2002; Dolan *et al.* 1996), the ranking exercise is typically regarded as a 'warm-up' task rather than as a basis for deriving cardinal valuations. There exists a strong methodological foundation, however, for estimating cardinal values from ordinal information, originating in psychology but commonly applied in areas as diverse as consumer marketing (Louviere *et al.* 2000), political science (Koop and Poirier 1994), transportation research (Beggs *et al.* 1981) and environmental economics (Adamowicz *et al.* 1994).

Potential advantages of ordinal data collection approaches include relative ease of comprehension and administration, and greater reliability corresponding to reduced measurement error. Particularly in settings or subpopulations in which educational attainment and numeracy are limited, an ordinal measurement strategy may have considerable practical advantages over more commonly applied techniques such as the SG and TTO, which place a greater cognitive burden on respondents and demand a relatively high degree of abstract reasoning.

Another advantage of ordinal data collection methods is that the preferences or judgements they elicit are not contaminated by values such as risk aversion (as in the standard gamble) or time preference (as in the TTO). As discussed in Chapter 5, the traditional methods that have been favoured in the health economics literature all elicit responses that reflect both valuations of the health levels associated with different states as well as other values, considerations or biases (see also Bleichrodt 2002; Salomon and Murray 2004). With ordinal methods, questions posed to respondents may be framed strictly in terms of choices over health states, without the need for 'calibrators' such as time or risk that can confound interpretation of responses as 'pure' valuations of health states.

7.2 Types of ordinal information

There are a variety of different types of ordinal information, corresponding to different modes of data collection.

7.2.1 Discrete choice

Discrete choice data are elicited by asking respondents to choose between two or more alternatives, typically described by their levels or attributes along several dimensions. In the context of health valuations, these choices are *stated choices* by which respondents indicate their selection from amongst a set of alternatives. The framing of the choice may be in terms of which state the respondent would choose to live in for some defined amount of time, or in terms of a judgement as to which state is associated with the best health level overall. Discrete choices may take the form of paired comparisons, in which respondents indicate the preferred option between two alternatives, or they may be presented as choices of the most preferred alternative amongst a choice set including more than two alternatives.

7.2.2 Ranking

Respondents may be asked to provide a complete ordering of a set of health states from the best to the worst (or vice versa). This information may be elicited either through an open-ended sorting task, or through a more structured interview protocol. As an example of the latter, respondents may first be asked to identify the best health state out of some set of states, followed by the worst state, followed by a state in the middle, and so on, until the complete ordering is obtained. The more structured mode of eliciting rankings bears a greater resemblance to the discrete choice methods described above.

7.2.3 Ordered categorical responses

Ordered categorical response scales constitute an alternative data collection mode, although this type of information differs from rankings or paired comparisons in that no direct comparison is made between health states. Rather, respondents are asked to rate each health state individually in terms of how good or bad they regard the level of health associated with that state overall, using a defined set of response categories. For example, respondents may be asked to characterize the overall health associated with a particular state as excellent, very good, good, fair or poor. In cases where there are more health states than response categories, a categorical rating task will provide an incomplete ordering of health states, since there will be multiple states with the same rating. Note that the type of question we are referring to here typically has a small number of categories marked by descriptive labels as response choices, which makes it different from a VAS task, which usually offers a continuous scale demarcated by numerical values.

For this chapter, we will focus in particular on rankings and paired comparisons data, although the models used to analyse these data have some similarities in functional form to those used to analyse ordered categorical data. For an example of estimating health valuations from categorical ratings, see Cutler and Richardson (1997).

In the context of health valuations, discrete choice and ranking exercises would take as stimuli health states described using standardized, generic descriptive systems such as EQ-5D, SF-6D or HUI, but could also take other stimuli, e.g. condition-specific vignettes. If stimuli are described by a standardized system with multiple dimensions, then modelling choices as a function of these dimensions allows estimation of scoring functions for the descriptive system, as we will describe below.

7.3 How can ordinal data be used to derive cardinal information?

We begin with an overview of the conceptual basis for deriving cardinal values from ordinal responses. Later we will elaborate on the statistical models that are used to formalize these intuitive notions. We first describe the concepts in terms of a discrete choice model, then consider how rankings over a choice set may be conceptualized in a discrete choice framework.

The starting point for imputing cardinal valuations from ordinal information is an assumption that choices over sets of items are related to latent cardinal values that are distributed around the mean levels for each item. Under this framework, a person may choose an item with a lower mean value than another item due to individual variability or random error. The frequency of these reversals is related to the proximity of the mean values for different items on the latent scale. Mean values that are far apart, in other words, will produce greater agreement in preferences than mean values that are close together.

A similar logic applies to a complete ordering of states if we regard this ordering as resulting from a series of discrete choices. For example, the ordering of three items A, B and C may be regarded as a sequence of discrete choices, either through paired comparisons (A over B, A over C and B over C) or choices within subsets (A from the set {A,B,C}, then B from the set {B,C}). The key assumption that allows this translation is called Luce's choice axiom, or *independence from irrelevant alternatives*, which we will discuss further below.

7.4 Historical foundations for ordinal approaches: Thurstone and beyond

The notion of inferring cardinal values from ordinal choices has its origins in the pioneering work of Thurstone (1927). Thurstone first proposed the *law of comparative judgement* as a measurement model representing 'discriminal processes' by which perceptions or judgements arise along some dimension of interest. Initially proposed in 1927 in reference to physical stimuli such as weights, Thurstone later extended the law to describe non-physical entities such as attitudes (Thurstone, 1928).

Thurstone's logic is as follows: a given stimulus, presented to a respondent, evokes a "discriminal process", which is subject to some random error, such that the same stimulus presented to the same respondent over multiple occasions will produce a distribution of discriminal processes, assumed to be normal. The distributions of discriminal processes cannot be observed directly, but can be inferred from comparisons between different stimuli. The *law of comparative judgement* comprises a set of mathematical relationships that imputes relative scale values (on a particular dimension) for two stimuli based on the frequency with which one stimulus is regarded as greater on that dimension than the other stimulus. Thurstone distinguished five 'cases' of his law, corresponding to different simplifying assumptions that would enable solution of the mathematical equations defining the law. The most commonly invoked assumption (representing Thurstone's 'case V') is that all stimuli are associated with distributions that are uncorrelated and have the same variance.

The estimation of relative scale values based on the law of comparative judgement involves matrix operations undertaken on data reporting the proportion of times a particular stimulus is judged as greater than each other stimulus. A requirement of the procedure is that comparisons between stimuli are replicated a large number of times, based either on repeated observations from a single individual, observations from multiple individuals or some combination of the two. In the standard approach to collecting data for Thurstone models, responses are elicited through paired comparisons, by which respondents consider two stimuli and indicate which one is greater on the attribute of interest.

Following Thurstone's original approach, there have been several modifications proposed by later contributors. Perhaps the most significant was the Bradley–Terry–Luce model (sometimes referred to as the Bradley–Terry model), which uses a logistic function in place of the normal density function (Bradley and Terry 1952; Luce 1959). The Bradley–Terry–Luce model is the basis of the regression approach to estimating valuation functions from ordinal data described later.

7.5 Applications

7.5.1 Thurstone modelling of paired comparisons

Application of Thurstone's paired comparison approach to estimate health valuations was first proposed by Fanshel and Bush (1970) in one of the earliest examples of a time-based health index model. Kind (1982) offered another early precedent in a comparison of Thurstone and Bradley–Terry models for scaling the sleep dimension of the Nottingham Health Profile. More recently, Kind has considered Thurstone scaling of EQ-5D values from the Measurement and Valuation of Health (MVH) study in the UK, which collected valuations for 44 states using VAS and TTO, but also included a preliminary ordinal ranking task (Kind 2005). Applying the law of comparative judgement, Kind estimated cardinal values for the 44 states in the study based on a matrix of pairwise ordinal preferences implied by TTO values or direct rankings. A strong linear correlation between the modelled ordinal data and the observed TTO values in the study confirmed the potential usefulness of ordinal data collection methods for deriving health valuations.

7.5.2 Modelling valuation functions from ranking data

The logic of Thurstone's law of comparative judgement provides the basic foundation for estimating cardinal values from ordinal information. This logic may also be extended in formal models that capture the relationships between rankings and attributes of the alternatives in the choice set. For the purposes of health state valuation, what this implies is that ordinal data may be used as the basis for models of valuation functions, allowing rank-based alternatives to the models described in Chapter 6.

Salomon (2003) proposed the use of a random utility approach to modelling health state valuations from data on ordinal rankings, and presented a first application to the MVH data from the UK. Here we review the basis of the model, summarize the findings from the application to EQ-5D data, and present results from a subsequent analysis of SF-6D and HUI2 ranking data (McCabe *et al.* 2006).

Conditional logit modelling of ranking data

The random utility model, attributed to Luce (1959) and McFadden (1974), is based on two functions: first, a statistical model that describes the probability of ranking a particular health state higher than another given the (unobserved) cardinal utility associated with each health state; and, secondly, a valuation function that relates the mean utility for a given health state to a set of explanatory variables. The model is summarized here, and readers are referred to the studies for further details (Salomon 2003; McCabe *et al.* 2006).

The basic random utility model may be operationalized using conditional logit regression, a modelling approach that has also been referred to as the rank-ordered logit (Koop and Poirier 1994) or exploded logit model (Chapman and Staelin 1982).

Each respondent is observed to rank J states, with Y_{ij} denoting the rank given to state j by respondent i (following the convention that 1 is the 'highest' ranking). It is assumed that respondent i has a latent utility value for state j, U_{ij}, that includes a systematic component and an error term:

$$U_{ij} = \mu_j + \varepsilon_{ij} \tag{7.1}$$

In this formulation, states are assumed to have the same expected latent utility value across all respondents; a more general specification of the model would allow for systematic variation in latent utility values that depends on attributes of the respondent as well.

A respondent will rank state j higher than state k if $U_{ij} > U_{ik}$. Allowing for the stochastic element in the model, the probability of this ordering is given by:

$$\text{Prob}(U_{ij} > U_{ik}) = \text{Prob}(\varepsilon_{ij} - \varepsilon_{ik} < \mu_j - \mu_k) \tag{7.2}$$

If the error terms are assumed to be independent and identically distributed with an extreme value distribution, then the odds of ranking j higher than k simplify to $\exp\{\mu_j - \mu_k\}$, and the likelihood for the complete ordering of a particular respondent may be expressed as

$$L_i = \prod_{j=1}^{J} \left[\frac{\exp\{\mu_j\}}{\sum_{k=1}^{J} \delta_{ijk} \exp\{\mu_k\}} \right] \qquad (7.3)$$

where $\delta_{ijk} = 1$ if $Y_{ik} \geq Y_{ij}$, and 0 otherwise (cf. Allison and Christakis 1994).

The extreme value distribution is a convenient option for the joint distribution of the error terms because it offers a simple closed-form expression for the choice probabilities. Given two variables X and Y with extreme value distributions, the difference $X - Y$ has a logistic distribution, hence the logit regression model. While other alternatives are possible, options such as the multinomial probit (which assumes normal distributions, as in Thurstone's original law of comparative judgement) require evaluation of complex integrals (Chapman and Staelin, 1982; Allison and Christakis 1994).

The name *exploded logit* has been used to describe the model because an observed rank ordering of J alternatives may be regarded as an 'explosion' into $J - 1$ independent observations, as described above. Based on this premise, the ranking $U_{i1} > U_{i2} > \ldots U_{iJ}$ is treated as equivalent to the following sequences of choices: $(U_{i1} > U_{ij}, j = 2, \ldots, J), (U_{i2} > U_{ij}, j = 3, \ldots, J), \ldots, (U_{i(J-1)} > U_{iJ})$ (Chapman and Staelin 1982). In other words, ranking data are treated as equivalent to one state being chosen over all other alternatives, a second state chosen over all except the first, and so on. This explosion is made possible by the assumption of *independence from irrelevant alternatives* (IIA), which states that the ordering of a given pair of items does not depend on the other alternatives available (Luce 1959).

In the formulation described here, μ_j represents the average valuation of a particular health state, and we may elaborate the model to express μ as a function of the multiple domain levels in the descriptive system, i.e. to specify the form of a valuation function. A range of different specifications is possible for the valuation function that relates the utility of a given health state to levels on different domains of health (see Chapter 6). The general specification may be represented as:

$$m_j = x'_j \theta \qquad (7.4)$$

with x_j a vector of indicator variables referring to levels on the relevant domains comprising the descriptive system and θ a vector of unknown parameters.

The conditional logit model produces estimated valuations on an interval scale, such that meaningful comparisons of differences are possible (Stevens 1946). However, the origin and units of the scale are defined arbitrarily by the identifying assumptions in the model. In other words, the rank order of a set of health states will be the same under any positive affine transformation of the latent utilities, which implies the following more general specification of equation 7.1 (cf. Chapman and Staelin 1982):

$$U_{ij} = \alpha(\mu_j + \varepsilon_{ij}) + \beta \qquad (7.5)$$

Substituting from equation 7.4, the predicted utility for a given health state, conditional on the parameter values estimated in the model, would be $\alpha x'_j \theta + \beta$.

In the context of health state valuations, there are certain conceptual constraints on the possible values for the parameters α and β, which lead to a limited number of logical alternatives. As applied here, β represents the value assigned to a state characterized by the best possible levels on all of the health dimensions in the relevant classification system. Intuitively, $\beta = 1$ is a reasonable choice that implies that a person with no difficulties on any dimension will have an expected health state valuation of 1.

For the value of α, which defines a normalizing constant for the model coefficients, there is a somewhat larger number of possibilities. Salomon (2003) and McCabe *et al.* (2006) describe three different possible choices.

- Normalization using the exogeneously defined value for at least one state. For example, the observed mean value (using TTO, VAS or SG values, for instance) for the state consisting of the worst levels on all dimensions, or the so-called 'pits' state, could anchor the lower end of the scale.

- Normalization to produce a utility of 0 for the 'pits' state.

- Normalization to produce a utility of 0 for dead. The scale may be defined with 'dead' at 0 if respondents have ranked 'dead' among the health states in the study. By including an indicator for 'dead' in the regression model alongside the indicator variables for the domain levels, the modelled utility for dead on the untransformed scale of the regression coefficients may be used to rescale the results with dead located at 0.

Modelling issues

The basic conditional logit model may be estimated using most statistical software packages, making it a practical choice for modelling ranking data. However, there are several key methodological issues worth noting.

1. *Reversibility.* The extreme value distribution is right-skewed, and as a result the exploded logit model does not give perfectly symmetric results when rank orderings are inverted. In other words, if states are ranked from best to worst in one analysis, an alternative analysis of rankings from worst to best would *not* produce coefficients that are identical but for opposite signs (Yellott 1977; Critchlow *et al.* 1991; Allison and Christakis 1994). While this

property may be unappealing intuitively, in practice the difference is usually minimal (Yellott 1977). In order to consider whether the lack of reversibility produces substantively important differences in this case, it is useful to run analyses with inverted rank orderings for purposes of comparison.

2. *Model evaluation and comparison.* It is important to evaluate the fit of the model to observable information. In health state valuations, the lack of a gold standard measurement instrument means that criterion validity cannot be established. Nevertheless, comparisons between the valuations estimated by modelling ordinal data with those observed using standard measurement techniques such as TTO or SG can provide information on convergent validity, which offers some critical perspective on the approach. In addition, models may be evaluated in terms of their predictive validity by withholding a portion of the data for validation purposes, fitting the model to the balance of data and comparing the model predictions against the empirical observations in the validation subset.

3. *Assessing independence from irrelevant alternatives.* The key assumption that accommodates the use of the conditional logit model to represent rank orderings is the IIA condition, which postulates that preferences over pairs of items are invariant to the other alternatives in the choice set. In the literature on models for ranking data, one possible violation of IIA that has been considered relates to a scenario in which the first several ranks are elicited with less measurement error than subsequent ranks, due either to less ambiguity at the upper end of the scale or to interview fatigue. This scenario may be evaluated formally using Hausman's specification test (Hausman and Ruud 1987).

Examples

Example 1: modelling ranking data from an EQ-5D study   Salomon (2003) presented a first application of conditional logit modelling for ranking data from the MVH study in the UK (Dolan *et al.* 1996; Kind *et al.* 1998). Health states in the survey were described using the EQ-5D descriptive system. Respondents completed the following tasks: (1) description of their own health using EQ-5D; (2) rank ordering, from best to worst, 13 different hypothetical states described by EQ-5D profiles, plus outcomes labelled as 'immediate death' and 'unconscious'; (3) ratings of the same states using a visual analogue scale; and (4) TTO valuations of the states, preceded by a question on whether or not a given state was preferred to death.

The conditional logit model was specified to be analogous to Dolan's widely cited model of the TTO values from the same study (Dolan 1997). The model included indicator variables for the second and third levels on each domain, plus an additional term for states with any domain at level 3. Three alternative rescalings of the model results were considered: matching to the mean TTO value for the 'pits' state; setting the valuation of the 'pits' state to 0; or setting the valuation of dead to 0 based on an extended model with a coefficient for dead estimated from the empirical rankings of dead in relation to the hypothetical states.

After fitting the model and using it to generate predicted valuations for the 42 EQ-5D states included in the study, these predictions (under the three alternative rescaling options) were compared with observed mean TTO values. The rank-based predictions were strongly correlated with observed TTO values; of the three rescaling alternatives, the rescaling to the lowest observed TTO was the best-fitting alternative (Fig. 7.1). Based on the intraclass correlation coefficient, the fit of this rank model was only marginally lower than the fit for predictions based on the directly estimated TTO tariff function reported previously by Dolan (1997).

Example 2: modelling ranking data from SF-6D and HUI2 studies   McCabe and colleagues (2006) fitted a similar conditional logit model to data from two other valuation surveys in the UK, which used the HUI2 and the SF-6D. In both surveys, respondents ranked health states and then valued the same states using the SG. Conditional logit models were estimated with indicator variables for each level on each domain. The models included an indicator variable for the state dead, and predictions from the model were rescaled based on setting the valuation of dead to 0.

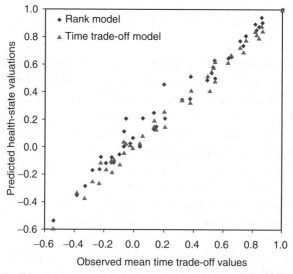

Fig. 7.1 Predicted valuations from the rank model compared with observed mean time trade-off values in the UK Measurement and Valuation of Health study. Source: Salomon (2003).

Models were assessed in terms of the logical consistency of the coefficients (i.e. that lower levels of functioning are associated with greater decrements in health valuations), and model predictions were compared with observed mean SG values. In the HUI2 data set, the rank-based model was very similar to a model estimated directly from the SG values. For the SF-6D data set, the rank-based and SG-based models were different, with fewer logical inconsistencies in the rank model, but lower predictive validity for the rank model compared with the SG model (Fig. 7.2).

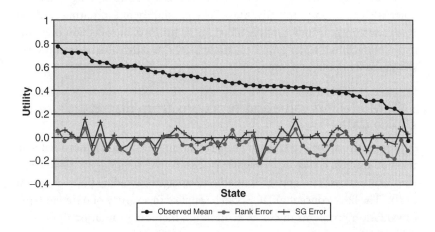

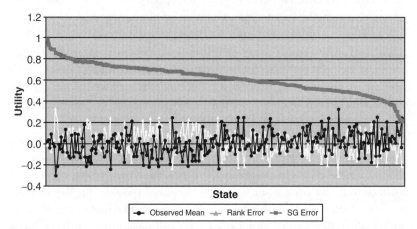

Fig. 7.2 Prediction errors for models of rank data and standard gamble data for the HUI2 (top panel) and SF-6D (bottom panel). The top line in each graph shows the observed mean standard gamble valuations, while the two lower lines show the average deviations from these for model predictions.
Source: Reprinted from *Journal of Health Economics*, 25(3), McCabe C, Brazier J, Gilks P, Tsuchiya A, Roberts J, O'Hagan A, Stevens K, 'Using rank data to estimate health state utility models' 418–431, © with permission from Elsevier.

McCabe *et al.* (2006) examined the assumption of IIA using the Hausman test and found that the models were sensitive to excluding the highest and lowest ranked states.

Taken together, the studies of Salomon (2003) and McCabe *et al.* (2006) offer encouraging evidence that models of health state valuations based on ordinal ranks can provide results that are similar to those obtained from more widely analysed valuation techniques such as the TTO or SG. This line of research suggests that the information content in aggregate ranking data is not currently exploited to full advantage. The possibility of estimating cardinal valuations from ordinal ranks could simplify future data collection dramatically and facilitate wider empirical study of health state valuations in diverse settings and population groups.

7.5.3 Modelling valuation functions from discrete choice data

An alternative approach to estimating valuation functions from ordinal data relies on discrete choice experiments (DCEs) to elicit respondents' preferences over health states. This approach has the advantage of avoiding the assumption of IIA. The basic concept of DCEs can be applied in a variety of different types of valuation problems in health economics, including valuation of generic classification systems, valuation of condition-specific classification systems, or valuation of vignettes based upon a common set of dimensions and levels.

Typically, the universe of multiattribute states defined by a particular classification system or array of relevant attributes is sampled using a fractional factorial design in order to generate an efficient selection of choice sets that are presented to respondents. Respondents are asked to indicate the option within a given choice set that is most preferred (or represents the highest health level, depending on how the question is framed).

Modelling of discrete choice data is analogous to the modelling of ranking data described above, based on regression models originating from a random utility framework. As in the models for rank data, the ordinal choices are assumed to derive from comparisons of latent utility values for the different options, which include both a systematic component related to the levels on the relevant dimensions and a stochastic component that follows some defined distribution. Several recent studies have applied this approach to modelling health state valuations based on DCEs.

Example 1: discrete choice modelling for EQ-5D   Hakim and Pathak (1999) compared models for valuation of EQ-5D health states based on a DCE with a model fit based on a multiattribute utility approach. Data were collected from out-patients treated at a veterans' clinic in the USA. Predictive validity of the alternative models was assessed with reference to valuations of a sample of states elicited directly through the SG or VAS. The authors found that both modelling approaches offered similar predictive validity, and that both approaches supported a multiplicative specification for the valuation function.

Example 2: discrete choice modelling for social care outcomes   More recently, Ryan *et al.* (2006) used a DCE to derive weights for a multidimensional measure of social care. They developed a five-dimensional profile measure and estimated regression models for the different attributes of the system based on the discrete choice responses. Ryan *et al.* examined test–retest reliability and convergent validity through rank correlation with rating scale responses, and concluded that the discrete choice approach was both reliable and valid.

Example 3: discrete choice modelling for a sexual quality of life questionnaire
Ratcliffe and Brazier (2006) used a DCE to estimate a value function for health states defined by the Sexual Quality of Life Questionnaire and compared the results with those obtained from ranking and TTO. A representative sample of the UK general population ($n = 207$) were interviewed and asked to rank a series of health states from best to worst. Following this exercise, the TTO technique was used to elicit utilities for each health state. Four weeks following the interview, consenting individuals received a postal self-completion questionnaire containing a DCE ($n = 102$). Rank data were analysed using a conditional logit model (normalized around zero) and DCE data by a random effects probit model (normalized on the TTO value for pits). The rank and DCE models produced significant coefficients that were consistent with the health state descriptive system, but with larger mean absolute errors compared with TTO in predicting actual TTO values.

Example 4: discrete choice modelling for an asthma quality of life questionnaire   Brazier *et al.* (2006) have taken the DCE method a stage further by including dead in a sample of pairwise choices, which allows rescaling of estimates to produce a zero for being dead (a step necessary for generating QALYs). A representative sample of the UK general population were interviewed and asked to rank a series of health states derived from the Asthma Quality of Life Questionnaire and being dead from best to worst, followed by a TTO elicitation exercise. Four weeks after the interview, consenting individuals received a postal self-completion questionnaire containing a DCE. A separate general population sample was sent the same postal questionnaire. DCE data were analysed using a random effects probit model. The rank model was found to predict actual TTO values very closely, but DCE predictions were substantively different and seemed to have a steeper gradient (i.e. poor states had a lower value and good states had a higher value). These results suggest that DCE may produce different values from those produced by rank methods.

7.6 **Conclusions**

The application of ordinal data collection methods for purposes of measuring and valuing health states remains an underexamined area at this time, but the examples that we have described in this chapter suggest that there is considerable promise in pursuing further research in this direction. Overall, the findings from studies to date have revealed that the information content in aggregate level ordinal data may be surprisingly similar to that in aggregated-data collected using more commonly recommended techniques in health economics such as the TTO or SG. Comparisons of discrete choice and rank-based results provide mixed results on the relationship between alternative modes of eliciting ordinal information, so conclusions about the optimal approach to ordinal data collection in health valuation awaits further empirical study.

A range of methodological issues highlighted here warrants further research, including testing the assumption of independence from irrelevant alternatives in ranking exercises and relaxing this assumption in models if needed. Other variants of ordinal and discrete choice data collection strategies, for example best–worst scaling (Marley and Louviere 2005), may prove to be attractive alternatives. As discussed in Chapter 5 in reference to methods such as the SG or TTO, ordinal valuation techniques may also be susceptible to important framing effects that produce significant differences in responses based on subtle variants in question wording, context and mode of administration.

Part of the appeal of ordinal data collection methods is their apparent ease of administration, particularly among populations in which other techniques may be difficult to implement because of their complexity or abstract nature. However, while we may postulate that ordinal methods will therefore reduce survey administration times and simplify data collection efforts, this issue should be evaluated more thoroughly. On balance, the combination of potential advantages of ordinal data collection methods with the promise shown in early examples of this approach justifies increased attention to this avenue of research.

References

Adamowicz W, Louviere J, Swait J (1994). Combining stated and revealed preference methods for valuing environmental amenities. *Journal of Environmental Economics and Management* 26:65–84.

Allison PD, Christakis NA (1994). Logit models for sets of ranked items. *Sociological Methodology* 24:199–228.

Beggs S, Cardell S, Hausman J (1981). Assessing the potential demand for electric cars. *Journal of Econometrics* 161:1–19.

Bleichrodt H (2002). A new explanation for the difference between time trade-off utilities and standard gamble utilities. *Health Economics* 11:447–56.

Bradley RA, Terry ME (1952). Rank analysis of incomplete block designs, I. The method of paired comparisons. *Biometrika* 39:324–45.

Brazier J, Roberts J, Deverill M (2002). The estimation of a preference-based measure of health from the SF-36. *Journal of Health Economics* 21:271–92.

Brazier JE, Yang Y, Tsuchiya A (2006). *Using DCE to value (asthma) health states for calculating quality adjusted life years.* Health Economics and Decision Science Discussion Paper 07/06, ScHARR, University of Sheffield.
http://www.sheffield.ac.uk/scharr/sections/heds/discussion.html

Chapman RG, Staelin R (1982). Exploiting rank ordered choice set data within the stochastic utility model. *Journal of Marketing Research* 19:288–301.

Critchlow DE, Fligner MA, Verducci J (1991). Probability models on rankings. *Journal of Mathematical Psychology* 35:294–318.

Cutler DM, Richardson E (1997). Measuring the health of the US population. *Brookings Papers on Economic Activity. Microeconomics* 1997:217–27.

Dolan P (1997). Modeling valuations for EuroQol health states. *Medical Care* 35:1095–108.

Dolan P, Gudex C, Kind P, Williams A (1996). The time trade-off method: results from a general population study. *Health Economics* 5:141–54.

Fanshel S, Bush JW (1970). A health status index and its application to health services outcomes. *Operations Research* 18:1021–66.

Fryback DG, Dasbach EJ, Klein R, Klein BE, Dorn N, Peterson K, Martin PA (1993). The Beaver Dam Health Outcomes Study: initial catalog of health-state quality factors. *Medical Decision Making* 13:89–102.

Hakim Z, Pathak DS (1999). Modelling the EuroQol data: a comparison of discrete choice conjoint and conditional preference modelling. *Health Economics* 82:103–16.

Hausman JA, Ruud PA (1987). Specifying and testing econometric models for rank-ordered data. *Journal of Econometrics* 34:83–104.

Kind P (1982). A comparison of two models for scaling health indicators. *International Journal of Epidemiology* 11:271–5.

Kind P, Dolan P, Gudex C, Williams A (1998). Variations in population health status: results from a United Kingdom national questionnaire survey. *British Medical Journal* 316:736–41.

Kind P (2005). Applying paired comparisons models to EQ-5D valuations—deriving TTO utilities from ordinal preferences data. In: Kind P, Brooks R, Rabin R, eds. *EQ-5D concepts and methods: a developmental history.* Springer, The Netherlands, pp. 201–220.

Koop G, Poirier DJ (1994). Rank-ordered logit models: an empirical analysis of Ontario voter preferences. *Journal of Applied Econometrics* 9:369–88.

Louviere JJ, Hensher DA, Swait JD (2000). *Stated choice methods: analysis and application.* Cambridge University Press, Cambridge.

Luce RD (1959) *Individual choice behavior: a theoretical analysis.* John Wiley & Sons, Inc., New York.

Marley AAJ, Louviere JJ (2005). Some probabilistic models of best, worst, and best–worst choices. *Journal of Mathematical Psychology* 49:464–80.

McCabe C, Brazier J, Gilks P, Tsuchiya A, Roberts J, O'Hagan A, Stevens K (2006). Using rank data to estimate health state utility models. *Journal of Health Economics* 25:418–31.

McFadden D (1974). Conditional logit analysis of qualitative choice behavior. In: Zarembka P, ed. *Frontiers in econometrics*. Academic Press, New York, pp. 105–142.

Ratcliffe J, Brazier JE (2006). *Estimation of a preference based single index from the sexual quality of life questionnaire (SQOL) using ordinal data*. Health Economics and Decision Science Discussion Paper 06/06, ScHARR, University of Sheffield. http://www.sheffield.ac.uk/scharr/sections/heds/discussion.html.

Ryan M, Netten A, Skatun D, Smith P (2006). Using discrete choice experiments to estimate a preference-based measure of outcome—an application to social care for older people. *Journal of Health Economics* 25:927–44.

Salomon JA (2003). Reconsidering the use of rankings in the valuation of health states: a model for estimating cardinal values from ordinal data. *Population Health Metrics* 1:12. http://www.pophealthmetrics.com/content/1/1/12.

Salomon JA, Murray CJ (2004). A multi-method approach to measuring health-state valuations. *Health Economics* 13:281–90.

Stevens SS (1946). On the theory of scales of measurement. *Science* 103:677–80.

Thurstone LL (1927). A law of comparative judgement. *Psychological Review* 34:273–86.

Thurstone LL (1928). Attitudes can be measured. *American Journal of Sociology* 33:529–54.

Yellott JI (1977). The relationship between Luce's choice axiom, Thurstone's theory of comparative judgment, and the double exponential distribution. *Journal of Mathematical Psychology* 15:109–44.

Chapter 8

Methods for obtaining health state values: generic preference-based measures of health and the alternatives

This chapter reviews the alternative instruments and methods for obtaining values for health states. It demonstrates how the conceptual and technical issues reviewed in the chapters on describing health (Chapter 4), valuing health (Chapter 5) and modelling health state values (Chapter 6) are addressed in the practical tools and methods used to generate health state values. There is a range of generic preference-based measures that could be used, and this chapter addresses the question about which to use. There are situations where a generic preference-based measure has not been used, and this chapter addresses what can be done in this situation. Generic measures might not be felt to be appropriate for the condition of patients in the study, and this concern has resulted in the development of standardized condition-specific preference-based measures. This approach is reviewed along with the option of developing bespoke vignettes or scenarios that might better take into account the condition and treatment, including the time profile of outcomes and their uncertainty. A final option is to elicit preferences directly from patients and avoid having to describe illness states (though normally it is still necessary to describe the upper anchor of full health).

This chapter also considers the use of health state values obtained from the published literature. With the increasing use of decision analytic models to examine the cost-effectiveness of health care interventions, it will become more important to synthesize evidence on the value of health states (see Chapter 9 for the implications of using health state values in models). This chapter concludes with a consideration of how to choose between these methods and the implications for decision makers concerned with making cross-programme comparisons in a consistent fashion.

8.1 **Generic preference-based measures of health**[1]

8.1.1 **Introduction**

Generic preference-based measures of health have two components, one a system for describing health or its impact on quality of life using a standardized descriptive system, and the second an algorithm for assigning values to each state described by the system. A health state descriptive system is composed of a number of multilevel dimensions that together describe a universe of health states. The EQ-5D, for example, has five dimensions each with three levels that together describe 243 states (see Table 2.5 in Chapter 2). The patient is usually asked to report their own health by using the descriptive system, though a proxy can do so on behalf of the patient. The scoring of each state is provided by an algorithm based on valuations obtained from a sample of the adult general population using one of the valuation techniques reviewed in Chapter 5. These instruments generate preference-based single index scores for each state of health on the scale required to construct QALYs, where full health is one and zero is equivalent to death.

Generic preference-based measures have become widely used in economic evaluation, and over the last decade have become the most popular method for obtaining health state values to calculate QALYs. This seems to stem from their ease of use, their alleged generic properties (i.e. validity across different patient groups) and their ability to meet a number of requirements of agencies such as National Institute for Health and Clinical Excellence (2004). Furthermore, they come 'off the shelf', with a questionnaire and set of weights already provided. The questionnaires for collecting the descriptive data can be readily incorporated into most clinical trials and routine data collection systems with little additional burden for respondents, and the valuation of their responses can be done easily using the scoring algorithms provided by the developers. They are generic and so should be relevant to all patient groups and provide a means of making comparisons between patient groups (see Chapter 4 for a discussion of this issue).

The number of generic preference-based measures has proliferated over the last two decades. These include the Quality of Well-Being (QWB) scale (Kaplan and Anderson, 1988); Rosser Classification of illness states (Rosser and Kind, 1978); Index of Health-related Quality of Life (Rosser *et al.* 1993); Health Utility Index (HUI) marks one, two and three (HUI1, HUI2 and HUI3) (Torrance 1982; Torrance *et al.* 1996; Feeny *et al.* 2002); EQ-5D (Dolan 1997; Shaw *et al.* 2005); 15D (Sintonen and Pekurin 1993); SF-6D—a derivative of the SF-36 and SF-12 (Brazier *et al.* 2002a; Brazier and Roberts 2004); and AQoL (Hawthorne *et al.* 1997). This list is not complete and does not account for some of the variants of these instruments, but it includes the vast majority of those that have been used. Whilst these measures all claim to be generic, they differ considerably in terms of the content and size of their descriptive system, the methods of valuation and the populations used to values the health states (though most aim for a general population sample).

This section reviews seven leading generic preference-based measures in some detail[2]. It provides a description of each instrument and then addresses how they compare, why they seem to generate different scores and how to choose between them.

8.1.2 Description of scales

A summary of the main characteristics of these seven generic preference-based generic measures of health is presented in Tables 8.1 and 8.2. Table 8.1 summarizes the descriptive content of these measures including their dimensions, dimension levels and mode of administration. Each instrument has a questionnaire for completion by the patient (or proxy), or for administration by interview, that is used to assign them a health state from the instruments descriptive system. These questions are mainly designed for adults, typically aged 16 or above, though the HUI2 is designed for children. Table 8.2 summarizes the valuation methods used in terms of the sampling frame used to generate the values, valuation technique and the method of modelling the preference data. These features are discussed in more detail in this section.

Quality of Well-Being scale

The QWB scale was developed from the Index of Well-Being and is the oldest of the QALY instruments (though its developers initially preferred the term 'well-year'). It was developed as part of a general health policy model to inform resource allocation in health services (Fanshel and Bush 1970; Patrick *et al.* 1973). The basic structure of the classification and its weighting has remained largely unchanged since the 1970s (Kaplan *et al.* 1976; Kaplan and Anderson 1988).

Descriptive system   The health state classification contains two components (Table 8.3a): three multilevel dimensions relating to function (mobility, physical activity and social activity) that produce a total of 46 functional levels (including death) and a list of 27 symptom and problem complexes (e.g. 'general tiredness, weakness or weight loss', 'wore eyeglasses or contact lenses'). The functional dimensions and the symptom/complexes combine to form 945 health states. It takes between 1 and 2 weeks to train interviewers to administer the questionnaire (Read *et al.* 1987). The interview involves detailed probing of the respondent. The developers claim it can take between 7 and 15 min to conduct

Table 8.1 Descriptive systems of generic preference-based measures

Instrument	Dimension	Levels	Health states
QWB	Mobility, physical activity, social functioning	3	945
	27 symptoms/problems	2	
HUI2	Sensory, mobility, emotion, cognitive, self-care, pain	4–5	24 000
	Fertility	3	
HUI3	Vision, hearing, speech, ambulation, dexterity, emotion, cognition, pain	5–6	972 000
EQ-5D	Mobility, self-care, usual activities, pain/discomfort, anxiety/depression	3	243
15D	Mobility, vision, hearing, breathing, sleeping, eating, speech, elimination, usual activities, mental function, discomfort/symptoms, depression, distress, vitality, sexual activity	4–5	31 billion
SF-6D	Physical functioning, role limitation, social functioning, pain, energy, mental health	4–6	18 000 (SF-36 version) 7500 (SF-12 version)
AQoL	Independent living (self-care, household tasks, mobility), social relationships (intimacy, friendships, family role), physical senses (seeing, hearing, communication), psychological well-being (sleep, anxiety and depression, pain)	4	16.8 million

Table 8.2 Valuation methods of generic preference-based measures

	Country[1]	Valuation technique[2]	Method of extrapolation
QWB	USA (San Diego)	VAS	Statistical—additive, except for symptom/problem complexes
HUI2	Canada (Hamilton), UK	VAS transformed into SG	MAUT—multiplicative
HUI3	Canada (Hamilton), France	VAS transformed into SG	MAUT—multiplicative
EQ-5D	Belgium, Denmark, Finland, Germany, Japan, The Netherlands, Slovenia, Spain, UK, USA, Zimbabwe	TTO, VAS, ranking	Statistical—additive, with interaction term
15D	Finland	VAS	MAUT—additive
SF-6D	Hong Kong, Japan, UK, Australia, Brazil	SG, ranking	Statistical—additive with interaction term
AQoL	Australia	TTO	MAUT—multiplicative

[1] For references see text or visit the instrument's website.

[2] VAS, visual analogue scale; TTO, time trade-off; SG, standard gamble; MAUT, multiattribute utility theory.

Table 8.3a Quality of Well-Being classification system

Part 1. Quality of Well-Being/general health policy model: function scales with step definitions and calculating weights

Step no.	Step definition	Weight
5	Mobility scale (MOB) No limitations for health reasons	−0.000
4	Did not drive a car, health related; did not ride in a car as usual for age (younger than 15 years), health related; and/or did not use public transportation, health related; or had or would have used more help than usual for age to use public transportation, health related	−0.062
2	In hospital, health related	−0.090
4	Physical activity (PAC) No limitations for health reasons	−0.000
3	In wheelchair, moved or controlled movement of wheelchair without	−0.060

Part 2. Quality of Well-Being/general health policy model: symptom/problem complexes (CPX) with calculating weight

CPX no.	CPX definition	Weight
1	Death (not on respondent's card)	−0.727
2	Loss of consciousness such as seizure (fits), fainting or coma (out cold or knocked out)	−0.407
3	Burn over large areas of face, body, arms or legs	−0.387
4	Pain, bleeding, itching or discharge (drainage) from sexual organs—does not include normal menstrual (monthly) bleeding	−0.349
5	Trouble learning, remembering or thinking clearly	−0.340
6	Any combination of one or more hands, feet, arms or legs either missing, deformed (crooked), paralysed (unable to move) or broken—including wearing artificial limbs or braces	−0.333
7	Pain, stiffness, weakness, numbness or other discomfort in chest, stomach (including	−0.299

No.	Description	Estimate
1	...help from someone else; or had trouble or did not try to lift, stoop, bend over or use stairs or inclines, health related; and/or limped, used a cane, crutches or walker, health related; and/or had any physical limitation in walking, or did not try to walk as far or as fast as others the same age are able, health related. In wheelchair, did not move or control the movement of wheelchair without help from someone else, or in bed, chair or couch for most or all the day, health related	−0.077
5	Social activity scale (SAC) No limitations for health reasons	−0.000
4	Limited in other (e.g. recreational) role activity, health related	−0.061
3	Limited in major (primary) role activity, health related	−0.061
2	Performed no major role activity, health related, but did not perform self-care activities	−0.061
1	Performed no major role activity, health related, and did not perform	−0.106
	hernia or rupture) side, neck, back, hips or any joint or hands, feet, arms or legs	
8	Pain, burning, bleeding, itching or other difficulty with rectum, bowel movement or urination (passing water)	−0.292
9	Sick or upset stomach, vomiting or loose bowel movement, with or without chills, or aching all over	−0.290
10	General tiredness, weakness, or weight loss	−0.259
11	Cough, wheezing or shortness of breath, with or without fever, chills or aching all over	−0.257
12	Spells of feeling, upset, being depressed or of crying	−0.257
13	Headache, or dizziness, or ringing in ears, or spells of feeling hot, nervous or shaky	−0.244
14	Burning or itching rash on large areas of face, body, arms or legs	−0.240

Table 8.3a (Continued) Quality of Well-Being classification system

Part 1. Quality of Well-Being/general health policy model: function scales with step definitions and calculating weights			Part 2. Quality of Well-Being/general health policy model: symptom/problem complexes (CPX) with calculating weight		
Step no.	Step definition	Weight	CPX no.	CPX definition	Weight
	or had more help than usual in performance of one or more self-care activities, health related		15	Trouble talking, such as lisp, stuttering, hoarseness, or being unable to speak	−0.237
			16	Pain or discomfort in one or both eyes (such as burning or itching) or any trouble seeing after correction	−0.230
			17	Overweight for age and height or skin defect of face, body, arms or legs, such as scars, pimples, warts, bruises or changes in colour	−0.188
			18	Pain in ear, tooth, jaw, throat, lips, tongue, several missing or crooked permanent teeth—includes wearing bridges or false teeth, stuffy, runny nose; or any trouble hearing—includes wearing a hearing aid	−0.170

19	Taking medication or staying on a prescribed diet for health reasons	−0.144
20	Wore eyeglasses or contact lenses	−0.101
21	Breathing smog or unpleasant air	−0.101
22	No symptom or problem (not on respondent's card)	−0.000
23	Standard symptom/problem	−0.257
X24	Trouble sleeping	−0.257
X25	Intoxication	−0.257
X26	Problems with sexual interest or performance	−0.257
X27	Excessive worry or anxiety	−0.257

X indicates that a standardized weight is used

Reproduced from Drummond, Sculpher, Torrance, O'Brien, Stoddart (2005), *Methods for the Economic Evaluation of Health Care Programmes* (3rd Edn) with permission from Oxford University Press and; Spilker, B. (ed) *Quality of Life and Pharmacoeconomics in Clinical Trials* (2nd Edn) pp 191–201, with permission from Lippincott, Williams and Wilkins.

an interview (Kaplan 1994), but the range reported in published studies has been up to 20 min (Bombardier and Raboud 1991). Since 1997 there has been a self-administered version that takes approximately 14 min (Andresen *et al.* 1998).

Valuation   Weights were estimated statistically from a sample of health states valued using a version of the visual analogue rating scale on a representative sample of 866 adults in San Diego, USA in 1974–1975. Each respondent valued 42 health states using a VAS (or category scale) where zero corresponded to death. An overall health state score shown in Table 8.3b has been calculated by a simple additive formula, i.e. one plus the decrement (i.e. negative weight) associated with the level of each of three functioning dimensions and the most highly weighted symptom/problem suffered by the patient[3].

The QWB questionnaire (including the self-administered version) and its scoring algorithm are available from the developers.

Health Utilities Index

The HUI has evolved over time into three different versions (HUI mark 1, 2 and 3). Torrance and others developed the first version in the late 1970s for use in an economic evaluation of neonatal intensive care (Torrance 1982). This version has been succeeded by the HUI2 and HUI3. The HUI2 was originally developed for use in studies of childhood cancer (Torrance *et al.* 1996) and is now used as a generic preference-based measure for children. The HUI3 is now designed for adults and is fast becoming the most widely used of the three (Feeny *et al.* 2002).

Descriptive systems   The HUI2 has seven dimensions: sensation, mobility, emotion, cognition, self-care, pain and fertility, with 3–5 levels to each dimension (Table 8.4a). The first six dimensions were developed from the literature and a survey of parents (Cadman and Goldsmith 1986). The first application of the HUI2 was to childhood cancer, and so fertility was added in order to capture the side effects of cancer. The seven dimensions of the HUI2 define 24 000 states in all. A six-dimensional version HUI2 can be used as a generic measure in children by assuming fertility is normal, and this reduces the number of states to 8000.

HUI3 has been adapted from HUI2. The number of dimensions was increased to eight and includes vision and hearing as separate dimensions, along with speech, ambulation, dexterity, emotion, cognition and pain, whilst fertility and self-care were removed. These changes were partly made to reduce the degree of structural dependence and to increase sensitivity. The number of levels has been increased to between five and six, and the new classification defines 972 000 health states (Table 8.5).

Table 8.3b Quality of Well-Being scoring formula

	Calculating formulas	
	Formula 1. Point-in-time well-being score for an individual (W): $W = 1+(CPX wt) + (MOB wt) + (PAC wt) + SAC wt)$	
	where wt is the preference-weighted measure for each factor and CPX is symptom/problem complex.	
	For example, the W score for a person with the following description profile may be calculated for 1 day as:	
CPX-11	Cough, wheezing or shortness of breath, with or without fever, chills, or aching all over	-0.257
MOB-5	No limitations	-0.000
PAC-1	In bed, chair, or couch for most of the day, health related	-0.077
SAC-2	Performed no major role activity health related, but did perform self-care	
	$W = 1 + (-0.257) + (-0.000) + (-0.077) + (-0.061) = 0.605$	
	Formula 2. Well-years (WY) as an output measure:	
	$WY = $ (No. of persons $\times$ (CPX wt + MOB wt + PAC wt + SAC wt) $\times$ time)	

Reproduced from Drummond, Sculpher, Torrance, O'Brien, Stoddart (2005), *Methods for the Economic Evaluation of Health Care Programmes* (3rd Edn) with permission from Oxford University Press and; Spilker, B. (ed) *Quality of Life and Pharmacoeconomics in Clinical Trials* (2nd Edn) pp 191–201, with permission from Lippincott, Williams and Wilkins.

Table 8.4a. Health Utilities Index Mark 2 (HUI2) classification

Attribute	Level	Description
Sensation	1	Able to see, hear and speak normally for age
	2	Requires equipment to see or hear or speak
	3	Sees, hears, or speaks with limitations even with equipment
	4	Blind, deaf or mute
Mobility	1	Able to walk, bend, lift, jump and run normally for age
	2	Able to walk bend, lift, jump or run with some limitations but does not require help
	3	Requires mechanical equipment (such as canes, crutches, braces or wheelchair) to walk or get around independently
	4	Requires the help of another person to walk or get around and requires mechanical equipment as well
	5	Unable to control or use arms and legs
Emotion	1	Generally happy and free from worry
	2	Occasionally fretful, angry, irritable, anxious, depressed or suffering 'night terrors'
	3	Often fretful, angry, irritable, anxious, depressed or suffering 'night terrors'
	4	Almost always fretful, angry, irritable, anxious or depressed
	5	Extremely fretful, angry, irritable, anxious or depressed, usually requiring hospitalization or psychiatric institutional care
Cognitive	1	Learns and remembers school work normally for age
	2	Learns and remembers school work more slowly than classmates as judged by parents and/or teachers
	3	Learns and remembers very slowly and usually requires special educational assistance
	4	Unable to learn and remember
Self-Care	1	Eats, bathes, dresses and uses the toilet normally for age
	2	Eats, bathes, dresses or uses the toilet independently with difficulty
	3	Requires mechanical equipment to eat, bathe, dress, or use the toilet independently
	4	Requires the help of another person to eat, bathe, dress or use the toilet

Pain	1	Free of pain and discomfort
	2	Occasional pain. Discomfort relieved by non-prescription drugs or self-control activity without disruption of normal activities
	3	Frequent pain. Discomfort relieved by oral medicines with occasional disruption of normal activities
	4	Frequent pain; frequent disruption of normal activities. Discomfort requires prescription narcotics for relief
	5	Severe pain. Pain not relieved by drugs and constantly disrupts normal activities
Fertility	1	Able to have children with a fertile spouse
	2	Difficulty in having children with a fertile spouse
	3	Unable to have children with a fertile spouse

The above level descriptions are worded here exactly as they were presented to interview subjects in the HUI2 preference survey.

Patients can be assigned to HUI2 and HUI3 using the same 15-item self-completed questionnaire, or from an interview version (administered face-to-face or by telephone) or by proxy (especially for younger children for the HUI2).

Valuation The original Canadian HUI2 weights were estimated from the responses of a sample of 293 parents of school age children in Hamilton, Ontario, Canada (Torrance *et al.* 1996). The response rate in the valuation survey was 72 per cent, though a large number of respondents were excluded because of missing data, poor quality interview or evidence of confusion with the valuation tasks. These problems resulted in the exclusion of a further 29 per cent of respondents. HUI3 has been valued by a representative sample of 504 adults from Hamilton, Ontario, obtained using a probability sample.

Published valuation functions for HUI2 and 3 were calculated using multi-attribute utility theory (MAUT). This approach has been detailed in Chapter 6, but essentially respondents are first asked to value single dimensional states to derive the single dimension utility functions. Then they are asked to value a set of 'corner' states where one dimension is presented at its worst level while all other dimensions are set to best. Finally, respondents are asked to value a multiattribute utility states. These valuation tasks were undertaken with a version of the VAS that uses a visual aid known as the feeling thermometer. Another three states were valued using VAS and SG in order to estimate a power function between VAS and SG to transform the VAS values into SG values. MAUT enabled the developers to estimate a multiplicative functional form that permits a limited degree of interaction between domains (Table 8.4b).

The HUI2 has been valued in the UK by McCabe *et al.* (2005*a*). They used the descriptive system without fertility, and values were obtained from a sample of 450 adults from the general population (rather than just parents), using the same valuation methods as the McMaster team. They examined alternative VAS to SG mapping functions and found a cubic function to perform better than a power function (Stevens *et al.* 2005) and estimated an additional function using statistical inference methods that (as reported in Chapter 6) was found to perform better than the MAUT functions (McCabe *et al.* 2006). They recommended that the SG weights estimated by statistical inference be used. The final weights were substantially different from the original Canadian values. McCabe and colleagues have also estimated weights using the rank data collected as part of the warm-up exercise, and these were found to be similar to those produced using statistical inference on the SG data (McCabe *et al.* 2006).

The HUI3 has been valued in France using the original methods on a sample of 365 members of the general population aged 20–65 (Le Gales *et al.* 2002). The authors found that the French results were relatively similar to those obtained in Canada.

Table 8.4b. HUI2 Canadian scoring algorithms

HUI2 single attribute utility functions

Level	Sensation	Mobility	Emotion	Cognition	Self-care	Pain	Fertility
1	1.00	1.00	1.00	1.00	1.00	1.00	1.00
2	0.87	0.92	0.86	0.86	0.85	0.95	0.75
3	0.65	0.61	0.60	0.66	0.55	0.75	0.00
4	0.00	0.34	0.37	0.00	0.00	0.42	
5		0.00	0.00			0.00	

HUI2 multiattribute utility function on dead–healthy scale

Sensation		Mobility		Emotion		Cognition		Self-care		Pain		Fertility	
x_1	b_1	x_1	b_1	x_1	b_1	x_1	b_1	x_1	b_1	x_1	b_1	x_1	b_1
1	1.00	1	1.00	1	1.00	1	1.00	1	1.00	1	1.00	1	1.00
2	0.95	2	0.97	2	0.93	2	0.95	2	0.97	2	0.97	2	0.97
3	0.86	3	0.84	3	0.81	3	0.88	3	0.91	3	0.85	3	0.88
4	0.61	4	0.73	4	0.70	4	0.65	4	0.80	4	0.64		
5	0.58	5	0.58	5	0.53	5	0.38	5	0.38				

Reproduced from Torrance GW, Feeny PM, Furlong WJ, Barr RD, Zhang Y, Wang Q (1996) 'A multi-attribute utility function for a comprehensive health status classification system: Health Utilities Mark 2' *Medical Care* 34(7): 702–722 with permission from Lippincott, Williams and Wilkins.

Where x_n is the attribute level and b_n is the attribute utility score

Formula (Dead–Perfect health scale) $u^* = 1.06(b_1 \times b_2 \times b_3 \times b_4 \times b_5 \times b_6 \times b_7) - 0.06$

Where u^* is the utility of a chronic health state on a utility scale where dead has a utility of 0.00 and healthy has a utility of 1.00. Because the worst possible health state was judged by respondents as worse than death, it has a negative utility of –0.03. The standard error of u^* is 0.015 for measurement error and sampling error, and 0.06 if model error is also included.

Table 8.5a Health Utilities Index Mark 3 (HUI3)

Attribute	Level	Description
Vision	1	Able to see well enough to read ordinary newsprint and recognize a friend on the other side of the street, without glasses or contact lenses
	2	Able to see well enough to read ordinary newsprint and recognize a friend on the other side of the street, but with glasses or contact lenses
	3	Able to read ordinary newsprint with or without glasses but unable to recognize a friend on the other side of the street, even with glasses or contact lenses
	4	Able to recognize a friend on the other side of the street with or without glasses but unable to read ordinary newsprint, even with glasses or contact lenses
	5	Unable to read ordinary newsprint and unable to recognize a friend on the other side of the street, even with glasses or contact lenses
	6	Unable to see at all
Hearing	1	Able to hear what is said in a group conversation with at least three other people, without a hearing aid
	2	Able to hear what is said in a conversation with one other person in a quiet room without a hearing aid, but requires a hearing aid to hear what is said in a group conversation with at least three other people
	3	Able to hear what is said in a conversation with one other person in a quiet room with a hearing aid, and able to hear what is said in a group conversation with at least three other people, with a hearing aid
	4	Able to hear what is said in a conversation with one other person in a quiet room with out a hearing aid, but unable to hear what is said in a group conversation with at least three other people even with a hearing aid
	5	Able to hear what is said in a conversation with one other person in a quiet room with a hearing aid, but unable to hear what is said in a group conversation with at least three other people even with a hearing aid
	6	Unable to hear at all

Speech	1	Able to be understood completely when speaking with strangers or people who know me well
	2	Able to be understood partially when speaking with strangers but able to be understood completely when speaking with people who know me well
	3	Able to be understood partially when speaking with strangers or people who know me well
	4	Unable to be understood when speaking with strangers but able to be understood partially by people who know me well
	5	Unable to be understood when speaking to other people (or unable to speak at all)
Ambulation	1	Able to walk around the neighbourhood without difficulty, and without walking equipment
	2	Able to walk around the neighbourhood with difficulty, but does not require walking equipment or the help of another person
	3	Able to walk around the neighbourhood with walking equipment, but without the help of another person
	4	Able to walk only short distances with walking equipment, and requires a wheelchair to get around the neighbourhood
	5	Unable to walk alone, even with walking equipment. Able to walk short distances with the help of another person and requires a wheelchair to get around the neighbourhood
	6	Cannot walk at all
Dexterity	1	Full use of two hands and 10 fingers
	2	Limitations in the use of hands or fingers, but does not require special tools or help of another person
	3	Limitations in the use of hands or fingers, is independent with use of special tools and does not require the help of another person
	4	Limitations in the use of hands or fingers, requires the help of another person for some tasks (not independent even with use of special tools)
	5	Limitations in the use of hands or fingers, requires the help of another person for most tasks (not independent even with use of special tools)
	6	Limitations in use of hands or fingers, requires the help of another person for all tasks (not independent even with use of special tools)
Emotion	1	Happy and interested in life

Table 8.5a Health Utilities Index Mark 3 (HUI3)

Attribute	Level	Description
	2	Somewhat happy
	3	Somewhat unhappy
	4	Very unhappy
	5	So unhappy that life is not worthwhile
Cognition	1	Able to remember most things, think clearly and solve day to day problems
	2	Able to remember most things, but has little difficulty when trying to think and solve day to day problems
	3	Somewhat forgetful, and has a little difficulty when trying to think or solve day to day problems
	4	Very forgetful, and has great difficulty when trying to think or solve day to day problems
	5	Unable to remember anything at all, and unable to think or solve day to day problems
Pain	1	Free of pain and discomfort
	2	Mild to moderate pain that prevents no activities
	3	Moderate pain that prevents a few activities
	4	Moderate to severe pain that prevents some activities
	5	Severe pain that prevents most activities

Table 8.5b HUI3 Canadian scoring algorithms

HUI3 single attribute utility functions

Level	Vision	Hearing	Speech	Ambulation	Dexterity	Emotion	Cognition	Pain
1	1.00	1.00	1.00	1.00	1.00	1.00	1.00	1.00
2	0.95	0.86	0.82	0.83	0.88	0.91	0.86	0.92
3	0.73	0.71	0.67	0.67	0.73	0.73	0.92	0.77
4	0.59	0.48	0.41	0.36	0.45	0.33	0.70	0.48
5	0.38	0.32	0.00	0.16	0.20	0.00	0.32	0.00
6	0.00	0.00		0.00	0.00		0.00	

HUI3 multiattribute utility function on dead–healthy scale

Vision		Hearing		Speech		Ambulation		Dexterity		Emotion		Cognition		Pain	
x_1	b_1	x_1	b_1	x_1	b_1	x_1	b_1	x_1	b_1	x_1	b_1	x_1	b_1	x_1	b_1
1	1.00	1	1.00	1	1.00	1	1.00	1	1.00	1	1.00	1	1.00	1	1.00
2	0.98	2	0.95	2	0.94	2	0.93	2	0.95	2	0.95	2	0.92	2	0.96
3	0.89	3	0.89	3	0.89	3	0.86	3	0.88	3	0.85	3	0.95	3	0.90
4	0.84	4	0.80	4	0.81	4	0.73	4	0.76	4	0.64	4	0.83	4	0.77

Table 8.5b (Continued) HUI3 Canadian scoring algorithms

HUI3 multiattribute utility function on dead–healthy scale

Vision		Hearing		Speech		Ambulation		Dexterity		Emotion		Cognition		Pain	
x_1	b_1	x_1	b_1	x_1	b_1	x_1	b_1	x_1	b_1	x_1	b_1	x_1	b_1	x_1	b_1
5	0.75	5	0.74	5	0.68	5	0.65	5	0.65	5	0.46	5	0.60	5	0.55
6	0.61	6	0.61	6	0.58	6	0.56	6	0.42						

From Furlong et al. (1998), Table 3.

Where x_n is the attribute level and b_n is the attribute utility score

Formula (dead–perfect health scale) $u^* = 1.371(b_1 \times b_2 \times b_3 \times b_4 \times b_5 \times b_6 \times b_7 \times b_8) - 0.371$

Where u^* is the utility of a chronic health state[1] on a utility scale where dead[2] has a utility of 0.00 and healthy has a utility of 1.00.

[1] Chronic states and healthy states are defined as lasting for a lifetime.

[2] Dead is defined as intermediate.

Copyright: Health Utilities Incorporated: www.healthutilities.com. Contact developers for application details and use registration

The HUI instruments can be obtained from the developers for a survey administration fee. Further information can be found at www.healthutilities.com.

The 15D

This scale originally had 12 dimensions and was revised to 15 dimensions (Sintonen and Pekurinen 1993). Further revisions have resulted in the 15D.2, and this is the recommended version for future applications (Sintonen 1994).

Descriptive system   This instrument covers most of the dimensions of any preference-based measure. The dimensions are mobility, vision, hearing, breathing, sleeping, eating, speech, elimination, usual activities, mental function, discomfort and symptoms, depression, distress, vitality and sexual activity (Table 8.6). Each dimension has either four or five levels and hence the classification is able to define many billions of health states. Patients are classified by a self-completed questionnaire where respondents are asked to indicate their level of health on each of the 15 dimensions.

Valuation   Health state values have been estimated from a simple additive formula, where a value is assigned to each dimension level, multiplied by a weight representing the relative importance of that dimension and summed to derive a single index. The valuation of the 15D.2 has been based on the survey of five random samples of the Finnish general population of 500 each (from response rates of 43, 46, 45, 52 and 72 per cent) (Sintonen 1994). The valuation method was a variant of a VAS where respondents are asked to regard the scale as having ratio properties. MAUT was used to estimate an additive function (see spss syntax file in Appendix 8.2).

Permission to use the 15D.2 and its scoring algorithm must be obtained from Professor Sintonen.

EQ-5D

This instrument was developed by a multidisciplinary group of researchers from seven centres across five countries (Euroqol Group 1990). The original version of the instrument was developed from a review of existing health status measures at the time. Kind (1996) has described the process as one where '... researchers principally drew on their own expertise and the evidence available from the literature in order to determine the dimensions of interest'. The aim was to develop an instrument which addressed a 'core' of domains common to other generic health status questionnaires and which reflected the most important concerns of patients themselves. It is the simplest of the instruments and was proposed to be used alongside more specific instruments.

Descriptive system   The original version had six dimensions (the EQ-6D), and this was succeeded by the five-dimensional EQ-5D. The group considered

Table 8.6 15D classification

Attribute	Level	Description
Mobility	1	I am able to walk normally (without difficulty) indoors, outdoors and on stairs
	2	I am able to walk without difficulty indoors, but outdoors and/or on stairs I have slight difficulties
	3	I am able to walk without help indoors (with or without an appliance), but outdoors and/or on stairs only with considerable difficulty or with help from others.
	4	I am able to walk indoors only with help from others
	5	I am completely bed-ridden and unable to move about
Vision	1	I see normally, i.e. I can read newspapers and TV text without difficulty (with or without glasses)
	2	I can read papers and/or TV text with slight difficulty (with or without glasses).
	3	I can read papers and/or TV text with considerable difficulty (with or without glasses)
	4	I cannot read papers or TV text either with glasses or without, but I can see enough to walk about without guidance
	5	I cannot see enough to walk about without a guide, i.e. I am almost or completely blind
Hearing	1	I can hear normally, i.e. normal speech (with or without a hearing aid).
	2	I hear normal speech with a little difficulty
	3	I hear normal speech with considerable difficulty; in conversation I need voices to be louder than normal
	4	I hear even loud voices poorly; I am almost deaf
	5	I am completely deaf
Breathing	1	I am able to breathe normally, i.e. with no shortness of breath or other breathing difficulty
	2	I have shortness of breath during heavy work or sports, or when walking briskly on flat ground or slightly uphill
	3	I have shortness of breath when walking on flat ground at the same speed as others my age

4	I get shortness of breath even after light activity, e.g. washing or dressing myself
5	I have breathing difficulties almost all the time, even when resting
Sleeping	
1	I am able to sleep normally, i.e. I have no problems with sleeping
2	I have slight problems with sleeping, e.g. difficulty in falling asleep, or sometimes waking at night
3	I have moderate problems with sleeping, e.g. disturbed sleep, or feeling I have not slept enough
4	I have great problems with sleeping, e.g. having to use sleeping pills often or routinely, or usually waking at night and/or too early in the morning
5	I suffer severe sleeplessness, e.g. sleep is almost impossible even with full use of sleeping pills, or staying awake most of the night
Eating	
1	I am able to eat normally, i.e. with no help from others
2	I am able to eat by myself with minor difficulty (e.g. slowly, clumsily, shakily, or with special appliances).
3	I need some help from another person in eating
4	I am unable to eat by myself at all, so I must be fed by another person
5	I am unable to eat at all, so I am fed either by tube or intravenously
Speech	
1	I am able to speak normally, i.e. clearly, audibly and fluently
2	I have slight speech difficulties, e.g. occasional fumbling for words, mumbling, or changes of pitch
3	I can make myself understood, but my speech is, e.g. disjointed, faltering, stuttering or stammering
4	Most people have great difficulty understanding my speech
5	I can only make myself understood by gestures
Elimination	
1	My bladder and bowel work normally and without problems
2	I have slight problems with my bladder and/or bowel function, e.g. difficulties with urination, or loose or hard bowels

Table 8.6 (Continued) 15D classification

Attribute	Level	Description
	3	I have marked problems with my bladder and/or bowel function, e.g. occasional 'accidents', or severe constipation or diarrhoea
	4	I have serious problems with my bladder and/or bowel function, e.g. routine 'accidents', or need of catheterization or enemas
	5	I have no control over my bladder and/or bowel function
Usual activities	1	I am able to perform my usual activities (e.g. employment, studying, housework, free-time activities) without difficulty
	2	I am able to perform my usual activities slightly less effectively or with minor difficulty
	3	I am able to perform my usual activities much less effectively, with considerable difficulty, or not completely
	4	I can only manage a small proportion of my previously usual activities
	5	I am unable to manage any of my previously usual activities
Mental function	1	I am able to think clearly and logically, and my memory functions well
	2	I have slight difficulties in thinking clearly and logically, or my memory sometimes fails me
	3	I have marked difficulties in thinking clearly and logically, or my memory is somewhat impaired
	4	I have great difficulties in thinking clearly and logically, or my memory is seriously impaired
	5	I am permanently confused and disoriented in place and time
Discomfort and symptoms	1	I have no physical discomfort or symptoms, e.g. pain, ache, nausea, itching etc.
	2	I have mild physical discomfort or symptoms, e.g. pain, ache, nausea, itching etc.
	3	I have marked physical discomfort or symptoms, e.g. pain, ache, nausea, itching etc.
	4	I have unbearable physical discomfort or symptoms e.g. pain, ache, nausea, itching etc.
Depression	1	I do not feel at all sad, melancholic or depressed

	2	I feel slightly sad, melancholic or depressed
	3	I feel moderately sad, melancholic or depressed.
	4	I feel very sad, melancholic or depressed.
	5	I feel extremely sad, melancholic or depressed.
Distress	1	I do not feel at all anxious, stressed or nervous
	2	I feel slightly anxious, stressed or nervous
	3	I feel moderately anxious, stressed or nervous
	4	I feel very anxious, stressed or nervous
	5	I feel extremely anxious, stressed or nervous
Vitality	1	I feel healthy and energetic
	2	I feel slightly weary, tired or feeble
	3	I feel moderately weary, tired or feeble
	4	I feel very weary, tired or feeble, almost exhausted
	5	I feel extremely weary, tired or feeble, totally exhausted
Sexual activity	1	My state of health has no adverse effect on my sexual activity
	2	My state of health has a slight effect on my sexual activity
	3	My state of health has a considerable effect on my sexual activity
	4	My state of health makes sexual activity almost impossible
	5	My state of health makes sexual activity impossible

The scoring algorithm has been provided by the author in spss (see Appendix 8.2) a dimension for energy, but it was found to have no additional impact on health state valuations (Bjork 1991). The final five dimensions of the EQ-5D are mobility, self-care, usual activities, pain/discomfort and anxiety/depression (Table 8.7a). They each have three levels and together define 243 health states. Patients are classified onto the EQ-5D by a simple one-page questionnaire that can be administered by post or via telephone, or by face-to-face interview. It takes about a minute to complete for the average responder, though older people may take longer. The EQ-5D is normally presented as having a sixth question, the EQ-VAS, but this is not a preference-based measure and has been reviewed as a variant of the VAS valuation technique in Chapter 5.

Valuation   The most widely used scoring algorithm has been estimated from the valuation survey undertaken by the UK Measurement and Valuation of Health (MVH) group at York. They used a variant of the VAS and TTO in an interview survey of 2997 members of the UK general population (response rate 56 per cent). Respondents were interviewed in their own home using TTO and VAS each to value 13 states. In all, 43 EQ-5D states were valued in this way. Regression techniques were used to model these data to estimate additive functions with decrements for the moderate and severe dysfunctional categories of the five dimensions, a constant term for any kind of dysfunction and the term 'N3' for whenever any of the dimensions are severe (Table 8.7b) (Dolan, 1997). Separate UK algorithms are available for different socio-demographic groups.

There has been a number of surveys conducted in other countries to value samples of EQ-5D health states using a VAS rating scale (van Agt *et al.* 1994; Badia *et al.* 1995; Selai and Rosser 1995) and TTO (Tsuchiya *et al.* 2002; Badia *et al.* 2001) and most recently the USA (Shaw *et al.* 2005). The US survey was the largest of these, with over 3773 respondents (a response rate of 59 per cent). The TTO valuations were often found to generate different values from those obtained in the first UK survey, and so this would suggest that country-specific values should be used where possible.

There has also been a valuation using rankings based on an analysis of existing data from the UK and US valuation surveys (Salomon 2003; Salomon and Craig 2005).

The Euroqol Group has placed the EQ-5D in the public domain. For further information, go to www.euroqol.org.

SF-6D

The SF-6D was developed by a team at the University of Sheffield (Brazier *et al.* 1998, 2002*a*) as a means of taking advantage of the most widely used health status measure in the world, the SF-36. The SF-36 was originally developed from the tools used in the RAND Health Insurance Experiment and

Table 8.7a EQ-5D classification

Dimension	Level	Description
Mobility	1	No problems walking about
	2	Some problems walking about
	3	Confined to bed
Self-Care	1	No problems with self-care
	2	Some problems washing or dressing self
	3	Unable to wash or dress self
Usual activities	1	No problems with performing usual activities (e.g. work, study, housework, family or leisure activities)
	2	Some problems with performing usual activities
	3	Unable to perform usual activities
Pain/discomfort	1	No pain or discomfort
	2	Moderate pain or discomfort
	3	Extreme pain or discomfort
Anxiety/depression	1	Not anxious or depressed
	2	Moderately anxious or depressed
	3	Extremely anxious or depressed

From Dolan *et al*. (1995).

Reproduced from Dolan P, 'Modelling valuations for EuroQol health states'. *Medical Care* 35(11): 1095–1108, (1997), with permission from Lippincott, Williams and Wilkins.

has been refined in a series of medical outcomes studies (Ware 2000). The original SF-36 yields scores across eight dimensions and two summary scores. The British team developed the SF-6D health state classification from the SF-36 to make it amenable to valuation. There are two versions of the SF-6D, one based on the 36-item version of the survey (Brazier *et al.* 2002*a*) and the other based on the 12-item version (Brazier and Roberts 2004).

Descriptive system   The SF-6D has six dimensions: physical functioning, role limitation, social functioning, pain, mental health and vitality (Table 8.8a and b). The number of levels per dimension is between four and six, depending on the response choice categories of the original items from the SF-36. The SF-36 version of the SF-6D defines 18,000 states and the SF-12 version defines 7,500 states. These can be derived from 11 items of the SF-36 and seven items of the SF-12, respectively, and from either versions one or two of these instruments.

Valuation   A representative sample of 836 members of the UK general population (response rate 65 per cent) was interviewed and asked to value a total of 249

Table 8.7b EQ-5D scoring algorithm

Full health	1.00
Constant	−0.081
Mobility	
Level 2	0.069
Level 3	0.314
Self-care	
Level 2	0.104
Level 3	0.214
Usual activity	
Level 2	0.036
Level 3	0.094
Pain/discomfort	
Level 2	0.386
Level 3	0.123
Anxiety/depression	
Level 2	0.071
Level 3	0.236
N3	0.269

Reproduced form Dolan P, 'Modelling valuations for EuroQol health states. *Medical Care* 35(11): 1095–1108, (1997), with permission from Lippincott, Williams and Wilkins.

EuroQol time trade-off scores are calculated by subtracting the relevant coefficients from 1.00. The constant term is used if there is any dysfunction at all. The N3 term is used if any dimension is at level 3. The term for each dimension is selected based on the level of that dimension. The algorithm for computing scores is quite straightforward. For example, for state 12123:

Full health	1.000
Constant term (for any dysfunctional health state)	−0.081
Mobility (level 1)	−0
Self-care (level 2)	−0.104
Usual activities (level 1)	−0
Pain or discomfort (level 2)	−0.123
Anxiety or depression (level 3)	−0.236
N3 (level 3 occurs within at least one dimension)	−0.269
Therefore the estimated value for 12123 is	0.187

Copyright: Euroqol group www.euroqol.org

Contact developers for application details and use registration.

Table 8.8a The SF-6D classification (SF-36 version)

Level		
	Physical functioning	
1	Your health does not limit you in *vigorous activities*	
2	Your health limits you a little in *vigorous activities*	
3	Your health limits you a little in *moderate activities*	
4	Your health limits you a lot in *moderate activities*	
5	Your health limits you *a little in bathing and dressing*	
6	Your health limits you *a lot in bathing and dressing*	
	Role limitations	
1	You have *no* problems with your work or other regular daily activities as a result of your physical health or any emotional problems	
2	You are limited in the kind of work or other activities as a result of your physical health	
3	You accomplish less than you would like as a result of emotional problems	
	Pain	
1	You have *no* pain	
2	You have pain but it does not interfere with your normal work (both outside the home and housework)	
3	You have pain that interferes with your normal work (both outside the home and housework) *a little bit*	
4	You have pain that interferes with your normal work (both outside the home and housework) *moderately*	
5	You have pain that interferes with your normal work (both outside the home and housework) *quite a bit*	
6	You have pain that interferes with your normal work (both outside the home and housework) *extremely*	
	Mental health	
1	You feel tense or downhearted and low *none of the time*	
2	You feel tense or downhearted and low *a little of the time*	
3	You feel tense or downhearted and low *some of the time*	

Table 8.8a (Continued) The SF-6D classification (SF-36 version)

Level	
4	You are limited in the kind of work or other activities as a result of your physical health and accomplish less than you would like as a result of emotional problems
4	You feel tense or downhearted and low *most of the time*
5	You feel tense or downhearted and low *all of the time*
	Social functioning
	Vitality
1	Your health limits your social activities *none of the time*
1	You have a lot of energy *all of the time*
2	Your health limits your social activities *a little of the time*
2	You have a lot of energy *most of the time*
3	Your health limits your social activities *some of the time*
3	You have a lot of energy *some of the time*
4	Your health limits your social activities *most of the time*
4	You have a lot of energy *a little of the time*
5	Your health limits your social activities *all of the time*
5	You have a lot of energy *none of the time*

The SF-36 items used to construct the SF-6D are as follows: physical functioning items 1, 2 and 10; role limitation due to physical problems item 3; role limitation due to emotional problems item 2; social functioning item 2; both pain items; mental health items 1 (alternative version) and 4; and vitality item 2.

Table 8.8b The SF-6D classification (SF-12 version)

Level		
Physical functioning		**Pain**	
1	Your health does not limit you in moderate *activities*	1	You have pain that does not interfere with your normal work (both outside the home and housework) *at all*
2	Your health limits you a little in *moderate activities*	2	You have pain that interferes with your normal work (both outside the home and housework) *a little bit*
3	Your health limits you a lot in *moderate activities*	3	You have pain that interferes with your normal work (both outside the home and housework) *moderately*
		4	You have pain that interferes with your normal work (both outside the home and housework) *quite a bit*
		5	You have pain that interferes with your normal work (both outside the home and housework) *extremely*
Role limitations		**Mental health**	
1	You have *no* problems with your work or other regular daily activities as a result of your physical health or any emotional problems	1	You feel downhearted and low *none of the time*
2	You are limited in the kind of work or other activities as a result of your physical health	2	You feel downhearted and low *a little of the time*
3	You accomplish less than you would like as a result of emotional problems	3	You feel downhearted and low *some of the time*
4	You are limited in the kind of work or other activities as a result of your physical health and accomplish less than you would like as a result of emotional problems	4	You feel downhearted and low *most of the time*

Table 8.8b (Continued) The SF-6D classification (SF-12 version)

Level	
5	You feel downhearted and low *all of the time*
	Vitality
1	You have a lot of energy *all of the time*
2	You have a lot of energy *most of the time*
3	You have a lot of energy *some of the time*
4	You have a lot of energy *a little of the time*
5	You have a lot of energy *none of the time*
	Social functioning
1	Your health limits your social activities *none of the time*
2	Your health limits your social activities *a little of the time*
3	Your health limits your social activities *some of the time*
4	Your health limits your social activities *most of the time*
5	Your health limits your social activities all of the time

states defined by the SF-6D using the SG (each respondent valued six states). There were 225 respondents excluded either for failing to value the pits state, producing fewer than two values or producing values without any variation. An SG valuation algorithm has been estimated for the SF-6D by random effects regression methods for the 36-item and 12-item versions (Table 8.8c and see Appendix 8.2 for the spss algorithm) (Brazier *et al.* 2002*a*; Brazier and Roberts 2004). The methods and results of this work have been summarized in Chapter 6.

More recently, a new algorithm has been estimated from the UK SG data using a non-parametric Bayesian approach that has been shown to perform better in terms of predictive ability and overcomes the bias (of underpredicting the better health states) found in the original model (Kharroubi *et al.* 2005). A model has also been estimated from the rank data that was found to generate weights similar to those from SG data (McCabe *et al.* 2006). There have been additional valuations undertaken in Japan (Brazier *et al.* 2006) and Hong Kong (Lam *et al.* 2004). The Japanese valuations were found to be significantly different from the UK valuation results, but the Hong Kong valuation was more similar. Further surveys are planned in Australia and Brazil.

The SF-36 and SF-12 are copyrighted and can be obtained from the Medical Outcomes Trust and Quality Metric. The SF-6D algorithms are readily available and free for non-commercial applications (see www.SF6D.com).

The Assessment of Quality of Life (AQoL)

Hawthorne, Richardson and others developed the AQoL at the Universities of Melbourne and Monash in Australia. On the basis of a literature review, consultations with health professionals and extensive psychometric testing, the team developed AQoL1 with five 'major' dimensions and 15 items (Hawthorne *et al.* 1997). This has been subjected to extensive revision, and the latest version is AQoL2 (Richardson *et al.* 2004).

Descriptive system   The structure of the AQoL differs from the previous preference-based measures in that it has three layers. The AQoL1 has five dimensions, with each dimension having a number of items, and the items having four levels (Fig. 8.1). The five dimensions and their items are illness (prescribed medicines, medication and aids, and medical treatments), independent living (self-care, household tasks and mobility), social relationships (relationships to others, social isolation and family role), physical senses (seeing, hearing and communication) and psychological well-being (sleep, anxiety and depression, and pain) (Table 8.9). A key advantage with this structure is that it uses a number of different items within a dimension. The AQoL2 structure is the same, except that it has six dimensions, 20 items and more

Table 8.8c Scoring for the SF-36 and SF-12 versions of the SF-6D

SF-36		SF-12	
c	1.000	c	1.000
PF23	−0.035		
PF4	−0.044		
PF5	−0.056	PF3	−0.045
PF6	−0.117		
RL234	−0.053		
		RL234	−0.063
SF2	−0.057	SF2	−0.063
SF3	−0.059	SF3	−0.066
SF4	−0.072	SF4	−0.081
SF5	−0.087	SF5	−0.093
PAIN23	−0.042		
PAIN4	−0.065	PAIN3	−0.042
PAIN5	−0.102	PAIN4	−0.077
PAIN6	−0.171	PAIN5	−0.137
MH23	−0.042	MH23	−0.059
MH4	−0.100	MH4	−0.113
MH5	−0.118	MH5	−0.134
VIT234	−0.071	VIT234	−0.078
VIT5	−0.092	VIT5	−0.106
MOST	−0.061	MOST	−0.077

These are the published UK scoring algorithms from Brazier and Roberts (2004). They are going to be replaced by new Bayesian non-parametric algorithms (see Kharroubi *et al*. 2005; see website for further information).

Reproduced from J Brazier and J Roberts, The estimation of a preference-based measure of health from the SF-12, *Medical Care* 42: 851–59 (2004) with permission from Lippincott, Williams and Wilkins.

than four levels. The six dimensions of the AQoL2 and their items are as follows: independent living (self-care, household tasks, mobility), social relationships (intimacy, friendships, family role) and physical senses (seeing, hearing, communication), psychological well-being (sleep, anxiety and depression, pain). Construction of the AQoL2 descriptive system was based on two samples: 143 hospital cases (response rate 90 per cent) and 112 randomly sampled community cases (response rate 78 per cent). Structural equation modelling tested the structure that defines many millions of states.

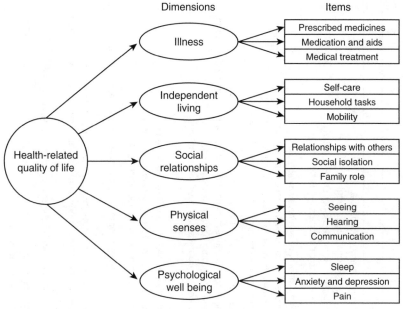

Fig. 8.1 AQoL1.

Valuation   The complex structure of the classification was dealt with by using a two-stage valuation procedure, starting with a valuation of the levels of each item and then combining the items within each dimension using a multiplicative model, and combining the dimensions by effectively a second multiplicative model. The valuation of item levels used VAS transformed into TTO, and then TTO was used to generate values for the corner states and multidimensional states. The 'utility' weights were obtained from a stratified sample of the population of Victoria (Australia) of 353. Initial results have been published in Richardson *et al.* (2004), but the final algorithm for AQoL1 is reproduced in Appendix 8.2.

8.1.3 **Comparison of measures**

In recent years there has been a growing interest in whether these different generic instruments produce the same values for a given population. If they did produce the same scores, then much of the debate about which measure to use would be redundant. Table 8.10 reports on the result of 24 studies published in the last 10 years that compared two or more of the instruments. These studies covered a diversity of populations and interventions.

Table 8.9 Assessment of Quality of Life (AQoL1)

Attribute description	Level	Description
Concerning my use of prescribed medicines	1	I do not or rarely use any medicines at all
	2	I use one or two medicinal drugs regularly
	3	I need to use three or four medicinal drugs regularly
	4	I use five or more medicinal drugs regularly
To what extent do I rely on medicines or a medical aid? (not glasses or a hearing aid) *e.g. walking frame, wheelchair, prosthesis, etc.*	1	I do not use any medicines and/or medical aids
	2	I occasionally use medicines and/or medicinal aids
	3	I regularly use medicines and/or medicinal aids
	4	I have constantly to take medicines or use a medicinal aid
Do I need regular medical treatment from a doctor or other health professional?	1	I do not need regular medical treatment
	2	Although I have some regular medical treatment, I am not dependent on this
	3	I am dependent on having regular medical treatment
	4	My life is dependent upon regular medical treatment
Do I need any help looking after myself?	1	I need no help at all
	2	Occasionally I need some help with personal care tasks
	3	I need help with the more difficult personal care tasks
	4	I need daily help with most or all household tasks
Thinking about how easily I can get around my home and community	1	I get around my home and community by myself without any difficulty
	2	I find it difficult to get around my home and community by myself
	3	I cannot get around the community by myself, but I can get around my home with some difficulty
	4	I cannot get around either the community or my home by myself
Because of my health, my relationships (e.g. with my friends, partner or parents) generally	1	Are very close and warm
	2	Are sometimes close and warm

	3	Are seldom close and warm
	4	I have no close and warm relationships
Thinking about my relationships with other people	1	I have plenty of friends and am never lonely
	2	Although I have friends, I am occasionally lonely
	3	I have some friends, but am often lonely for company
	4	I am socially isolated and feel lonely
Thinking about my health and my relationship with my family	1	My role in the family is unaffected by my health
	2	There are some parts of my family role I cannot carry out
	3	There are many parts of my family role I cannot carry out
	4	I cannot carry out any part of my family role
Thinking about my vision, including when using my glasses or contact lenses if needed	1	I see normally
	2	I have some difficulty focusing on things, or I do not see them sharply, *e.g. small print, a newspaper or seeing objects in the distance*
	3	I have a lot of difficulty seeing things. My vision is blurred, *e.g. I can see just enough to get by with*
	4	I can only see general shapes or am blind, *e.g. I need a guide to move around*
Thinking about my hearing, including using my hearing aid if needed	1	I hear normally
	2	I have some difficulty hearing or I do not hear clearly, e.g. I ask people to speak up, or turn up the TV or radio volume
	3	I have difficulty hearing things clearly, e.g. often I do not understand what is said. I usually do not take part in conversations because I cannot hear what is said
	4	I hear very little indeed, e.g. I cannot fully understand loud voices speaking directly to me
When I communicate with others (*e.g. by talking, listening, writing or signing*)	1	I have no trouble speaking to then or understanding what they are saying
	2	I have some difficulty being understood by people who do not know me. I have no trouble understanding what others are saying to me
	3	I am only understood by people who know me well. I have great trouble

Table 8.9 (Continued) Assessment of Quality of Life (AQoL1)

Attribute description	Level	Description
	4	understanding what others are saying to me
		I cannot adequately communicate with others
If I think about how I sleep	1	I am able to sleep without difficulty most of the time
	2	My sleep is interrupted some of the time, but I am usually able to go back to sleep without difficulty
	3	My sleep is interrupted most nights, but I am usually able to go back to sleep without difficulty
	4	I sleep in short bursts only. I am awake most of the night
Thinking about how I generally feel	1	I do not feel anxious, worried or depressed
	2	I am slightly anxious, worried or depressed
	3	I feel moderately anxious, worried or depressed
	4	I am extremely anxious, worried or depressed
How much pain or discomfort do I experience?	1	None at all
	2	I have moderate pain
	3	I suffer from severe pain
	4	I suffer unbearable pain

Source: Hawthorne et al. 1997. © Graeme Hawthorne and Jeff Richardson. Reproduced with permission.

http://www.acpmh.unimelb.edu.au/aqol/default.html

See Appendix 8.2 for spss syntax file for scoring AQoL1.

Table 8.10 Empirical comparisons of preference-based measures of health

Study measures compared	Preference-based	Population group	Summary of findings Completion	Agreement	Validity
Nord et al. (1993)	EQ-5D, QWB, HUI, Rosser	General population		EQ-5D and HUI were found to give lower values than QWB	
Elvik (1995)	EQ-5D, Rosser, QWB, HUI	Road traffic injury cases (n = 1174).		Poor agreement reported across instruments	Evidence of validity not strong for any instrument, but thought to be better for EQ-5D
Glick et al. (1999)	EQ-5D, HUI2	Subarachnoid haemorrhage (n = 561)		Scores converged. Similar for poorer states, but more different for better states	Concerns about comparability of best states
Bosch and Hunink (2000)	EQ-5D, HUI3	Intermittent claudication (n = 88)		ICC at baseline 0.49. HUI3 0.66 and EQ-5D 0.57 before treatment but similar after treatment. ICC for change 0.30.	Both showed some lack of discriminatory power in this condition, but responsive to change. EQ-5D showed larger gain
Suarez-Almazor et al. (2000)	EQ-5D, HUI2	Low back pain (n = 46)		Moderate correlation between	HUI2 more discriminating at one assessment

Table 8.10 (Continued) Empirical comparisons of preference-based measures of health

Study measures compared	Preference-based	Population group	Summary of findings Completion	Agreement	Validity
				instruments (r < 0.6)	(3 months), but not the other (6 mths)
Hawthorne et al. (2001)	EQ-5D, SF-6D, HUI3, 15D, AQoL	General population (n = 396), out-patients (n = 334) and in-patients (n = 266)		Correlations 0.64–0.80. Largest range of scores given by EQ-5D, HUI3 and AQOL 1 and predicted similar scores, whereas 15D and SF-6D gave higher scores	AQOL, 15D and SF-6D found to be most sensitive (at upper end)
Lubetkin and Gold (2003)	EQ-5D, HUI3	Community health centre (n = 301)		Correlations between scores: 0.69	
Spady and Suarez-Almazor (2001)	EQ-5D, HUI3	Musculoskeletal disease		Moderate correlations. EQ-5D has largest range	EQ-5D most sensitive to change over 12 months
Stavem et al. (2001)	EQ-5D, 15D	Epilepsy (n = 397)		Mean 15D was 0.88 and EQ-5D was 0.81. r = 0.78	Evidence for test-re-test reliability. Construct validity similar for both instruments

Schulz et al. (2002)	EQ-5D, HUI2	Benign prostatic hyperplasia (n = 29)		r = 0.325. EQ-5D has largest range of scores	EQ-5D most responsive over time
Bosch et al. (2002)	SF-6D, HUI3	Intermittent claudication (n = 87)		Both 0.66 at baseline. Correlation over time 0.49	Both responsive after treatment, but HUI3 produced a larger gain
Longworth and Bryan (2003)	EQ-5D, SF-6D	Liver transplantation (n = 524)	Completion rates: EQ-5D 91 per cent versus SF-6D 89 per cent	Baseline EQ-5D 0.517 and SF-6D 0.606	EQ-5D responsive to transplant, but not the SF-6D. SF-6D suffers from floor effects, but more responsive to changes at the top end
Brazier et al. (2004)	EQ-5D, SF-6D	Chronic obstructive airway disease, osteoarthritis, irritable bowel syndrome, low back pain, leg ulcers, menopause, elderly (n = 2436)		ICC 0.51; mean difference 0.045. SF-6D has smaller range and lower variance	Evidence of floor effect in SF-6D (e.g. 26.6 per cent at lowest level of PF and 38.4 per cent of RL) and ceiling effects in EQ-5D (e.g. mobility 40 per cent)
Holland et al. (2004)	EQ-5D, AQOL1	Hospitalized elderly (n = 141)	Completion rates: EQ-5D 81 per cent versus AQOL 65 per cent	ICC 0.55. Baseline EQ-5D range −0.35 to 1.0 and negatively skewed and bimodal versus AQOL of 0.45, 0–1.0 and positively skewed	Authors argued the AQOL had a more favourable descriptive system, but EQ-5D better completion rate, slightly more responsive
Moock S, Kohlman T (2004)	QWB, EQ-5D, HUI2, 15D and SF-6D	Medical rehabilitation (n = 127)	Maximum 3 per cent	Mean scores ranged from 0.52 to 0.81	SF-6D most responsive according to standardized effect sizes: SF-6D (0.56),

Table 8.10 (Continued) Empirical comparisons of preference-based measures of health

Study measures compared	Preference-based	Population group	Summary of findings Completion	Agreement	Validity
					15D (0.36), HUI2 (0.26), EQ-5D (0.12)
Epstein and Marra (2003)	EQ-5D, SF-6D	Neck pain ($n = 139$)		Baseline 0.696 (EQ-5D) versus 0.735 (SF-6D)	EQ-5D found to be insensitive to improvement
McDonough et al. (2005)	EQ-5D, HUI3, SF-6D	Spinal patients ($n = 2097$)		Baseline mean values: EQ-5D (0.39), HUI3 (0.45) and SF-6D (0.57). Correlations: 0.67–0.72	All responsive to improvement, but larger for EQ-5D (0.30) than HUI3 (0.22) and SF-6D (0.11). Floors 1) pain dimension: EQ-5D (38 per cent), HUI3 (24.2 per cent) and 22.4 percent for SF-6D. 2) Physical functioning: 1 per cent for EQ-5D and HUI3 and 11 per cent for SF-6D
Feeny et al. (2004)	HUI3, HUI2, SF-6D	Osteoarthritis ($n = 83$)			All responsive, but size of gain larger for HUI3 (0.23) compared with SF-6D (0.1)
Gerard et al. (2004)	EQ-5D, SF-6D	Older, chronically ill patient group	EQ-5D completion rate was 93 per cent compared with SF-6D of 79 per cent	EQ-5D 0.616 and SF-6D 0.639, but former had larger range and was bimodal	'Performed similarly'

Hatoum et al. (2004)	HUI3, SF-6D	Patients undergoing percutaneous coronary intervention prior to hospital discharge (n = 331)	Completion: SF-6D 91 per cent and the HUI3 97 per cent	SF-6D was 0.67 and HUI3 0.63. r = 0.616 and ICC = 0.4	Both instruments reflected known differences between groups and were responsive between baseline and 6 months, but change was 0.08 for SF-6D and 0.154 for HUI3
Espallargues et al. (2005)	EQ-5D, SF-6D, HUI3	Age-related macular degeneration (n = 209)	Item completion exceeded 95 per cent for all instruments	Baseline scores: EQ-5D 0.72, SF-6D 0.66 and HUI3 0.34	HUI3, and to a lesser extent SF-6D, reflected differences in visual impairment confirmed by patients' own TTO and VAS that were not found by EQ-5D.
Barton et al. (2004)	EQ-5D, HUI3, SF-6D	Hearing impaired adults (n = 609)		Baseline scores: EQ-5D 0.80, SF-6D 0.78 and HUI3 0.58	HUI3 and SF-6D significantly changed after hearing aid provision, but EQ-5D did not. HUI3 estimated largest gain
Stavem et al. (2005)	EQ-5D, 15D, SF-6D	HIV/AIDS (n = 60)		15D gave highest score 0.86, EQ-5D 0.77 and SF-6D 0.73. Lowest score was −0.30, 0.40 and 0.43, respectively. Correlations 0.74–0.80	Similar discriminative properties. Maximal value obtained in 29 per cent cases for EQ-5D, compared with 10% for 15D and SF-6D. SF-6D most responsive to improvement and EQ-5D to worsening (but numbers very small)

Table 8.10 (Continued) Empirical comparisons of preference-based measures of health

Study measures compared	Preference-based	Population group	Summary of findings Completion	Agreement	Validity
Marra *et al.* (2005)	EQ-5D, HUI2, HUI3, SF-6D	Rheumatoid arthritis (*n* = 239)			HUI3 and SF6D appear to be the most responsive, and HUI3 generated the largest magnitude of change
Petrou and Hockley (2005)	EQ-5D, SF-6D	General population (*n* = 16 443)	Completion 97.6 per cent for EQ-5D and 89.6 per cent for SF-6D	Mean EQ-5D score 0.845 and SF-6D 0.799. Bland Altman plots showed lack of agreement, particularly at lower end	SF-6D found to be more 'efficient' at detecting differences

Developed from Bryan and Longworth (2005).

[1] These measures have also been called multiattribute utility scales (MAUS) in the literature (Drummond *et al.* 2005) on the grounds that they have been developed from utility theory. We believe the MAUS terminology may be confused with the use of multiattribute utility theory (MAUT), and while a number of the measures have used MAUT to derive their preference-function, there are a significant number which have not. Another potential source of confusion is whether these are measures of health or measures of the impact of health on quality of life. The descriptive systems differ in terms of whether they are limited to a narrow definition of health that is concerned with impairment or whether they describe health further along the spectrum towards quality of life, including disability and function, through to participation (see Fig. 4.1, Chapter 4). For those who regard participation as a quality of life dimension rather than health, then the descriptive systems are not concerned with health *per se*. However, the purpose of all these measures is to assess the preference-based value of the impact of health on quality of life or well-being in some way, whether or not the impact on quality of life is included in the descriptive system, and so to that extent we believe our terminology is appropriate.

[2] See Appendix 8.1 for a review of a description of the Rosser scale and the Index of Health Related Quality of Life.

[3] $W = 1 + (CPXwt) + (MOBwt) + (PACwt) + (SACwt)$

where: W is the health state score, CPX the worst symptom/problem, MOB the mobility scale, PAC the physical activity scale and SAC the social activity scale (Kaplan 1989).

The agreement between measures was generally found to be poor to moderate (~0.3–0.5 as measured by the intraclass correlation coefficient). Whilst differences in mean scores have often been found to be little more than 0.05 between SF-6D, EQ-5D and HUI3 (Brazier *et al.* 2004*a*; Hatoum *et al.* 2004; O'Brien *et al.* 2004), this mean statistic masks considerable differences in the distribution of scores. A comparison of the SF-6D and EQ-5D across seven patient groups shows this quite clearly (Brazier *et al.* 2004*a*) in a plot of EQ-5D to SF-6D (Fig. 8.1). There is a substantial disagreement between the scores at the individual level, with negative indices on the EQ-5D being associated with values on the SF-6D as high as 0.75. The ranges also differ markedly, with the range for the EQ-5D covering –0.4 to 1.0 compared with 0.3 to 1.0 for the SF-6D. On the other hand, there is a wide range in SF-6D values for those with EQ-5D values of 1.00 (i.e. state 11111). Some of these respondents can have SF-6D values as low as 0.56. There are discrete steps in the EQ-5D values that are most noticeable between those with 1.00 and those less with than 1.00, and at around 0.45 that probably reflects the role of the 'N3' term. Furthermore, the relationship between EQ-5D and SF-6D varied across conditions.

Comparisons of the HUI3 and SF-6D have also found that similarities in mean scores mask major differences in the distribution by severity, with considerable divergence at the lower end (Feeny *et al.* 2004; Hatoum *et al.* 2004; O'Brien *et al.* 2004). Comparisons of EQ-5D and HUI2 and 3 have been mixed, with some finding HUI3 to be higher (Bosch and Hunink 2000; McDonough *et al.* 2005), one finding them to be very similar (Bosch *et al.* 2002) and another finding HUI3 scores to be lower (Barton *et al.* 2004; Espallargues *et al.* 2005). Such variation in findings suggests that differences between these may depend on the characteristics of the patient group. One of the few studies comparing more than three instruments found that QWB, 15D and SF-6D generate higher mean values than the EQ-5D, HUIs and AQoL (Hawthorne *et al.* 2001). Longitudinal differences in estimates of change have been more marked, such as a mean gain from total hip arthroplasty of 0.10 for SF-6D and 0.23 for HUI3 (Feeny *et al.* 2004).

8.1.4 **Do these differences matter?**

While mean differences may seem quite small at around 0.03–0.05, a review by Drummond (1991) suggested a difference of 0.03 to be the minimal value for use in sample size calculations. For the SG task this represents a difference in risk of 3 per cent of death, and for TTO 3.5 months over 10 years. Intuitively these seem important. Empirical estimates of minimally important differences in the quality of life literature, as indicated by a patient reporting a change in their health status, suggested values of 0.04 for SF-6D and 0.075 for EQ-5D

(Walters and Brazier 2005). Such differences are likely to have an important effect on cost per QALY ratios, particularly some of the large differences in estimates of change.

8.1.5 Why do these differences exist?

Given the differences in coverage of the dimensions and the different methods used to value the health states (summarized in Tables 9.1 and 9.2), it is not surprising the measures have been found to generate different values. The likely role of these differences is discussed below.

Coverage of descriptive systems

The scales do not cover the same aspects of health. To begin with, they all include physical functioning, but there are differences in whether the concept is described in terms of capacity (e.g. HUI) or actual behaviour and performance (e.g. QWB). The coverage of symptoms, mental health and social health is variable. The QWB explicitly excludes mental health as a separate dimension, but has a long list of symptoms and problems that includes excessive worry or anxiety. The HUI3 covers some symptoms and a number of key impairments (such as vision and hearing loss), but does not examine role or social function, since these are regarded as 'out of skin' and not appropriate in a measure of individual health preferences (see Chapter 4 for a review of this debate). The SF-6D and EQ-5D have dimensions for role and social function, and pain and mood, but no other symptoms or impairments. Of course, the fact that EQ-5D and SF-6D, for example, do not have dimensions for particular impairments should not matter, provided the impact on health-related quality of life is reflected in other dimensions such as usual activity, role and social functioning. Whether this is the case or not is an empirical issue. The 15D and AQoL cover the most number of dimensions of any generic preference-based measure.

There is little systematic comparative evidence on the impact of coverage and the types of dimensions covered by an instrument. Existing evidence is limited to studies of vision and hearing loss, which found that EQ-5D and SF-6D failed to reflect the impact of these functions as well as HUI3 (Barton *et al.* 2004; Espallargues *et al.* 2005).

Sensitivity of dimensions

The instruments differ considerably in the number of levels in each dimension and the range of severity that they cover. The AQoL, 15D and HUI3, for example, define many millions of states compared with the SF-6D with 18, 000 and the EQ-5D with just 243. However, does this extra size result in different values?

There is some evidence on this question from comparisons of the SF-6D and EQ-5D, where many of the dimensions seem to be tapping the same underlying domains (e.g. EQ-5D mobility and self-care dimensions cover similar concepts to the physical functioning dimension from SF-6D, usual activities is related to role and social activities, pain and distress to pain, and depression and anxiety to mental health). Responses to the SF-6D suggest that physical functioning, role limitations and social functioning dimensions suffer from having a significant number of respondents at the lowest level for patient groups with more severe problems (Longworth and Bryan 2003; Brazier *et al.* 2004*a*). This does not appear to be the case with pain, mental health and vitality dimensions. This 'floor effect' in the SF-6D seems to be reflected in the larger differences between SF-6D and EQ-5D for conditions focused more on physical health problems, such as leg ulcers and osteoarthritis, compared with conditions such as lower back pain and irritable bowel syndrome that are more focused on pain, a dimension that does not suffer from such a floor effect (Brazier *et al.* 2004*a*).

At the other end of the scale, EQ-5D arguably suffers from a ceiling effect, because a large proportion of respondents indicate no problem (i.e. state 11111) and yet many of these respondents report problems on other instruments. The study of seven patient groups found that most people in state 11111 of the EQ-5D had problems according to the SF-6D (Brazier *et al.* 2004*a*). This seems to result in milder problems getting higher mean values according to the EQ-5D than the SF-6D (Epstein and Marra 2003; Petrou and Hockley 2005).

A potential limitation of the EQ-5D, from having three levels per dimension, has been raised in the literature (McDowell and Newell 1996), but there has been little systematic work to examine the consequences of this. There has been some evidence of the EQ-5D being insensitive for some conditions, such as chronic respiratory disease and leg reconstruction, but whether the low number of levels caused this problem was not examined (Harper *et al.* 1997; Burton *et al.* 2002). Indeed there are many more cases where this apparent limitation does not seem to have impaired its sensitivity (e.g. Gerard *et al.* 2004; Marra *et al.* 2005).

Valuation methods

The HUI2, HUI3 and SF-6D used SG; EQ-5D and AQoL used TTO; and 15D and QWB used VAS. These three valuation methods have been shown to generate different values for the same health states. In over 30 studies reporting comparisons of VAS and SG (Brazier *et al.* 1999), SG values consistently exceeded those of VAS in most cases (e.g. Torrance 1976; Bombadier *et al.* 1982; Llewellyn-Thomas *et al.* 1984; Read *et al.* 1987; Bass *et al.* 1994).

A survey undertaken at York found a crossover at around 0.8, with milder health states having lower SG values than the adjusted VAS ratings (Dolan and Sutton 1997). The 18 studies reporting TTO and VAS results found a less consistent relationship, though in the majority of studies TTO values exceeded VAS.

It has been suggested that SG would be expected to generate higher values than TTO due to risk aversion and positive time preference, and this has been supported in a number of studies (Brazier *et al.* 1999). However, a study undertaken in York found evidence for a crossover (Dolan and Sutton 1997). SG props values exceeded TTO props up to VAS values of 0.4, but then there was a crossover with TTO values exceeding SG values. They also found that the difference between TTO and SG depended on the variants of the two techniques being used.

The only empirical attempt to estimate the likely impact of the valuation method on the generic instruments was by Tsuchiya and colleagues (2006). They undertook an empirical study to compare the protocols used in estimating health state values for EQ-5D (TTO) and SF-6D (SG). Respondents were assigned one of the two protocols and asked to value four states each from EQ-5D and SF-6D. TTO values for milder states were higher than SG values, and there was some suggestion that TTO generated lower values for poor states.

Another source of difference could be the use of 'chained' SG values (Brazier *et al.* 2002*a*; Feeny *et al.* 2002), where the intermediate health state is valued against full health and a poorer state, and so the value has to be transformed using the value of the poorer state against full health and dead (see the explanation in Chapter 5 for temporary states). That is, first a set of intermediate health states are valued using perfect health and the worst health state as anchor points. Then the worst state is valued using an SG with the anchor points perfect health and death, and this is used to transform the intermediate states onto the full health–death scale. There is evidence that 'chained' values may be higher than values obtained directly (see review in Brazier *et al.* 1999). This would mean that the values of the SF-6D would be shifted upward compared with the TTO valuation of the EQ-5D that did not use a chained procedure. Finally, the HUI2 and HUI3 did not directly use SG, but a function for mapping between VAS values to SG values, and this has implications for the values generated (Stevens *et al.* 2005).

8.1.6 Which measure should be used?

The choice of generic measure has been a point of some contention, since the respective instrument developers have academic and in some cases commercial interests in promoting their own measure (including one of the authors of this book!). Therefore, it is important to have a clear set of criteria for selecting the best measure. Below we set out the criteria and then compare the measures against them.

Review criteria

The criteria of practicality, reliability and validity are important concerns for assessing the performance of any measurement instrument (Table 8.11). The *practicality* of an instrument depends on its acceptability to respondents and cost of administration (e.g. in terms of time). This can be assessed in terms of how long the instrument takes to administer, method of administration and the proportion of completed questionnaires. *Reliability* is the ability of a measure to reproduce the same value on two separate administrations when there has been no change in health. This can be over time or between methods of administration.

The assessment of *validity*, however, is more controversial. The purpose of a preference-based measure is to reflect preferences *revealed* in real market transactions. Unfortunately, in the field of health care, data on revealed preferences over health states are not available in a useable form for testing validity. Furthermore, this would only tap into one concept of value, namely the extent to which individuals' stated preferences for a state are reflected in their actual decisions. For those interested in using patients' own experience-based valuation of the state (Dolan and Kahneman 2005) or social valuation of a state (as advocated by Nord *et al.* 1993), this would not be appropriate.

Despite these conceptual problems, it is important to examine the validity of a measure, since there is little point in having a practical and reliable measure if it cannot be shown to be measuring the right concept. A three-part approach has been proposed for examining the validity of preference-based measures (Brazier and Deverill 1999). The first part is to examine the validity of the health state descriptive system. This has been described in Chapter 4 in terms of content, face and construct validity of the descriptions of the health state classification used by the measure.

The second concerns the way the health states were valued, including the question of whose values were elicited, the technique for eliciting preferences (and the quality of the data) and the method of extrapolating from the sample of health state valuations to all health states defined by the system. For most generic preference-based instruments, the values have been obtained from a sample of the general population (the exception being HUI2 where the original values were obtained from parents), since this constituency is thought to be most relevant for social decision making.

Where the measures differ is in terms of valuation technique and methods of extrapolation. The main conclusion from the review of valuation techniques

Table 8.11 Checklist for judging the merits of preference-based measures of health

		Components
Practicality		How long does the instrument take to complete?
		What is the response rate to the instrument?
		What is the rate of completion?
Reliability		What is the test–re-test reliability?
		What are the implications for sample size?
		What is the inter-rater reliability?
		What is the reliability between places of administration?
Validity	Description	Content validity:
		Does the instrument cover all dimensions of interest?
		Do the items appear sensitive enough?
		Face validity
		Are the items relevant and appropriate for the population?
		Construct validity:
		Can the unscored classification of the instrument detect known or expected differences or changes in health?
	Valuation	Whose values have been used?
		Technique of valuation
		Is it choice based?
		Which choice based method has been used?
		Quality of data

Is the sample representative?

What is the rate of response and level of missing data

Is there evidence of the respondents' understanding of the task

(e.g. level of logical inconsistency in responses)?

What was the method of extrapolation?

Empirical

Is there any evidence for the empirical validity of the instrument against:

Revealed preferences?

Stated preferences?

Hypothesized preferences?

Adapted from Brazier and Deverill (1999). A checklist for judging preference-based measures of health related quality of life: learning from psychometrics. *Health Economics* 8(1), 41–52. Copyright: John Wiley and Sons Ltd. Reproduced with permission.

presented in Chapter 5 is that for measures purporting to be preference based, then the valuation technique should present a choice-based context, such as SG (where the choice is between a certain and risky outcome) or TTO (where the choice is between some period in a chronic state and a shorter period in full health), rather than VAS which really only asks about a person's feelings rather than their strength of preference. There is, however, considerable disagreement in the health economics literature regarding the appropriateness of TTO compared with SG. The extrapolation of values from the valuation of a sample of health states is also the subject of some debate that is reviewed in Chapter 6, primarily between statistical estimation and an algebraic approach based on MAUT. More evidence is needed on the relative predictive validity of these approaches before it is possible to use this as a means of differentiating between the instruments.

Together these two parts form the basis for instrument validity in theory, but it is important not to lose sight of *empirical validity*, and this forms the third part. There are two tests of the empirical validity of preference-based measures (other than revealed preferences), one based on stated preferences and the other on hypothetical preferences. One test of stated preferences is to administer a preference-based measure alongside another method of preference elicitation, such as another preference-based measure or the ranking of states, and to examine the degree of convergence. Another might be to assess convergence against directly administered TTO or SG, or, as Nord *et al.* (1993) have argued, against social values elicited by the person trade-off (PTO) technique, where the aim is to measure one of these concepts of value. These approaches can provide some support for the validity of a measure against the concept of interest, but never prove validity. For hypothetical tests of validity, the researcher must assume expected differences in preferences (e.g. a patient would prefer a less severe condition and hence it should be associated with a higher score). The hypothesis must be chosen with care, and again cannot be said to prove the validity of a measure.

These criteria have been summarized in a checklist of questions shown in Table 8.11 and are designed to guide a researcher in the selection of a preference-based instrument for an economic evaluation.

The review

This is not a systematic review of all published studies using these instruments, although it does draw on earlier reviews (such as Coons *et al.* 2000; Brazier *et al.* 2004a). Where it uses empirical studies, it focuses on the 24 comparative studies listed in Table 8.10. The results of this review are summarized in Box 8.1.

Box 8.1 Summary of comparison of generic preference-based measures

Generic preference-based measures do not generate the same values for a given group of patients, and this is a consequence of major differences in their respective descriptive systems and methods of valuation (though their relative importance is not clear). This leaves the question of which instrument should be chosen. At the present time, it is possible to argue that the QWB and 15D should not be chosen on the grounds that they are valued using a non-choice-based method (VAS). The decision can be further narrowed by those who strongly favour SG or TTO (though it must be borne in mind that HUI2 and HUI3 do not use SG directly). Another consideration would be the source of values. Although they have all been valued by general population samples, surveys have not been undertaken in all countries, and where a policymaker insists the values come from their own country (as is the case with NICE, 2004), then this will also be an important selection criterion. These may be temporary considerations as instruments become valued in different countries and perhaps using different valuation methods.

Choosing between the instruments is also handicapped by a lack of evidence on the validity of the measures in different patient groups. What does exist suggests that the appropriateness of the descriptive systems varies between patient groups. The HUI2 is the only generic instrument designed for use in children (though there are plans to develop the EQ-5D for children), but there is little evidence on validity. The EQ-5D offers a greater range of scores than the SF-6D and so may be preferred in populations with more severe health problems, but it seems less sensitive for milder problems. The HUI3 seems to perform better for patients with sensory problems. However, the evidence base for these conclusions is weak. It is not possible to select one generic preference-based measure as being superior to the others in all patient groups. The implications of this last conclusion are addressed at the end of this chapter.

Practicality All the generic preference-based measures can be administered using brief and easy to use self-completed questionnaires that are practical to use in most settings. They involve asking between five (EQ-5D) and 36 (SF-6D) questions and take between a few minutes and 20 or so minutes when self-completed. Interviewer-administered versions tend to take longer.

In many studies completion rates were over 95 per cent for all instruments (Table 8.3). However, completion rates for the EQ-5D were found to be significantly better that the longer SF-6D (based on SF-36) and AQoL in two studies with older people (Gerard *et al.* 2004; Holland *et al.* 2004). The completion rate of the SF-6D might be improved by using the SF-12 version and indeed using the SF-6D classification directly (though there is little experience of doing this).

Reliability   Published evidence suggests an acceptable degree of test–re-test reliability across the measures (Brazier *et al.* 1999). Evidence was found of differences between the assessments by patients of their own health compared with that of health professionals using HUI (Feeny *et al.* 1993; Barr *et al.* 1994). Where the aim is to make cross-programme comparisons, this implies that the methods of administering these instruments need to be standardized.

Descriptive validity   The difference in coverage of the instruments has been reviewed above. All instruments are the product of a compromise between comprehensiveness and the need to keep the instrument simple enough for the chosen valuation strategy, namely the valuation of entire health states. All measures exclude dimensions that may be regarded as important for many specific medical conditions. The choice of instrument partly depends on what aspects of health the potential user wishes to cover, and will depend on the disease group and age of the patients being evaluated. The HUI3 may be better suited to study visually impaired patients, for example, than the EQ-5D or SF-6D.

Another aspect of content validity is the sensitivity of the scales. The QWB has just two or three levels in its functioning scale, and EQ-5D just three levels; this would seem to permit little scope for measuring change. However, the developers argue that it is the instrument as a whole that should be judged. It is claimed that the symptom/problem complex list of the QWB, for example, achieves sensitivity by selecting the worst symptoms or problems associated with a given state of ill health. Ultimately the issue of sensitivity can only be assessed empirically using evidence of discriminative validity.

There is evidence that all measures can detect differences in group comparisons, and the scores were significantly correlated with each other and other measures of self-perceived health (Brazier *et al.* 1999). As shown in Table 8.10, scores have been shown also to reflect changes in population health. Despite the 24 studies found to date, there are not enough studies using the measures on the same populations to be able to draw any firm conclusions. Evidence for the AQoL and 15D is even more limited. Furthermore, existing evidence tends to focus on scores rather than the performance of the descriptive systems.

Valuation   The QWB and the 15D can be regarded as inferior to the other preference-based measures due to their use of VAS to value the health descriptions.

HUI2 and 3 would be preferred to the EQ-5D by those who regard the SG as the 'gold standard', but this is not a universally held view in health economics (Chapter 5). A further complication is that the SG utilities for the HUIs have been derived from VAS values using a power transformation that has been criticized in the literature (Brazier *et al.* 1999; Stevens *et al.* 2005).

Most measures were valued by samples of the general population though not all were representative of their countries' populations. Some instruments have been valued by general population samples from one city or region (e.g. QWB and HUI3), and there is some evidence of regional variation (Kind *et al.* 1998). Response rates to the surveys were typically between 50-65 per cent. The role of background characteristics is examined in Chapter 6, but existing evidence suggests that they play a minor role in explaining variation in health state values. Furthermore, it is possible to re-weight the estimates to allow for measurable differences in the sample and the general population (Shaw *et al.* 2005). Of more concern are the characteristics of non-responders that are not typically measured, such as attitudinal variables (e.g. over time preference or risk). There is an accumulating evidence base of variation in health state values between countries (at least in TTO and SG), and this is addressed in Chapter 11.

Empirical validity Comparative evidence on empirical validity is very limited. What there is suggests that the scores produced by these measures can detect expected differences between patient groups and expected changes over time (e.g. Marra *et al.* 2005). The EQ-5D was found to be more responsive than HUI3 (Spady and Suarez-Almazo, 2001) in musculoskeletal disease and was found to be more responsive than SF-6D in liver disease (Longworth and Bryan 2003). However, it was less responsive in rehabilitation patients (Kohlman *et al.* 2005), and in patients with visual impairment and hearing loss where EQ-5D scores did not reflect differences that were picked up by the HUI3 (Barton *et al.* 2004 Espallargues *et al.* 2005). In the study of patients with macular degeneration, there was further evidence from the stated preferences of patients (i.e. own TTO and VAS ratings) that visual impairment had an impact on quality of life, something that was reflected by the HUI3, but not the EQ-5D. Such evidence is difficult to interpret, since its value depends on establishing that the differences or changes over time represent preferences between the states. Furthermore, studies showing one measure to be more 'responsive' than another have to be viewed with some scepticism, since the measure showing a larger difference is not necessarily more valid (see Chapter 4 for a discussion of this issue).

8.2 Mapping or cross-walking from non-preference-based measures onto generic preference-based measures

Key trials or studies often do not use one of the generic preference-based measures, but have used a non-preference-based health or quality of life measure. This situation is far from ideal, but surprisingly common. This section considers how such measures might be mapped onto one of the generic preference-based measures by judgement-based methods (e.g. using panels of experts) or empirically (using a data set containing the non-preference-based measure and generic preference-based measure). These methods could also be used to map between generic preference-based measures.

8.2.1 Mapping using judgement

In this approach, components of a non-preference-based measure of health or quality of life would be assigned by judgement to specific domains and levels of a generic preference-based measure (such as the EQ-5D) (e.g. Coast 1992). For a valid translation process to be possible, the non-preference-based measure must include the dimensions of the preference-based measure (though it may have more) and have items which readily equate to the dimension levels of it. The process can be based on the judgements of professionals or researchers. It can involve the development of an explicit set of decision rules or simply be an aggregation of expert opinion (Bryan and Longworth 2005).

This mapping can be undertaken by dimension or by item. By dimension, a score range would be judged to be equivalent to a given level on a given domain of EQ-5D. For instance, scores in the range 30–50 on the SF-36 pain dimension (see Chapter 2) might be mapped to level 2 on the pain dimension of EQ-5D, or levels 4 and 5 of the SF-6D pain dimension might be mapped onto EQ-5D pain/discomfort level 3. Needless to say, mapping by dimension scores assumes that the items within a given dimension carry equal weight.

Another method is to take some specific health states and to assign these onto a generic health state descriptive system. Gerard *et al.* (1999), for example, identified four states associated with breast cancer screening and used the assessment of patients to map these onto various EQ-5D states. This approach is not feasible for mapping whole measures, but is potentially useful for specific health states (such as those used in economic models).

The main criticism of this approach is its arbitrariness. Furthermore, it does not involve any attempt to estimate the uncertainty around the mapping. This could be overcome by testing the judgements against real data (if there were any) to see whether or not patients who score between 30 to 50 on the pain dimension of the SF-36 report themselves as being on level 2 for pain in

EQ-5D. This ultimately might lead to estimating a relationship between the measures empirically (say by regression), which offers a much better approach to mapping.

8.2.2 Empirical mapping of a non-preference-based measure onto a preference-based generic measure

Introduction

The approach of empirically mapping a health measure onto a preference-based measure is also known as 'cross-walking' or estimating exchange rates between instruments. It requires the preference-based measure and the non-preference-based measure to be administered to the same population. The approach was used by Fryback *et al.* (1993) in the Beaver Dam study and by Nichol *et al.* (2001), both of whom mapped the SF-36 onto generic preference-based measures. Studies have since examined the mapping of condition-specific non-preference-based measures onto generic preference-based measures (Tsuchiya *et al.* 2002; Dixon *et al.* 2003; Brazier *et al.* 2004*b*). These studies have regressed the non-preference-based measure onto the preference-based measure in various ways. A case study of mapping the Asthma Quality of Life Questionnaire onto the generic preference-based EQ-5D is presented in Appendix 8.3.

Published studies mapping between measures have often used a number of limiting assumptions depending on the specification of the model. The simplest model regresses the total QoL score onto the EQ-5D preference index. This is the most limiting specification, since it assumes that the dimensions are equally important (say in the case of the SF-36 where each dimension has the same score), all items carry equal weight and response choices to each item lie on an interval scale. It is possible to relax these assumptions by modelling the following as explanatory variables: dimension scores, item scores or each item response as a dummy variable (though there usually needs to be some method for reducing the number of variables). It is also possible to consider interaction terms. More sophisticated modelling approaches have been using the QoL instrument to predict responses to individual EQ-5D dimensions [Tsuchiya *et al.* 2002 (see Appendix 8.3); Gray *et al.* 2006].

Studies estimating mapping functions have met with varying success. Some of the earlier models tended to be presented without adequate reporting of the performance of the models, so it was difficult to judge them. Those that do present a more thorough testing report some success in terms of predictive validity (Dixon *et al.* 2003; Brazier *et al.* 2004*a*), whilst others have encountered problems (Tsuchiya *et al.* 2002). The mapping of the Asthma Quality of Life Questionnaire (AQLQ) onto EQ-5D showed that it could be done, but the predictions of EQ-5D using the mapping function were associated with a large margin of error and was rather worse at predicting severe states. These problems may have arisen from an inherent skewness in the data, with some levels of severity not well represented in the data set, or it may have arisen from a more fundamental limitation with this approach.

A major limitation of this approach is the assumption that the preference-based measure covers all important aspects of health covered by the non-preference-based measure. In other words, the strength of the mapping function depends on the degree of overlap between the descriptive systems. Where there are important dimensions of one instrument not covered by the other, then this may undermine the model. The generic measure may not cover certain dimensions of the non-preference-based measures that are regarded as important.

Whatever one's view on the role of condition-specific measures of health or other non-preference-based measures, mapping of any kind is only ever a second best to either: (1) using the generic preference-based measure in the trial in the first place or (2) estimating preference weights for the non-preference-based measure (as was done for the SF-36; Brazier *et al.* 2002*a*).

8.3 Deriving a preference-based instrument from the non-preference-based measure

This approach takes an existing non-reference-based measure such as the SF-36, or a condition-specific measure such as the King's Health Questionnaire for urinary incontinence, and develops them into preference-based measures. This has been done with the SF-36 (Brazier *et al.* 1998, 2002), the King's Health Questionnaire (Brazier *et al.* 2005) and the Asthma Quality of Life Questionnaire (Yang *et al.* 2006). The methods for doing this have been described elsewhere in this book (Chapters 4, 5 and 6). The first stage is to derive a health state descriptive classification that is amenable to valuation using a preference elicitation technique; this means selecting a sample of the best items from the original instrument and using them to form dimensions with multiple levels that combine to create health states (this has been described in Chapter 4).

The advantage of estimating a preference-based measure from an existing non-preference based instrument is that it then can be applied to any data set containing the original instrument. Using an existing and established condition-specific instrument may also improve its acceptability to the clinical community. However, existing measures were not designed for this purpose and may prove to be intractable in some cases. At best, the simplification required to produce a health state classification results in a significant loss of information from losing content, and at worst would result in the loss of any advantage in sensitivity over the generic measures.

8.4 **Deriving a new preference-based measure**

A second approach would involve developing a preference-based condition-specific instrument *de novo* (e.g. Revicki *et al.* 1998*a*, *b*). Using an existing instrument may be rather limiting, and designing a bespoke instrument means it may be better suited to the task. There are important issues in the construction of preference-based measures that are detailed in Chapter 4 (see also Brazier and Roberts 2006). To be done properly, it requires a rigorous process of interviewing relevant groups to discover what aspects of health or quality of life matter to them (Coast *et al.* 2006), followed by a careful process of testing and refinement using techniques such as focus groups, cognitive interviewing and psychometrics to develop a final classification system. Such work takes time and can be costly. Furthermore, it cannot be applied retrospectively and so could not be used until it had been used in a number of studies.

8.5 **Valuing vignettes**

This approach involves constructing a vignette or scenario to describe frequently occurring states or pathways associated with a condition and its treatment for respondents to value. The vignettes are usually based on interviews with patients and professionals. They can incorporate a range of information about the condition, the treatment and the long-term profile of health states likely to be experienced. The vignettes can be presented in a more narrative format rather than the abstract descriptions used in the generic preference-based measures (see Chapter 4 for a discussion of this issue). For those wishing to take a more holistic approach to valuing the benefits of health care, vignettes can incorporate such things as temporary states, different sequences of states and risk. This approach can be used to estimate health year equivalents (HYEs) or the valuation of profiles in general, as an alternative to QALYs.

Issues in the construction of vignettes are described in Chapter 4. A key problem is that the linkage of such vignettes to the clinical evidence tends to be weak. Aspects of symptoms, functioning and well-being tend be included in a deterministic fashion and take little account of uncertainty. The distributions around key health parameters found in clinical trials are often lost in a few vignettes. The validity of the content of vignettes and scenarios needs to be rigorously assessed. Furthermore, this approach is less flexible than using structured measures directly in trials, since new vignettes need to be constructed to take into account new evidence. While the construction of vignettes and their valuation can take more time than using structured questionnaires in a trial, it can provide a way to examine the value of different outcomes in the absence of other evidence. It offers a quick alternative where an analyst has no other empirical data.

8.6 **Direct preference elicitation**

Direct preference elicitation is where the patient is asked to value his or her own health using a preference elicitation technique such as TTO or SG. This differs fundamentally from the other approaches reviewed so far where respondents (whether or not they have the condition) are asked to value hypothetical states selected by the researcher. Direct elicitation avoids the need to describe a state of health, since the patient is experiencing it. This has the attraction of avoiding all the problems of poor coverage, insensitivity and lack of meaning associated with many health state descriptive systems.

However, this approach raises some important technical and ethical problems. Patients could be prone to strategic behaviour, in that they may change their valuations in order to influence the result of the trial, though there is little evidence for it in the health care field to date. A more fundamental limitation is that patients may be too ill to complete the instrument in valuation exercises. Tasks such as SG and TTO are cognitively demanding, and respondents may not be able to do them due to their state of health. Furthermore, these tasks can be upsetting to respondents in some situations, such as those with terminal conditions. There are ethical limitations to asking children, very elderly, mentally ill or other vulnerable groups to valuing their own health (particularly those tasks that involve them thinking about their own death).

The valuations of health states by patients in those states have been found to be consistently higher than those obtained from respondents asked to imagine the states. This raises the question of whose values should be used in economic evaluation, and this has been addressed in Chapter 5. Ultimately this is a normative question and not one to be resolved technically.

8.7 **Using values from the literature**

There are now published lists of health state values for a wide range of conditions (e.g. Tengs and Wallace 2000). This literature will grow over time and may offer analysts more opportunities to use existing published values rather than having to obtain new data. This is especially important in populating an economic model, where it may not be valid to draw on the results of one trial. To obtain the best estimate for a model, the parameter values should be obtained from a review of the literature (Drummond *et al.* 2005). A review of the literature for health state values needs to be as systematic as it would be for clinical evidence. The selection of values needs to be justified and reproducible by an independent reviewer and they will need to be analysed appropriately. There is significantly less expertise at reviewing published health state values than clinical data and so this section is far from definitive.

An important starting point is a thorough search of the literature using appropriate terms and ensuring all the main databases are examined (see for example Brazier *et al.* 2002*b*). What is often found is a large array of values available in the literature and considerable variation in the values for what seem to be similar states. A review of values for use in an economic model of osteoporosis, for example, found values for hip fracture to vary from 0.28 to 0.72 and vertebral fracture from 0.31 to 0.8 (Brazier *et al.* 2002*b*). This leaves considerable scope for discretion in the selection of values for an economic model. Methods must be developed for selecting appropriate values for economic models that take account of this variation.

Published values have been obtained using a considerable diversity of methods, similar to those reviewed in this chapter, so it is not surprising that such large differences exist. These values come from studies using different ways of describing health, different valuation techniques and different respondents (including patients and members of the general population). Some have used a recognized generic preference-based measure and others have constructed their own vignettes. The first task for the reviewer is to decide in advance on the appropriate methods. As discussed later in this section, there may be a reference case for determining what instruments can be used, or at least which valuation technique should be used and which source of values. This should reduce the number of useable values.

Values in the literature cannot often be used directly in an economic model without some modification. The aim is to estimate the loss from having a condition and then any impact of the treatment on the mean value associated with a state. In a clinical trial, the impact of the treatment can be estimated as the difference between mean scores in different arms of the trial, and this may provide the correct estimate for the model (see Chapter 10). In the context of an economic model, the analyst is usually looking for values for a finite set of health states. The main outcomes of treatment in the osteoporosis, for example, were reductions in the incidence of fractures, breast cancer and heart disease (Stevenson *et al.* 2005). Health state values in the literature are not usually for the impact of (say) fractures on health-related quality of life; rather they provide values for a population who had recently experienced a fracture. To use these to estimate the impact of a fracture, it is necessary to know what their health state values would have been without a fracture (i.e. the counterfactual). A common assumption is that the loss associated with the fracture is equivalent to 1.0 minus the value in the literature, but this overestimates the value, since people prone to having fractures are likely to be less healthy [a view confirmed in a recent prospective study of hip fractures by Murray *et al.* (2002)]. Some analysts have taken the age/sex norm of the general population to provide values for the control arm, but this only partially compensates for this problem. More accurate estimates of the impact of a condition require large-scale longitudinal studies.

Values published in the literature have usually been collected for another purpose, so patients will probably not be the same as those in the economic model in a number of key respects including age, disease severity, social background or country, or in terms of period of follow-up in the study (usually too short). The values need to be adjusted for the characteristics of the population in the model, such as the age of the population in the model. Ideally, the impact of age and other characteristics would be estimated from the published data, such as a meta regression across a number of studies. This was not possible in the osteoporosis study, so the simplifying assumption was made that the impact on health state values is proportionate to the baseline health state values of patients receiving the intervention (on the grounds that people in poorer health have less to lose), but an equally viable assumption would have been to assume the impact is additive regardless of baseline values. These assumptions need to be replaced with properly adjusted estimates as they become available.

8.8 Implications for decision making

Recent years has seen the increasing use of preference-based measures of health, including different generic measures, those designed for specific groups [such as those for older people (Coast *et al.* 2006), children (Torrance *et al.* 1996) and social care (Netten *et al.* 2002)] and those designed for specific medical conditions. If all these measures are preference based, measured on an interval scale, with the upper anchor at full health (=1) and the lower anchor at dead (=0), then it might be thought that they should generate comparable values for the same patient. However, this does not hold in practice. Even the generic measures for adults have been shown to generate different health state values on the same populations. This is a practical problem for researchers wishing to synthesize evidence from studies that used different instruments. More importantly, it creates problems for policy makers wishing to make cross-programme comparisons, since there is no means of comparing scores generated by different measures.

One solution to cross-programme comparison would be to use one generic preference-based measure in all economic evaluation (Dowie 2002). However, this is not possible for all groups of patients, such as children (where there are special considerations regarding language comprehension and development). It has also been argued that there are special considerations in very elderly people (Coast *et al.* 2006) and for those receiving social care. Furthermore, generic measures of health have been found to be inappropriate or insensitive for many medical conditions. Whether or not these arguments are accepted, the fact remains that different measures have been developed and used and will continue to be developed and used around the world (where there is no international agreement on what measure to use).

Another solution would be to undertake an empirical mapping or cross-walking exercise between the main generic preference-based measures (e.g. Fryback *et al.* 1993; Nichol *et al.* 2001; Gray *et al.* 2006). This would provide a basis for making comparisons. However, evidence from some early work on mapping functions between EQ-5D and SF-6D suggests that separate functions would have to be estimated for different conditions (Brazier *et al.* 2004*a*). More importantly, this approach suffers from the weaknesses identified earlier, that it assumes sufficient overlap between descriptive systems. It assumes that it is appropriate to use all the instruments on the same population, but for the reasons given above this may not be the case. More generally, trying to map between measures in this way seems to miss the point. What is needed is a means of relating the responses on different measures on a common metric and preserving the advantages that each descriptive system may bring.

Comparability could be partly achieved is all the descriptive systems could be valued using an agreed set of valuation methods. The valuation method, for example, needs to be standardized in terms of technique of valuation (and its variant) and source of values. There also needs to be a common yardstick at the very least, that uses common upper and lower anchors (such as best imaginable and worst imaginable, regardless of descriptive system). However, as discussed in Chapter 4, this does not ensure comparability, because there will be focusing effects and preference interactions between those dimensions included in any given descriptive system and those excluded. The problems of focusing could be addressed by specifying more carefully what is happening to dimensions of health not included in the descriptive system being valued. The extent of the problem of preference interactions with excluded dimensions would also need to be examined.

8.9 Conclusion

This chapter has presented a review of different approaches to obtaining health state values, including generic preference measures, condition-specific preference-based measures, vignettes and direct preference elicitation from patients. The decision about approach and, within the chosen approach, the precise instrumentation, should be determined on the basis of practicality, reliability and validity. The choice of valuation methods depends on theoretical preferences for one technique over another, and the source of values is a normative question for policy makers. Selection amongst the instruments depends largely on the validity of the descriptive system, and this relates to the condition and treatment outcomes associated with the treatment being evaluated.

The analyst looking to populate their model needs to understand the main effects of the condition and its treatment on health-related quality of life. There needs to be a rigorous search of the literature for existing values to see whether any of these would be suitable. In many cases they will not, and means must be found of obtaining more appropriate health state values either in clinical trials or in observational studies. If the policy maker for whom the model is being developed does not have any requirement, then the choice of instrument for the study should depend on whether one of the generics is suitable and, if so, which one. If not, then the analyst may want to develop a condition-specific measure or set of vignettes. Of course, the analyst may decide to opt for directly eliciting patient preference elicitation. This chapter provides a basis for making these choices.

For policy makers wishing to make cross-programme decisions, the plethora of approaches and instruments is a cause for concern. For this reason, some agencies (such as NICE) have introduced the notion of a reference case that has a default for one or other of the (usually generic) measures. Given that more than one measure is likely to be used for the foreseeable future, and perhaps for good reason, there is a need for research into mapping between measures using either their descriptive systems and indices or an alternative common metric.

References

Andresen EM, Rothenburg BM, Kaplan RM (1998). Performance of a self-administered mailed version of the Quality of Well-being (QWB-SA) questionnaire among older adults. *Medical Care* 36:1349–60.

Badia X, Fernandez E, Segura A (1995). Influence of socio-demographic and health status variables on evaluation of health states in a Spanish population. *European Journal of Public Health* 5:87–93.

Badia X, Roset M, Herdman M, Kind P (2001). A comparison of United Kingdom and Spanish general population time trade-off values for EQ-5D health states. *Medical Decision Making* 21:7–16.

Barr RD, Pai MKR, Weitzman S, Feeny D, Furlong W, Rosenbaum P, Torrance GW (1994). A multi-attribute approach to health status measurement and clinical management illustrated by an application to brain tumors in childhood. *International Journal of Oncology* 4:639–48.

Barton GR, Bankart J, Davis AC, Summerfield QA (2004). Comparing utility scores before and after hearing-aid provision. *Applied Health Economics and Health Policy* 3:103–5.

Bass EB, Steinberg EP, Pitt HA, Griffiths RI, Lillemore KD, Saba GP, Ohns C (1994). Comparison of the rating scale and the standard gamble in measuring patient preferences for outcomes of gallstone disease. *Medical Decision Making* 14:307–14.

Bjork S (1991). *Euroqol Conference Proceedings*. Swedish Health Economics Institute Discussion paper 1.

Bombardier C, Raboud J (1991). A comparison of health-related quality-of-life measures for rheumatoid-arthritis research. *Controlled Clinical Trials* 12, S243–56.

Bombadier C, Wolfson AD, Sinclair AJ, McGreer A (1982). Comparison of three measurement methodologies in the evaluation of functional status index. In: Deber R, Thompson G, eds. *Choices in health care: decision making and evaluation of effectiveness.* University of Toronto, Toronto.

Bosch J, Hunink M (2000). Comparison of the Health Utilities Index mark 3 (HUI3) and the EuroQol EQ-5D in patients treated for intermittent claudication. *Quality of Life Research* 9:591–601.

Bosch JL, Halpern EF, Gazelle GS (2002) Comparison of preference-based utilities of the short-form 36 health survey and health utilities index before and after treatment of patients with intermittent claudication. *Medical Decision Making* 22:403–9.

Brazier JE, Deverill M (1999) A checklist for judging preference-based measures of health related quality of life: learning from psychometrics. *Health Economics* 8:41–52.

Brazier JE, Roberts J (2004). Estimating a preference-based index from the SF-12. *Medical Care* 42:851–9.

Brazier J, Roberts J (2006). Methods for developing preference-based measures of health. In: Jones A, ed. *The Elgar companion to health economics*. Edward Elgar, Cheltenham, UK. pp. 529–548.

Brazier JE, Usherwood TP, Harper R, Jones NMB, Thomas K (1998). Deriving a preference based single index measure for health from the SF-36 *Journal of Clinical Epidemiology* 51:1115–29.

Brazier JE, Deverill M, Green C, Harper R, Booth A (1999). A review of the use of health status measures in economic evaluation. *Health Technology Assessment* 3(9):1–164

Brazier J, Roberts J, Deverill M (2002*a*). The estimation of a preference-based single index measure for health from the SF-36. *Journal of Health Economics* 21:271–92.

Brazier JE, Green G, Kanis J (2002*b*). A systematic review of health state utility values for osteoporosis related conditions. *Osteoporosis International* 13:768–76.

Brazier JE, Tsuchiya A, Roberts J, Busschbach J (2004*a*). A comparison of the EQ-5D and the SF-6D across seven patient groups. *Health Economics* 13:873–884.

Brazier JE, Kolotkin RL, Crosby RD, Williams GR (2004*b*). Estimating a preference-based index from the Impact of Weight on Quality of Life Instrument (IWQOL-Lite) from the SF-6D. *Value in Health* 7:490–8.

Brazier J, Murray C, Roberts J, Brown M, Symonds T, Kelleher C (2005). *Estimation of a preference-based index from a condition specific measure: the King's Health Questionnaire.* HEDS Discussion Paper 02/05.

Brazier JE, Fukahara S, Roberts J, Kharroubi S, Ikeda S (2006). *Estimating a preference-based index from the SF-36: the case of Japan.* HEDS 06 Discussion Paper, University of Sheffield.

Bryan S, Longworth L (2005). Measuring health related quality utility: why the disparity between EQ-5D and SF-6D? *European Journal of Health Economics* 6:253–60.

Burton M, Walters SJ, Brazier J, Saleh M (2002). Measuring outcome in leg reconstruction and complex trauma—what to use. *Quality of Life Research* 11:660.

Cadman D, Goldsmith C (1986). Construction of social value or utility-based health indices: the usefulness of factorial experimental design plans. *Journal of Chronic Disease* 39:643–51.

Coast J (1992). Reprocessing data to form QALYs. *British Medical Journal* 305:87–90.

Coast J, Flynn T, Grewal I, Natarajan L, Lewis J, Sproston K (2006). *Developing an index of capability for health and social policy evaluation for older people: theoretical and method-ological challenges.* HESG, January 2006.

Coons S, Rao S, Keininger D, Hays R (2000). A comparative review of generic quality of life instruments. *Pharmacoeconomics* 17:13–35.

Dixon S, McEwen P, Currie CJ (2003). Estimating the health utility in adults with growth hormone deficiency. *Journal of Outcomes Research* 7:1–12.

Dolan P (1997). Modeling valuations for EuroQol health states. *Medical Care* 35:1095–108.

Dolan P, Gudex C, Kind P, Williams A (1985). A Social Traits for Euroqol: Results from UK general population survey, Discussion paper, 38, Centre for Health Economics, University of York, York.

Dolan P, Kahneman D (2005). *Interpretations of utility and their implications for the valua-tion of health.* Princeton University, NJ.

Dolan P, Sutton M (1997). Mapping VAS scores onto TTO and SG utilities. *Social Science and Medicine* 44:1289–97.

Dowie J (2002). Decision validity should determine whether generic or condition-specific HRQOL measure is used in health care decisions. *Health Economics* 11:1–8.

Drummond MF (1991). Introducing economic and quality of life measures into clinical trials. *Annals of Medicine* 33:344–9.

Drummond MF, Sculpher M, O'Brien B, Stoddart GL, Torrance GW (2005). *Methods for the economic evaluation of health care programmes.* Oxford Medical Publications, Oxford.

Elvik R (1995). The validity of using health state indexes in measuring the consequences of traffic injury for public health. *Social Science and Medicine* 40:1385–98.

Epstein D, Marra A (2003). A comparison of the SF-6D and the EQ-5D: how does the choice of health outcome measure matter? Presented at the Health Economists Study Group, July 2003.

Espallargues M, Czoski-Murray C, Bansback N, Carlton J, Lewis G, Hughes L, Brand C, Brazier J (2005). The impact of age related macular degeneration on health state utility values. *Investigative Ophthalmology and Visual Science* 46:4016–23.

Euroqol group (1990). Euroqol—a new facility for the measurement of health-related quality-of-life. *Health Policy* 16:199–208.

Fanshel S, Bush J (1970). A health status index and its application to health service outcomes. *Operations Research* 18:1021–66.

Feeny D, Leiper A, Barr RD, Furlong W, Torrance GW, Rosenbaum P, Weitzman S (1993). The comprehensive assessment of health status in survivors of childhood cancer: application to high-risk acute lymphoblastic leukaemia. *British Journal of Cancer* 67:1047–52.

Feeny DH, Furlong WJ, Torrance GW, Goldsmith CH, Zenglong Z, Depauw S, Denton M, Boyle M (2002). Multiattribute and single-attribute utility function: the Health Utility Index Mark 3 system. *Medical Care* 40:113–28.

Feeny D, Wu L, Eng K (2004). Comparing short form 6D, standard gamble, and health utilities index Mark 2 and Mark 3 utility scores: results from total hip arthroplasty patients. *Quality of Life Research* 13:1659–70.

Fryback DG, Dasbach EJ, Klein R, Klein BE, Dorn N, Peterson K, Martin PA (1993). The Beaver Dam Health Outcomes Study: initial catalog of health-state quality factors. *Medical Decision Making* 13:89–102.

Furlong W, Feeny D, Torrance GW, Goldsmith CH, Zenglong Z, Depauw S, Denton M, Boyle M (1998). Multiplicative multi-attribute utility function for the health utilities index mark 3 (HUI 3) system: A technical report (CHEPA working paper no. 98/11). McMatser University, Centre for Health Economics and Policy, Hamilton, Ontario.

Gerard K, Johnstone K, Brown J (1999). The role of a pre-scored multiattribute health state classification in validating condition specific health state descriptions. *Health Economics* 8:685–99.

Gerard K, Nicholson T, Mullee M, Mehta R, Roderick P (2004). EQ-5D versus SF-6D in an older, chronically ill patient group. *Applied Health Economics and Health Policy* 3:91–102.

Glick H, Polsky D, Willke R, Schulman K (1999). A comparison of preference assessment instruments used in a clinical trial: responses to the visual analog scale from the EuroQol EQ-5D and the Health Utilities Index. *Medical Decision Making* 19:265–74.

Gray AM, Rivero-Arias O, Clarke PM (2006). Estimating the association between SF-12 responses and EQ-5D utility values by response mapping. *Medical Decision Making* 26:18–29.

Gudex C, Kind P (1988). *The QALY toolkit.* Centre for Health Economics Discussion Paper 93, University of York.

Gudex C, Kind P, van Dalen H, Durand M-A, Morris J, Williams A (1993). *Comparing scaling methods for health state valuations: Rosser revisited.* Centre for Health Economics Discussion Paper 107, University of York.

Harper R, Brazier JE, Waterhouse JC, Walters SJ, Jones NMB, Howard P (1997). A comparison of outcome measures for patients with chronic obstructive pulmonary disease (COPD) in an outpatient setting *Thorax* 52:879–87

Hatoum H, Brazier JE, Ahkras K (2004). Comparison of the HUI3 with the SF-36 preference based single index in a clinical setting. *Value in Health* 7:602–9.

Hawthorne G, Richardson J, Osborne R, McNeil H (1997). *The Australian Quality of Life (AQoL) instrument.* Monash University Working Paper 66.

Hawthorne G, Richardson J, Day NA (2001). A comparison of the assessment of quality of life (AQoL) with four other generic utility instruments. *Annals of Internal Medicine* 33:358–70.

Holland R, Smith RD, Harvey I, Swift L, Lenaghan E (2004). Assessing quality of life in the elderly: a direct comparison of the EQ-5D and AQoL. *Health Economics* 13:793–805.

Kaplan RM (1989). Health outcome models for policy analysis. *Health Psychology* 8:723–35.

Kaplan RM (1994). Using quality-of-life information to set priorities in health-policy. *Social Indicators Research* 33:121–63.

Kaplan RM, Anderson JP (1988). A general health policy model: update and application. *Health Services Research* 23:203–35.

Kaplan RM, Bush JW, Berry CC (1976). Health status: types of validity and the index of well-being. *Health Services Research* 11:478–507.

Kharroubi SA, O'Hagan A, Brazier JE (2005). Estimating utilities from individual health preference data: a nonparametric Bayesian method. *Applied Statistics* 54:879–95.

Kind P (1996). The Euroqol instrument: an index of health-related quality of life. In: Spilker B, ed. *Quality of life and pharmacoeconomics in clinical trials*, 2nd edn. Lippincott-Rivera, Philadelphia, PA, pp. 191–201.

Kind P, Dolan P, Gudex C, Williams A (1998). Variations in population health status: results from a United Kingdom national questionnaire survey. *British Medical Journal* 316:736–41.

Moock J, Kohlman T (2004). Comparing the EQ-5D, SF-6D, HU12, QWB-5A and 15D: which measure can be recommended for use in the German System of medical rehabilitation. Proceeded of WH Meeting @ the Euroqol Group, Chicago, USA. Available at www.Euroqol.org.

Lam C, Brazier J, McGhee S (2004). Feasibility, reliability and validity of valuation of the SF-6D health states in a Chinese. *Quality of Life Research* 13(9):1509.

Le Gales C, Buron C, Costet N, Rosman S (2002). Development of preference-wieghted health status clasifiction system in France: the Health Utilities Index 3. *Health Care Management Science* 5:41–51.

Llewellyn-Thomas H, Sutherland HJ, Tibshirani R, Ciampi A, Till JE, Boyd NF (1984). Describing health states: methodological issues in obtaining values for health states. *Medical Care* 22:543–52.

Longworth L, Bryan S (2003). An empirical comparison of EQ-5D and SF-6D in liver transplantation patients. *Health Economics* 12:1061–7.

Lubetkin EI, Gold MR (2003). Areas of decrement in health-related quality of life (HRQL): comparing the SF-12, EQ-5D, and HUI 3. *Quality of Life Research* 12:1059–67.

Macran S, Kind P (1999). Valuing EQ-5D health states using a modified MVH protocol: preliminary results. In: Badia X, Herdman M, Roset M, eds. *Proceedings of the Euroqol Plenary Meeting 1999*. Sitges, 6–9 November 1999.

Marra CA, Woolcott JC, Kopec JA, Shojania KI, Offer R, Brazier JE, Esdaile JM, Anis AH (2005). A comparison of generic, indirect utility measures (the HU12, HU13, SF-6D, and the EQ-5D) and disease-specific instruments (the RAQoL and the HAQ) in rheumatoid arthritis. *Social Science and Medicine* 60:1571–82.

McCabe C, Stevens K, Roberts J, Brazier JE (2005*a*). Health state values from the HUI-2 descriptive system: results from a UK survey. *Health Economics* 14:231–44.

McCabe C, Stevens K, Brazier J, Roberts J (2005*b*). Multi-attribute utility function or statistical inference models: a comparison of health state valuation models using the HUI2 health state classification system. Presentation at iHEA 5th World Congress, Barcelona, Spain, July 2005. www.shef.ac.uk/scharr/section/heds/ihea2005.

McCabe C, Brazier J, Gilks P, Tsuchiya A, Roberts J, O'Hagan A, Stevens K (2006). Estimating population cardinal health state valuation models from individual ordinal (rank) health state preference data. *Journal of Health Economics* 25:418–31.

McDonough CM, Grove MR, Tosteson TD, Lurie JD, Hilibrand AS, Tosteson ANA (2005). Comparison of EQ-5D, HUI, and SF-36-derived societal health state values among spine patient outcomes research trial (SPORT) participants. *Quality of Life Research* 14:1321–32.

McDowell I, Newell C (1996). *Measuring health: a guide to rating scales and questionnaires.* Oxford University Press, Oxford.

Murray C, Brazier J, Walters S (2002). Utility following a fracture in a group of elderly women. *Quality of Life Research* 11: 642.

National Institute for Health and Clinical Excellence (NICE) (2004). *Guide to the methods of technology appraisal.* National Health Service, London.

Netten A, Ryan M, Smith P, Skatun D, Healey A, Knapp A, Wykes (2005). *The development of a measure of social care outcomes for older people.* DP 1690/2, Personal Social Services Research Unit, Canterbury, University of Kent. http://www.ukc.ac.uk/pssru

Nichol MB, Sengupta N, Globe DR (2001). Evaluating quality-adjusted adjusted life years: estimation of the health utility index (HUI2) from the SF-36. *Medical Decision Making* 21:105–12.

Nord E, Richardson J, Macarounas Kirchmann K (1993). Social evaluation of health care versus personal evaluation of health states. Evidence on the validity of four health-state scaling instruments using Norwegian and Australian surveys. *International Journal of Technology Assessment in Health Care* 9:463–78.

O'Brien BJ, Spath M, Blackhouse G, Severens JL, Brazier JE (2004). A view from the bridge: agreement between the SF-6D utility algorithm and the health utilities index. *Health Economics* 12:975–82.

Patrick DL, Bush JW, Chen MM (1973). Methods for measuring levels of well-being for a health status index. *Health Services Research* 8:228–45.

Petrou S, Hockley C (2005). An investigation into the empirical validity of the EQ-5D and SF-6D based on hypothetical preferences in a general population. *Health Economics* 14:1169–1189.

Read JL, Quinn RJ, Hoefer MA (1987). Measuring overall health: an evaluation of three important approaches. *Journal of Chronic Disease* 40 Supplement 1:7S–26S.

Revicki DA, Leidy NK, Brennan-Diemer F, Sorenson S, Togias A (1998*a*). Integrating patients' preferences into health outcomes assessment: the multi-attribute asthma symptom utility index. *Chest* 114:998–1007.

Revicki DA, Leidy NK, Brennan-Diemer F, Thompson C, Togias A (1998*b*). Development and preliminary validation of multi-attribute rhinitis symptom utility index. *Chest* 114:693–702.

Richardson J, Atherton Day N, Peacock S, Iezzi A (2004). Measurement of the quality of life for economics evaluation and the Assessment of Quality of Life (AQoL) Mark 2 instrument. *The Australian Economic Review* 37:62–88.

Rosser RM, Kind P (1978). A scale of valuations of states of illness: is there a social consensus? *International Journal of Epidemiology* 7:347–58.

Rosser RM, Watts VC (1972). The measurement of hospital output. *International Journal of Epidemiolology* 1:361–8.

Rosser R, Allison R, Butler C, Cottee M, Rabin R, Selai C (1993). The Index of Health-related Quality of Life (IHQL): a new tool for audit and cost-per-QALY analysis. In: Walker SR, Rosser RM, eds. *Quality of life assessment: key issues in the 1990s.* pp. 179–184. Kluwer Academic Publishers, Dordrecht, Netherlands.

Salomon JA (2003). Reconsidering the use of rankings in the valuation of health states: a model for estimating cardinal values from ordinal data. *Population Health Metrics* 1:12.

Salomon JA, Craig BR (2005). *Estimating health state valuation functions based on ordinal data: findings from the US EQ-5D study*. International Health Economics Association 5th World Congress, July 2005, Barcelona, Spain.

Schulz M, Chen J, Woo H, Keech M, Watson M, Davey P (2002). A comparison of techniques for eliciting patient preferences in patients with benign prostatic hyperplasia. *Journal of Urology* 168:155–9.

Selai C, Rosser R (1995). Eliciting Euroqol descriptive data and utility scale values from inpatients—a feasibility study. *PharmacoEconomics* 8:147–58.

Shaw JK, Johnson JA, Coons SJ (2005). US valuation of the EQ-5D health states: development and testing of the D1 model. *Medical Care* 43:203–20.

Sintonen H (1994) *The 15D measure of HRQoL: reliability, validity, and the sensitivity of it's health state descriptive system*. NCFPE Working paper 41, Monash University/The University of Melbourne.

Sintonen H, Pekurinen M (1993). A fifteen-dimensional measure of health-related quality of life (15D) and its applications. In: Anonymous, *Quality of life assessment: key issues in the 1990s.* pp. 185–195. Kluwer Academic Publishers, Dordrecht, Netherlands.

Sloan J, Symonds T, Vargas-Chanes D, Fridley B (2003). Practical guidelines for assessing the clinical significance of health-related quality of life changes within clinical trials. *Drug Information Journal* 37:23–31.

Spady B, Suarez-Almazor M (2001). *A comparison of preference-based health status tools in patients with msculosketal disease*. Proceedings of the 18th Plenary Meeting of the Euroqol Group.

Stavem K, Bjornaes H, Lossius M (2001). Properties of the 15D and EQ-5D utility measures in a community sample of people with epilepsy. *Epilepsy Research* 44:179–89.

Stavem K, Fr⁻land SS, Hellum KB (2005). Comparison of preference-based utiltities of the 15D, EQ-5D and SF-6D in patients with HIV/AIDS. *Quality of Life Research* 14:971–80.

Stevens KJ, McCabe CJ, Brazier JE (2005). Mapping between visual analogue and standard gamble data; results from the UK Health Utilities Index 2 valuation. *Health Economics* 15:527–34.

Stevenson MD, Brazier JE, Calvert NW, Lloyd-Jones M, Oakley J, Kanis JA (2005). Description of an individual patient methodology for calculating the cost-effectiveness of treatments for osteoporosis in women. *Journal of the Operational Research Society* 56:214–21.

Suarez-Almazor M, Kendall C, Johnson SK, Vincent D (2000). Use of health status measures in patients with low back pain in clinical settings. Comparison of specific, generic and preference-based instruments. *Rheumatology (Oxford)* 39:783–90.

Tengs TO, Wallace A (2000). One thousand health-related quality-of-life estimates. *Medical Care* 38:583–637.

Torrance GW (1976). Social preferences for health states: an empirical evaluation of three measurement techniques. *Socio-Economic Planning Sciences* 10:129–36.

Torrance GW (1982). Multi-attribute utility theory as a method of measuring social preferences for health states in long-term care. In: Kane RL, Kane RA, eds. *Values in long-term care.* Lovington Books, DC Heath & Co., pp. 127–156.

Torrance GW (1986). Measurement of health state utilities for economic appraisal: a review. *Journal of Health Economics* 5:1–30.

Torrance GW, Boyle MH, Horwood SP (1982). Applications of multi-attribute utility theory to measure social preferences for health states. *Operations Research* 30:1043–69.

Torrance GW, Feeny DH, Furlong WJ, Barr RD, Zhang Y, Wang Q (1996). A multi-attribute utility function for a comprehensive health status classification system: Health Utilities Mark 2. *Medical Care* 34:702–22

Tsuchiya A, Brazier J, McColl E, Parkin D (2002). *Deriving preference-based condition-specific instruments: converting AQLQ into EQ-5D indices.* Sheffield Health Economics Group Discussion Paper 02/01, School of Health and Related Research, University of Sheffield.

Tsuchiya A, Brazier JE, Roberts J (2006). Comparison of valuation methods used to generate the EQ5D and the SF6D value sets in the UK. *Journal of Health Economics* 25:334–46.

van-Agt HM, Essink-Bot ML, Krabbe PF, Bonsel GJ (1994). Test–retest reliability of health state valuations collected with the EuroQol questionnaire. *Social Science and Medicine* 39:1537–44.

Ware JE (2000). SF-36 health survey update. *Spine* 25:3130–9.

Walters S, Brazier JE (2005). Comparison of the minimally important difference for two health state measures: EQ-5D and SF-6D. *Quality of Life Research* 14:1523–32.

Williams A (1995). *The role of the Euroqol instrument in QALY calculations. DP130.* Centre for Health Economics, University of York

Yang Y, Tsuchiya A, Brazier J, Young Y (2006). *Deriving a preference-based measure for health from the AQLQ.* HESG, City University.

Appendix 8.1 Rosser disability/distress scale

This classification was developed by Rosser and others in the 1970s as a measure of hospital output (Rosser and Watts 1972; Rosser and Kind 1978), and in the 1980s it became the most widely used instrument for deriving QALYs in the UK. The content of the classification has remained largely unaltered, though different methods of administration have been developed, including a self-completed version.

The classification has two dimensions, disability and distress, with eight and four levels, respectively. The disability dimension has descriptions for each level, for example level three is 'Severe social disability and/or slight impairment of performance at work. Able to do all housework except very heavy tasks', whereas the four distress levels are simply none, mild, moderate and severe. Together the two dimensions define a total of 29 health states (the matrix defines 32 states, but the worst level of disability is unconsciousness and hence there is no distinction between the four states defined by the different levels of distress). Patients were originally classified by clinician assessment. A self-completed instrument called the Health Measurement Questionnaire (HMQ) has also been developed (Gudex and Kind 1988).

The most commonly used weights were obtained by Rosser and her colleagues from 70 respondents using a version of magnitude estimation (Kind *et al*, 1982). The classification has since been revalued by a larger, general population sample using magnitude estimation, visual analogue scaling and time trade-off (Gudex *et al*. 1993). These methods produced different values, and the authors recommend a matrix of weights based on a synthesis of the results.

This instrument was widely used in the 1980s, but has largely fallen into disuse with the development of alternatives, such as the EQ-5D.

Index of Health related Quality of Life

The Index of Health related Quality of Life (IHQL) was developed by Rosser and colleagues from the disability/distress classification (Rosser *et al*. 1992, 1993). In the first stage of its development, distress was subdivided into physical discomfort and emotional distress. This '3-D' version defines 175 composite health states. The three dimensions have been further divided into seven attributes and these in turn into 44 scales. The scales have been divided into 107 descriptors, which in total have 225 levels. This hierarchical classification of the IHQL defines many millions of states. The 3D has been valued using SG, and a matrix of health state values has been published in an edited volume (Rosser *et al*. 1992). The IHQL was valued using VAS and provisional results presented in the same volume.

Descriptions of the methods of valuation have not been published elsewhere and it has not been possible to review this work critically on the basis of what is available. No applications were found in peer-reviewed journals from an extensive search of the literature (Brazier *et al.* 1999).

Appendix 8.2 SPSS scoring algorithms provided by developers of the 15D and AQoL1

These scoring algorithms have been reproduced in good faith, but the authors accept no responsibility for any remaining errors. Researchers wishing to use them should check the relevant instrument website (see text) or and obtain permission from the developer.

15D

```
COMPUTE MOVE1=MOVE.
COOMPUTE SEE1=SEE.
COMPUTE HEAR1=HEAR.
COMPUTE BREATH1=BREATH.
COMPUTE SLEEP1=SLEEP.
COMPUTE EAT1=EAT.
COMPUTE SPEECH1=SPEECH.
COMPUTE ELIM1=ELIM.
COMPUTE UACT1=UACT.
COMPUTE MENTAL1=MENTAL.
COMPUTE DISCO1=DISCO.
COMPUTE DEPR1=DEPR.
COMPUTE DISTR1=DISTR.
COMPUTE VITAL1=VITAL.
COMPUTE SEX1=SEX.
RECODE MOVE1 (1=1) (2=0.7129) (3=0.4729) (4=0.2526) (5=0.0780).
RECODE SEE1 (1=1) (2=0.7840) (3=0.4901) (4=0.3137) (5=0.1089).
RECODE HEAR1 (1=1) (2=0.7497) (3=0.4611) (4=0.2353) (5=0.1003).
RECODE BREATH1 (1=1) (2=0.6976) (3=0.4771) (4=0.2581) (5=0.0879).
RECODE SLEEP1 (1=1) (2=0.7615) (3=0.5124) (4=0.3015) (5=0.1115).
RECODE EAT1 (1=1) (2=0.6462) (3=0.4267) (4=0.1984) (5=0.0710).
RECODE SPEECH1 (1=1) (2=0.7033) (3=0.4322) (4=0.2471) (5=0.1298).
RECODE ELIM1 (1=1) (2=0.6845) (3=0.3958) (4=0.1764) (5=0.0558).
RECODE UACT1 (1=1) (2=0.7210) (3=0.4133) (4=0.2182) (5=0.0785).
RECODE MENTAL1 (1=1) (2=0.6434) (3=0.3750) (4=0.1956) (5=0.0489).
RECODE DISCO1 (1=1) (2=0.7024) (3=0.3960) (4=0.2083) (5=0.0617).
```

```
RECODE DEPR1 (1=1) (2=0.7651) (3=0.5148) (4=0.3053) (5=0.1576).
RECODE DISTR1 (1=1) (2=0.7251) (3=0.4786) (4=0.2633) (5=0.1255).
RECODE VITAL1 (1=1) (2=0.7713) (3=0.5152) (4=0.2957) (5=0.1253).
RECODE SEX1 (1=1) (2=0.7095) (3=0.4424) (4=0.2486) (5=0.1318).
COMPUTE MOVE2=MOVE.
COMPUTE SEE2=SEE.
COMPUTE HEAR2=HEAR.
COMPUTE BREATH2=BREATH.
COMPUTE SLEEP2=SLEEP.
COMPUTE EAT2=EAT.
COMPUTE SPEECH2=SPEECH.
COMPUTE ELIM2=ELIM.
COMPUTE UACT2=UACT.
COMPUTE VITAL2=VITAL.
COMPUTE MENTAL2=MENTAL.
COMPUTE DISCO2=DISCO.
COMPUTE DEPR2=DEPR.
COMPUTE DISTR2=DISTR.
COMPUTE SEX2=SEX.
RECODE MOVE2 (1=0.0704) (2=0.0440) (3=0.0236) (4=0.0104) (5=0.0027).
RECODE SEE2 (1=0.0518) (2=0.0444) (3=0.0309) (4=0.0210) (5=0.0078).
RECODE HEAR2 (1=0.0590) (2=0.0540) (3=0.0401) (4=0.0232) (5=0.0106).
RECODE BREATH2 (1=0.0839) (2=0.0562) (3=0.0373) (4=0.0195)
(5=0.0065).
RECODE SLEEP2 (1=0.0695) (2=0.0555) (3=0.0391) (4=0.0239) (5=0.0091).
RECODE EAT2 (1=0.0707) (2=0.0384) (3=0.0224) (4=0.0090) (5=0.0029).
RECODE SPEECH2 (1=0.0664) (2=0.0459) (3=0.0277) (4=0.0156)
(5=0.0081).
RECODE ELIM2 (1=0.0615) (2=0.0379) (3=0.0196) (4=0.0080) (5=0.0024).
RECODE UACT2 (1=0.0760) (2=0.0515) (3=0.0274) (4=0.0137) (5=0.0048).
RECODE VITAL2 (1=0.0756) (2=0.0596) (3=0.0408) (4=0.0239) (5=0.0111).
RECODE MENTAL2 (1=0.0852) (2=0.0445) (3=0.0214) (4=0.0096)
(5=0.0021).
RECODE DISCO2 (1=0.0624) (2=0.0395) (3=0.0198) (4=0.0096) (5=0.0027).
RECODE DEPR2 (1=0.0520) (2=0.0458) (3=0.0350) (4=0.0229) (5=0.0125).
RECODE DISTR2 (1=0.0610) (2=0.0487) (3=0.0347) (4=0.0203) (5=0.0101).
RECODE SEX2 (1=0.0546) (2=0.0489) (3=0.0363) (4=0.0228) (5=0.0128).
COMPUTE D15SCORE=MOVE2+SEE2+HEAR2+BREATH2+SLEEP2+EAT2
+SPEECH2+ELIM2+UACT2+VITAL2+MENTAL2+DISCO2
+DEPR2+DISTR2+SEX2.
```
Execute.

AQoL1 soring algorithm

```
*** REM This file analyses the AQoL and produces utilities for each
dimension ***
*** and the instrument overall. ***
*** REM The AQoL uses D2, D3, D4 & D5 ***
*** when calculating the utilities, ***
*** although dimension values are calculated for D1. ***
*** REM The dimensions are scaled on a ***
*** 'Dimension Worst Health State-Dimension Best Health State'
scale***
*** where DWHS = 0.00 and DBHS = 1.00. ***
*** These are not strict utility values as they have not been
evaluated on ***
*** a life-death scale. ***
*** REM The AQoL utility scores are scaled such that the: ***
*** 'AQoL worst health state' = -0.04 (i.e. this is worse than
Death, where ***
*** Death = 0.00). ***
*** 'AQoL best health state' = 1.00 (i.e. this is good HRQoL) ***
*** REM Copyright. Version 3. Release date: September 1999. ***
*** REM Version 3 is an interim release which replaces Versions 1 &
2. ***
*** This version will increase utility scores by about 3% ***
*** at the bottom end of the utility scale when compared with
Version 1. ***
*** REM Note that missing data are handled by imputing values within
each ***
*** dimension. Regression analysis should not be used because this
may ***
*** violate the statistical independence of each dimension and
result in ***
*** double-counting. ***
*** REM THIS IS AN INTERIM RELEASE WHICH IS SUBJECT TO REVISION
WITHOUT
NOTICE. ***
*** REM RESEARCHERS SHOULD CHECK WITH THE AQOL TEAM FOR SUBSEQUENT
MODIFICATION ***
*** REM Note: 'AQoL1' etc. are the variables in your questionnaire
or database; ***
```

```
*** you will need to replace these with your variable names. ***
*** This only applies to the first 15 COMPUTE statements. ***
*** Once these have been changed, your variables are no longer
used***
*** anywhere in the program. ***
**********************************************************************
**************
Compute Q1 = AQOL1.
Compute Q2 = AQOL2.
Compute Q3 = AQOL3.
Compute Q4 = AQOL4.
Compute Q5 = AQOL5.
Compute Q6 = AQOL6.
Compute Q7 = AQOL7.
Compute Q8 = AQOL8.
Compute Q9 = AQOL9.
Compute Q10 = AQOL10.
Compute Q11 = AQOL11.
Compute Q12 = AQOL12.
Compute Q13 = AQOL13.
Compute Q14 = AQOL14.
Compute Q15 = AQOL15.
Execute
Compute ILLmiss = Nmiss (Q1 to Q3).
Do if ILLmiss = 1.
Do repeat
A = Q1 to Q3.
If (Missing (A)) A = RND(Mean (Q1 to Q3)).
End repeat.
End if.
Compute ADLmiss = Nmiss (Q4 to Q6).
Do if ADLmiss < 2.
Do repeat
A = Q4 to Q6.
If (Missing (A)) A = RND(Mean (Q4 to Q6)).
End repeat.
End if.
```

```
Compute SOCmiss = Nmiss (Q7 to Q9).
Do if SOCmiss < 2.
```

```
Do repeat
A = Q7 to Q9.
If (Missing (A)) A = RND(Mean (Q7 to Q9)).
End repeat.
End if.
Compute PHYmiss = Nmiss (Q10 to Q12).
Do if PHYmiss < 2.
Do repeat
A = Q10 to Q12.
If (Missing (A)) A = RND(Mean (Q10 to Q12)).
End repeat.
End if.
Compute PSYmiss = Nmiss (Q13 to Q15).
Do if PSYmiss < 2.
Do repeat
A = Q13 to Q15.
If (Missing (A)) A = RND(Mean (Q13 to Q15)).
End repeat.
End if.
Execute.
Compute U1 = Q1.
Compute U2 = Q2.
Compute U3 = Q3.
Compute U4 = Q4.
Compute U5 = Q5.
Compute U6 = Q6.
Compute U7 = Q7.
Compute U8 = Q8.
Compute U9 = Q9.
Compute U10 = Q10.
Compute U11 = Q11.
Compute U12 = Q12.
Compute U13 = Q13.
Compute U14 = Q14.
Compute U15 = Q15.
If (U1 eq 1)U1 = 0.000.
If (U1 eq 2)U1 = 0.328.
If (U1 eq 3)U1 = 0.534.
If (U1 eq 4)U1 = 1.000.
If (U2 eq 1)U2 = 0.000.
```

```
If (U2 eq 2)U2 = 0.269.
If (U2 eq 3)U2 = 0.467.
If (U2 eq 4)U2 = 1.000.
```

```
If (U3 eq 1)U3 = 0.000.
If (U3 eq 2)U3 = 0.166.
If (U3 eq 3)U3 = 0.440.
If (U3 eq 4)U3 = 1.000.
If (U4 eq 1)U4 = 0.000.
If (U4 eq 2)U4 = 0.154.
If (U4 eq 3)U4 = 0.403.
If (U4 eq 4)U4 = 1.000.
If (U5 eq 1)U5 = 0.000.
If (U5 eq 2)U5 = 0.244.
If (U5 eq 3)U5 = 0.343.
If (U5 eq 4)U5 = 1.000.
If (U6 eq 1)U6 = 0.000.
If (U6 eq 2)U6 = 0.326.
If (U6 eq 3)U6 = 0.415.
If (U6 eq 4)U6 = 1.000.
If (U7 eq 1)U7 = 0.000.
If (U7 eq 2)U7 = 0.169.
If (U7 eq 3)U7 = 0.396.
If (U7 eq 4)U7 = 1.000.
If (U8 eq 1)U8 = 0.000.
If (U8 eq 2)U8 = 0.095.
If (U8 eq 3)U8 = 0.191.
If (U8 eq 4)U8 = 1.000.
If (U9 eq 1)U9 = 0.000.
If (U9 eq 2)U9 = 0.147.
If (U9 eq 3)U9 = 0.297.
If (U9 eq 4)U9 = 1.000.
If (U10 eq 1)U10 = 0.000.
If (U10 eq 2)U10 = 0.145.
If (U10 eq 3)U10 = 0.288.
If (U10 eq 4)U10 = 1.000.
If (U11 eq 1)U11 = 0.000.
If (U11 eq 2)U11 = 0.253.
If (U11 eq 3)U11 = 0.478.
If (U11 eq 4)U11 = 1.000.
If (U12 eq 1)U12 = 0.000.
```

```
If (U12 eq 2)U12 = 0.219.
If (U12 eq 3)U12 = 0.343.
If (U12 eq 4)U12 = 1.000.
If (U13 eq 1)U13 = 0.000.
If (U13 eq 2)U13 = 0.107.
If (U13 eq 3)U13 = 0.109.
If (U13 eq 4)U13 = 1.000.
If (U14 eq 1)U14 = 0.000.
If (U14 eq 2)U14 = 0.141.
If (U14 eq 3)U14 = 0.199.
If (U14 eq 4)U14 = 1.000.
If (U15 eq 1)U15 = 0.000.
If (U15 eq 2)U15 = 0.104.
If (U15 eq 3)U15 = 0.312.
If (U15 eq 4)U15 = 1.000.
Compute DU1 = (1.1641*(1-(1-0.3350*U1)*(1-0.5927*U2)*(1-0.4896*U3))).
Compute DU2 = (1.0989*(1-(1-0.6097*U4)*(1-0.4641*U5)*(1-0.5733*U6))).
Compute DU3 = (1.0395*(1-(1-0.7023*U7)*(1-0.6253*U8)*(1-0.6638*U9))).
Compute DU4 = (1.6556*(1-(1-0.2476*U10)*(1-0.2054*U11)*(1-0.3382*U12))).
Compute DU5 = (1.2920*(1-(1-0.1703*U13)*(1-0.2554*U14)*(1-0.6347*U15))).
```

```
Compute UD1 = 1-DU1.
Compute UD2 = 1-DU2.
Compute UD3 = 1-DU3.
Compute UD4 = 1-DU4.
Compute UD5 = 1-DU5.
*** REM This model uses W = 1.04.
Compute AQOL = ((1.04*((1-(0.613*0))*
(1-(0.841*DU2))*
(1-(0.855*DU3))*
(1-(0.931*DU4))*
(1-(0.997*DU5)))) - 0.04).
```
Execute.

Appendix 8.3 A case study of mapping the Asthma Quality of Life Questionnaire onto the EQ-5D

This appendix presents a summary of a study involving the mapping of the condition-specific Asthma Quality of Life Questionnaire (AQLQ) onto the EQ-5D (Tsuchiya *et al.* 2002). The AQLQ is typical of many non-preference-based instruments. It has 32 items and each item has seven levels, where 1 is an

Table 8.A1 Summary of models used to map AQLQ onto EQ-5D

Model	Dependent variable	D/C	Independent variables	D/C
1	EQ-5D index	C	AQLQ overall score	C
2	EQ-5D index	C	All AQLQ domain scores	C
3	EQ-5D index	C	All AQLQ item levels	C
3'	EQ-5D index	C	All AQLQ item levels + interactions	C
4	EQ-5D index	C	Selected AQLQ item levels	D
4'	EQ-5D index	C	Further selected AQLQ item levels	D
5	EQ-5D dimension level	C	All AQLQ item levels	C
6	EQ5D dimension-level	D	Selected AQLQ item levels	D

Where AQLQ is the Asthma Quality of Life Measure that contains four dimensions and 32 items (each with seven levels).

D, discrete variable; C, continuous variable.

Source: Tsuchiya *et al.* (2002).

extreme problem and 7 is for no problem. These items form four domains (12 items for symptoms, 11 items for activities, five items for emotions and four items for environment). Results can be reported in terms of domain scores (average score across the items within each domain), or in terms of overall score (average across all 32 items). It is scored by a simple summing of responses (see Chapter 2 for a discussion of this method).

The task was to map this onto the EQ-5D. The study applied regression techniques to a data set that included the AQLQ and EQ-5D. There are a number of different ways to specify the relationship between these measures. There are at least six additive regression models, and two supplementary models, which could be used to estimate the relationship between AQLQ and EQ5D (Table 8.A1).

The first three were basic additive models that treated the independent and dependent variables as continuous.

1. $Q = a + \beta A + u,$

2. $Q = a + \beta_1 A_S + \beta_2 A_A + \beta_3 A_{Em} + \beta_4 A_{Ev} + u,$

3. $Q = a + \beta_1 A_1 + \beta_2 A_2 + \ldots \beta_{32} A_{32} + u,$

where Q is the preference-based EQ5D index (range: −0.59,1); A is the AQLQ overall score (1,7); A_d is the score of an AQLQ domain (1,7), where $d = S, A,$ *Em*, *Ev*; A_i is the level of an AQLQ item (1,7), where $i = 1, 2, \ldots 32$; A_{ix} is a dummy variable that $= 1$ when the level of an AQLQ item i is x; E_d is the level of an EQ5D dimension (1,3), where $d = M, SC, UA, PD, A$; and u represents the error term. Model 1 is the most restrictive since it assumes: the relative importance of the dimensions is reflected in the number of items (for the SF-36 it would assume the dimensions are equally important); all items carry equal weight; and item levels represent preferences on an interval scale. Model 2 relaxes the first of these, and model 3 relaxes the second. These three models assume no interactions and have been estimated using ordinary least squares (OLS), with independent variables treated as continuous.

The next model permits interactions:

$$3'. \quad Q = a + \beta_1 A_1 + \ldots \beta_{32} A_{32} + b\,Z + u,$$

where the subscript *in* represents item *i* and item *n* of AQLQ and Z is a vector of selected items for interaction. For model 2 this could be interactions between dimensions. The independent variables (*i* to *n*) used to form the interaction terms can be selected according to the results of model (3) (e.g. on the basis of statistical significance) to reduce to a tractable number (otherwise there are potentially thousands). The next model breaks the AQLQ down further and uses item levels as variables:

$$4. \quad Q = a + \beta_{i\cdot2} A_{i.2} + \beta_{i\cdot3} A_{i.3} + \ldots \beta_{i\cdot7} A_{i.7} + \ldots \beta_{n\cdot7} A_{n.7} + u, \, (i \ldots n\text{: selected items})$$

where subscript *ix* represents level *x* on item *i* of AQLQ. The independent variables are a subset of the AQLQ items that can be selected according to the results of model 3 to make it more manageable. This model continues to use OLS, but now the independent variable s are treated as categorical variables. Thus, the number of independent variables will be $n - 1$ times the number of items selected. Again this can be expanded to incorporate interactions:

$$4'. \quad Q = a + \beta_{i\cdot2} A_{i.2} + \beta_{i\cdot3} A_{i.3} + \ldots \beta_{i\cdot7} A_{i.7} + \ldots \beta_{m\cdot7} A_{m.7} + u,$$
$$(i \ldots m\text{: further selected items})$$

Here, the independent variables are restricted further by excluding *whole* items, as opposed to excluding individual variables. This is because each variable represents different levels within a given item, and it becomes difficult to interpret if not all the levels of a given item were either included or excluded as one set.

The models so far have been using the EQ-5D score as the dependent variable. It may be possible to extract more information by using the AQLQ to predict each EQ-5D dimension.

5. Regress the five EQ5D dimensions on the 32 AQLQ item levels so that

$$E_M = a + \beta_1 A_1 + \beta_2 A_2 + \ldots \beta_{32} A_{32} + u,$$

$$E_{SC} = a + \beta_1 A_1 + \beta_2 A_2 + \ldots \beta_{32} A_{32} + u,$$

$$E_{AD} = \ldots.$$

Again, OLS is used, and both the dependent and the independent variables are treated as continuous. The predictions obtained from this model for each of the EQ-5D dimensions are on a continuous scale. Thus, this model cannot be used to generate predictions for the overall score. Rather, the objective of this model is to enable the selection of the independent variables used in the next model. In addition, this model can be useful to explore empirically the relationship between the descriptive content of two instruments. This is taken a stage further below:

6. Regress the five EQ-5D dimensions on a subset of the AQLQ item levels so that

$$E_M = a + \beta_i A_i + \beta_j A_j + \ldots \beta_n A_n + u, (i \ldots n: \text{selected items})$$

$$E_{SC} = a + \beta_i A_i + \beta_j A_j + \ldots \beta_n A_n + u, (i \ldots n: \text{selected items})$$

$$\ldots E_{AD} = \ldots.$$

Here multinomial regression is used since the dependent variable is categorical (rather than a continuous variable as for the previous models).

The performance of the models can be assessed using tests presented in Chapter 6.

Chapter 9

Design and analysis of health state valuation data for trial- and model-based economic evaluations

9.1 **Introduction**

The primary purpose of collecting and analysing health state valuation data is to use the data in an economic evaluation (Chapter 2). There are two main vehicles for undertaking economic evaluation: one is to undertake the evaluation along-side a clinical trial, and the other is to use a decision analytic model. Overall methodological issues associated with these two approaches have been described in Drummond *et al.* (2005). This chapter focuses on the needs of these two approaches in terms of the design and analysis of health state valuation data.

The design and analysis of health state valuation data also differ depending on the approach chosen for obtaining such data. As described in Chapter 8, there are generic or condition-specific preference-based measures that use a standardized health state classification and come with a set of preference weights, bespoke vignettes or scenarios, and direct elicitation of preferences from patients. For standardized instruments, there are a set of issues relating to the administration of the descriptive system including who should be asked, the relevant question/s to ask, time points for administration, mode of administration and sample size (see later). There are similar design issues around the direct use of preference-based measures including who to ask, technique and sample size. This chapter deals with the practical issues of implementing these two approaches.

The development of vignettes from clinical trials has been less common, since they have tended not be directly linked to evidence. However, it has some attractions for a researcher wishing to use informed patient preferences for deciding which treatment is preferred and then to estimate the QALY benefit. In principle, this approach could also be used to obtain general population preferences for different vignettes. The construction of vignettes was examined in Chapter 4, and the design of studies to value health states has been described in Chapter 5 (including who to ask, technique of valuation and sample size).

Standardized generic instruments and preference elicitation techniques are often used on patients in clinical trials. This raises a host of analytical questions about how to summarize such data, how to handle missing data and uncertainty.

These questions are examined in this chapter. Collecting and analysing data for economic models raises some additional issues. Economic models can be populated from a range of sources and typically involve using data from studies undertaken by other researchers that may not always be reported in an ideal form.

The first section presents the requirements of trial- and model-based evaluations. The next section considers issues surrounding the design and analysis of data collection in clinical trials, and the last section considers the additional requirements of models.

9.2 Some basics—what do trial- and model-based economic evaluations require?

9.2.1 Economic evaluations alongside a clinical trial

Clinical trials use an outcome measure for assessing the impact of the intervention. Where an economic analysis is planned, then one of the methods discussed in Chapter 8 should be used. This may be to use an instrument in the trial, either a preference-based instrument or a preference elicitation technique, or it may involve awaiting the completion of the trial to construct a set of vignettes or scenarios for a preference study.

The former requires a suitable instrument to administer at different points in time in order to be able to estimate an incremental difference in change in QALYs over the duration of the trial. This requires a researcher to select their preferred approach and instrument to use. The bases for such a selection have been discussed in Chapter 8 and include the psychometric concerns of practicality, reliability and validity of the measure, along with the requirements of policy makers (such as any requirement for a generic preference-based instrument). There will be cases where one of the accepted preference-based measures has not been used, and the analyst will need to explore one of the other methods outlined in the previous chapter to derive health state values (such as mapping onto a generic preference-based measure). Whichever instrument is used, the researcher is left with issues concerning who to ask, time points of assessment, mode of administration and sample size. These issues are addressed in the next section.

The data generated from trials require analysis in order to estimate the difference in mean QALYs over the duration of the trial. This raises important questions about how this should be estimated, how missing data should be handled and how uncertainty should be incorporated into any estimate.

9.2.2 Model-based evaluations

It is increasingly being recognized that the aim of economic evaluation is to inform decisions, and that it is unlikely that a single trial will be able to collect all the relevant data for informing such a decision. Trials are often not aimed at a particular resource allocation decision, and, furthermore, there may be other important sources of evidence on efficacy, cost and quality of life. The purpose of modelling is to synthesize evidence from a range of sources in order to determine the relative cost-effectiveness of different uses of resources in order to inform decisions. Such evidence may come from several clinical trials and other observational data on clinical efficacy, as well as specific studies on costs, quality of life and health state valuations.

An example of a simple decision analytic model has been reproduced in Fig. 9.1, which compares surgical and medical interventions for some undefined medical condition. A patient is assumed to end up in one of three states following treatment, either a good, intermediate or bad outcome, but it is not known in advance which of these states the patient will ultimately be in. A decision analytic model will have probabilities associated with the different

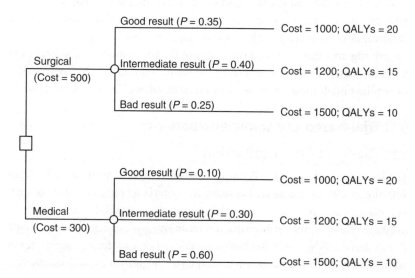

Expected cost of surgery: $500 + (0.35 \times 1000) + (0.40 \times 1200) + (0.25 \times 1500) = 1705$
Expected QALYs of surgery: $(0.35 \times 20) + (0.40 \times 15) + (0.25 \times 10) = 15.5$
Expected cost of medicine: $300 + (0.10 \times 1000) + (0.30 \times 1200) + (0.60 \times 1500) = 1660$
Expected QALYs of medicine: $(0.10 \times 20) + (0.30 \times 15) + (0.60 \times 10) = 12.5$

Incremental cost per QALY gained of surgery: $(1705 - 1660)/(15.5 - 12.5) = 15$

Fig. 9.1 Simple decision analytic model.

Reproduced from 'Methods for the Economic Evaluation of Health Care Programmes' (3rd Edn) by Drummond, Sculpher, Torrance, O'Brien, Stoddart (2005). By permission of Oxford University Press.

outcomes, as indicated in the figure, and these will differ between treatments. Each outcome is associated with a cost and a certain number of QALYs. The expected cost of each intervention is the cost of the respective interventions plus the therapy-specific sum of the cost associated with each of the three outcomes, weighted by the probability of the outcome occurring. The expected QALY of each treatment is then estimated in the same way.

In practice, economic models for economic evaluation tend to be considerably more complex and may have many more branches than the simple model presented in Fig. 9.1. An alternative structure is the Markov model, which assumes that a patient is always in one of a finite number of health states. Probabilities are used to determine the movement between these states, and only designated transitions are allowed. The overall time duration of patients in each state, along with their associated cost and health state values, is used to estimate the expected costs and QALYs associated with each treatment.

These types of model require mean values for each health state in the model in order to be able to estimate QALYs. In addition, there needs to be some account taken of the uncertainties surrounding these values. Conventional deterministic sensitivity analysis would need at least a range to reflect any underlying uncertainty in order to explore the consequences of varying the mean estimate. More sophisticated probabilistic methods of sensitivity analysis require distributions over the likely range of values. This is explored later.

9.3 Trial-based economic evaluations

9.3.1 Design of data collection

The basic method of data collection is assumed to have been selected, along with the specific instrumentation using the criteria set out in Chapter 8, such as a standardized generic (or condition-specific) preference-based measure or the direct use of a preference elicitation technique with patients. Having made this choice, then the researcher has to consider a range of design issues: who to ask, mode of administration, when to administer the instrument and sample size.

9.3.2 Who to ask

It has become common practice to obtain quality of life data directly from patients where possible (Bowling 2004). Patients are usually in the best position to know how their health has impacted on their functioning and well-being. There is evidence from a range of sources that proxies do not give the same response as patients themselves (Coucill *et al.* 2001; Eiser and Morse 2001; Brunner *et al.* 2005; Bryan *et al.* 2005; Sloane *et al.* 2005). Therefore, it seems appropriate to administer preference-based measures and preference elicitation techniques in cases where patients are able and willing to provide such data.

However, there may be circumstances where it is not possible to ask patients questions about their own health, such as people with severe mental health problems or patients who are simply too ill. This may be more of a problem with the preference elicitation techniques, since these tasks require a higher level of cognitive ability than the descriptive components of generic health-related quality of life measures. In such instances, proxy measures may be obtained from family members or carers or from parents in the case of young children (see Box. 9.1).

Box 9.1. Patient versus proxy measurement of health-related quality of life?

Sometimes it is unclear whether it is appropriate to ask the patient or not about their own health-related quality of life, for example in patients with dementia or in children. In a study of patients with dementia, Coucill *et al.* (2001) found that patients' carers reported higher levels of disability across all five dimensions of the EQ-5D than patients themselves, whereas clinicians reported fewer problems on the 'pain/discomfort' and 'anxiety/depression' dimensions. Overall, the level of agreement was only fair (using a statistical measure of agreement known as the weighted kappa score). However, it is unclear as to the level of dementia severity at which patients are able to provide valid ratings of health-related quality of life using the EQ-5D instrument.

Eiser and Morse (2001) undertook a review of using quality of life measures in children, and considered how far ratings made by children and parents or carers were identical or whether systematic differences might occur. They noted that the results may be influenced by the specific measure of quality of life utilized, and differences in the quality of the individual measures may contribute to the findings. However, their review found only limited support for the widely held view that parents are better able to judge the child's quality of life in terms of physical rather than social or emotional domains, as contrary data were found in some studies. In addition, there was no clear evidence to suggest that parents tended to over- or underestimate their child's quality of life. Although there have been very few studies which have considered the issue of concordance based upon age, gender or illness status, Eiser and Morse found that where it had been studied there was greater concordance for parent–child agreement in groups of chronically sick compared with healthy children. They concluded that until more conclusive evidence is available on this issue indicating that one informant is more reliable, information relating to the child's quality of life should be collected from multiple informants wherever possible.

9.3.3 **Mode of administration**

To date, the vast majority of clinical trials using generic preference-based measures have used self-administered questionnaire formats or 'paper and pencil' versions. There are some examples of clinical trials which have used telephone or face-to-face interviews (Selai *et al.* 2000; Kiebert *et al.* 2001; Coyne *et al.* 2003). Interviews have been used most often where values have been elicited for bespoke descriptions of health states (Brazier *et al.* 2006; Milne *et al.* 2006). For eliciting preferences directly from patients, most investigators have used interviewer administration (with various props). More recently, computer-based methods have started to be used for preference-based measures and preference elicitation (Lenert 2000; Lenert *et al.* 2002).

Each mode of administration has its advantages and disadvantages. These have been reviewed for health status quality of life instruments in general, and the results of this review are summarized in Table 9.1. These issues apply just as much to preference-based measures, but even more so for preference elicitation.

Table 9.1 Pros and cons of alternative modes of administration

	Face-to-face interviews	Telephone interviews	Postal questionnaires
Response rates			
General population samples	Usually best	Usually lower than face-to-face	Poor to good
Special population samples, e.g. patients	Usually good	Satisfactory to best	Satisfactory to good
Representative samples			
Avoidance of refusal bias	Depends on good interviewer technique	Depends on good interviewer technique	Poor
Control over who completes the questionnaire	Good	Moderate	Poor to good
Gaining access to a named selected person	Good	Good for those with telephones	Poor to good
Locating the named selected person	Good	Good	Good
Ability to handle			
Long questionnaire	Good	Moderate	Satisfactory to poor

Table 9.1 (Continued) Pros and cons of alternative modes of administration

Complex questions	Good	Moderate	Moderate to poor
Boring questions	Good	Moderate	Poor
Item non-response	Good	Good	Moderate
Filter questions	Good	Good	Moderate to poor
Question sequence control	Good	Good	Poor
Open-ended questions	Good	Good	Poor
Quality of answers			
Minimize social desirability responses	Poor	Moderate	Satisfactory
Ability to avoid distortion due to			
Interviewer's characteristics	Poor	Moderate	Good
Interviewer's opinions	Moderate	Moderate	Good
Influence of other people	Moderate	Good	Poor
Allows opportunities to consult	Moderate	Poor	Good
Implementing the survey			
Ease of finding suitable staff	Poor	Moderate	Good
Speed	Poor	Good	Poor
Cost	Poor	Moderate	Good

Reproduced from McColl E, Jacoby A, Thomas L, Soutter J, Bamford C, Steen N, Thomas R, Harvey E, Garratt A, Bond J (2001). Design and use of questionnaires: a review of best practice applicable to surveys of health service staff and patients. *Health Technology Assessment* 5(31):1–256. © Crown copyright material is reproduced with the permission of the Controller of HMSO and Queen's Printer for Scotland.

Face-to-face interviews

In a face-to-face interview, the interviewer rather than the respondent holds the responsibility of recording the responses. As a consequence, interviewer-administered questionnaires facilitate the collection of larger amounts of information and more detailed and complex data. Response rates to interview surveys are typically much higher than for postal surveys due to their interactive and personal nature. Sample composition bias is typically reduced by ensuring that information is obtained from the target respondents. Interviews also enable responses from people with reading and writing difficulties and from ethnic minorities whose first language is not English. The quality of the data collected may be enhanced through an interview because the interviewer is on hand to offer clarification and reduce any misunderstandings. These advantages are particularly important in the context of eliciting preferences.

The disadvantages of interviews include their expense and the possibility of interviewer bias due to differences in the way in which questions are posed or responses are recorded. There may also be a degree of respondents trying to please the interviewer.

Telephone interviews

Telephone interviews are a relatively low cost and speedy method of data collection, although the response rate may not be as high as with face-to-face interviews due to the lack of direct contact between the interviewer and the respondent. An advantage of telephone interviews is that strict control and close supervision of interviewers is possible because (with the consent of the respondent and the interviewer) interviewers can be monitored by supervisors listening in. Complex questions should be avoided in a telephone interview as it is more difficult for the respondent to answer reliably when there are a large number of possible responses. Similarly, long interviews should be avoided as respondents are more likely to terminate the call. In this respect, the EQ-5D would have an advantage over other off-the-shelf instruments because it is reasonably short and relatively easy to complete. Sample composition bias may be a problem for telephone interviews as those on lower incomes and ethnic minorities are less likely to have a telephone (Oppenheim 1992).

This approach has been used to elicit preferences for health states using rating scales, most notably forming one component of the Oregon Medicaid experiment in the USA in the mid 1990s where combinations of medical conditions and treatments were prioritized (Kaplan 1994). It would be more difficult to operationalize in the case of more complex preference elicitation techniques such as SG and TTO. Furthermore, the more commonly used versions of these techniques require props (Brazier *et al.* 1999).

Self-completion questionnaires

Postal surveys are the most common format for self-completion, although supervised self-completion questionnaires (where the respondent completes the questionnaire in the presence of a researcher who is able to offer assistance and explanation where required) are also frequently used in assessing health status or quality of life. The main advantage of self-completion questionnaires is their low cost, which enables researchers to study large groups within a study population. Postal surveys are generally quicker to administer than interviewer-based surveys, and respondents may feel that they are able to respond more truthfully to sensitive questions using this approach.

The main disadvantage of self-completion questionnaires is that typically they result in lower response rates. Data collection periods may therefore extend over several months to allow for follow-up mailings and possibly telephone reminders to try and boost the response rate. It is also often quite difficult to obtain a complete and accurate list of the population needed to act as sampling frame. Responder bias, whereby respondents differ from non-respondents in terms of their socio-demographic characteristics, is also a real possibility. Such responder bias leads to a bias in the estimates obtained from a given sampling frame. Self-completion questionnaires are best suited to clear uncomplicated research questions which can be easily explained. Unfortunately, there is no opportunity to probe beyond the answer given. Respondents may be more likely to exhibit primacy effects where they select the first response which seems applicable instead of considering the full range of alternatives available.

There are self-completed versions of all the main generic preference-based measures, and this tends to be the most popular format. Preference elicitation techniques are not often used in this format, though there are some notable examples (Lundberg *et al.* 1999).

Computer-assisted approaches

Computer-assisted approaches may be used for either interviewer-administered or self-completion questionnaires. In this approach, the interviewer or the respondent keys in answers to questions which appear on a computer screen. Computer-assisted approaches often facilitate skipping of irrelevant questions and branching. The results tend to be made more quickly available because the data entry process is not required. This is not necessary for the preference-based measures since they are quite simple and require all items to be completed. However, this is potentially a real advantage for preference elicitation, such as those that use 'ping–pong' and other iterative methods.

The use of the Web or e-mail to deliver questionnaires is also becoming more popular (see Box 9.2). There are examples of computer- and Internet-based surveys to elicit health state values from patients themselves and from members of the general public who are asked to imagine that they themselves are in the health state in question (Baron and Ubel 2001; Lenert *et al.* 2004).

Overall the choice of mode of administration depends upon (1) the type of instrument (preference-based instrument or preference elicitation) and (2) the abilities of the respondents. These two factors interact to affect the reliability and validity of responses. Most of the literature has been concerned with quality of life measurement in general, and there has been little focus on direct preference elicitation. Current advice is best summarized in Table 9.1.

Box 9.2. Example of an Internet-based survey

Public preferences for health states with schizophrenia and a mapping function to estimate utilities from positive and negative symptom scale scores: Lenert LA, Sturley AP, Rapaport MH, Chavez A, Mohr PE, Rupnow M (2004). *Schizophrenia Research* 71:155–65.

A model was developed to describe the health effects of schizophrenia comprising eight health states. A description of the symptom profiles of patients in each state was developed. A script for a brief teleplay used to convey the health impact of the state to subjects was then composed. The script describing each state had two main components—a simulated session between the patient and his psychiatrist illustrating the most important impairments, and a summing up by the psychiatrist of the overall effects of this impairment upon quality of life. Eight professional actors were then employed to portray patients in each of the states. A website was then developed which both displayed the digital videos describing each health state and measured values for those states using a visual analogue scale (VAS) and the standard gamble (SG) (for a detailed description of each of these methods, see Chapter 5). The survey was completed by 620 members of the general population (representing 49 per cent of the total who signed an online consent form to participate). VAS ratings were elicited on a vertical scale with 20 divisions, anchored on perfect health at the top and death at the bottom. In the SG, participants determined the risk of death they would accept to live without the displayed health condition. The SG procedure presented differing risks of death starting at 1 per cent and increasing upwards. Whilst the program performed well in obtaining plausible utilities for each health state, the authors note that there may be certain biases in the administration of an Internet-based research panel relating to access to the Internet and the appropriate technology required to view the video materials in the survey.

Ultimately, the researcher needs to make the necessary judgements about the relevance of each mode of administration to their own study.

9.3.4 Timing of assessments

The timing of quality of life assessments is an important design consideration. In a review of methodological considerations for the assessment of health-related quality of life in clinical trials, Calvert and Freemantle (2004) recommend that the timing of assessments should be driven by the objectives of the trial and any practical considerations, e.g. the clinical relevance of a particular time point within the trial and the scheduling of treatment or clinic visits. The potential for a treatment or clinic visit to affect the quality of life scores obtained should, however, be borne in mind. For example, patients' responses to a health-related quality of life questionnaire may be affected at a clinic visit in a situation where the clinician has had to convey bad news to the patient. If such a scenario is anticipated in advance, then it is important that the patient's health-related quality of life is assessed prior to the visit and that this is specified in the trial protocol to maintain consistency for all patients.

All patients in a clinical trial should have a quality of life assessment at baseline. This provides useful pre-treatment data which can be compared with any post-treatment data obtained. It also allows a characterization, in quality of life terms, of the trial population. This assessment should preferably be made prior to randomization, because there is some evidence to suggest that patients who complete their baseline assessment prior to randomization tend to have better health-related quality of life scores than patients who have already been randomly assigned and are aware of their treatment allocation (Brooks *et al.* 1998).

Decisions relating to the frequency and timing of any follow-up assessments need to be made in relation to a number of factors including the length of the trial, the aims of the study, the type and severity of disease and the type and expected response to treatment. It may be thought appropriate to time any follow-up assessments to coincide with clinic visits in order to reduce administrative burden and improve completion rates, although it is also important to aim to choose timings that will not bias against a particular treatment. Assessments may be made to coincide with treatment schedules or to a particular time point that is independent of a treatment schedule.

9.3.5 Sample size

Once a decision has been made as to what to measure, from whom and when, the next stage is to determine how many individuals are required to be sampled. In clinical trials, where instruments to measure health from the patient's perspective (e.g. EQ-5D and SF-36) are being increasingly used as primary outcome measures, it is common practice to determine a minimally important difference between treatments and then use existing data on variation and assumed levels of power (e.g. 80 per cent) and significance (e.g. 95 per cent) to calculate the required sample size (Walters and Brazier 2003).

The key variables in this calculation are the minimally important difference, power and level of significance. The former has been developed in the quality of life literature, since its meaning is not obvious from the conventional and often arbitrary scoring rules of non-preference-based measures. To date, two broad strategies have been used to interpret changes in health status and quality of life measures in health care: distribution-based approaches using the effects size, and anchor-based measures that use the concept of a minimum clinically important difference (Guyatt *et al.* 2002).

Distribution-based approaches relate the difference in health between treatment and control groups within the context of a clinical trial or other experimental design to some measure of variability. Cohen's standardized effect size is the most commonly utilized distribution-based approach (Cohen 1988). This estimates the mean change in health-related quality of life for treatment and control groups divided by the standard deviation of the change to produce an effect size index which can then be used for sample size estimation. Cohen has suggested that standardized effect sizes of 0.2–0.5 should be regarded as 'small', 0.5–0.8 as 'moderate' and those above 0.8 as 'large'. Cohen's effect size may be influenced by the degree of homogeneity or heterogeneity in the sample. Distribution-based methods express an effect in terms of the underlying distribution of the results.

Anchor-based methods examine the relationship between a measure of health and an independent measure to determine the significance of a particular degree of change. Therefore, anchor-based methods require an independent standard or anchor that can be easily interpreted and which has some overlapping elements with the instrument being assessed. One item that has been used to provide an independent anchor has been the self-reported global rating of change scale that contains responses from much better through to much worse (Guyatt *et al.* 2002; Walters and Brazier 2003). What is a minimally important change on such a scale may be open to some debate, with some arguing a half point change on a 7-point scale.

There has been some interest in the economics literature in applying the concept of minimally important difference. It has been suggested that differences of 0.03 may be important, and there is some empirical evidence to support this using the methods outlined above (Walters and Brazier 2003). However, as Drummond suggests, if the ultimate objective is to influence resource allocation decisions, as is the case within economic evaluation of health care, then it is the difference in cost-effectiveness between alternative treatments that is important and not the change in health-related quality of life. Therefore, changes in health alone may not be of interest without also considering the cost of bringing about such changes.

Ultimately, the sample size of a clinical trial or any study seeking to provide estimates of health state values should be based on careful weighing up of the marginal value of additional information against the marginal cost of collecting such data. The former is linked to the notion of the value of information, which requires a model that is populated with distributions around parameter inputs that reflects the extent of current uncertainty and then to explore the impact of reducing uncertainty around mean health state values. Whilst the techniques for undertaking such a calculation are still being developed (see Karnon, 2002; Drummond *et al.* 2005), the principle is clear. A sample calculation for a health state valuation study should not be based on the idea of a minimally important clinical difference, standardized effects sizes or arbitrary cut-off levels of significance.

9.3.6 Analysis

QALY estimation

When using preference-based meaures (e.g. EQ-5D) or preference elicitation techniques (e.g. SG or TTO), there will be health state values for each patient at each assessment (when completed). These assessments can be most easily converted into QALYs by using a well established method for assessing repeated measures, known as the area under the curve method (Mathews *et al.* 1990). A simple QALY calculation for a treatment versus control therapy for patients in a 12 month clinical trial using the EQ-5D is illustrated in Fig. 9.2. A patient in the treatment group has a baseline EQ-5D health state of 22322, a 6 month EQ-5D health state of 21222 and a 12 month EQ-5D health state of 12211. A patient in the control group has a baseline EQ-5D health state of 22322, a 6 month EQ-5D health state of 22222 and a 12 month EQ-5D health state of 21122 (see Table 9.2). An assumption is made that health status changes between measurements are smooth and gradual over time so that changes in utility scores can be approximated by a straight line. The area

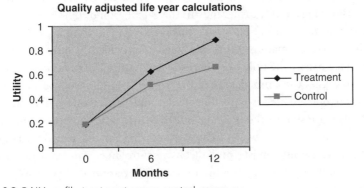

Fig. 9.2 QALY profile treatment versus control group.

Table 9.2 EQ5D health states and corresponding tariff scores at each time point

Time	Health state	EQ-5D score
Treatment		
0 months	22322	0.189
6 months	21222	0.62
12 months	11211	0.883
Control		
0 months	22322	0.189
6 months	22222	0.516
12 months	21122	0.656

under the curve for each of the treatment and control profiles is then estimated using the trapezium rule (Appendix 9.1).

The beauty of applying the area under the curve methods to health state values is that given that duration is expressed in years or a fraction of a year, the product will be the number of QALYs experienced during the trial. For the treatment group patient, the QALY gain is 1.981 {[0.5(0.189+0.620)6 + 0.5(0.620 + 0.883]6)/12} and for the patient in the control group it is 0.998 {[0.5(0.189+0.516)6 + 0.5(0.516 + 0.656)6]/12}.

Although in this simple example the baseline EQ-5D health state of patients in the treatment and control group are equivalent, Manca and colleagues (2005) point out that in practice it is quite common for baseline mean utility values to be imbalanced between treatment arms. They argue that this imbalance in baseline utility needs to be taken into account in the estimation of QALY differences between treatment arms because it typically contributes to the QALY calculation. This is because a patient's baseline utility is likely to be highly correlated with their QALYs over the follow-up period. A recent review of methodology and transparency in the calculation of QALYs in the published literature found that most clinical trial-based economic evaluations studies to date estimating QALYs had failed to recognize the need to adjust for imbalance in baseline utility (Richardson and Manca 2004). However, Manca and colleagues use a practical example from a large clinical trial comparing lapararoscopic-assisted hysterectomy with standard methods to illustrate how multiple regression methods can be utilized to generate appropriate estimates of QALY differences between treatment arms and an associated measure of sampling variability, whilst simultaneously controlling for differences in baseline mean utility between treatment arms. They argue that controlling for baseline utility in estimating QALY differences between treatment arms should become standard practice in the future for any economic evaluation that uses patient-level data.

Intention to treat

In common with clinical data, QALY data within clinical trials should be analysed on the basis of intention-to-treat analysis. This form of data analysis provides a strategy for analysing data in which all participants are included in the treatment group to which they were originally assigned at randomization, whether or not they completed the intervention given to the group. Intention-to-treat analysis prevents bias caused by the loss of participants over the period of the trial, which may disrupt the baseline equivalence established by random assignment and which may reflect non-adherence to the clinical trial treatment protocol.

Handling missing data

The majority of clinical trials relate to an extended time period and, as discussed above, typically the health-related quality of life of patients needs to be assessed at several time points during the course of follow-up, often by means of a self-completion questionnaire. In such studies, it is common for a proportion of health-related quality of life data to be missing at one or more time points. Responses missing at a particular time point (t) can be categorized in three main ways (Little and Rubin 2002). First, responses may be missing completely at random, where the probability of response at time point t is independent of both the previously observed value and the unobserved value at time t and other variables collected at this, or previous, time points, for example measures of disease severity. Secondly, responses may be missing at random where the probability of response at time t depends on the previously observed value or other variables collected during the study but not on the unobserved values at time t. The third category of missing response is non-ignorable non-response when the probability of response at time t depends on the unobserved values at time t and possibly also on the previously observed values.

Where the intervention being considered involves treatment for a severe condition, patients may be very ill before receiving the intervention and it is common for a proportion of participants to fail to complete questionnaires because of death or the severity of their illness at any time point. Such data represent non-ignorable non-response because the missing data are directly dependent on the health status of the patient, hence this type of data is often referred to as representing 'informative drop-out'. Where patients choose not to respond to the questionnaire at one or multiple time points, such data may be assumed to be missing completely at random because the probability of response is independent of any previously observed values.

Approaches for handling missing data may be classified into simple and more sophisticated imputation approaches.

Simple approaches   Simple approaches for handling missing data include complete case analysis and available case analysis. Complete case analysis is the default approach for handling missing data utilized by the vast majority of statistical software packages. This approach involves deletion of those patients where data is incomplete. The advantages of this approach are its simplicity and the fact that it allows analysis of the same sample of patients for all analyses. However, this approach is inefficient because some potentially informative data are discarded. Alternatively, available case analysis avoids the inefficiency of complete case analysis by estimating the mean for the complete cases for each variable. However, the main problem with this approach is that different samples of patients will contribute to the estimation of different variables, leading to problems in comparability between variables.

Imputation-based approaches   Imputation methods for handling missing data attempt to overcome the disadvantages of complete and available case analyses. Imputation is where the missing data can be replaced with statistical estimates of the missing values. A complete data set is therefore made available which can be analysed using statistical methods for complete data. Imputation methods include mean imputation, regression-based approaches, last value carried forward, maximum likelihood approaches and the more recently employed technique of multiple imputation.

1. *Mean imputation*. This involves the calculation of the mean value for the variable under consideration. Accordingly, all patients with missing data for that particular variable will be assigned the mean value. However, this approach, although relatively popular in health services research, is problematic since it leads to an underestimation of the sample variance or standard deviation and weakens the estimates of correlations and covariances for the variable under consideration. Furthermore, it does not allow for any bias created by non-response.

2. *Regression imputation*. Regression analysis can be used to provide estimates of the missing data conditional upon the complete cases for the variable under consideration within the data analysis. Missing data are usually multivariate, and it is possible to extend the procedure of regression-based imputation to deal with multivariate missing data. It is possible to fit a model for each missing value within the dataset using the complete cases for all the other variables (Buck 1960). Alternatively, an iterative regression approach can be adopted (Brick and Kalton 1996) whereby

missing values in a given variable are predicted from a regression of that variable on the complete cases of all other variables in the data set. This process is repeated for all variables with missing values using complete cases of the other variables (including previously imputed values) until a completed rectangular data set has been generated. The imputation of missing values for each variable is then re-estimated in turn using the complete set of data, and the process continues until the imputed values stop changing (Briggs *et al.* 2003).

3. *Last value carried forward/backward.* This approach is widely used in the calculation of QALY data where health status data at particular time point(s) are missing for individual patients whilst still being available at other relevant time points. This approach is quite simple to employ, hence its popularity. It involves carrying forwards the last observed health status value for an individual in order to complete the data set. The main disadvantage of this approach is that, in practice, it is unlikely that the health status of a patient in a clinical trial remains at exactly the same point over a period of time. It is far more likely to fluctuate. Hence, extensive use of the last value carried forward/backward may lead to a situation whereby the actual variability in health state values across patient groups is lost.

4. *Maximum likelihood approaches.* The maximum likelihood (ML) approach involves formulating a statistical model and basing inference on the likelihood function of the incomplete data (Briggs *et al.* 2003). For multivariate missingness, the expectation maximization (EM) algorithm can be applied. This involves iterating between an estimation step (E) and a maximization step (M). The E step involves estimating the missing data by averaging the complete data likelihood over the predictive distribution of the missing data given the parameters of the model to be estimated. The M step involves providing updated estimates of the parameters through maximization of the likelihood given the complete data set. Following convergence (Wu 1983), predicted values for the missing data can be obtained directly by using the parameters.

5. *Multiple imputation.* This method is a Monte Carlo simulation technique where each missing data case is replaced by a set of plausible estimates, which are drawn from the predictive distribution of the missing data given the observed data. In contrast to the more naïve approaches previously highlighted, multiple imputation has the advantage that it includes a random component to reflect the fact that imputed values are estimated rather than treating the imputed values as if they are known with certainty. As such, it is likely to produce more accurate estimates of the standard

errors (SE) and variances of mean health state values at each time point than other methods of imputation (Manca and Palmer 2005).

There are three main stages to multiple imputation. First, a number of imputed data sets are produced by estimating missing values for incomplete observations based upon values generated from their predictive distributions. The number of imputed data sets required is determined by the rate of missing information for the variable being estimated (Rubin 1987). Secondly, these data sets are analysed using standard statistical methods. Thirdly, the results from each of these analyses are pooled to provide estimates and confidence intervals which incorporate the uncertainty relating to the missing data (see Box 9.3).

Rubin (1987) recommends that the imputed data sets are created using a Bayesian approach which involves the specification of a parametric model

---

Box 9.3. A practical example of the impact of imputing values for EQ-5D health states

Ratcliffe J, Longworth L, Young T, Buxton M (2005). An assessment of the impact of informative drop out and non-response in measuring the health–related quality of life of liver transplant recipients using the EQ-5D descriptive system. *Value in Health* 8:53–8.

This study investigated the impact of imputing EQ-5D values to allow for informative drop-out and non-response in a longitudinal assessment of the health-related quality of life of liver transplant recipients. The EQ-5D was administered at defined time intervals pre- and post-transplantation to all adults who were listed to receive a liver transplant at each of the Department of Health-designated treatment centres in England and Wales over a time period of 36 months. During the course of the study, missing data arose due to informative drop-out and non-response. Informative drop-out was accounted for by giving those patients who died an EQ-5D score of 0 and those patient who were too ill to respond an EQ-5D score equivalent to the 5th percentile of respondents for each time point pre-transplantation. Non-response was accounted for using relatively naïve approaches (last value carried forward and upper/lower 95 per cent confidence interval around the mean) and contrasted with a more sophisticated multiple imputation method based upon the approach described by Schafer (1999) using the software package NORM.

Box 9.3. A practical example of the impact of imputing values for EQ-5D
health states *(continued)*

Of the 400 patients surveyed, 31 patients became too ill to participate at some point during the course of the study, and 81 patients dropped out due to death. Within the non-response group, 114 individuals chose not to respond to the questionnaire at one or more time point, and 16 individuals' responses were unusable as they were incomplete. Adjusting for informative drop-out in isolation resulted in a marked deterioration in mean scores over time pre-transplant relative to the base case situation in which no such adjustments were made. Post-transplant data indicated highly statistically significant improvements in quality of life over time for the base case ($P < 0.001$), whereas no statistically significant improvements over time were found when informative drop-out was allowed for in isolation ($P = 0.402$) or when informative drop-out and non-response were allowed for simultaneously ($P = 0.95–0.185$).

The authors conclude by recommending that future studies which purport to assess the health-related quality of life over time of patients, such as those with end-stage liver disease, include an allowance for informative drop-out and non-response within the analysis.

for the complete data. A prior distribution is then applied to the unknown model parameters and a number of independent draws are simulated from the conditional distribution of the missing data given the observed data. Alternative approaches for the creation of the imputed data sets include an approximate Bayesian bootstrap whereby the values to be imputed are drawn by re-sampling, with replacement, from the set of observed data [this approach can be implemented in the software SOLAS (Statistical Solutions 1999)] or a Bayesian regression method known as a data augmentation algorithm, a class of Markov Chain Monte Carlo techniques (Schafer 1999). This can be implemented in the freely available software NORM: http://www.stat.psu.edu/~jls/misoftwa.html).

Following the imputation procedure the subsequent data sets can be analysed and pooled using standard complete data methods in statistical software packages.

9.3.7 Discounting future QALYs

It is standard practice in economic evaluation to discount future costs and benefits arising from health care interventions to reflect individuals' and society's time preference (Severens and Milne 2004; Drummond *et al.* 2005). In order to compare the costs and benefits that occur over time, both must be adjusted to relate to the same fixed point in time or 'present value'. Calculations for discounting involve multiplying the value of costs and benefits for each year in the future by the following formula: $(1/(1 + D)^y)$, where the discount rate is denoted by D (Drummond *et al.* 2005) and y is the number of years over which future costs and benefits are to be valued. The higher the discount rate, the lower the net present value. A constant discount rate produces values that decline exponentially with time. The impact of discounting tends to be greatest for those health care programmes where the costs are incurred initially but health benefits are expected to occur in the far future, e.g. screening programmes for cancer or paediatric vaccination programmes. In the context of clinical trials, discounting is only relevant where the trial lasts for more than a year.

Prescribed discount rates in the guidelines for economic evaluation in health care produced by several developed countries vary between 3 and 5 per cent (Smith and Gravelle 2001). In the UK, until recently, it was widely accepted that the life years or QALYs generated by health care programmes in future years should be discounted at a lower rate than costs. However, the recent guidance published by NICE (National Institute for Health and Clinical Excellence 2004) in its report: 'Guide to the methods of technology appraisal' recommends an annual discount rate of 3.5 per cent for both costs and benefits, based upon the latest recommendations from the UK Treasury (Great Britain HM Treasury 2003). Given the variability in prescribed discount rates over time and across countries, it is important to test the impact of the use of different discount rates upon the results obtained by sensitivity analysis.

9.3.8 Linking QALYs and costs

Typically the costs and QALYs associated with an intervention are combined to form incremental cost-effectiveness ratios (ICERs) which estimate the additional cost per QALY associated with a new intervention relative to other interventions and/or standard treatment. The cost-effectiveness plane (CE plane) is often employed to show how decisions can be related to both costs and QALYs (see Chapter 2). The plane is divided into four quadrants indicating four possible situations relating to the additional costs and additional QALYs associated with a new therapy compared with a standard therapy. When one therapy is clearly less costly and more effective than the other (quadrants II and IV of the CE plane: see Fig. 9.3) then it is said to be dominant and it is obvious which of the therapies should be chosen over the other. However, the more common situation is where one intervention (typically the

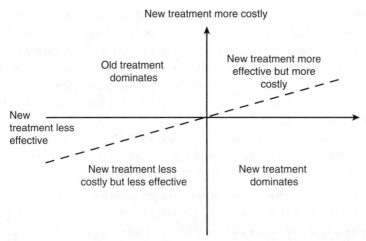

Fig. 9.3 The cost-effectiveness plane comparing a new treatment with a currently provided control treatment.

new intervention) is both more costly and more effective in terms of additional QALYs generated, and hence the decision as to its possible adoption is no longer clear. A decision has to be made as to whether the additional costs are justified by the additional QALYs which would be generated should the new intervention be adopted.

If it is possible to define a maximum willingness to pay (WTP) for a QALY, then this ceiling value can be used to judge whether the intervention under consideration is cost-effective. The ceiling value of the ICER can be represented by the slope of the dashed line on the CE plane. All incremental costs and QALYs plotted to the right of this line may be considered cost-effective, whilst points to the left of the line represent cost-ineffective interventions. The steeper the gradient of the dashed line, the higher the cost per QALY threshold.

The aim of an economic evaluation alongside a clinical trial is to estimate the expected value of the incremental cost per QALY. In the context of a trial, there will be uncertainty surrounding the costs and QALY data, and this uncertainty needs to be represented.

9.3.9 Handling uncertainty

In a clinical trial situation, one method of handling stochastic uncertainty is to present a confidence interval estimate around the mean cost per QALY to represent uncertainty due to sampling variation (methods for handling other forms of uncertainty are discussed in Drummond *et al.* 2005). Due to the unknown nature of the ICER's sampling distribution, commentators have suggested the non-parametric approach of bootstrapping as an appropriate method of estimating confidence limits for the ICER (Briggs and Fenn 1998). This approach has since been employed in a variety of studies using clinical trial data (see for example Dijkgraaf *et al.* 2005; Ratcliffe *et al.* 2006). The bootstrap method uses the original data to provide an empirical estimate of the sampling distribution through repeated re-sampling from the observed data (Polsky *et al.* 1997).

In the case of the ICER, where data on costs and QALYs exist for two groups of patients, with sample sizes n_a and n_b receiving treatments **a** and **b**, respectively, the bootstrap method involves three key stages (Briggs and Fenn, 1998):

1. Sample with replacement n_a cost/QALY pairs from the sample of patients who received treatment **a** and calculate the mean of the bootstrapped estimate of costs and QALYs for the bootstrap sample.

2. Sample with replacement n_b cost/QALY pairs from the sample of patients who received treatment **b** and calculate the mean of the bootstrapped estimate of costs and QALYs for the bootstrap sample.

3. Calculate the bootstrap replicate of the ICER generated by the ratio of the bootstrapped incremental costs divided by the bootstrapped incremental QALYs.

This three-stage process is repeated many times to produce a vector of bootstrapped estimates which provide an empirical estimate of the sampling distribution of the ICER. The percentile method, which employs the $(\acute{\alpha}/2)90$ and $(1 - \acute{\alpha}/2)90$ percentiles of the empirical sampling distribution, then offers the most straightforward method for estimating confidence limits around the ICER.

An alternative approach to estimating confidence intervals around ICERs to represent the uncertainty surrounding the cost-effectiveness of a health care intervention in the case of decision making involving two interventions is to estimate cost-effectiveness acceptability curves (CEACs). A CEAC represents the probability that an intervention is cost-effective at each value of WTP for a QALY (or whatever measure of effect is used).

The methods for deriving CEACs for decisions involving two interventions or multiple interventions are broadly similar. Firstly, stochastic analysis is applied to generate a distribution of costs and QALYs for each intervention. For clinical trial-based data analyses these estimates are estimated by bootstrapping. The cost and effect distributions for each intervention are then combined to form a series of distributions, one for each intervention and each level of λ. The probability that the intervention of interest is optimal is quantified and plotted graphically for every conceivably possible value of λ.

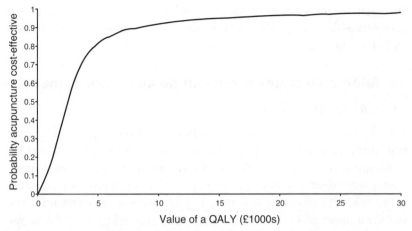

Fig. 9.4 Cost-effectiveness acceptability curve (CEAC): two interventions.

Where two interventions are being considered, the analysis can be undertaken using incremental net benefits (INBs). For any particular simulation, the intervention of interest is considered to be optimal compared with the alternative intervention when the INB is positive. Hence for each value of λ, the technique involves determining the proportion of iterations in which the intervention of interest has a positive INB. Figure 9.4 illustrates a standard CEAC curve for an intervention which has a single comparator.

The vertical axis represents the probability that the intervention (in this case acupuncture for low back pain relative to standard treatment) is cost-effective, and the horizontal axis represents alternative values of λ or WTP for a QALY. Assuming an implicit threshold maximum WTP value of £20 000 for a QALY, Fig. 9.4 illustrates that the probability of the cost per QALY of the intervention of interest falling below this threshold value is close to 90 per cent.

CEACs provide a geographical representation of the probability that a particular intervention is cost-effective over a range of maximum WTP for a QALY values (Fenwick *et al.* 2001). They can be constructed for decisions involving any number of interventions, although the literature has largely concentrated upon the case of two interventions being compared with each other. CEACs indicate the probability that an intervention is optimal for any externally set limit (λ) or maximum WTP for a QALY [currently set at between £20 000 and £30 000 per QALY in the UK (National Institute for Health and Clinical Excellence 2004)]. CEACs may be considered as a more flexible approach to representing uncertainty than estimation of confidence limits around the ICER, since they directly address the decision problem relating to the probability that the intervention is cost-effective for all poten-tial values of the ceiling ratio, and CEACs avoid the issue of negative values for the ICER, which conveys no useful meaning.

9.4 Additional issues in populating an economic model

9.4.1 Model structure

A model-based economic evaluation requires health state values in order to estimate the incremental QALY gains from multiple interventions. Indeed the values given to health states in a model may form driving variables in deter-mining the cost-effectiveness of a new intervention (e.g. Bansback *et al.* 2005).

The needs of a model are determined by its structure, since this differenti-ates the number and definition of the health states to be valued. Economic models require mean values (and their distributions) for a number of health states. Health states may be distinguished according to clinical events, e.g. myocardial infarction or angina in treatments for coronary heart disease (Lindgren *et al.* 2004), or according to the severity of symptoms, e.g. normal, mild, moderate and severe depression (Kaltenthaler *et al.* 2005). However, it is important to note that reducing the large range of health state values typically found in a clinical trial context to a few health states for incorporation into an economic model may result in a loss of information, thereby reducing the sen-sitivity of the model to detect confirmed differences between interventions. If this loss of information is important, then the structure of the model needs to be modified to take account of this by expanding the number of states repre-sented in the model. The structure of a model needs to take into account not just the patient care pathway, but also the appropriateness of the health states as a summary of the resource use and costs and the associated utilities experi-enced by patients over time.

9.4.2 Estimating distributions

For a model it is necessary to specify a mean health state value and its associ-ated distribution. For this it is necessary to specify a shape to the distribution. For health states which are very unlikely to be associated with utility values of less than 0, the most pragmatic approach is to fit a beta distribution, a flexible class of parametric distributions. A standard beta distribution is supported on the interval (0, 1) and is specified by its mean and variance (Karnon and Brown 2002).

For health states that may have utility values of less than zero, various alter-native approaches have been suggested. The simplest approach is to use the triangular distribution, the parameters for which are the most likely value, a minimum value and a maximum value (Karnon *et al.* 2005). However, the triangular distribution draws straight lines from the mode down to the minimum and maximum values that assign too much probability to values near the furthest extreme, and as such overemphasizes the tail of the distribution. An alternative to the triangular distribution is the PERT distribution, which is related to the beta distribution. The PERT distribution has the same three parameters as the triangular distribution, but interprets them with a smooth curve that places less emphasis on the furthest extreme (Oscar 2004).

Alternatively, utility values can be described as decrements from perfect health, i.e. as a simple transformation of $X = 1 - U$ where U is the utility decrement. If a lower constraint is placed on possible utility value, for example, the worst EQ-5D health state where a patient has severe problems associated with each dimension of the scale has a tariff value of -0.6, a scaled beta distribution may be used where the standard beta distribution is scaled upwards by a height parameter (λ), so that the distribution is supported on a $(0, \lambda)$ scale. If no lower constraint is assumed, a log normal or gamma distribution can be applied to the utility decrement, such that the utility decrement is on an interval between 0 and positive infinity.

9.4.3 Source of values

Models are able to take their values from a variety of sources. As reported in Chapter 8, an increasingly important source of health state value data is the literature. For many health states, there are already multiple values. A model needs a central value with a distribution to reflect the uncertainty around that value. The first problem is selecting an appropriate value from the literature, or perhaps in the future synthesizing values, in order to obtain the best estimates for health states in a model. As demonstrated in Chapter 8, the basis for selection is partly determined by the requirements of the policy maker who will be using the results of the model, but also by the appropriateness of the descriptions and methods of valuation. The problems are made even more difficult by the fact that published sources may not have values for the same patient group as the one in your model. Adjustments will need to be made for the background characteristics of the patients in the trial, and some methods for doing this were described in Chapter 8.

9.5 Conclusions

This chapter has considered the issue of how to value the quality adjustment weight component of QALYs for use within the methodology of economic evaluation. The requirements of clinical trial- and model-based economic evaluations were considered. In a clinical trial context, it has become common practice to obtain quality of life data directly from patients wherever possible, since patients are often most aware of how their health has impacted upon their functioning and well-being. Generic preference-based measures, e.g. EQ-5D and SF-6D, have tended to be used most often in a clinical trial setting, typically in a self-administered format, although interviews have been used. For model-based economic evaluations, many of the issues relating to trial-based economic evaluations apply. A typical economic model requires mean values for each health state in the model in order to be able to estimate QALYs. It is also necessary to specify a distribution around the mean health state value. There are various distribution types which can be applied, although the most pragmatic approach (a standard beta distribution) is not suitable for health states that may have values of less than zero

It is important to note that if the ultimate objective of economic evaluation is to influence resource allocation decisions, then sample size calculations based upon expected differences in health-related quality of life between alternative treatment groups may not be sufficient. It will also be necessary to consider the costs of bringing about such changes. Techniques such as value of information analysis offer a promising way forward in this area.

References

Bansback NJ, Brennan A, Ghatnekar O (2005). Cost effectiveness of adalimumab in the treatment of patients with moderate to severe rheumatoid arthritis in Sweden. *Annals of Rheumatic Diseases* 64:995–1002.

Baron J, Ubel PA (2001). Revising a priority list based on cost-effectiveness: the role of the prominence effect and distorted utility judgments. *Medical Decision Making* 21:278–87.

Bowling A (2004). *Measuring health: a review of quality of life measurement scales.* Open University Press, Milton Keynes, UK.

Brazier J, Deverill M, Green C, Harper R, Booth A (1999). A review of the use of health status measures in economic evaluation. *Health Technology Assessment* 3(9):1–164.

Brazier J, Dolan P, Karampela K, Towers I (2006). Does the whole equal the sum of the parts? Patient assigned utility scores for IBS-related health states and profiles. *Health Economics* Jan 3; [Epub ahead of print] 15:543–541.

Brick JM, Kalton G (1996). Handling missing data in survey research. *Statistical Methods in Medical Research* 5:215–38.

Briggs A, Clark T, Wolstenholme J, Clarke P (2003). Missing presumed at random: cost analysis of incomplete data. *Health Economics* 12:377–92.

Briggs A, Fenn P (1998). Confidence intervals or surfaces? Uncertainty on the cost-effectiveness plane. *Health Economics* 7:723–40.

Brooks MM, Jenkins LS, Schron EB, Steinberg JS, Cross JA, Paeth DS for the AVID investigators (1998). Quality of life at baseline: is assessment after randomization valid? *Medical Care* 36:1515–9.

Brunner HI, Johnson AL, Barron AC, Passo MH, Griffin TA, Graham TB, Lovell DJ (2005). Gastrointestinal symptoms and their association with health related quality of life of children with juvenile rheumatoid arthritis: validation of a gastrointestinal symptom questionnaire. *Journal of Clinical Rheumatology* 11:194–204.

Bryan S, Hardyman W, Bentham P, Buckley A, Laight A (2005). Proxy completion of EQ-5D in patients with dementia. *Quality of Life Research* 14:97–118.

Buck SF (1960). A method of estimation of missing values in multivariate data suitable for use with an electronic computer. *Journal of the Royal Statistical Society Series B* 22:302–6.

Calvert MJ, Freemantle N (2004). Use of health-related quality of life in prescribing research. Part 2: methodological considerations for the assessment of health-related quality of life in clinical trials. *Journal of Clinical Pharmacology and Therapeutics* 29:85–94.

Cohen J (1998). *Statistical power analysis for the behavioural sciences*. Lawrence Erlbaum, Mahwah, New Jersey.

Coucill W, Bryan S, Bentham P, Buckley A, Laight A (2001). EQ-5D in patients with dementia: an investigation of inter-rater agreement. *Medical Care* 39:760–1.

Coyne KS, Margolis MK, Gilchrist KA, Grandy SP, Hiatt WR, Ratchford A, Revicki DA, Weintraub WS, Regensteiner JG (2003). Evaluating effects of administration on Walking Impairment Questionnaire. *Journal of Vascular Surgery* 38:296–304.

Dijkgraaf MG, van der Zanden BP, de Borgie CA, Balnken P, van Ree JM, van den Brink W (2005). Cost utility analysis of co-prescribed heroin compared with methadone maintenance treatment in heroin addicts in two randomised trials. *British Medical Journal* 330:1297.

Drummond MF, Sculpher MJ, Torrance GW, O'Brien BJ, Stoddart GL (2005). *Methods for the economic evaluation of health care programmes*. Oxford University Press, Oxford.

Eiser C, Morse R (2001). Quality of life measures in chronic diseases of childhood. *Health Technology Assessment* 5(4):1–157.

Fenwick E, Claxton K, Sculpher M (2001). Representing uncertainty: the role of cost-effectiveness acceptability curves. *Health Economics* 9:779–87.

Great Britain HM Treasury (2003). *The green book appraisal and evaluation in central government*. HMSO, London.

Guyatt GH, Osoba D, Wu AW, Wyrwich KW, Norman GR and the Clinical Signficance Consensus Meeting Group (2002). Methods to explain the clinical significance of health status measures. *Mayo Clinic Proceedings* 77:371–83.

Kaltenthaler E, Shackley P, Stevens K, Beverley C, Parry G, Chilcott J (2002). A systematic review and economic evaluation of computerised cognitive behaviour therapy for depression and anxiety. *Health Technology Assessment* 22:1–89.

Kaplan RM (1994). Value judgements in the Oregon Medicaid experiment. *Medical Care* 32:975–88.

Karnon J (2002). Planning the efficient allocation of research funds: an adapted application of a non-parametric Bayesian value of information analysis. *Health Policy* 61:329–47.

Karnon J, Brown J (2002). Tamoxifen plus chemotherapy versus tamoxifen alone as adjuvant therapies for node-positive postmenopausal women with early breast cancer—a stochastic economic evaluation. *Pharmacoeconomics* 20:119–37.

Karnon J, Brennan A, Pandor A, Fowkes G, Lee A, Gray D, Coshall C, Nicholls C, Akehurst R (2005). Modelling the long term cost effectiveness of clopidogrel for the secondary prevention of occlusive vascular events in the UK. *Current Medical Research and Opinion* 21:91–12.

Kiebert GM, Green C, Murphy C, Mitchell JD, O'Brien M, Burrell A, Leigh PN (2001). Patient's health related quality of life and utilities associated with different stages of amyotrophic lateral sclerosis. *Journal of Neurological Sciences* 191:87–93.

Lenert LA (2000). The reliability and internal consistency of an Internet-capable computer program for measuring utilities. *Quality of Life Research* 7:811–7.

Lenert LA, Sturley A, Watson ME (2002). iMPACT3: Internet-based development and administration of utility elicitation protocols. *Medical Decision Making* 22:464–74.

Lindgren P, Jonsson B, Yusuf S (2004). Cost-effectiveness of clopidogrel in acute coronary syndromes in Sweden: a long-term model based on the cure trial. *Journal of Internal Medicine* 255:562–70.

Little DB, Rubin RJA (2002). *Statistical analysis with missing data*, 2nd edn. Wiley Series on probability and statistics. John Wiley and Sons Inc., New York.

Lundberg L, Johannesson M, Isacson DG, Borgquist L (1999). The relationship between health state utilities and the SF-12 in a general population. *Medical Decision Making* 19:128–40.

Manca A, Hawkins N, Sculpher MJ (2005). Estimating mean QALYs in trial-based cost-effectiveness analysis: the importance of controlling for baseline utility. *Health Economics* 14:487–96.

Manca A, Palmer S (2005). Handling missing data in patient-level cost-effectiveness analysis alongside randomized clinical trials. *Applied Health Economics and Health Policy* 4(2):65–75.

Mathews JNS, Altman D, Campbell MJ (1990). Analysis of serial measurements in medical research. *British Medical Journal* 300:230–235

McColl E, Jacoby A, Thomas L, Soutter J, Bamford C, Steen N, Thomas R, Harvey E, Garratt A, Bond J (2001). Design and use of questionnaires: a review of best practice applicable to surveys of health service staff and patients. *Health Technology Assessment* 5(31):1–256.

Milne RJ, Heaton-Brown KH, Hansen P, Thomas D, Harvey V, Cubitt A (2006). Quality of life valuations of advanced breast cancer by New Zealand women. *Pharmacoeconomics* 24:281–92.

National Institute for Health and Clinical Excellence (2004). *Guide to the methods of technology appraisal*. National Institute of Clinical Excellence, London.

Oppenheim AN (1992). *Questionnaire design, interviewing and attitude measurement*, 2nd edn. London, Pinter Pub Ltd.

Oscar T (2004). Dosenresponse model for thirteen strains of salmonella. *Risk Analysis* 24:41–9.

Polsky D, Glick HA, Wilke R, Schulman K (1997). Confidence intervals for cost-effectiveness ratios: a comparison of four methods. *Health Economics* 6:243–52.

Ratcliffe J, Brazier JE, Campbell WB, Palfreyman S, MacIntyre JB, Michaels JA (2006). Cost-effectiveness analysis of surgery versus conservative treatment for uncomplicated varicose veins in a randomized clinical trial. *British Journal of Surgery* 93:182–6.

Richardson G, Manca A (2004). Calculation of quality adjusted life years in the published literature: a review of methodology and transparency. *Health Economics* 13:1203–10.

Rubin DB (1987). *Multiple imputation for non-response in surveys*. Wiley, New York.

Schafer JL (1999). Multiple imputation: a primer. *Statistical Methods in Medical Research* 8:3–16.

Selai CE, Elstner K, Trimble MR (2000). Quality of life pre and post epilepsy surgery. *Epilepsy Research* 38:67–74.

Severens JL, Milne RJ (2004). Discounting health outcomes in economic evaluation: the ongoing debate. *Value in Health* 7:397–401.

Sloane PD, Zimmerman S, Williams CS, Reed PS, Gill KS, Preisser JS (2005). Evaluating the quality of life of long term care residents with dementia. *Gerontologist* Special issue 1:37–49.

Smith DH, Gravelle H (2001). The practice of discounting in economic evaluations of healthcare interventions. *International Journal of Technology Assessment in Health Care* 17:236–43.

Walters S, Brazier J (2003). What is the relationship between the minimally important difference and health state utility values? The case of the SF-6D. *Health and Quality of Life Outcomes* 11:1–4.

Wu (1983). On the convergence properties of the EM algorithm. *Annals of Statistics* 11:95–103.

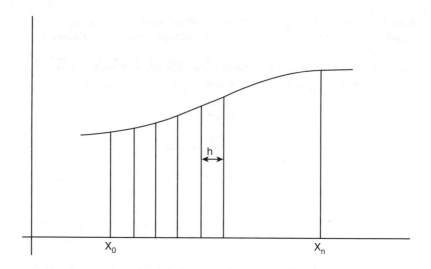

Appendix 9.1 The trapezium rule

The trapezium rule is a way of estimating the area under a curve. The area under a curve is calculated using a mathematical technique known as integration, and so the trapezium rule gives a method of estimating integrals. The trapezium rule works by splitting the area under a curve into a number of trapeziums.

If we want to find the area under a curve between the points x_0 and x_n, we divide this interval up into smaller intervals, each of which has length h (see diagram above).

Then we find that:

$$\int_{x_0}^{x_n} f(x)dx = \frac{1}{2}h\left[(y_0 + y_n) + 2(y_1 + y_2 + \cdots + y_{n-1})\right]$$

where $y_0 = f(x_0)$ and $y_1 = f(x_1)$ etc

If the original interval was split up into n smaller intervals, then h is given by: $h = (x_n - x_0)/n$.

Chapter 10

A QALY is a QALY is a QALY—or is it not?

10.1 **Introduction**

To recap, there are two main reasons why the allocation of health care resources is not left to the market mechanism but is subjected to government intervention. First, the market for health care fails to satisfy the main conditions for a perfect market and therefore outcomes of a free unregulated market are expected to be inefficient; and secondly, health care is a special commodity requiring not only efficient distributions but also equitable ones. To generalize somewhat brutally, the 'welfarist' school of economic evaluation gives less weight to the second reason and regards CBA as the theoretically correct type of economic evaluation, whereas the 'non-welfarist' school of economic evaluation gives more weight to the issue of equity and prefers cost per QALY analysis over CBA. This chapter revisits this debate, and then goes on to show how equity considerations can be incorporated into the aggregation of QALYs in non-welfarist CEAs.

To give an example, let us go back to CBA. Because CBA is based on monetary representations of the gains and losses (see Chapter 2), it may in practice be unfair towards those with lower income. Imagine the maximum amount of money an individual can pay to improve or to protect their own health. It is very likely that this will be determined largely by that person's level of income. If this is the case, then a CBA of a (somewhat contrived) public health programme that improved the health of the rich by some degree and damaged the health of the same number of the poor by the same degree (at no other costs) will conclude that this programme will improve efficiency. Note that CEA is an approach that accounts for this concern, by removing the monetary representation of health benefits from the equation: all changes in health, both positive and negative, are called health outcomes, and all changes in resources, both resources used and resources saved, are called inputs. Also, since outcomes and inputs are no longer measured in the same units, the results are no longer reported in terms of net benefits, but of ratios of inputs required to produce a unit of output, or costs per QALY. The different monetary amounts that the rich and the poor may associate with a unit of health change have no bearing on the results. In other words, a QALY to the rich and a QALY to the poor are valued equally, so that the net health benefit of the above example is zero. It should be noted, however, that achieving equity is not without costs. In this case, resource allocation by CEA will be less efficient compared with resource allocation by CBA, because it fails to represent the different monetary values attached to the health of the rich and the health of the poor, which would lead to satisfying the Kaldor–Hicks criteria. However, if the notion of equity upheld in society is one that contends that everybody's unit health is of equal societal value, then this equity consideration will favour CEAs over CBAs.

In Chapter 3, there was a brief mention of 'distributional weights' in CBA based on the 'marginal social welfare of individual income', to reflect the difference in the ability to pay between the rich and the poor. As was pointed out there, one of the difficulties of this is how to determine what the correct distributional weights should be. The crux of welfarism is that the only information that goes into the assessment of social good is on choices that individuals make for themselves. However, by definition, distributional preferences are not reflected in choices that people make for themselves: distributional preferences involve a concern for others alongside oneself, or possibly beyond oneself. Theoretical texts on this issue typically present the objective function with inequality aversion, but do not discuss where this might come from (Johansson 1995; Johannesson 1996). The practical way forward would be for researchers or policy makers simply to impose some 'reasonable' level of inequality aversion (with possible sensitivity tests). However, then note that, strictly speaking, this is no longer welfarist, because the judgement of social welfare now includes information other than individual revealed preference. Welfarism narrowly defined and distributional weights seem to be incompatible with each other (see Box 10.1).

Let us take a step back, to CBA (without distributional weights) and CEA with QALYs. The claim in favour of CEA with QALYs was that this is fairer than CBA. However, one may ask further whether this is enough. The use of CEA over CBA will involve valuing a unit change in health between the rich and the poor equally, but it only guarantees that two programmes that improve the health of the rich and of the poor by the same degree will be regarded as equally cost-effective *if the two programmes cost the same*. In reality, it is quite likely that it is less costly to improve the health of the rich by a given degree than to improve the health of the poor by the same degree. This is because the rich (and the middle class) in general have a healthier lifestyle in terms of diet, exercise, not smoking, drinking in moderation, have access to

Box 10.1 The marginal social welfare of individual income and inequality aversion

Where social welfare is represented by W, and individual i's income by y_i, marginal social welfare of individual income is the partial derivative of the former by the latter: $\partial W/\partial y_i$. This concept can be further broken down into two factors: the marginal social welfare of individual utility, $\partial W/\partial u_i$, where u_i represents individual i's utility; and the marginal individual utility of own income, $\partial u_i/\partial y_i$.

Based on a cardinal concept of utility, the latter is a factual concept that may (or may not) be measured accurately: the extent to which one derives additional utility from one's own income increase is a positive matter. However, the former notion of marginal social welfare of individual utility is not a factual matter: it depends on the functional form of the social welfare function, in particular the degree of inequality aversion represented in the particular specification.

Aversion to inequality in distribution of income (or health) means that if the total income (or total health) across the population is the same, then an even distribution within the population is more preferable to a less even distribution. The implication is that a smaller total with a more even distribution can be equally preferable to a larger total with a less even distribution.

The issue here is: preferable to whom?

better heated and ventilated housing, and have safer jobs. They also tend to be more aware of health issues, and have higher compliance with complex and/or restrictive treatment regimens. So they are likely to be more cost-effective to treat than the poor even when the value of health is equalized. If so, should we be giving more weight to a QALY to a person who is more costly to treat, and, furthermore, how? What other characteristics require similar attention? That is the issue addressed in the rest of this chapter.

10.2 Weighted cost per QALY analyses

Recall the cost-consequences analysis (CCA), briefly introduced in Chapter 2. This was a type of economic evaluation that tried to note down all relevant and legitimate concerns. These are typically concerns beyond resource use and health benefits, so they are not reflected in a cost per QALY analysis (see Box 10.2 for examples). As one can see, some of them stem from a concern for efficiency, whilst others are related to a concern for equity, and some of these

Box 10.2 Candidate considerations for weighted QALYs
(not all of which are theoretically justifiable)

- The size of the health benefit
- Severity of health before receiving treatment
- Severity of health should patients not receive treatment
- The nature and size of non-health benefits
- The nature and size of the costs
- Age and life stage of a typical patient
- Socio-economic background of a typical patient
- Whether or not patients brought the ill health on to themselves
- Whether or not the NHS has caused the ill health
- How long patients have had the condition for
- The number of patients involved and whether or not they are 'identifiable'
- Whether there are alternative treatments available
- Whether the treatment cures the disease or merely controls the symptoms
- The degree of uncertainty associated with the predicted costs and outcomes

can be reflected in CBA. For instance, if it is more important for people to receive an intervention when the condition they have is severe than when it is not, or there are no other treatments available than when there are, then, other things being the same, the monetary valuation of the benefit of the intervention will reflect these concerns and be higher. Nevertheless, if it means that the rich will be able to make higher bids and receive such care but the poor will not, then although these might be real concerns of consumers, reflecting them in decision making via CBA might not be in line with the policy objectives of a public health care system.

The argument in support of CCA is that to the extent that these are valid and relevant considerations in public policy they should, and can, be presented as part of the information base based on which the decision maker makes their decisions (Coast 2004). The decision maker can take account of the extra weight given to severity of the condition without treatment, or the fact that the intervention is the only one available, and weigh this against other considerations for all patients, not just for rich patients. On the other hand, the criticism against CCA is that once researchers report all the relevant infor-mation, some of which are in favour and others against the provision of the health care intervention in question, it is not clear how actual decisions would, or should, then be made. The only way to achieve transparent and accountable decision making would be to have a published 'tariff' that stated explicitly and exactly how much consideration is given to, for example, a less cost-effective intervention that treats a disease with very severe symptoms as opposed to a more cost-effective treatment for one with only mild symptoms; or a less cost-effective intervention that is the only one available for the relevant condition as opposed to a more cost-effective intervention which is just one of several treatments available for the relevant condition. However, if such a tariff is possi-ble, then there is no reason to be content with a CCA, because the tariff prices, which in effect will be the relative weights given to different considerations, can be incorporated into CEAs in the form of a cost per weighted QALY analysis: it can then have all those additional considerations reflected in the analysis.

Efficient and equitable use of public health care resources is not the only rel-evant consideration. People are also concerned about the procedural justice of decision making. More specifically, it is not only the allocation of health care resources and the resulting distribution of health across the population that matter, but also the ways in which these allocation decisions are made. Decisions need to be made in a transparent manner, based on accurate information, reflecting the voice of stake holders (patients and the tax-paying public in particular), independent of vested interests of a minority of experts or business organizations, based on a consistent set of decision rules, and with appropriate scope for people to challenge and reverse the decisions (Tsuchiya *et al.* 2005). Regarding these procedural justice considerations, compared with a health care resource allocation system that relies on CCA, systems that are based on cost per weighted QALY analyses will improve transparency and consistency.

In what follows, the associated issues are briefly discussed. As with health valuation, the topics addressed are: what considerations are to be valued; who is to value them; and how to value them. These topics are followed by a further discussion regarding the actual process of reflecting these weights in cost per QALY analyses.

10.3 Theory and evidence for the relative value of QALYs

10.3.1 Theory on what considerations should be valued

The first issue to be addressed is which are the legitimate considerations. The list given in Box 10.2 is loosely based on considerations that have been raised in the literature in some form or other: some come from the theoretical literature,

others from more observational sources. The judgement regarding the legiti-
macy of considerations must start from their theoretical position, but not all
of the items on the list are accompanied by satisfactory justifications.
Theoretical arguments put forward to support different considerations can be
divided into those that are based on efficiency reasons and those that are based
on equity reasons.

An example of an efficiency-based argument is the one in favour of giving
priority to those with dependents, because treating the parent will also benefit
the child, and therefore produce more good than treating a non-parent. As
such, there is scope to use efficiency-based weights to reflect non-health benefits that CEA with QALYs typically does not handle very well. Note that giving
priority to parents of young children is sometimes treated as an issue of
equity, but then the relevant comparison becomes that between a child with
an unwell parent and a child with a well parent, not the comparison between a
patient with a young child versus a patient with no young children. A similar
example of efficiency-based consideration is age: young people and very old
people rely on others to support them, not just on an individual basis, but in
terms of sustaining an economy, a political system, a community, and, in this
respect, treating an adult will be more efficient than a child or a very old person. Efficiency-based age weights have been used in CEAs (World Bank 1993).

However, it is also possible to argue in favour of giving higher weight to
young people than adults (including the elderly) because the former group
have not yet had the life opportunity the latter group by definition have. This
then, would be an argument based on equity. There can be two types of
equity-based considerations. One is based on the principle of equal *outcomes*,
i.e. people's *health* should be equal. There are many ways to measure health of
people, such as current health utility, risk of certain conditions, life expectancy
at birth, lifetime expected QALYs, and so on, but the reality is that regardless
of which measure is used, people's health is not equal. So this can lead to
equity weights that give higher priority to those with worse health. Other
things equal, being older means expected lifetime health is higher, so if lifetime health is to be the relevant measure of health, less equity weight should
be given to a unit health improvement of an older person compared with that
of a younger person, i.e. the 'fair innings argument' (Williams 1997). Similarly,
other things being equal, improving the health of patients in a more severe
health state or those with a poorer prognosis by a given amount can be valued
more highly than improving the health of other patients by the same amount
(Harris 1991; Nord 1999).

Another possible example of equity concerns based on the principle of
equal outcomes is ill health, or being more costly to treat, because of factors

beyond one's control. This can include ill health caused by, for instance, low income, genetics (including one's sex), pollution, accidents, medical negligence or malpractice, and so on. To the extent that it is perceived as a health disadvantage caused by external forces, alleviating or preventing such ill health can be given larger weight than attending to ill health caused by deliberate choice made by informed and competent individuals.

Note that it is not the socio-economic disadvantage *per se* that calls for larger weights here, even if being poor was beyond one's own control. To give higher weights to socio-economic disadvantage *per se* in the context of cost per QALY analyses (where the disadvantage in ability to pay is no longer an issue) would require further justifications, since it implies that the poor would be given priority over the rich even when their health benefits and the cost of treating them are the same, so that the health care system would be used in effect as a means to achieve some social justice beyond fairness in health. This is not to say it is wrong (or right) to use the health care system as a means to correct for social injustices even where it does not affect health: the justifications and implications of such usage need to be made clear and discussed.

Giving higher priority to treating ill health caused by medical negligence and malpractice may also require additional justifications. With the other factors, the relationship between those who are affected by the factor and those who are not is in some sense symmetric. If those with higher efficiency are given a larger weight, then those with lower efficiency are given a smaller weight. If those who have caused their own ill health are given a smaller weight, then those who have not caused their own ill health will be assigned a larger weight. If one agrees that one party should get a larger weight, then one must also agree that the counter-party should get a smaller weight. With the medical negligence and malpractice case, the health care service should be held accountable and 'pay' for the damage caused. However, if we give those whose ill health was caused by the health care services a larger weight, then it is those whose ill health was not caused by the health care services who 'pay' by being given a smaller weight.

The other type of equity-based consideration is based on the principle of equal *opportunities*, i.e. the opportunity of *receiving health care* should be distributed equally across people. An example of this is geographical access. If there are 'economies of scale' in the way hospitals operate, so that larger hospitals were more efficient than smaller ones, this will be an efficiency-based justification for having a smaller number of larger hospitals across the country. However, if this is going to compromise how people in remote areas are going to reach hospital health care, then there is scope to consider a trade-off between securing equal geographical access and achieving maximum health improvements.

10.3.2 **Theory on who should value them**

Most empirical studies exploring the relative value of a QALY are based on the idea that a representative sample of the general public, or the tax-paying citizenry, should be surveyed. For instance, the Citizens' Council convened by NICE is a body that aims to elicit the views of exactly such a group of people. Parallel to the health valuation literature, the two alternative groups to this might be to survey stakeholders such as patients and carers, and to survey experts in health care. The obvious immediate shortcoming of surveying stakeholders is that they are stakeholders. The valuation of relative value of QALYs requires comparing the societal value of a health gain to one group relative to the same health gain to another group. Although surveying patients in the context of health valuations has its attractions because this is the group that knows best about a given health problem, the same reason makes them less attractive for the present context. The neutrality aspect of procedural justice requires that those who can be expected to be detached and unbiased judges should provide the relative values across different groups of patients.

The justification of surveying the tax-paying public also comes from procedural justice: since the issue is about how to allocate publicly funded health care resources, the voice of those who are paying should be reflected, not the views of health care policy makers that are not democratically elected representatives. Note that there is some, unpublished, empirical evidence to suggest that the views on weighted QALYs held by members of the general public and the views of health care policy makers may differ (Dolan *et al.* 2006).

10.3.3 **Theory on how to value them**

The empirical survey can be an individual face-to-face interview or a discussion session in small groups. The relevant issues are complex, so there should be ample time to hear and to understand the various opinions and their implications. This point makes postal questionnaires less attractive. However, on the other hand, if the existence of an interviewer or fellow study participants is going to make people react in ways that they think, rightly or wrongly, are more socially acceptable and politically correct than ways that reflect their genuine opinions, then there may be some merit in study designs that protect the anonymity of responses.

Another interesting matter is that the more evidence and the more opportunity for deliberation participants are given, the farther away they become from the average voter on the street. There is the danger that their participation in the survey transforms them into mini-experts, undermining the objective of eliciting the views held by a representative sample of the general public. For further discussion on study design issues, see Dolan and Tsuchiya (2006).

10.3.4 The empirical evidence: people's views on the relative value of QALYs

There is enough evidence to suggest that members of the general public do not always support the assumption that all QALYs are of equal value. Evidence has shown that, for example, there is a tendency to prefer giving higher priority to treat patients in worse health (for example Nord 1993; Ubel and Loewenstien 1995; Cookson and Dolan 1999; Ubel 1999), younger patients (Charny *et al.* 1989; Busschbach *et al.* 1993; Cropper *et al.* 1994; Nord *et al.* 1996; Johannesson and Johansson 1997; Rodriguez and Pinto 2000), and those who are not responsible for their ill health (Lewis and Charny 1989; Nord *et al.* 1995; Ubel *et al.* 1999; Ratcliffe 2000). However, very few studies have gone beyond identifying the direction of the preference actually to quantify the size of the weights to be used in such contexts. For more extensive reviews of the empirical literature, see Schwappach (2002) and Dolan *et al.* (2005).

It is important to note here the relationship between theoretical arguments and empirical evidence. For cost per weighted QALY analyses actually to succeed, both theoretical arguments and empirical evidence need to be in place. On the one hand, theory can be useful in identifying the legitimate considerations, but on its own it cannot be used to identify what size the relative weights should be. On the other hand, simply because people seem to support certain types of priorities, if this cannot be underwritten by a theoretical justification, it should not form the basis of policy making. For example, in modern liberal societies, it is unacceptable to give different weights to the health of people according to their ethnicity, religious beliefs or sexual orientation.

10.4 Practical concerns for cost per weighted QALY analyses

A more practical issue to address is the logistics of cost per weighted QALY analyses. If the relevant weights to be given to different patients remain constant throughout the time horizon of an analysis, then there can be one reference case analysis based on the population group that will be given a conventional weight of one. Applying the relevant weights will then be equivalent to making decisions with reference to differentiated cost-effectiveness thresholds. So, suppose the reference group was given a cost-effectiveness threshold of £20 000 per QALY. Then a population group whose weight is two with respect to the reference group will be given a cost-effectiveness threshold of £40 000 per QALY, and a group with weight 0.8 will have a threshold of £16 000 per QALY, and so on. There will be a handful of characteristics that fall into this first category, such as patient gender or the responsibility associated with the cause of the condition.

The category that comes next in terms of complexity is where weights are to reflect characters such as age and how long patients have had the condition. These characteristics do not stay constant through the time horizon of the analysis, but the weights of all surviving patients through time are completely predictable with no uncertainty, and they change at the same rate across everybody. In this case, weights can be applied at the end of the analysis in the form of differential thresholds, but the actual weight will have to be derived from the distribution of different patients across the relevant time horizon.

However, these two categories are likely to be exceptional rather than the norm. Weights may well change within the time horizon of a chronic condition, and they may or may not be systematically related to the progress of the condition and the effectiveness of treatment, as with severity or employment status. If so, the weight relevant to the time period in question needs to be reflected in each stage of the CEA, making the process far more complicated. At the extreme, individual-level modelling may be required.

The final issue to be addressed is how to reflect the weighted results in policy decision making. It is clear that if weights are to be used in health care resource allocation, they will be used at the macro, central planning level; and meso level (i.e. the regional, or institution level) decisions could also be expected to reflect the weights. However, would it be ethically acceptable to deny treatment to an individual patient because her condition is not severe enough, or because she has caused her condition herself some years ago? It has been observed that members of the public who support the use of priority setting based on such characteristics at the macro level may well refuse to use the same characteristics for selecting individual patients at the bedside level (Dolan and Cookson 1999). In a way, this debate is not only an issue for weights, and the same arguments apply to cost per (unweighted) QALY analysis. Would it be ethically acceptable to deny treatment to an individual patient because she is too costly to treat given her expected health gain (or vice versa, because her expected health gain is too small given the costs required to treat her)?

10.5 **Conclusion**

This chapter has looked at the possibility of cost per weighted QALY analyses. At one level, the movement towards health care decision making based on economic evaluation is in line with a demand for improved efficiency in resource allocation. At another level, however, there is a demand for equitable health care resource allocation. This can have two facets. One is in terms of procedural justice: we need a decision-making process that is transparent and accountable, using information derived through mechanisms that reflect the voice of the people in an unbiased way. The other is in terms of the equity of opportunities and outcomes: there are additional considerations beyond levels of health benefits and resource use that need to be reflected in economic evaluation. Both facets are consistent with cost per weighted QALY analyses.

The weights to be used in cost per weighted QALY analyses need to be supported by both normative arguments justifying the use of such weights, and empirical evidence justifying their size. Furthermore, the chapter has identified two areas that are currently distinctly underdeveloped, which are the actual mechanism by which the weights will be incorporated in the cost per QALY analysis, and the process by which the results of the cost per weighted QALY analyses will be reflected in decision making regarding the allocation of public health care resources.

References

Busschbach JJV, Hessing DJ, Decharro FT (1993). The utility of health at different stages in life—a quantitative approach. *Social Science and Medicine* 37:153–8.

Charny MC, Lewis PA, Farrow SC (1989). Choosing who shall not be treated in the NHS. *Social Science and Medicine* 28:1331–8.

Coast J (2004). Is economic evaluation in touch with society's health values? *British Medical Journal* 329:1233–6.

Cookson R, Dolan P (1999). Public views on health care rationing: a group discussion study. *Health Policy* 49:63–74.

Cropper ML, Aydede SK, Portney PR (1994). Preferences for life saving programs—how the public discounts time and age. *Journal of Risk and Uncertainty* 8:243–65.

Dolan P, Cookson R (2000). A qualitative study of the extent to which health gain matters when choosing between groups of patients. *Health Policy* 51:19–30.

Dolan P, Tsuchiya A (2006). The elicitation of distributional judgements in the context of economic evaluation. In Jones A, ed. *Companion to health economics*. Cheltenham Elgar, pp. 382–391.

Dolan P, Shaw R, Tsuchiya A, Williams A (2005). QALY maximisation and people's preferences: a methodological review of the literature. *Health Economics* 14:197–208.

Dolan P, Bekker H, Brennan A, Edlin R, Goyder R, Kennedy S, Michaels J, Murray C, Payne N, Ratcliffe J, Roberts J, Oluboyede Y, Shiekle D, Tsuchiya (2006). The relative importance attached to access, equity and cost-effectiveness by people and organisations providing health services. Unpublished report to the NHS Service Delivery and Organisation Research & Development Programme.

Harris J (1991). Unprincipled QALYs—a response to Cubbon. *Journal of Medical Ethics* 17(4):185–8.

Johannesson M (1996). *Theory and methods of economic evaluation of health care*. Kluwer Academic Publishers, Dordrecht, The Netherlands.

Johannesson M, Johansson P-O (1997). Is the valuation of a QALY gained independent of age? Some empirical evidence. *Journal of Health Economics* 16:589–99.

Johansson P-O (1995). *Evaluating health risks: an economic approach*. Cambridge University Press, Cambridge.

Lewis PA, Charny M (1989). Which of 2 individuals do you treat when only their ages are different and you can't treat both? *Journal of Medical Ethics* 15:28–32.

Nord E (1999). *Cost-value analysis in healthcare: making sense out of QALYs*. Cambridge University Press, Cambridge.

Nord E (1993). The trade-off between severity of illness and treatment effect in cost-value analysis of health-care. *Health Policy* 24:227–38.

Nord E, Richardson J, Street A, Kuhse H, Singer P (1995). Maximizing health benefits vs egalitarianism—an Australian survey of health issues. *Social Science and Medicine* 41:1429–37.

Nord E, Street A, Richardson J, Kuhse H, Singer P (1996). The significance of age and duration of effect in social evaluation of health care. *Health Care Analysis* 4:103–11.

Ratcliffe J (2000). Public preferences for the allocation of donor liver grafts for transplantation. *Health Economics* 9:137–48.

Rodriguez E, Pinto JL (2000). The social value of health programmes: is age a relevant factor? *Health Economics* 9:611–21.

Schwappach, DLB (2002). Resource allocation, social values and the QALY: a review of the debate and empirical evidence. *Health Expectations* 5:210–22.

Tsuchiya A, Miguel LS, Edlin R, Wailoo A, Dolan P (2005). NICE and procedural justice: *Journal of Applied Health Economics and Policy* 4:119–27.

Ubel PA (1999). How stable are people's preferences for giving priority to severely ill patients? *Social Science and Medicine* 49:895–903.

Ubel PA, Loewenstein G (1995). The efficacy and equity of retransplantation—an experimental survey of public attitudes. *Health Policy* 34:145–51.

Ubel PA, Baron J, Asch DA (1999). Social responsibility, personal responsibility, and prognosis in public judgments about transplant allocation. *Bioethics* 13:57–68.

Williams A (1997). Intergenerational equity: an exploration of the 'fair innings' argument. *Health Economics* 6:117–32.

World Bank (1993). *World development report 1993: investing in health*. Oxford University Press, Oxford.

Chapter 11

Measuring and valuing health: an international perspective

So far in this book our primary consideration has been the measurement and valuation of health for economic evaluations in settings such as the UK, where the National Institute for Health and Clinical Excellence has formalized the requirement for evidence on cost-effectiveness of interventions, expressed in terms of costs per QALY, as an input to national decision making on health technologies. Somewhat paradoxically, the institutionalized demand for cost-effectiveness evidence in low- and middle-income countries—where this sort of information is arguably even more urgently required—has yet to gain traction in the way that it has in various countries in the industrialized world. Nevertheless, there has been rising interest in undertaking CEAs in developing countries, and notable products of this interest have included the body of work from the World Health Organization's CHOICE (CHOosing Interventions that are Cost Effective) project, which has generated guidelines on conducting 'generalized cost-effectiveness analysis' (Tan-Torres Edejer *et al.* 2003), and the recent update from the World Bank's Disease Control Priorities Project on cost-effectiveness for a range of interventions related to major health problems in low- and middle-income countries (Jamison *et al.* 2006).

In this chapter, we briefly revisit some of the key topics covered in the preceding chapters of this volume through the particular lens of the developing country perspective. We provide a brief introduction to the disability-adjusted life year (DALY), which is an alternative to the QALY that has been favoured in much of the cost-effectiveness work in developing countries; and extend the discussions of key issues in the definition, description and valuation of health to address some of the added considerations demanded by cross-cultural applications of the methods and tools that are the focus of this book.

11.1 The disability-adjusted life year

The DALY was first developed for the primary purpose of quantifying the global burden of disease (Murray and Lopez 1994). In this context, it was constructed as a summary measure of population health—specifically, to be used as an indicator of the relative magnitude of losses of healthy life associated with different causes of diseases and injuries. The construction of summary measures of population health has much in common with the construction of measures of the benefits from health interventions (Box 11.1). Indeed, the developers of the DALY explicitly intended that the measure could be used as

Box 11.1 Summary measures of population health

Broadly, there are two families of summary measures of population health, with distinct features and uses: health expectancy measures capture the overall, average level of health in a population, useful as a single summary index of population health; health gaps, typically decomposed by cause, indicate the overall loss of health associated with a given problem in reference to some defined target for healthy survivorship (Murray *et al.* 2000). Both health expectancies and health gaps combine information on mortality with information on non-fatal health outcomes and express these outcomes in time-based units, i.e. as healthy years lived or healthy years lost. In both families of population health measures, as in measures of intervention benefits such as QALYs, health state valuations provide the critical link between the mortality and non-fatal outcomes. By quantifying health levels on a continuum from the best to the worst levels, and scaling these values in reference to optimal health and dead, extensions (or reductions) in longevity and improvements (or decrements) in health levels can be aggregated in composite measures.

The mechanics of combining information on health levels with information on longevity or premature mortality in population health measures is similar to that in the measurement of intervention benefits (see Chapter 9). For CEAs, the benefits of interventions are estimated by computing the difference between the estimated life expectancy with or without the intervention, weighting each life year in a way that reflects the levels of health (or utility or quality of life) associated with the sequence of health states that are experienced in either case. For the health expectancy family of population health measures, an analogous operation at the aggregate level extends the demographic measure of life expectancy to account for the levels of health experienced in the population at different ages. For health gap measures, such as the DALY, losses associated with a particular problem are measured in terms of years of life lost, reflecting premature mortality compared with some yardstick for longevity at each age, combined with years lived with disability, which reflect the severity and duration of non-fatal health decrements.

both a unit of account for the burden of disease, and a metric for health bene-fits in the denominator of cost-effectiveness ratios (Murray *et al.* 1994). The major debut of the DALY in the World Bank's *World development report 1993* introduced applications of the measure toward both ends (World Bank, 1993). More recently, the guidelines from the WHO-CHOICE project on conducting generalized CEAs have included an explicit recommendation to use DALYs as the measure of benefit in these analyses (Tan-Torres Edejer *et al.* 2003).

As discussed in this book with reference to QALYs, a key issue in the con-struction of DALYs is the definition and interpretation of the weights attached to non-fatal health outcomes. As described in Chapters 2 and 3, there have been a range of different interpretations of the weights that are included in QALYs, originating from alternative theoretical perspectives (welfarist versus non-welfarist) and complicated by the diversity of measures that are used to elicit these weights. In computing weights for QALYs, some researchers have explicitly defined valuations in terms of the individual utility associated with health states, while others have favoured an alternative view of QALYs as an indicator of changes in population health to be used as the maximand in a social objective function (see Chapter 3 for a full discussion). The interpreta-tion of the 'disability weights' used in DALYs has been more closely aligned with the latter position in the competing views of QALYs. However, the approach used to elicit these weights has evolved through successive iterations of the DALY measure, as described in the following section.

11.1.1 Development of disability weights for DALYs

The development of the DALY as a metric for the global burden of disease has required as one input a set of disability weights that reflect the relative severity of each of the approximately 500 disabling sequelae following from the 100 or so different disease and injury causes included in the study. As the name implies, disability weights reflect a construct that resides at an intermediate point in the spectrum from impairment to handicap proposed in the International Classification of Impairments, Disabilities and Handicaps (ICIDH), appearing in revised form as the International Classification of Functioning, Disability and Health (see Chapter 4). The choice of disability rather than handicap as the relevant measure was based on the argument that a focus on handicap could further exacerbate disparities by placing a greater emphasis on the impact of a particular disability amongst those who already have a relative advantage. As quoted in Murray (1994), one example of this thinking appeared in the ICIDH manual: 'Subnormality of intelligence is an impairment, but it may not lead to appreciable activity restriction; factors other than the impairment may determine the handicap because the disadvantage may be minimal if the individual lives in a remote rural community, whereas it could be severe in the child of university graduates living in a large city, of whom more might be expected'.

Assignment of disability weights to the range of sequelae in the first iteration of the Global Burden of Disease study was based on first defining six different disability classes, and then mapping from each sequela into the class or classes that applied to incident cases of that sequela (Murray 1994; Murray and Lopez 1994). The six disability classes were defined in reference to limitations in activities of daily living such as eating and personal hygiene; instrumental activities of daily living such as meal preparation; and four other domains (procreation, occupation, education and recreation). Weights were assigned to the different classes by a panel of public health experts using a rating scale approach. Once the weights associated with the six classes were determined (by averaging the values from the expert panel), the disability weight for a particular sequela was estimated by distributing incident cases across the different classes—reflecting either the proportion of time an average incident case would spend in different disability classes, or the proportion of incident cases that would be characterized by different severity levels—and computing the average weight.

For the revision of the Global Burden of Disease study published in 1996, a new approach to estimating disability weights was devised based on the person trade-off (PTO) method. The revision of the approach was inspired by some specific criticisms of the original approach: (1) that the disability classes were appropriate only for adults (since, for example, children were naturally dependent on adults for various of the referenced activities); (2) that no formal, replicable protocol was available to guide those aspiring to undertake a national burden of disease exercise; (3) that the class with the lowest level of disability was valued at 0.096 (on a scale on which 0 represents no disability and 1 represents disability equivalent to being dead), which produced a scale that was too blunt to capture very mild conditions; and, finally, (4) that the valuation task itself did not allow the expert panellists to reflect on the policy implications of their values (Murray 1996). New health state valuations were elicited from a panel of health professionals following an explicit protocol. In the protocol, a series of 22 indicator conditions was evaluated through an intensive group exercise involving two variants of the PTO and incorporating a deliberative process to encourage reflection on the values that emerged during the exercise. The first type of PTO question asked participants to trade off life extension in a population of healthy individuals versus life extension in a population of individuals having a particular condition. The second type of PTO question asked participants to trade off life extension for healthy individuals versus health improvements in individuals with the reference condition. Participants were required to resolve inconsistencies in the numerical weights implied by the two alternative framings of the PTO. The final consistent values implied by the reconciled PTO responses, averaged across participants, defined the disability weights for the 22 indicator conditions, which were then clustered into seven different severity classes (Box 11.2).

To generate disability weights for the remainder of the approximately 500 disabling sequelae in the study, participants were asked to estimate distributions across the seven classes for each sequela. As described above for the first iteration, these distributions were intended to reflect either the proportion of time a typical case for a given sequela would spend in each of the

---

Box 11.2 Disability weights in the Global Burden of Disease study, 1996 revision

Based on a deliberative protocol built around the PTO method, disability weights for 22 indicator conditions were estimated, and the conditions were then grouped into seven different classes reflecting a spectrum of severity levels:

- Class 1, with weights ranging from 0.00 to 0.02, included vitiligo on face; and weight-for-height 2 SDs or more below the reference median

- Class 2, with weights ranging from 0.02 to 0.12, included watery diarrhoea; severe sore throat; and severe anaemia

- Class 3, with weights ranging from 0.12 to 0.24, included radius fracture in a stiff cast; infertility; erectile dysfunction; rheumatoid arthritis; and angina

- Class 4, with weights ranging from 0.24 to 0.36, included below-the-knee amputation; and deafness

- Class 5, with weights ranging from 0.36 to 0.50, included rectovaginal fistula; mild mental retardation; and Down syndrome

- Class 6, with weights ranging from 0.50 to 0.70, included unipolar major depression; blindness; and paraplegia

- Class 7, with weights ranging from 0.70 to 1.00, included active psychosis; dementia; severe migraine; and quadriplegia

Weights for the full range of sequelae in the study were derived by estimating the distribution of incident cases across these seven classes, using

---

Box 11.2 Disability weights in the Global Burden of Disease study, 1996 revision *(continued)*

the indicator conditions in each class as illustrative benchmarks. Examples of the resulting weights include:

- Episodes of otitis media: 0.02
- Cases of asthma: 0.10 (untreated); 0.06 (treated)
- Episodes of malaria: 0.21 (ages 0–4 years); 0.17 (ages 15 and older)
- Rheumatoid arthritis cases: 0.23 (untreated); 0.17 (treated)
- Episodes of meningitis: 0.62
- Terminal cancer: 0.81

Source: Murray (1996)

---

disability classes; or the percentage of cases that would be categorized in each of the different classes. Distributions across disability classes were estimated separately for treated and untreated cases where relevant, and weights could also vary by age group. Box 11.2 presents a few examples of the resulting disability weights for common causes.

More recently, prompted by a more general research agenda on developing internationally comparable summary measures of population health at the World Health Organization, the use of the PTO as the basis for disability weights in DALYs has been reconsidered. The most recent thinking on DALYs reflects an effort to delineate the concept embodied in the non-fatal component of the measure more precisely, which has led to the explicit definition of disability weights as measures of overall levels of health associated with health states rather than as measures of the utility associated with these states or the contribution of health to overall welfare (Salomon *et al.* 2003*a*). Part of this effort has included an attempt to separate out some of the other values that combine with judgments about health levels in valuation elicitation techniques such as the TTO, SG and PTO, either by formally modelling responses as a function of both underlying health judgements and these other values (Salomon and Murray 2004) (see Chapter 5 for a discussion of these non-health factors), or by choosing alternative valuation methods such as ones based on ordinal data collection strategies (Salomon 2003; see also Chapter 7).

11.1.2 Other social value choices in DALYs

Another feature of DALYs that should be mentioned relates to the inclusion of other social value choices, besides the valuations of health states used to construct disability weights. Many of the arguments around discounting invoked in the context of QALY measures (see Chapter 9) have also been rehearsed in the discussion of DALYs as population health measures. As debate continues, the use of a three per cent annual discount rate has become the default standard in the construction of the DALY, as in the recommended base case analysis for cost-effectiveness studies; in both cases it is advised that alternatives should be considered in sensitivity analyses. In addition to discounting, some have argued for assigning unequal weights to life years lived at different ages, and the standard DALY includes weights that give the highest values to years lived in young adulthood. A range of arguments have been considered in relation to age weighting, with reference to empirical findings on weights that people attach to years over the life course (Busschbach *et al.* 1993; Jelsma *et al.* 2002). The developers of the DALY measure argue for unequal age weighting based on the social roles played at different ages (Murray 1996), but age weights remain controversial (see for example, Anand and Hansen 1997). The question of age weighting is considered more fully in Chapter 10.

In summary, for use in economic evaluations of health interventions, the DALY is best viewed as a close relative of the QALY, with a few key differences, summarized in Box 11.3.

Box 11.3 DALYs and QALYs

The relationship between DALYs and QALYs has been characterized as follows by developers of the DALY: 'DALYs can be considered as a variant of QALYs which have been standardized for comparative use' (Murray and Acharya 1997).

Key distinctions between DALYs and QALYs include the following:

♦ Because DALYs are negative measures that reflect health losses, the scale used to quantify non-fatal health outcomes in DALYs is inverted compared with the scale used in QALYs, i.e. numbers near zero represent relatively good health levels (or small losses) in DALYs, while numbers near one represent relatively poor health levels (or large losses). The inverted scale means that interventions that improve health result in DALYs *averted*, whereas QALYs are *gained*.

♦ Disability weights in DALYs are intended to reflect the degree to which health is reduced by the presence of different conditions, whereas at least one interpretation of the weights in QALYs is based on the individual utility derived from different states.

Box 11.3 DALYs and QALYs *(continued)*

- The standard formulation of DALYs weights healthy life lived at different ages according to a variable function that peaks at young adult ages, while QALYs do not typically incorporate unequal age weights (though these can be added; see Chapter 10). (It should be noted that DALYs may also be computed with equal age weights.)

- For measuring the burden of disease, years of life lost due to premature mortality at different ages are computed in reference to a standard life table, defined by the period life expectancy at birth for Japanese females at the time of the original Global Burden of Disease study. For purposes of cost-effectiveness, this distinction is largely inconsequential, since the standard life expectancy essentially cancels out when benefits of inter- ventions are computed as the *change in* DALYs. As a simplified example, imagine an intervention that defers one death from age 50 to age 70, and suppose that the normative target lifespan used as the yardstick for DALYs is 80 years (irrespective of one's current age). Then the number of DALYs averted through intervention is a change from $80 - 50 = 30$, to $80 - 70 = 10$, for a net of 20 DALYs averted, which is the same as the number of QALYs gained through the intervention. (Note that in the actual standard life table that is used, as in most life tables, the target lifespan, equal to the age at death, x plus the number of years of remaini- ing life expectancy at age x, rises slightly with advancing adult ages rather than remaining constant as per the simple example here. This will produce a slight discrepancy between DALYs averted and QALYs gained, but this difference is usually negligible.)

11.2 International comparisons of health state valuations

Stepping back from the specifics of the DALY measure in international CEA, we turn now to more general issues around measurement and valuation of health for cross-national applications. While we will refer to applications that span both developed and developing countries here, we will note in particular where work has taken place in low- and middle-income settings.

11.2.1 International adaptation of health status measures

There has been significant interest in adapting health status measurement instruments to varied cultural settings, and several reviews of these efforts are available (for example, Guillemin *et al.* 1993; Anderson *et al.* 1996). A recent review on cross-cultural adaptation of health status measures (Sommerfeld *et al.* 2002) notes further the growing range of studies on cross-cultural adaptations of condition-specific instruments for health problems ranging from epilepsy (Cramer *et al.* 1998) to genital herpes (Doward *et al.* 1998).

Certain generic health measurement instruments, including the SF-36 and the EQ-5D, have been the focus of large-scale efforts at adaptation and translation into a wide range of languages and settings. The IQOLA project has produced translations of the SF-36 for use in more than 50 countries (see, for example, Keller *et al.* 1998; Ware *et al.* 1995; or the IQOLA website at www.iqola.org). The EQ-5D instrument has also been translated widely, with official language versions available for 60 countries as of January 2006 (see www.euroqol.org).

These extensive efforts to translate and adapt health measurement instruments to diverse settings have given considerable attention to issues of linguistic equivalence in translation, and various guidelines have been proposed to help standardize the translation of health survey instruments (Guillemin *et al.* 1993; Sartorius and Kuyken 1994; Bullinger *et al.* 1998). However, concerns have been raised about the cultural equivalence of translations (Herdman *et al.* 1997, 1998), and a review of 58 papers reporting on the translation of eight generic instruments concluded that more attention must be given to ensuring conceptual equivalence (Bowden and Fox-Rushby 2003).

In general, most efforts to translate and adapt instruments—either generic or condition-specific—have focused nearly exclusively on high-income countries; examples from low- and middle-income countries are relatively rare. For the standardized instruments discussed extensively in this book, exceptions to this general rule include adaptations of the SF-36 in China (Li *et al.* 2003), Mexico (Zuniga *et al.* 1999), Bangladesh (Ahmed *et al.* 2002), Tanzania (Wagner *et al.* 1999) and several other developing countries; and the EQ-5D in China (Wang *et al.* 2005), Zimbabwe (Jelsma *et al.* 2003) and South Africa (Jelsma *et al.* 2004), among others.

Large-scale examples of adapting and applying standardized health measurement instruments in developing countries come from two waves of surveys conducted by the World Health Organization: the Multi-Country Survey Study on Health and Responsiveness (MCSS), conducted in 61 countries during 2000–2001 (Üstün *et al.* 2003*a*), and the World Health Surveys, conducted in 72 countries during 2002–2003 (Üstün *et al.* 2003*b*). The MCSS included a generic health status module including items with five-category response scales on six core domains (affect, cognition, mobility, pain, self-care and usual activities). The World Health Survey included a modified health module with items on eight domains (affect, cognition, energy, interpersonal activities, mobility, pain, self-care and vision).

11.2.2 International research on valuation approaches

To date, international research on health state valuations has been less extensive than research on adapting existing health status instruments. The great majority of studies on valuation approaches such as the TTO, SG and PTO have been conducted in the USA, Western Europe and Australia. A handful of studies have been conducted in developing countries to consider the feasibility of administering valuation techniques where educational attainment, literacy and numeracy are low. Application of these techniques across cultures introduces a range of additional challenges that compound the universal concerns about the abstract nature and cognitive demands of questions such as the SG. Sommerfeld *et al.* (2002) provide a concise summary of some of the considerations for cross-cultural application of these techniques, including varying notions of illness, risk and probability, and time.

The following examples illustrate some of the key findings from the few studies that have been conducted outside the industrialized world.

Sadana (2002) undertook a valuation study in Phnom Penh, Cambodia in order to investigate the feasibility of different valuation techniques in a developing country setting. In the study, pre-tests of the PTO, SG and VAS were conducted in a sample of women ages 18–45 years. For the PTO, the pre-tests indicated that respondents were reluctant to answer both variants of the question used in the study, although the author concluded that comprehension problems were not a major concern. For the SG, the pre-test found that no respondents could complete the task. Of the three methods examined, only the VAS was successfully implemented in pre-test, yielding consistent orderings of the five indicator conditions in the study (blindness, infertility, below-the-knee amputation, severe headache and unipolar major depression).

Mahapatra *et al.* (2002) conducted a valuation study in Andhra Pradesh State, India, including two components: (1) a multimethod study using ranking, VAS, TTO and PTO among a convenience sample of more educated respondents; and (2) a community sample survey in a rural village using ranking and VAS. The community survey included graphical depictions of domain levels for the range of hypothetical states to facilitate communication to respondents. The study found reasonable agreement between responses from the different valuation approaches in the multimethod component, with the smallest number of logically inconsistent responses on the VAS. In the community survey, while substantial measurement error appeared to characterize the VAS responses, the aggregate results were compared with VAS responses from a similar study in the Netherlands, and a high correlation was observed.

Baltussen *et al.* (2002) developed and applied a culturally adapted version of the VAS in a rural village in Burkina Faso. Considering nine hypothetical states, respondents were asked to indicate the severity of overall health decrements associated with those states using wooden blocks as physical units. The authors found that this procedure had high test–retest reliability (0.90 using Pearson's *r*) and concluded that the adapted approach to eliciting VAS responses was feasible to implement in a rural African setting.

The most extensive effort to date to implement health state valuations in developing countries was undertaken as part of a survey programme led by the World Health Organization (Salomon *et al.* 2003*b*). Household surveys including a health state valuation module were conducted in 14 countries: China, Colombia, Egypt, Georgia, India, Iran, Lebanon, Indonesia, Mexico, Nigeria, Singapore, Slovakia, Syria and Turkey. The surveys were nationally representative except in China, India and Nigeria. Each country fielded both a sample survey in the general community using ranking and VAS, as well as a more detailed survey among respondents with high levels of educational attainment using ranking, VAS, TTO, SG and PTO. The multimethod study found systematically different results by methods, with the lowest valuations from the VAS and the highest valuations from PTO. SG valuations were close to PTO valuations for most states, and TTO valuations tended to be nearer to VAS. The degree of measurement error varied widely across countries, but the broad patterns of differences across methods were consistent in the range of settings. The community survey revealed consistent orderings of the valuations for the 33 hypothetical states in the study using the VAS, although for any given state there was variation across countries in the mean VAS values (Fig. 11.1).

11.2.3 Estimation of valuation functions across countries

Several of the major health status descriptive systems have been linked to valuation functions estimated in multiple countries, although the number of published international valuation functions remains relatively small. Given the high cost of undertaking valuation surveys, early work using preference-based measures has tended to use the valuation results from just one or two countries, which for the EQ-5D and SF-6D has been the UK and for the HUI has been Canada. However, there is increasing interest in cross-country variation in health state valuations, and some emerging evidence suggests that the results from one country cannot necessarily be transferred to other countries.

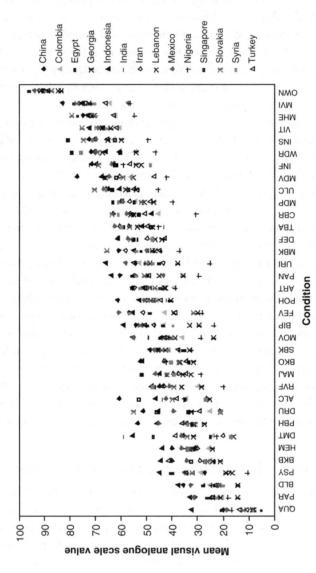

Fig. 11.1 Average visual analogue scores across countries in the World Health Organization Multi-country Survey Study on Health and Responsiveness, 2000–2001. The three letter condition labels on the horizontal axis refer to brief descriptions of problems presented to respondents, ranging from quadriplegia (QUA) to mild vision problems (MVI). Also shown are respondents' valuation of their own health (OWN) Source: Salomon et al. (2003b).

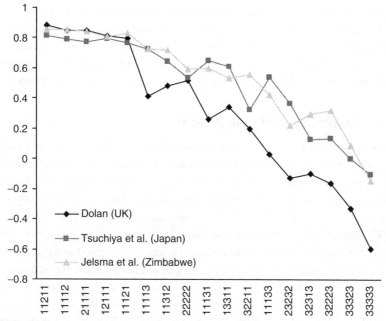

Fig. 11.2 Predicted valuations for selected EQ-5D states based on published valuation functions estimated from surveys in the UK, Japan and Zimbabwe. Sources: Dolan (1997); Tsuchiya *et al.* (2002); Jelsma *et al.* (2003).

We have already reported on comparative results from several of the major systems in Chapter 8, but review selected examples here.

The instrument with the largest number of country-specific valuation functions is the EQ-5D, through the efforts of the EuroQol group. EQ-5D valuation functions have been estimated for 13 countries, and for six European countries combined (see www.euroqol.org). Outside Europe, the countries include Japan, New Zealand, the USA and Zimbabwe. For some countries including Denmark, Germany, Spain and the UK, alternative valuation functions are available based on either VAS or TTO responses. A comparison of the valuations predicted using the country-specific functions reveals certain differences. Figure 11.2 shows an example of predictions from published EQ-5D valuation functions that were estimated based on TTO surveys in the UK, Japan and Zimbabwe (Dolan 1997; Tsuchiya *et al.* 2002; Jelsma *et al.* 2003). Perhaps surprisingly the predictions from the Tsuchiya *et al.* (2002) model based on a study in Japan and the Jelsma *et al.* (2003) model based on a study in Zimbabwe are very similar, while the Dolan (1997) model estimated from a UK study produces predictions that diverge from both of these, particularly for severe health states.

As reported in Chapter 8, valuations for SF-6D have been undertaken in Japan and Hong Kong in addition to the UK, and valuations for HUI2 have been undertaken in the UK and for HUI3 in France. Along with the EQ-5D research, the findings from these studies suggest that there are often significant differences in the values given to the same states as defined by these systems.

11.3 Summary and conclusions

This chapter has provided a brief introduction to the DALY as an alternative to the QALY used increasingly in economic evaluations in low- and middle-income countries. We have highlighted similarities and differences in the two measures and traced the evolution of conceptual and empirical work supporting the measurement and valuation of non-fatal outcomes in DALYs.

We also have discussed the expanding interest in adapting instruments for describing and valuing health in diverse settings and reviewed some of the key developments in this area. As the number of adaptations and translations of existing instruments grows, it is important to think critically about various ways of evaluating equivalence. In the realm of valuation, it is essential to continue to examine whether prevailing modes of data collection and analysis are suitable in settings of varying educational levels and diverse cultures.

Evidence on cross-cultural variation in valuations is limited, but some of the research thus far points to possible differences. A clear understanding of the extent, direction and substantive importance of these differences awaits further empirical research, and understanding the reasons for variation that has been observed to date is challenging. Differences in observed valuations may reflect genuine differences in population values for health; differences in attitudes toward time (in the TTO) or risk (in the SG), or different uses of response scales (in the VAS); or differences in the interpretations of health state labels and descriptions across countries. As the evidence base on valuations across settings widens, parsing out the possible determinants of variation, and thinking carefully about the policy implications of these findings, remains a priority.

References

Ahmed SM, Rana AK, Chowdhury M, Bhuiya A (2002). Measuring perceived health outcomes in non-western culture: does SF-36 have a place? *Journal of Health, Population, and Nutrition* 20:334–42.

Anand S, Hanson K (1997). Disability-adjusted life years: a critical review. *Journal of Health Economics* 16:685–702.

Anderson RT, Aaronson NK, Bullinger M, McBee WL (1996). A review of the progress towards developing health-related quality-of-life instruments for international clinical studies and outcomes research. *Phamacoeconomics* 10:336–55.

Baltussen RMPM, Sanon M, Sommerfeld J, Würthwein R (2002). Obtaining disability weights in rural Burkina Faso using a culturally adapted visual analogue scale. *Health Economics*, 11:155–63.

Bowden A, Fox-Rushby JA (2003). A systematic and critical review of the process of translation and adaptation of generic health-related quality of life measures in Africa, Asia, Eastern Europe, the Middle East, South America. *Social Science and Medicine* 57:1289–306.

Bullinger M, Alonso J, Apolone G, Leplege A, Sullivan M, Wood-Dauphinee S, Gandek B, Wagner A, Aaronson N, Bech P, Fukuhara S, Kaasa S, Ware JE Jr. (1998). Translating health status questionnaires and evaluating their quality: the IQOLA Project approach. International Quality of Life Assessment. *Journal of Clinical Epidemiology* 51:913–23.

Busschbach JJ, Hessing DJ, de Charro FT (1993). The utility of health at different stages in life: a quantitative approach. *Social Science and Medicine* 37:153–8.

Cramer JA, Perrine K, Devinsky O, Bryant-Comstock L, Meador K, Hermann B (1998). Development and cross-cultural translations of a 31-item quality of life in epilepsy inventory. *Epilepsia* 39:81–88.

Dolan P (1997) Modelling valuations for EuroQol health states. *Medical Care* 35:1095–108.

Doward LC, McKenna SP, Kohlmann T, Niero M, Patrick D, Spencer B, Thorsen H (1998). The international development of the RGHQoL: a quality of life measure for recurrent genital herpes. *Quality of Life Research* 7:143–53.

Guillemin F, Bombardier C, Beaton D (1993). Cross-cultural adaptation of health related quality of life measures: literature review and proposed guidelines. *Journal of Clinical Epidemiology* 46:1417–32.

Herdman M, Fox-Rushby J, Badia X (1997). 'Equivalence' and the translation and adaptation of health-related quality of life questionnaires. *Quality of Life Research* 6:237–47.

Herdman M, Fox-Rushby J, Badia X (1998). A model of equivalence in the cultural adaptation of HRQoL instruments: the universalist approach. *Quality of Life Research* 7:323–35.

Jamison DT, Breman JG, Measham AR, Alleyne G, Claeson M, Evans DB, Jha P, Mills A, Musgrooe P. eds (2006). *Disease control priorities in developing countries*, 2nd edn. Oxford University Press, New York.

Jelsma J, Mkoka S, Amosun L, Nieuwveldt J (2004). The reliability and validity of the Xhosa version of the EQ-5D. *Disability abd Rehabilitation* 26:103–8.

Jelsma J, Hansen K, De Weerdt W, De Cock P, Kind P (2003). How do Zimbabweans value health states? *Population Health Metrics* 1(1):11.

Jelsma J, Shumba D, Kristian H, De Weerdt W, De Cock P (2002). Preferences of urban Zimbabweans for health and life lived at different ages. *Bulletin of the World Health Organisation* 80:204–9.

Keller SD, Ware JE, Gandek B (1998). Testing the equivalence of translations of widely used response choice labels: results from the IQOLA project, International Quality of Life Assessment. *Journal of Clinical Epidemiology* 51:933–44.

Li L, Wang HM, Shen Y (2003). Chinese SF-36 Health Survey: translation, cultural adaptation, validation, and normalization. *Journal of Epidemiology and Community Health* 57:259–63.

Mahapatra P, Salomon JA, Nanda L (2002). Measuring health state values in developing countries—results from a community survey in Andhra Pradesh. In: Murray CJL,

Salomon JA, Mathers CD, Lopez AD, eds. *Summary measures of population health: concepts, ethics, measurement and applications.* World Health Organization, Geneva, pp. 473–486.

Murray CJL (1994). Quantifying the burden of disease: the technical basis for disability-adjusted life years. *Bulletin of the World Health Organisation* 72:429–45.

Murray CJL (1996). Rethinking DALYs. In: Murray CJL, Lopez AD, eds. *The global burden of disease: a comprehensive assessment of mortality and disability from diseases, injuries, and risk factors in 1990 and projected to 2020.* Harvard School of Public Health, Cambridge, MA, pp. 1–98.

Murray CJL, Acharya AK (1997). Understanding DALYs. *Journal of Health Economics* 16:703–30.

Murray CJL, Lopez AD (1994). Quantifying disability: data, methods and results. *Bulletin of the World Health Organisation* 72:481–94.

Murray CJL, Lopez AD, Jamison DT (1994). The global burden of disease in 1990: summary results, sensitivity analysis and future directions. *Bulletin of the World Health Organisation* 72:495–509.

Murray CJL, Salomon JA, Mathers CD (2000). A critical examination of summary measures of population health. *Bulletin of the World Health Organisation* 78: 981–94.

Sadana R (2002). Measurement of variance in health state valuations in Phnom Penh, Cambodia. In: Murray CJL, Salomon JA, Mathers CD, Lopez AD, eds. *Summary measures of population health: concepts, ethics, measurement and applications.* World Health Organization, Geneva, pp. 593–618.

Salomon JA (2003). Reconsidering the use of rankings in the valuation of health states: a model for estimating cardinal values from ordinal data. *Population Health Metrics* 1(1):12. http://www.pophealthmetrics.com/content/1/1/12.

Salomon JA, Murray CJL (2004). A multi-method approach to measuring health-state valuations. *Health Economics* 13:281–90.

Salomon JA, Mathers CD, Chatterji S, Sadana R, Üstün TB, Murray CJL (2003*a*). Quantifying individual levels of health: definitions, concepts and measurement issues. In: Murray CJL, Evans DB, eds. *Health systems performance assessment: debates, measures and empiricism.* World Health Organization, Geneva, pp. 301–318.

Salomon JA, Murray CJL, Üstün TB, Chatterji S (2003*b*). Health state valuations in summary measures of population health. In: Murray CJL, Evans DB, eds. *Health systems performance assessment: debates, measures and empiricism.* World Health Organization, Geneva, pp. 409–436.

Sartorius N, Kuyken W (1994). Translation of health status instruments. In: Orley J, Kuyken W, eds. *Proceedings of the joint meeting organised by the World Health Organisation and the foundation IPSEN.* Springer, Paris, pp. 3–18.

Sommerfeld J, Baltussen RMPM, Metz Lm Sanon M, Sauerborn R (2002). Determinants of variance in health state valuations. In: Murray CJL, Salomon JA, Mathers CD, Lopez AD, eds. *Summary measures of population health: concepts, ethics, measurement and applications.* World Health Organization, Geneva, pp. 549–580.

Tan-Torres Edejer T, Baltussen R, Adam T, Hutubessy R, Acharya A, Evans DB, Murray CJL (2003). *Making choices in health: WHO guide to cost effectiveness analysis.* World Health Organization, Geneva.

Tsuchiya A, Ikeda S, Ikegami N, Nishimura S, Sakai I, Fukuda T, Hamashima C, Hisashige A, Tamura M (2002). Estimating an EQ-5D population value set: the case of Japan. *Health Economics* 11:341–53.

Üstün TB, Chatterji S, Villanueva M, Zendeb L, Celik C, Sadaon R, Valentine NB, Ortiz JB, Tandon A, Salomon JA, Cao Y, Xie WJ, Özalten E, Mathers CD, Murray CJL (2003a). WHO Multi-country Survey Study on Health and Responsiveness 2000–2001. In: Murray CJL, Evans DB, eds. *Health systems performance assessment: debates, measures and empiricism*. World Health Organization, Geneva, pp. 761–796.

Üstün TB, Chatterji S, Mechbal A, Murray CJL, WHS Collaborating Group. (2003a). The World Health Surveys. In: Murray CJL, Evans DB, eds. *Health systems performance assessment: debates, measures and empiricism*. World Health Organization, Geneva, pp. 797–808.

Wagner AK, Wyss K, Gandek B, Kilima PM, Lorenz S, Whiting D (1999). A Kiswahili version of the SF-36 Health Survey for use in Tanzania: translation and tests of scaling assumptions. *Quality of Life Research* 8:101–10.

Wang H, Kindig DA, Mullahy J (2005). Variation in Chinese population health related quality of life: results from a EuroQol study in Beijing, China. *Quality of Life Research* 14:119–32.

Ware JE, Keller SD, Gandek B, Brazier JE, Sullivan M (1995). Evaluating translations of health status questionnaires: methods from the IQOLA project. *International Journal of Technology Assessment in Health Care* 11:525–551.

World Bank (1993). *World development report 1993*. Oxford University Press, New York.

Zuniga MA, Carrillo-Jimenez GT, Fos PJ, Gandek B, Medina-Moreno MR (1999). Evaluation of health status using the SF-36 survey: preliminary results in Mexico [in Spanish]. *Salud Pública de México* 41:110–8.

Chapter 12

Conclusions

In this book we set out to address the main questions surrounding the measurement and valuation of health and its consequences for well-being. What emerges from even a casual reading of this book is the wide range of ways available for addressing the core questions such as the definition of health, the techniques of valuation, who should provide the values, techniques for modelling health state values, and so forth. The last three decades have seen a substantial body of research seeking to address these questions and the development of new tools and instruments for putting the 'q' into the QALY. We hope we have fully reflected these developments.

This content of this book begs the question as to which combination of answers to these questions should be used. In economic evaluation, the precise choice of methods depends on normative judgement as well as technical considerations, and none more so than in the measurement and valuation of health. It is difficult to get a group of health economists to agree on whether the main outcome of health care is health or on a single definition of health, let alone who should value the states and by which valuation technique.

Economic theory might suggest that individuals have a uni-dimensional latent utility variable along which people's utility for all sorts of health states can be represented. The methods described in this book are offering a different view of this single value. Whether or not a single latent variable exists, we know that the different methods themselves help fashion the value respondents provide. As Llewellyn-Thomas *et al.* (1984, p. 550) pointed out a number of years ago, it is '... naive to think of any state of health as possessing a single utility or value. Rather, numerical values for health states are influenced by the state itself, the way in which information about the state is presented to a rater, the method used to elicit judgements and other circumstances of the rating task'. At the time of being asked, respondents are constructing their preferences over the things they have given little thought to prior to the interview. So it is not surprising that their responses are influenced by the way they are asked. This problem is well recognized in psychology and has started to be taken seriously in health economics, but what is the solution?

One response might be that health state values are so labile and prone to external influence that they are largely meaningless. We would argue strongly that this is not the case. The values we obtain using different methods reflect the underlying views of respondents. It is important that researchers think hard about what they want to value, the theoretical basis of the technique (such as whether they want a preference-based technique like SG or TTO rather than VAS), avoid obvious biases (such as from anchoring effects) and use modelling methods with the best predictive validity. There are also important options that require policy makers to make normative judgements. To inform resource allocation across a health care system it is necessary to achieve a degree of standardization in terms of the combination of key attributes, such as whose values, the technique and variant of valuation (including the appropriate upper and lower anchors states). This was the approach recommended by the Washington Panel on Cost Effectiveness in Health and Medicine (Gold *et al.* 1996) and later adopted by the National Institute for Health and Clinical Excellence (2004). The extent to which this also requires a single descriptive system remains an open question.

There are important differences in the methods being adopted around the world. Across eight sets of guidelines from seven countries reviewed in Table 12.1, most guidelines currently permit a range of methods to be used. Some express a preference, but this does not seem to rule out other methods. Even where there is a preference between methods, there is no clear agreement between guidelines. However, it would seem that CEA or cost per QALY analysis is usually preferred to CBA, and that most agencies want general population values to be used. Beyond this, the specifics are often unclear (even from the public guidelines). Over time, these guidelines could be revised, and readers are advised to consult www.ispor.org/PEguidelines/index.asp regularly.

The adoption of a reference case does not imply that other methods are wrong. Any set of methods implies compromises and may be thought to work against the interests of some conditions and treatments that should be recognized. We still have much to learn about the measurement and valuation of health and its consequences for well-being in the context of economic evaluation, such as the role of descriptive systems, how values are influenced by the techniques and their variants, the development of better techniques for eliciting values (particularly in more vulnerable groups), the role of cross-cultural variation, why experience-based values differ from preferences, how best to model data and so forth. We cannot predict the way the field is likely to develop over the next decade, but we are sure it will lose none of its intellectual challenge and controversy.

Table 12.1 Comparison of economic guidelines on valuation of benefits (as of January 2006)

Country	Agency	Year	Preferred form of economic evaluation	Descriptive system	Whose values	Method of obtaining values	Questionnaire recommended	Other information
England and Wales	NICE	2004	CEA using QALYs	Generic	UK population public preferences	Choice based method	No—though does mention EQ-5D	This is for the reference case. Additional analyses may be submitted using disease-specific instruments or patient preferences. Although not compulsory to use EQ-5D, it is mentioned as it meets all the criteria.

Table 12.1 (Continued) Comparison of economic guidelines on valuation of benefits (as of January 2006)

Country	Agency	Year	Preferred form of economic evaluation	Descriptive system	Whose values	Method of obtaining values	Questionnaire recommended	Other information
Canada	CCOHTA	1997 (2nd edn.)	Cost per QALY/CBA preferred But CMA, CCA plus CEA	Where possible, use a specific, a generic and a preference-based Measure	Informed general public	Not specified but must be 'scientifically sound'	Mentions QWB, HUI, EQ-5D and says these would be satisfactory	Scores must be based on preferences and measured on an interval scale where dead = 0 and healthy = 1. Patient values may be used as a suitable proxy
Canada	Ontario	1994	Minimum of cost comparison and CCA. Probably CEA as well	Prefer generic	Not specified	Not specified	Not specified	CEA not compulsory. If doing a CUA, then utility should be estimated in a sample of subjects with the of interest. In some cases, proxies are appropriate.

The Baltic	2002	CEA/cost per QALY/CMA	Either	Not specified	Not specified	Recommend Euroqol or HUI	Mentions that it is useful to carry out more than one type of analysis. Idea of cost value analysis in addition to CUA
Norway Norwegian Medicines Agency		2002	An analysis should be done which includes the patient utility (outcome). If a cost per QALY is done, supplement with a cost value analysis	Not specified	Not specified	Mention Euroqol as an example, but not a recommendation	

Table 12.1 (Continued) Comparison of economic guidelines on valuation of benefits (as of January 2006)

Country	Agency	Year	Preferred form of economic evaluation	Descriptive system	Whose values	Method of obtaining values	Questionnaire recommended	Other information
The Netherlands	Health Insurance Council	1999	CEA and/or cost per QALY	Recommends both	If doing a CUA—random sample of the population	Not specified	Euro-QoL and HUI mentioned as suitable	CBA allowed only if a CEA/CUA has been done
Australia	Commonwealth Department of Health and Ageing	2002	CEA/cost per QALY/CMA as appropriate	Not specified	Not specified	Not specified	Not specified	CBA not encouraged. Prefer final outcomes, i.e. deaths prevented, LYG or QALYs. Whilst recognizes that it would be useful to have most outcomes valued as QALYs, recognizes that research/data not there yet to allow this

| Finland | Ministry of Social Affairs and Health | 1999 | CMA/CEA/cost per QALY/CBA dependent on how therapies impact on patients' health condition. Must justify choice | None | Not specified | Not specified | None |
| Sweden | | | CUA/CBA | None | III person | Choice-based | None |

Source: Tarn, Tony YH, and Smith, Marilyn D, 'Pharmacoeconomic Guidelines Around the World'. ISPOR connections 10 (2004, July/August): 5–15.

References

Gold MR, Siegel JE, Russell LB, Weinstein MC (1996). *Cost-effectiveness in health and medicine.* Oxford University Press, Oxford.

Llewellyn-Thomas H, Sutherland HJ, Tibshirani R, Ciampi A, Till JE, Boyd NF (1984). Describing health states: methodological issues in obtaining values for health states. *Medical Care* 22:543–52.

National Institute for Clinical Excellence (NICE) (2004). *Guide to the methods of technology appraisal.* National Health Service, London, pp. 1–54. Available at http://www.nice.org.uk/pdf/tap_methods.pdf.

Glossary

Terms in italics are defined elsewhere in the glossary.

additive separability One of the conditions to be satisfied if the *QALY* is to be interpreted as a representation of individual utility. It requires that the preference for a given state of health is not affected by the states of health that precede or follow it.

Bayesian method A branch of statistics that uses prior information on beliefs for estimation and inference.

bootstrapping A simulation method for deriving non-parametric estimates of variables of interest (e.g. the variance in the C/E ratio) from a data set.

category rating scales Scales that are composed of distinct categories. The categories are often numerical, such as 0, 1, 2,... 10; the phenomenon being rated must be assigned to one and only one category. Numerical categories often are treated as equal-interval in analyses. In psychology, sometimes referred to as the method of equal-appearing intervals.

compensation test In economics, a gauge of the desirability of a programme. A programme is considered to be welfare enhancing if those who gain from it are willing to pay enough for their gains to compensate the losers. Actual payment of the compensation is not required. (Also *potential Pareto improvement* or *Kaldor–Hicks criterion*.)

construct validity An instrument exhibits construct validity when it is seen to correlate with other measures of the phenomenon being measured and it is able to discriminate between groups that have known differences.

contingent valuation A method of placing a monetary value on a good or service that is not available in the marketplace by determining, contingent on it being available in the marketplace, the maximum amount that people would be *willing to pay* for it (buying price) and/or the minimum amount that people would be willing to accept to part with it (selling price).

convergent validity An instrument exhibits convergent validity when it is shown to co-vary (in the fashion expected of a good measure for the *construct* or phenomenon of interest) with a number of other distinct measures, each of which is thought to be a direct or indirect correlate for some distinct aspect of the *construct* or phenomenon. The correlations between the instrument being evaluated and these other measures are conceived of as representing convergent lines of evidence for the *validity* of the instrument.

cost-benefit analysis (CBA) A technique of economic evaluation for estimating the net social benefit of a programme or intervention as the incremental benefit of the programme less the *incremental cost*, with all benefits and costs measured in dollars.

cost-consequence analysis A technique of economic evaluation in which the components of *incremental costs* and consequences of alternative programmes are computed and listed, without any attempt to aggregate these results.

cost-effectiveness analysis (CEA) A technique of economic evaluation in which costs and effects of a programme and at least one alternative are calculated and presented in a ratio of *incremental cost* to incremental effect. Effects are health outcomes, such as cases of a disease prevented, years of life gained or *quality-adjusted life years*, rather than monetary measures as in *cost-benefit analysis*.

cost-effectiveness ratio The *incremental cost* of obtaining a unit of health effect (such as dollars per year, or per quality-adjusted year, of life expectancy) from a given health intervention, when compared with an alternative.

cost-minimization analysis (CMA) A technique of economic evaluation that compares the net costs of programmes that achieve the same outcome.

cost-per QALY analysis A special case of CEA where the health effects of the intervention is represented in terms of *QALYs*. Also known as cost-utility analysis.

cost-utility analysis See *cost per QALY analysis*.

decision analysis An explicit, quantitative, systematic approach to decision making under conditions of *uncertainty* in which *probabilities* of each possible event, along with the consequences of those events, are stated explicitly.

decision tree A graphical representation of a decision, incorporating alternative choices, uncertain events (and their *probabilities*) and outcomes.

dimension(s) Component(s) of health status, also called health attributes.

direct preference elicitation A term used in the health economics literature meaning health state values obtained from patients for their own current state.

disability-adjusted life years (DALYs) An indicator developed to assess the global burden of disease. DALYs are computed by adjusting age-specific life expectancy for loss of healthy life due to disability. The value of a year of life at each age is weighted, as are decrements to health from disability from specified diseases and injuries.

discounting The process of converting future money and future health outcomes to their *present value*.

discount rate The interest rate used to compute *present value*, or the interest rate used in *discounting* future sums.

discriminant validity An instrument exhibits discriminant validity to the extent that it does not correlate with variables and measures thought to be unrelated to the *construct* being measured.

discrete choice experiments Elicited by asking respondents to choose between two or more alternatives, typically described by their levels along several dimensions of health and/or *non-health benefit*. Can be converted into valuations with interval properties (see Chapter 7).

economic model An attempt to simplify reality into structure such a *decision tree* of *Markov* process in order to help with the application of one of the techniques of economic evaluation (e.g. *CEA, cost per QALY, CBA*).

effectiveness The extent to which medical interventions achieve health improvements in real practice settings.

effect size A standardized measure (some time known as a 'standardized' effect size) of change over time or between groups. For measuring change over time (such as in a 'before and after' design in a group or a difference in such changes between two groups), a commonly used version is the standardized response mean which is the mean change divided by the standard deviation of changes across individuals.

efficacy The extent to which medical interventions achieve health improvements under ideal circumstances.

equity weights Weights attached to *QALYs* to take into account social relative values of health, due to equity-based concerns. Also see *weighted QALYs*.

ex ante A situation viewed from beforehand, i.e. before the event occurs, before an action is taken or before an outcome is known. This is as opposed to ex post.

expected utility A quantity used to represent the relative desirability of a specified course of action(s) where the outcome of the action cannot be specified before the fact with certainty. Each potential outcome is assigned a *utility*, to represent its desirability, and a *probability*, to represent the likelihood of its occurring if the course of action were adopted. The expected utility is the probability-weighted average *utility* of the potential outcomes.

expected utility theory A framework for analysing decisions under *uncertainty* positing that alternative actions are characterized by a set of possible outcomes and a set of *probabilities* corresponding to each outcome. The sum of the products of the *probability* of each outcome and the *utility* of that outcome is the expected value of *utility* and reflects the preferences of the decision maker. First axiomatized by J. von Neumann and O. Morgenstern in their 1947 book, *Theory of games and economic behavior*, the theory sets forth conditions under which there exists a numerical measure of subjective attractiveness of outcomes (called a *utility function*) with the following properties: (1) this function represents the *ordinal* preferences of the decision maker if outcomes were to be received with certainty; and (2) the order of the expected utilities associated with various uncertain decision strategies represents the rankings of these strategies according to the decision maker's preferences.

experienced-based utility A form of utility concerned with a respondents experience of the moment, in contrast to preference-based utility which concerns views about future states.

externalities The positive (beneficial) or negative (harmful) effects that market exchanges have on people who do not participate directly in those exchanges. Also called 'spillover' effects.

extra welfarism. See *non-welfarism*.

face validity A judgment of the *validity* or reasonableness of a measurement or model based on its examination by persons with expertise in the health problem and intervention being measured or modelled.

generic preference-based measure An instrument for deriving health state values that uses a generic health state descriptive system and a tariff or algorithm for assigning values to each state described by the classification (examples include the EQ-5D or HUI3).

health-related quality of life As a *construct*, health-related quality of life (HRQOL) refers to the impact of the health aspects of an individual's life on that person's *quality of life*, or overall well-being. Also used to refer to the value of a *health state* to an individual.

health state The health of an individual at any particular point in time. A health state may be modified by the impairments, functional states, perceptions, and social opportunities that are influenced by disease, injury, treatment or health policy.

health status measures Systems used to define and describe *health states* (e.g. a multiattribute health status classification system).

health status profile An instrument that describes the health status of a person on each of a comprehensive set of *dimensionss.*

healthy-years equivalent (HYE) The number of years of perfect health (followed by death) that has the same *utility* as (is seen as equivalent to) the lifetime path of *health states* under consideration. It can be measured by two *standard gamble* questions or by one *time trade-off* question.

incremental cost-effectiveness (ratio) The ratio of the difference in costs between two alternatives to the difference in *effectiveness* between the same two alternatives.

inequality aversion The extent to which people prefer a more even distribution of the good in question (e.g. health) than a less even distribution.

Inter-rater reliability A measure of consistency among multiple judges.

interval scale A scale on which equal intervals (e.g., 0.1–0.2, 0.8–0.9) have an equivalent interpretation. An interval scale may have two arbitrarily anchored points.

intrarater reliability A measure of the stability of the rating an individual judge gives to the same question presented more than once during the same or a subsequent administration.

Kaldor–Hicks criterion See *compensation test.*

league table A table in which interventions are ranked by their (incremental) *cost-effectiveness ratios.*

magnitude estimation A technique from psychophysics wherein judges are asked to rate the magnitude of the sensation produced by one stimulus versus another as a ratio (e.g. '2.5 times as much').

marginal benefit The added benefit generated by the next unit consumed.

marginal cost The added cost of producing one additional unit of output.

marginal cost-effectiveness (ratio) The *incremental cost-effectiveness ratio* between two alternatives that differ by one unit along some quantitative scale of intensity, dose or duration. (This term is often used incorrectly as a synonym for *incremental cost- effectiveness.*)

Markov models A type of mathematical model containing a finite number of mutually exclusive and exhaustive *health states*, having time periods of uniform length, and in which the *probability* of movement from one state to another depends on the current state and remains constant over time.

multiattribute utility theory An extension of *expected utility theory* by Keeny and Raiffa (1976) that uses an additional assumption that utility independence among dimensions (or attributes) can be represented by at least one of three forms (additive, multiplicaticative or multilinear). Used to extrapolate values from a subset of states to all possible states defined by a descriptive system.

non-health benefit Benefits from health care that go beyond patient health.

Non-welfarism An alternative approach to modern *welfare economics* that holds that judgements of *social welfare* can be based on information other than individual utility, such as their level of health, independently of how health is valued by the individuals themselves. Also known as *extra welfarism*.

normative theory A coherent group of general propositions or principles of which the objective is to define a norm or standard of correctness.

normative theory of social choice Any group of coherent propositions that lead to prescriptions about the choices society ought to make under well defined circumstances.

objective function The summary quantity, expressed as a mathematical function of independent variables, that an investigator wished to maximize or minimize, e.g. total cost.

opportunity cost The value of time or any other 'input' in its highest value use. The benefits lost because the next best alternative was not selected.

ordinal preference elictiation techniques In relation to health, a ranking of two or more health states. See also *discrete choice experiments*. Contrasts with techniques such as *standard gamble* or *time trade-off* that it is claimed can generate values on an *interval scale*.

parameter uncertainty *Uncertainty* about the true numerical values of the parameters used as inputs.

Pareto improvement A reallocation that makes at least one person better off and no one worse off.

Pareto optimality A distribution of resources such that any change in the distribution must make at least one person worse off.

perspective The view point from which health state valuations are conducted (e.g. own current health state, own future hypothetical state or someone else's state).

Ping–pong method A method of eliciting preferences by converging to the final answer while alternating steps from both sides. For example, finding the difference *probability* in a *standard gamble* question by alternatingly asking about *probabilities* that are too high and too low while converging inward.

person trade-off A technique for valuing health states where a respondent in areas to indicate how many people (y) in health (x) state B are equivalent to a specified member of people in health state A. The undesirability of health state B is the ratio x/y times as great as that of health state A.

point estimate A single estimate of a parameter of interest. Potential Pareto improvement See *compensation test.*

power See *statistical power.*

predictive validity The ability of a model to make verifiably accurate predictions of quantities of interest. A measurement instrument that has predictive validity is one that allows accurate predictions of future states of the *construct* being measured.

preference function A mathematical expression describing preferences or *utility function* of specific variables. See also *utility function.*

preference score See *preference weight.*

preference subgroup A group of individuals within a larger population whose preferences for particular *health states* are relatively homogeneous and differ systematically from the average preferences of the population.

preference weight A numerical judgement of the desirability of a particular outcome or situation. Also known as preference score or value.

present value The value to the decision maker now of outcomes occurring in the future.

prevalence The proportion of individuals in a population who have a disease or condition at a specific point in time.

probabilistic sensitivity analysis A method of *decision analysis* in which *probability distributions* are specified for each uncertain parameter (e.g. *probabilities, utilities,* costs); a simulation is performed whereby values of each parameter are randomly drawn from the corresponding distribution; and the resulting *probability distribution* of *expected utilities* (and costs) is displayed.

probability An expression of the degree of certainty that an event will occur, on a scale from 0 (certainty that the event will not occur) to 1 (certainty that the event will occur).

probability distribution A numerical or mathematical representation of the relative likelihood of each possible value that a variable may take on (technically, a 'probability density function').

psychophysical methods Methods (or protocols) for asking judges to give numerical assessments representing the psychological perception or sensation produced by physical stimuli. These methods have been adapted to ask people to give numerical responses to represent preferences or degrees of preference for *health states.*

quality-adjusted life expectancy Life expectancy computed using *quality-adjusted life years* rather than nominal life years.

quality-adjusted life years (QALYs) A measure of health outcome which assigns to each period of time a weight, ranging from negative infinity (or negative one for one transformation) to 1, corresponding to the *health-related quality of life* during that period, where a weight of 1 corresponds to optimal health, and a weight of 0 corresponds to a *health state* judged equivalent to death; these are then aggregated across time periods.

quality of life A broad *construct* reflecting subjective or objective judgement concerning all aspects of an individual's existence, including health, economic, political, cultural, environmental, aesthetic and spiritual aspects.

randomized clinical trial (RCT) A clinical trial in which the treatments are randomly assigned to the subjects. The random allocation eliminates bias in the assignment of treatments to patients and establishes the basis for statistical analysis.

recall bias Bias that arises when the study subjects are asked to report past events based on their memory. May arise because individuals with a particular exposure or adverse health outcome are likely to remember their experiences differently from those who are not similarly affected.

relative risk An estimate of the magnitude of an association between exposure and disease which also indicates the likelihood of developing the disease among persons who are exposed relative to those who are not. It is defined as the ratio of incidence of disease in the exposed group divided by the corresponding incidence of disease in the non-exposed group.

reliability Consistency in repeated measures of a phenomenon by the same individual or across different groups of observers. The higher the reliability, the higher the test–re-test correlation between replications of the measurement. Technically, the fraction of the variance in a measure that is the true value rather than measurement error. See also *intrarater reliability*, *inter-rater reliability* and *test–retest reliability.*

response shift A change in the way a person perceives their *health-related quality of life* despite no objective difference over time in health status caused by changes in their internal standards, their way they weight the life goals and their very goals themselves.

risk aversion The extent to which an individual prefers a distribution of outcomes with a narrower spread to a wider one with the same expected value.

risk neutrality The risk attitude of an individual whose preference over different distributions of outcomes is determined by the expected value of the distribution and not affected by the spread.

social rate of time preference The rate at which the social decision maker is willing to trade-off present for future consumption. Frequently approximated by the real (inflation-adjusted) return on low-risk government investments.

social welfare An indication of how good or desirable a given state of affairs is for society as a whole.

standard gamble In *cost-effectiveness analysis*, an approach to determining the *utility* of a particular outcome from a particular *perspective*. Judges are asked to compare life in a particular given *health state* that is 'a sure thing' to a gamble with a *probability P* that perfect health is the outcome and $1 - P$ that immediate death is the outcome. The *probability P* is varied until the preference for the sure thing, the certainty of the particular *health state*, is equal to the preference for the gamble. The *probability P* for which the *expected utility* of the two choices is equal is then a measure of the preference for the *health state* and for all intents and purposes satisfies (by construction) the requirements for a *von Neumann–Morgenstern (nVM) utility*.

state-transition models Models which allocate, and subsequently reallocate, members of a population among several categories or *health states*. Transitions from one state to another occur at defined, recurring time intervals according to transition *probabilities*. Through simulation, or mathematical calculation, the number of members of the population passing through each state at each point in time can be estimated. State-transition models can be used to calculate life expectancy or *quality-adjusted life expectancy*.

statistical power The *probability* of detecting (as 'statistically significant') a postulated level of effect. Technically, the *probability* of (correctly) rejecting the null hypothesis, i.e. the *probability* of rejecting the null hypothesis when in fact the alternative is true.

study arm A group of patients assigned to the same treatment (or control condition) in a controlled study.

test–retest reliability The correlation between scores on the same measure administered on two separate occasions.

Thurstone's Law of Comparative Judgement One of the earliest methods for deriving psychological scales; it is based on paired-comparison judgements. Thurstone's law holds that stimulus differences which are detected equally often are subjectively equal.

time preference The rate at which the decision maker is just willing to trade present for future consumption of some commodity of interest. A positive rate of time preference means the decision maker is willing to forgo some current consumption of the commodity in return for a sufficiently large gain in future consumption.

time trade-off A method of measuring *health state utilities* in which patients are asked to trade-off life years in a state of less than perfect health for a shorter life span in a state of perfect health. The ratio of the number of years of perfect health that is equivalent to a longer life span in less than perfect health provides a measure of the preference for that *health state.*

uncertainty A state in which the true value of a parameter or the structure of a process is unknown.

utility A concept in economics, psychology and *decision analysis* sometime used to refer to the preference for, or desirability of, a particular outcome. In the context of *health-related quality of life* measurement, utility is used to refer to the preference of the rater (usually a patient or a member of the general public) for a particular health outcome or *health state.* For technical use in *decision analysis,* see *von Neumann–Morgenstern (vNM) utility.*

utility function An algebraic expression stating that a decision maker's satisfaction is dependent on the types and amounts of commodities she consumes. Symbolically, $U = U(XI, X2...)$, where XI, $X2$ ... are valued outcome attributes. According to *expected utility theory*, individuals behave so as to maximize the expected value of *utility*, subject to constraints.

utilitarianism A theory of social justice that holds the policies that produce the greatest good for the greatest number improve social welfare. This theory incorporates everyone's well-being into the social process by balancing the *utility* of persons who gain from a given policy with the *utility* of those who lose as a result of the same policy.

validity The extent to which a technique measures what it is intended to measure. See also *construct validity, convergent validity, discriminant validity, face validity* and *predictive validity.*

value See *preference weight.*

valuation technique A technique (such as *standard gamble* or *time trade-off*) for valuaing health states, also known as preference elicitation technique.

veil of ignorance A philosophical *construct* in which a rational public decides what is the best course of action when blind to its own self-interest.

visual analogue scales Direct rating methods using a line on paper (or similar visual device) without internal markings; raters are asked to place a mark at some point between the two anchor states appearing at the ends of the line.

von Neumann–Morgenstern (vNM) utility A number representing relative desirability that satisfies axioms set forth by von Neumann and Morgenstern (1947) and suitable for computation of *expected utilities* to represent preferences among alternatives with uncertain outcomes.

weighted QALYs The outcome measure of a *CEA* when it is corrected to reflect various concerns implying that the relative societal value of health may differ depending on the circumstance. Weights can be applied to *QALYs* for equity reasons and efficiency reasons.

welfare economics A normative branch of economics concerned with the development of principles for maximizing social welfare and economic output. It is based on the assumptions (1) that individuals maximize a well defined *preference function* and (2) that the overall welfare of society is a function of these individual preferences.

welfarism One of the key requirements of modern *welfare economics* that holds that judgements of *social welfare* must be a function of individual utility. See also *non-welfarism*.

willingness to pay A method of measuring the value an individual places on a good, service, or reduction in the risk of death and illness by estimating the maximum dollar amount an individual would pay in order to obtain the good, service or risk reduction.

years of healthy life (YHL) The duration of an individual's life, as modified by the changes in health and well-being experienced over a lifetime. Also called *quality-adjusted life years* or health-adjusted life years.

This glossary has drawn heavily on the Glossary presented in Gold *et al.* (1996), though any remaining error are those of the authors.

Index